THE ANCIENT LANGUAGES OF A AMERICAS

This book, derived from the acclaimed *Cambridge Encyclopedia of the World's Ancient Languages*, describes the ancient languages of Asia and the Americas, for the convenience of students and specialists working in that area. Each chapter of the work focuses on an individual language or, in some instances, a set of closely related varieties of a language. Providing a full descriptive presentation, each of these chapters examines the writing system(s), phonology, morphology, syntax, and lexicon of that language, and places the language within its proper linguistic and historical context. The volume brings together an international array of scholars, each a leading specialist in ancient language study. While designed primarily for scholars and students of linguistics, this work will prove invaluable to all whose studies take them into the realm of ancient language.

Roger D. Woodard is the Andrew Van Vranken Raymond Professor of the Classics at the University of Buffalo. His chief research interests lie generally within the areas of Greek and Roman myth and religion, Indo-European culture and linguistics, the origin and development of writing among the Greeks, and the interaction between Greece and the ancient Near East. His other books include *The Cambridge Companion to Greek Mythology* (2007), *Indo-European Sacred Space* (2006), *The Cambridge Encyclopedia of the World's Ancient Languages* (2004), *Ovid's Fasti* (with A. J. Boyle, 2000), *Greek Writing from Knossos to Homer: A Linguistic Interpretation of the Origins of the Greek Alphabet* (1997), and *On Interpreting Morphological Change* (1990). He has also published numerous articles and served as President of the Society for the Study of Greek and Latin Language and Linguistics from 1992 to 2001.

The Ancient Languages of Asia and the Americas

Edited by
ROGER D. WOODARD

CAMBRIDGE
UNIVERSITY PRESS

CAMBRIDGE UNIVERSITY PRESS
Cambridge, New York, Melbourne, Madrid, Cape Town, Singapore, São Paulo, Delhi

Cambridge University Press
The Edinburgh Building, Cambridge CB2 8RU, UK

Published in the United States of America by Cambridge University Press, New York

www.cambridge.org
Information on this title: www.cambridge.org/9780521684941

Previously published in 2004 as chapters 26–30 and 41–4 of Woodard, Roger D.,
The Cambridge Encyclopedia of the World's Ancient Languages
© Cambridge University Press 2004

First published 2008

Printed in the United Kingdom at the University Press, Cambridge

A catalogue record for this publication is available from the British Library

ISBN 978-0-521-68494-1 paperback

Contents

Figures

For full captions for Figures 9.1–9.17, please see Figure 43.1–43.17 in the *Cambridge Encyclopedia of the World's Ancient Languages* (*WAL*) list of figures

Tables

Map

Contributors

VICTORIA R. BRICKER	Tulane University
MARK HALE	Concordia University, Montreal
STEPHANIE W. JAMISON	University of California at Los Angeles
JOHN JUSTESON	State University of New York at Albany
TERRENCE KAUFMAN	University of Pittsburgh
ALAIN PEYRAUBE	Université de Paris
DON RINGE	University of Pennsylvania
RÜDIGER SCHMITT	Universität des Saarlandes
SANFORD B. STEEVER	New Canaan, Connecticut
ROGER D. WOODARD	University of Buffalo (The State University of New York)

Notes on numbering and cross-referencing

This volume is one of five paperbacks derived from *The Cambridge Encyclopedia of the World's Ancient Languages* (*WAL*), with the content now organized by region for the convenience of students and specialists wishing to focus on a given area of the ancient world.

Cross-references to material within this volume use its own internal chapter numbers. Any cross-references to other chapters of the original *WAL* refer to the chapter numbers in that work, and are prefixed by *WAL*. The contents list of *WAL* is reproduced at the back of this volume, as are the contents of the respective volumes of the paperback series derived from it.

Abbreviations

Any abbreviation that deviates from the form given below is noted within the text of the individual chapter or within a chapter-specific list.

Linguistic terms

abl.	ablative
abs.	absolutive
acc.	accusative
act.	active
adj.	adjective
adv.	adverb (adverbial)
all.	allative
anim.	animate
aor.	aorist
art.	article
asp.	aspirated
aux.	auxiliary (verb)
caus.	causative
cl.	clause
coll.	collective
com.	common
comp.	comparative
comt.	comitative
conj.	conjunction
conjv.	conjunctive
conn.	connective
cons.	consonant
constr.	construct (state)
cont.	continuant
cop.	copula
dat.	dative
def. art.	definite article
dem.	demonstrative
det.	determinate
detv.	determinative
dial.	dialect
dir.	directive
dir. obj.	direct object
disj.	disjunctive
du.	dual
dur.	durative
emph.-pcl.	emphatic particle
encl.	enclitic
eq.	equative
erg.	ergative
ext.	extended
fem.	feminine
final-pcl.	final-particle
fut.	future
gdve.	gerundive
gen.	genitive
ger.	gerund
impf.	imperfect
impftv.	imperfective
impv.	imperative
inan.	inanimate
inc.	inclusive
indef. art.	indefinite article
indet.	indeterminate
indic.	indicative
inf.	infinitive
instr.	instrumental
interr.	interrogative
intr.	intransitive
iter.	iterative
juss.	jussive
loc.	locative
mediopass.	mediopassive
mid.	middle

N.	noun
neg.	negative
neut.	neuter
nom.	nominative
NP	noun phrase
num.	number
obj.	object
obl.	oblique
opt.	optative
part.	participle
pass.	passive
pcl.	particle
per.	person
perf.	perfect
perfv.	perfective
perfvz.	perfectivizer
pert.	pertinentive
pl.	plural
pluperf.	pluperfect
poss. suff.	possessive suffix
postp.	postposition
PP	prepositional phrase
prec.	precative
preC.	preconsonantal
pref.	prefix
prep.	preposition
pres.	present
pret.	preterite
preV.	prevocalic
pro.	pronoun
prosp.	prospective
quot.	quotative particle
refl.	reflexive
rel. pro.	relative (pronoun)
rel./connec.	relative/connective
sg.	singular
soc.	sociative case
SOV	Subject–Object–Verb (word order)
spec.	specifier
splv.	superlative
stat.	stative
subj.	subject
subjunc.	subjunctive
subord.	subordinate/subordinator/ subordination marker
subord.-pcl.	subordinating particle
suff.	suffix
s.v.	*sub voce*
top.	topicalizer
tr.	transitive
V.	verb
var.	variant
vent.	ventive
voc.	vocative
vow.	vowel
VP	verbal phrase

Languages

Akk.	Akkadian
Ar.	Arabic
Ass.	Assyrian
Av.	Avestan
Bab.	Babylonian
Cis. Gaul.	Cisalpine Gaulish
Eg.	Egyptian (Old, Late, Earlier)
Eng.	English
Etr.	Etruscan
Gk.	Greek
Gmc.	Germanic
Go.	Gothic
Hisp.-Celt.	Hispano-Celtic
Hitt.	Hittite
IE	Indo-European
Lat.	Latin
Lep.	Lepontic
Luv.	Luvian
Lyc.	Lycian
MA	Middle Assyrian
MB	Middle Babylonian
NA	Neo-Assyrian
NB	Neo-Babylonian
OA	Old Assyrian
O. Akk.	Old Akkadian
O. Av.	Old Avestan
OB	Old Babylonian
OHG	Old High German
OP	Old Persian
PG	Proto-Greek
PGmc.	Proto-Germanic
PIE	Proto-Indo-European
PIIr.	Proto-Indo-Iranian
PIr.	Proto-Iranian
PMS	Proto-Mije-Sokean
PS	Proto-Semitic
PSo.	Proto-Sokean
SB	Standard Babylonian

Skt.	Sanskrit
Sum.	Sumerian
Y. Av.	Young Avestan

Other

abbr.	abbreviation
dict.	dictionary
intro.	introduction
lit.	literally
NA	not applicable
NS	new series
trad.	traditional
translit.	transliteration

Preface

Preliminary remarks

What makes a language ancient? The term conjures up images, often romantic, of archeologists feverishly copying hieroglyphs by torchlight in a freshly discovered burial chamber; of philologists dangling over a precipice in some remote corner of the earth, taking impressions of an inscription carved in a cliff-face; of a solitary scholar working far into the night, puzzling out some ancient secret, long forgotten by humankind, from a brittle-leafed manuscript or patina-encrusted tablet. The allure is undeniable, and the literary and film worlds have made full use of it.

An ancient language is indeed a thing of wonder – but so is every other language, all remarkable systems of conveying thoughts and ideas across time and space. And ancient languages, as far back as the very earliest attested, operate just like those to which the linguist has more immediate access, all with the same familiar elements – phonological, morphological, syntactic – and no perceptible vestiges of Neanderthal oddities. If there was a time when human language was characterized by features and strategies fundamentally unlike those we presently know, it was a time prior to the development of any attested or reconstructed language of antiquity. Perhaps, then, what makes an ancient language different is our awareness that it has outlived those for whom it was an intimate element of the psyche, not so unlike those rays of light now reaching our eyes that were emitted by their long-extinguished source when dinosaurs still roamed across the earth (or earlier) – both phantasms of energy flying to our senses from distant sources, long gone out.

That being said, and rightly enough, we must return to the question of what counts as an ancient language. As *ancient* the editor chose the upward delimitation of the fifth century AD. This *terminus ante quem* is one which is admittedly "traditional"; the fifth is the century of the fall of the western Roman Empire (AD 476), a benchmark which has been commonly (though certainly not unanimously) identified as marking the end of the historical period of *antiquity*. Any such chronological demarcation is of necessity arbitrary – far too arbitrary – as linguists accustomed to making such diachronic distinctions as *Old English, Middle English, Modern English* or *Old Hittite, Middle Hittite, Neo-Hittite* are keenly aware. Linguistic divisions of this sort are commonly based upon significant political events and clearly perceptible cultural shifts rather than upon language phenomena (though they are surely not without linguistic import as every historical linguist knows). The choice of the boundary in the present concern – the ancient-language boundary – is, likewise (as has already been confessed), not mandated by linguistic features and characteristics of the languages concerned.

However, this arbitrary choice, establishing a *terminus ante quem* of the fifth century, is somewhat buttressed by quite pragmatic linguistic considerations (themselves consequent to the whim of historical accident), namely the co-occurrence of a watershed in language documentation. Several early languages first make a significant appearance in the historical record in the fourth/fifth century: thus, Gothic (fourth century; see *WAL* Ch. 36), Ge'ez (fourth/fifth century; see *WAL* Ch. 14, §1.3.1), Classical Armenian (fifth century; see *WAL* Ch. 38), Early Old Georgian (fifth century; see *WAL* Ch. 40). What newly comes into clear light in the sixth century is a bit more meager – Tocharian and perhaps the very earliest Old Kannada and Old Telegu from the end of the century. Moreover, the dating of these languages to the sixth century cannot be made precisely (not to suggest this is an especially unusual state of affairs) and it is equally possible that the earliest attestation of all three should be dated to the seventh century. Beginning with the seventh century the pace of language attestation begins to accelerate, with languages documented such as Old English, Old Khmer, and Classical Arabic (though a few earlier inscriptions preserving a "transitional" form of Arabic are known; see *WAL* Ch. 16, §1.1.1). The ensuing centuries bring an avalanche of medieval European languages and their Asian contemporaries into view. Aside from the matter of a culturally dependent analytic scheme of historical periodization, there are thus considerations of language history that motivate the upper boundary of the fifth century.

On the other hand, identifying a *terminus post quem* for the inclusion of a language in the present volume was a completely straightforward and noncontroversial procedure. The low boundary is determined by the appearance of writing in human society, a graphic means for recording human speech. A system of writing appears to have been first developed by the Sumerians of southern Mesopotamia in the late fourth millennium BC (see *WAL* Ch. 2, §§1.2; 2). Not much later (beginning in about 3100 BC), a people of ancient Iran began to record their still undeciphered language of Proto-Elamite on clay tablets (see *WAL* Ch. 3, §2.1). From roughly the same period, the Egyptian hieroglyphic writing system emerges in the historical record (see *WAL* Ch. 7, §2). Hence, Sumerian and Egyptian are the earliest attested, understood languages and, *ipso facto*, the earliest languages treated in this volume.

It is conjectured that humans have been speaking and understanding language for at least 100,000 years. If in the great gulf of time which separates the advent of language and the appearance of Sumerian, Proto-Elamite, and Egyptian societies, there were any people giving written expression to their spoken language, all evidence of such records and the language or languages they record has fallen victim to the decay of time. Or the evidence has at least eluded the archeologists.

Format and conventions

Each chapter, with only the occasional exception, adheres to a common format. The chapter begins with an overview of the history (including prehistory) of the language, at least up to the latest stage of the language treated in the chapter, and of those peoples who spoke the language (§1, HISTORICAL AND CULTURAL CONTEXTS). Then follows a discussion of the development and use of the script(s) in which the language is recorded (§2, WRITING SYSTEMS); note that the complex Mesopotamian cuneiform script, which is utilized for several languages of the ancient Near East – Sumerian (*WAL* Ch. 2), Elamite (*WAL* Ch. 3), Hurrian (*WAL* Ch. 4), Urartian (*WAL* Ch. 5), Akkadian and Eblaite (*WAL* Ch. 8), Hittite (*WAL* Ch. 18), Luvian (*WAL* Ch. 19) – and which provides the inspiration and graphic raw materials for others – Ugaritic (*WAL* Ch. 9) and Old Persian (Ch. 5) – is treated in most detail in *WAL* Chapter 8, §2. The next section presents a discussion of phonological elements of the language (§3, PHONOLOGY), identifying consonant and vowel phonemes, and treating matters such as allophonic and morphophonemic variation, syllable structure and phonotaxis, segmental length, accent (pitch and stress), and synchronic and diachronic phonological processes. Following next is discussion of morphological phenomena (§4, MORPHOLOGY), focusing on topics such as word structure, nominal and pronominal categories and systems, the categories and systems of finite verbs and other verbal elements (for explanation of the system of classifying Semitic verb stems – G stem, etc. – see *WAL* Ch. 6, §3.3.5.2), compounds, diachronic morphology, and the system of numerals. Treatment of syntactic matters then follows (§5, SYNTAX), presenting discussion of word order and coordinate and subordinate clause structure, and phenomena such as agreement, cliticism and various other syntactic processes, both synchronic and diachronic. The description of the grammar closes with a consideration of the lexical component (§6, LEXICON); and the chapter comes to an end with a list of references cited in the chapter and of other pertinent works (BIBLIOGRAPHY).

To a great extent, the linguistic presentations in the ensuing chapters have remained faithful to the grammatical conventions of the various language disciplines. From discipline to discipline, the most obvious variation lies in the methods of transcribing sounds. Thus, for example, the symbols *ś*, *ṣ*, and *ṭ* in the traditional orthography of Indic language scholarship represent, respectively, a voiceless palatal (palato-alveolar) fricative, a voiceless retroflex fricative, and a voiceless retroflex stop. In Semitic studies, however, the same symbols are used to denote very different phonetic realities: *ś* represents a voiceless lateral fricative while *ṣ* and *ṭ* transcribe two of the so-called emphatic consonants – the latter a voiceless stop produced with a secondary articulation (velarization, pharyngealization, or glottalization), the former either a voiceless fricative or affricate, also with a secondary articulation. Such conventional symbols are employed herein, but for any given language, the reader can readily determine phonetic values of these symbols by consulting the discussion of consonant and vowel sounds in the relevant phonology section.

Broad phonetic transcription is accomplished by means of a slightly modified form of the International Phonetic Alphabet (IPA). Most notably, the IPA symbols for the palato-alveolar fricatives and affricates, voiceless [ʃ] and [tʃ] and voiced [ʒ] and [dʒ], have been replaced by the more familiar [š], [č], [ž], and [ǰ] respectively. Similarly, [y] is used for the palatal glide rather than [j]. Long vowels are marked by either a macron or a colon.

In the phonology sections, phonemic transcription, in keeping with standard phonological practice, is placed within slashes (e.g., /p/) and phonetic transcription within square brackets (e.g., [p]; note that square brackets are also used to fill out the meaning of a gloss and are employed as an element of the transcription and transliteration conventions for certain languages, such as Elamite [*WAL* Ch. 3] and Pahlavi [Ch. 7]). The general treatment adopted in phonological discussions has been to present transcriptions as phonetic rather than phonemic, except in those instances in which explicit reference is made to the phonemic level. Outside of the phonological sections, transcriptions are usually presented using the conventional orthography of the pertinent language discipline. When potential for confusion would seem to exist, transcriptions are enclosed within angled brackets (e.g., <p>) to make clear to the reader that what is being specified is the *spelling* of a word and not its *pronunciation.*

Further acknowledgments

The enthusiastic reception of the first edition of this work – and the broad interest in the ancient languages of humankind that it demonstrates – has been and remains immensely gratifying to both editor and contributors. The editor would like to take this opportunity, on behalf of all the contributors, to express his deepest appreciation to all who have had a hand in the success of the first edition. We wish too to acknowledge our debt of gratitude to Cambridge University Press and to Dr. Kate Brett for continued support of this project and for making possible the publication of this new multivolume edition and the increased accessibility to the work that it will inevitably provide. Thanks also go to the many kind readers who have provided positive and helpful feedback since the publication of the first edition, and to the editors of *CHOICE* for bestowing upon the work the designation of Outstanding Academic Title of 2006.

Roger D. Woodard
Vernal Equinox 2007

Preface to the first edition

In the following pages, the reader will discover what is, in effect, a linguistic description of all known ancient languages. Never before in the history of language study has such a collection appeared within the covers of a single work. This volume brings to student and to scholar convenient, systematic presentations of grammars which, in the best of cases, were heretofore accessible only by consulting multiple sources, and which in all too many instances could only be retrieved from scattered, out-of-the-way, disparate treatments. For some languages, the only existing comprehensive grammatical description is to be found herein.

This work has come to fruition through the efforts and encouragement of many, to all of whom the editor wishes to express his heartfelt gratitude. To attempt to list all – colleagues, students, friends – would, however, certainly result in the unintentional and unhappy neglect of some, and so only a much more modest attempt at acknowledgments will be made. Among those to whom special thanks are due are first and foremost the contributors to this volume, scholars who have devoted their lives to the study of the languages of ancient humanity, without whose expertise and dedication this work would still be only a *desideratum.* Very special thanks also go to Dr. Kate Brett of Cambridge University Press for her professionalism, her wise and expert guidance, and her unending patience, also to her predecessor, Judith Ayling, for permitting me to persuade her of the project's importance. I cannot neglect mentioning my former colleague, Professor Bernard Comrie, now of the Max Planck Institute, for his unflagging friendship and support. Kudos to those who masterfully translated the chapters that were written in languages other than English: Karine Megardoomian for Phrygian, Dr. Margaret Whatmough for Etruscan, Professor John Huehnergard for Ancient South Arabian. Last of all, but not least of all, I wish to thank Katherine and Paul – my inspiration, my joy.

Roger D. Woodard
Christmas Eve 2002

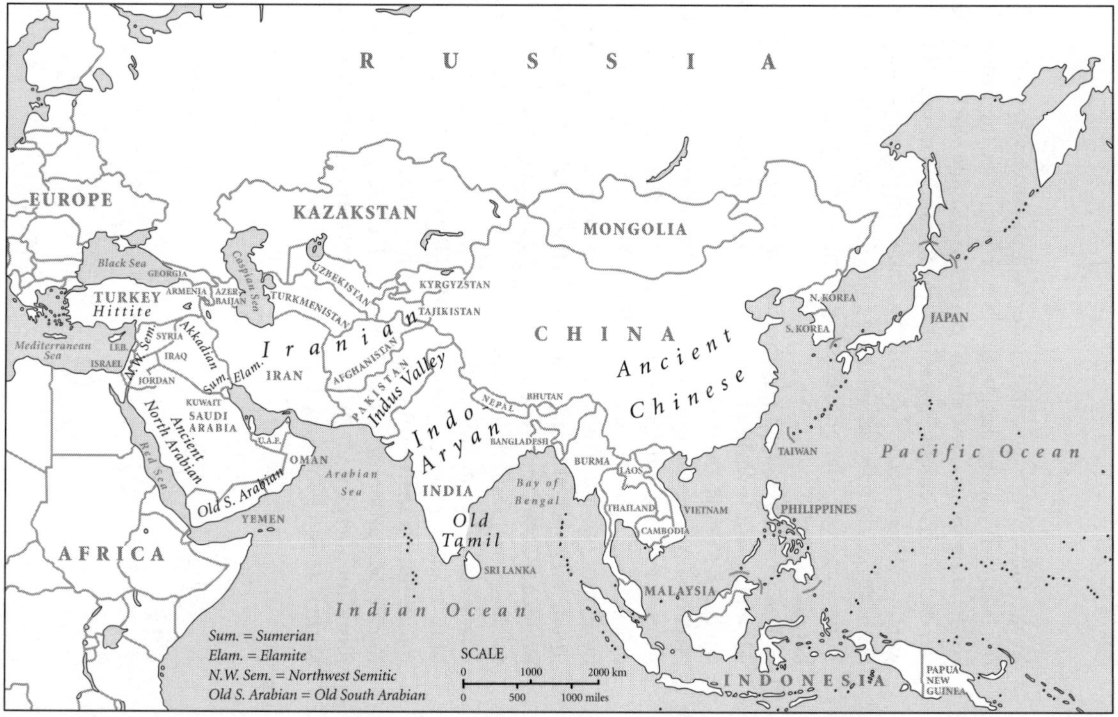

Map 1. The distribution of attested ancient languages within Asia

CHAPTER 1

Language in Ancient Asia and the Americas: an introduction

ROGER D. WOODARD

1 O Bṛhaspati. When in giving names they first set forth the beginning of Language,
Their most excellent and spotless secret was laid bare through love.
2 When the wise ones formed Language with their mind, purifying it like grain with a winnowing fan,
Then friends knew friendships – an auspicious mark placed on their language.
3 Through sacrifice they tracked the path of Language, and within the poets found it.
Bearing it, they spread it abroad – in many places; the seven singers together spoke it loud.
4 One looking did not see Language; another listening did not hear it;
Language unfolds itself to another – like a wife, beautifully adorned and willing, to her husband.

Rig-veda 10.71.1–4

The present volume covers far greater geographic space than any of its companion volumes: all of Asia is included – excepting the linguistically rich regions of Asia Minor, with Transcaucasia (see *The Ancient Languages of Asia Minor*) and southwest Asia (which readers will find covered within the volumes entitled *The Ancient Languages of Mesopotamia, Egypt, and Aksum* and *The Ancient Languages of Syria-Palestine and Arabia*) – as well as the American continents (or continent, as one prefers). Over half of the languages examined in the chapters that follow were spoken in ancient Iran, central Asia, and the Indian subcontinent; and of these, all were Indo-European languages, with the exception of the Dravidian language of Old Tamil. From more easterly Asian locales, the only language to be preserved out of antiquity is Chinese – the speech of a culture whose influence dominated ancient east Asia – occupying a position of prestige and primacy comparable to that of Egypt in the ancient Mediterranean world – and which, as the third millennium AD begins, gives every sign of being poised for resurgence in a world gone global. Continuing farther east, across the Bering Strait, one finds a place, the Americas, that provides only limited evidence for the linguistic life of its ancient peoples – all of it emanating from the cinctured waist of the continent(s) that is Central America.

Of the languages described in the chapters that follow, the "oldest" is Sanskrit, an ancient language of India (see Ch. 2). Sanskrit is a member of the Indo-European language family, belonging to the subgroup called Indo-Iranian, which is itself divided into two branches: Indo-Aryan (or simply Indic) and Iranian. The earliest form of this "oldest" language, Sanskrit, is the one found in the ancient Brahmanic text called the *Rig-veda*, composed *c.* 1500 BC. The date makes Sanskrit one of the three earliest of the well-documented

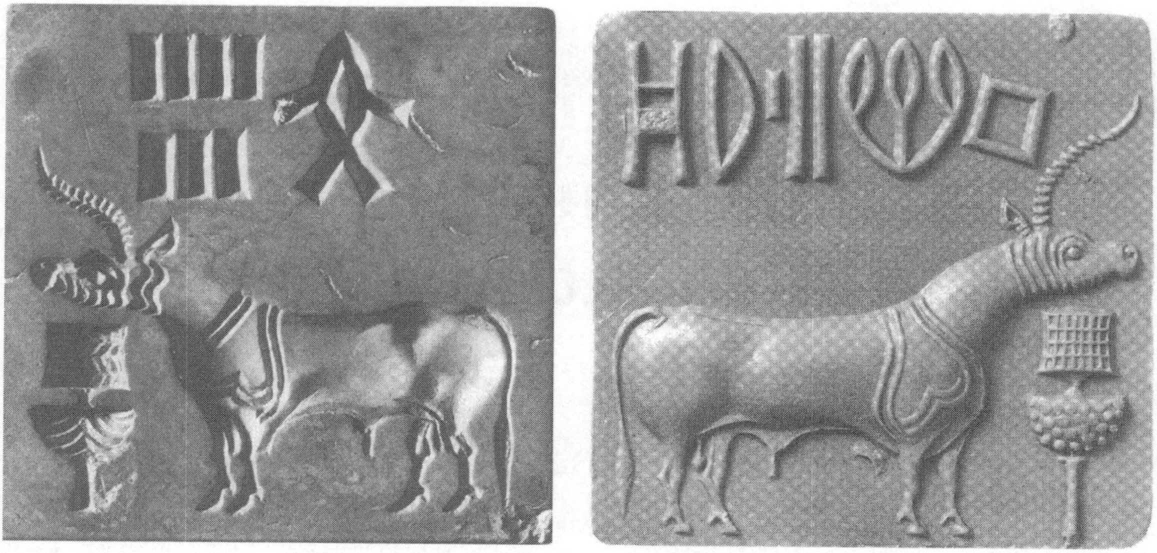

Figure 1.1 Indus Valley inscriptions

languages of the Indo-European family – the other two being Old Hittite (see *WAL* Ch. 18, §1) and Mycenaean Greek (see *WAL* Ch. 25, §1.2) – and, in keeping with its early appearance, Sanskrit has been a cornerstone in the reconstruction of the parent language of the Indo-European family – Proto-Indo-European (see the Appendix in the companion volume, *The Ancient Languages of Europe*).

Sanskrit is not, however, the oldest *documented* language of South Asia. That distinction belongs to a language that is not presently understood – the language of an undeciphered script – and, hence, a language that cannot be given any sort of well-informed linguistic description. In the mid third millennium BC, writing emerges in the archeological record of the Harappan culture of the Indus Valley. The characters of this Indus Valley script (see Figure 1.1) are of a well-developed, somewhat conventionalized pictographic nature at the earliest phase of the script's attestation (possibly suggesting some earlier unattested developmental stage). The number of characters identified likely reveals that the script operates with both logograms (symbols representing entire words) and syllabograms (phonetic symbols having the value of a syllable). Lying behind the Indus Valley script may well be a Dravidian language (see Ch. 4, §1) or possibly an early form of Indo-Aryan (see Ch. 2, §1). On the Indus Valley script and its attempted decipherment, see Parpola 1996 and 1994.

In point of fact, Sanskrit is not even the earliest (demonstrably) Indo-European language of South Asia to be attested by inscriptional evidence. While Vedic Sanskrit represents the *earliest preserved* language of those languages described in this volume, the *Rig-veda*, like all of the Vedas (see Ch. 2, §1), was passed along orally for many centuries before being given written form. The earliest surviving Indo-European *texts* of South Asia are the inscriptions left by Aśoka, ruler of the Maurya Empire of India during the second and third quarters of the third century BC (see, *inter alia*, Keay 2003:1:88–113, especially pp. 98–113). The language of these inscriptions constitutes one particular form of Middle Indic, "the designation for a range of Indo-Aryan languages displaying characteristic phonological and grammatical developments from Old Indic (i.e. Sanskrit)" (see Ch. 3).

When Indo-Europeans entered the subcontinent of India at some point in the second millennium BC, among the peoples whom they there encountered, some were undoubtedly speakers of languages belonging to the Dravidian family. The earliest known of the Dravidian languages is Old Tamil (see Ch. 4), a language spoken in southern India and northern Śri Lanka. As with Indo-Aryan (i.e. Middle Indic), the Dravidian language of Old Tamil is first attested in inscriptions produced during the third century BC.

The Iranian branch of the Indo-Iranian subfamily of Indo-European is represented by several languages known from antiquity. Avestan (see Ch. 6), closely related to Sanskrit, is the language of the Zoroastrian legal and religious documents that comprise the *Avesta*. The date of the composition of the earliest Avestan materials is uncertain, but to situate them in the late second millennium BC, while controversial in some circles, would not be unreasonable from a linguistic perspective. The earliest portion of the *Avesta*, the set of hymns called the Gāthās, has traditionally been attributed to Zarathuštra, the prophetic founder of the Zoroastrian religion. Later Avestan documents, among many other types of texts, were recorded in Middle Iranian languages, often collectively designated by the name Pahlavi (see Ch. 7).

From a different sacred textual tradition comes – perhaps somewhat unexpectedly – a reference to another influential Iranian figure of antiquity:

> . . . "He is my shepherd,
>   and he shall fulfill all my purpose";
> saying of Jerusalem, "She shall be built,"
>   and of the temple, "Your foundation shall be laid."
> Thus says the Lord to his anointed, to Cyrus,
>   whose right hand I have grasped,
> to subdue nations before him
>   and ungird the loins of kings,
> to open doors before him
>   that gates may not be closed.
>   Isaiah 44.28–45.1 (Revised Standard Version)

The Biblical prophet who composed these lines in which Yahweh proclaims "Cyrus" to be "his anointed" speaks of the Iranian monarch Cyrus the Great (d. 530 BC) – founder of the Achaemenid Empire of Persia – who had overthrown the Babylonian king Nabonidus, opening the way for exiled Jews in Babylonia to return to Jerusalem and rebuild their ruined temple. The Western Iranian language of the Achaemenid Empire is Old Persian (see Ch. 5), far less robustly attested than Avestan. No Old Persian inscriptions survive from the reign of Cyrus; all come from the era of his successors, stretching from Darius I to Artaxerxes III (the period 522–338/7 BC). For their recording, a unique cuneiform script is used (see Ch. 5, §2) – one based stylistically on Mesopotamian cuneiform (see *WAL* Ch. 8, §2 and the Appendix accompanying that chapter) but operationally quite distinct from it.

On its eastern fringe, the speech area of the Iranian languages in antiquity stretched to Chinese Turkestan. Here, speakers of known Middle Iranian languages such as Saka and Sogdian interfaced not only with other Indo-Europeans – the Tocharians (whose language is first attested too recently to be included in the present volume) – but with speakers of Chinese and Tibetan as well (see Narain 1994:173–176). Concerning these extreme eastern Indo-European peoples, Narain writes (p. 176):

> It is their movement which brought China into contact with the Western world as well as with India. These Indo-Europeans held the key to world trade for a long period . . . They acted as carriers of religious doctrines and artistic traditions from the east to the west and vice versa . . . In the process of their own transformation, these Indo-Europeans influenced the world around them more than any other people before the rise of Islam.

The groups with which these Indo-Europeans were interacting so as to exert such a far-ranging influence – the people activating such influence – were, of course, first and foremost Chinese. The earliest surviving Ancient Chinese documents are "oracle bone" inscriptions of the fourteenth century BC (thus almost contemporaneous with the composition of the Vedas), written in that form of the near-hypnotically intriguing Chinese script called *jiaguwen* – having recognizably pictographic characters in many instances (see Ch. 8, §2 and Table 8.1). Here too – in China – writing was first employed for purposes of the sacred – or at least first survived in such usages. Tortoise-shell or bones – often ovine or bovine scapulas – were engraved with text and then heated until they cracked; oracular responses were then divined by reading the text demarcated by the fracture-lines.

Long, long before Indo-Europeans had made their way into Chinese Turkestan, long, long before the Chinese language was ever committed to writing on tortoise-shell and bone, when ice still bridged Asia and America, some group, or groups, of Asian peoples trekked across that ice and began the long process of settling the New World. But the specifics of such settlement are a matter of great uncertainty and disagreement; as Campbell (1997:93) observes: "opinions concerning the origins of Native American languages at present differ widely and the topic is surrounded by controversy. These different views reflect different approaches to the classification of American Indian Languages, and the different classifications which have been proposed have distinct implications for the origins of the languages." The very number of distinct native American languages that can be identified is disputed – perhaps about 900 still spoken (see Campbell 1997:3), with many, many others long or recently extinct (on which see generally Crystal 2002) – as is the number of linguistic families that these individual languages comprise, though "most [scholars] believe that there are approximately 150 different language families in the Western Hemisphere which cannot at present be shown to be related to each other" (Campbell 1997:105).

The earliest graphic remains of native America are rock carvings – petroglyphs – many certainly dating back thousands of years before the present time (though precise dating is often difficult; see Bahn 1998, especially pp. 142–169). But these widely occurring, often starkly beautiful, artistic images of ancient American peoples do not constitute writing – that is, they do not preserve *language* in graphic form. With the exception of only a few languages of Mesoamerica – Mayan, Epi-Olmec, Zapotec – the native American languages of antiquity are known solely through linguistic reconstruction – the remarkable method that allows for the scientific recovery of unattested proto-languages (i.e. ancestral languages) by comparing the attested descendant languages. The reader will find a careful treatment of the comparative method in Appendix 1 located at the end of this volume.

Regarding the above-mentioned ancient Mesoamerican languages, only two are, at present, sufficiently well understood to be given a full linguistic description: Mayan, the better-known, is treated in Chapter 9 and Epi-Olmec in Chapter 10. Zapotec inscriptions, carved in stone like those of the Mayans and Epi-Olmecs, may date to as early as 500 or 600 BC (though the earliest uncontroversial dates are between 400 and 200 BC) and are last attested in about AD 900 (Zapotec manuscripts also occur in the sixteenth century, though the corpus is small). Several dozen short inscriptions exist, as well as a large number of calendrical citations, providing perhaps 100–300 distinct glyphic components. Owing to the difficulty in obtaining information on this language, a brief grammatical sketch of Zapotec, based on our present, limited understanding of the language, has been included as an Appendix to Chapter 10.

Since the evidence for language in early America is so limited, mention should also be made of the early Mesoamerican languages of Mixtec and Aztec. Both are attested by about AD 1100 (and so fall outside of the chronological scope of this volume) but are best known from sixteenth-century AD manuscripts. For Mixtec see, *inter alia*, Marcus 1992:57–67 and Jansen 1992; for Aztec, see Marcus 1992:46–57 and Prem 1992. In addition, on the pictographic records of the Tlapanecs, see Vega Sosa 1992.

Bibliography

Bahn, P. 1998. *The Cambridge Illustrated History of Prehistoric Art*. Cambridge: Cambridge University Press.

Bricker, V. 1992. *Epigraphy*. Supplement to the Handbook of Middle American Indians, vol. V. Austin: University of Texas Press.

Campbell, L. 1997. *American Indian Languages: The Historical Linguistics of Native America*. Oxford: Oxford University Press.

Crystal, D. 2002. *Language Death*. Revised edition. Cambridge: Cambridge University Press.

Jansen, M. 1992. "Mixtec pictography: conventions and contents." In Bricker 1992, pp. 20–33.

Keay, J. 2003. *India: A History* (2 vols.). London: The Folio Society.

Marcus, J. 1992. *Mesoamerican Writing Systems*. Princeton: Princeton University Press.

Narain, A. 1994. "Indo-Europeans in Inner Asia." In D. Sinor (ed.), *The Cambridge History of Early Inner Asia*, pp. 151–176. Reprint. Cambridge: Cambridge University Press.

Parpola, A. 1994. *Deciphering the Indus Script*. Cambridge: Cambridge University Press.

_______. 1996. "The Indus Script." In Daniels and Bright 1996, pp. 165–171.

Prem, H. 1992. "Aztec writing." In Bricker 1992, pp. 53–69.

Vega Sosa, C. 1992. "The annals of the Tlapanecs." In Bricker 1992, pp. 34–52.

Whittaker, G. 1992. "The Zapotec writing system." In Bricker 1992, pp. 5–19.

CHAPTER 2

Sanskrit

STEPHANIE W. JAMISON

1. HISTORICAL AND CULTURAL CONTEXTS

Sanskrit is an Indo-European language, a member of the Indo-Aryan branch of the Indo-Iranian subgroup of that family. It is chronologically and in terms of linguistic development the "oldest" Indo-Aryan language and consequently often referred to as *Old Indic* (Altindisch) or *Old Indo-Aryan*; its descendants include a range of linguistic varieties classified under the rubric Middle Indic (or Prākrit, see Ch. 3), as well as the Modern Indic (New Indo-Aryan) languages spoken today, such as Hindi, Gujarati, Bengali. It is not related genetically to the Dravidian languages of South India, such as Tamil and Telegu.

The oldest form of Sanskrit is so-called *Vedic Sanskrit*, the language of the four collections of liturgical texts known as the Vedas and of the early exegetical literature on these texts. The oldest Veda is the *R̥gveda* (*Rig-veda*), a compilation of 1,028 hymns which took shape around 1500 BC in northwest India, though the composition and collection of hymns clearly occupied several centuries. In language, style, and phraseology the *R̥gveda* resembles the earliest texts of its closest linguistic relative, the *Gāthās* attributed to the prophet Zarathustra, composed in Old Avestan (see Ch. 6).

Though the composition of Vedic texts can be dated with fair confidence to the period of *c.* 1500–500 BC, direct records of them are only found several millennia later. The "texts" were transmitted orally, with minimal alteration, and even after they were also committed to writing, the manuscripts were perishable and less reliable than the oral tradition.

Through the approximately thousand years of Vedic textual composition, the language shows gradual changes, especially in the loss of certain grammatical categories and the reduction of variant forms. Around 500 BC the Sanskrit then current among cultivated speakers received a magnificent description by the grammarian Pāṇini in his treatise, the *Aṣṭādhyāyī* ("[Work] consisting of eight chapters"), whose level of detail and theoretical sophistication has not been equaled to this day.

Pāṇini inadvertently froze the language in this particular form forever. What was composed as a *descriptive* grammar (though descriptive of a geographically and socio-culturally limited speech form, not the speech of the whole society) became a *prescriptive* grammar of a learned language. All subsequent Sanskrit follows, or attempts to follow, the rules of Pāṇini. Though there are systematic variations in later texts, these are essentially stylistic and distributed according to textual genre. The language of the great epics, the *Mahābhārata* and the *Rāmāyaṇa*, deviates somewhat from the Pāṇinian norm and is therefore sometimes distinguished as *Epic Sanskrit*; it displays some Middle Indic tendencies. Inscriptional Sanskrit also commonly shows nonsanctioned forms. Despite these minor exceptions, Sanskrit no longer had a history in the accepted linguistic sense of this term – even though the greater part of its literature remained to be composed. The great flourishing of Sanskrit literary production lasted through the first millennium AD.

The language as fixed by Pāṇini is commonly known as *Classical Sanskrit*, or *Sanskrit* proper. Indeed, the term *saṃskṛta* means "perfected" and refers to the language generated according to Pāṇini's rules, as opposed to the vernacular Prākrits, from *prākṛta* "natural, unrefined." Strictly speaking, the pre-Pāṇinian language of the Vedic texts is not "Sanskrit," and is sometimes called simply *Vedic*, rather than Vedic Sanskrit. In this work, however, *Sanskrit* will denote all varieties of Old Indic.

2. WRITING SYSTEM

The earliest Sanskrit texts were composed and transmitted orally, not written down for centuries after their first "attestation." Indeed, the first documentary evidence of Indo-Aryan languages in the Indian subcontinent comes not from Old Indic but Middle Indic: the inscriptions of the ruler Aśoka in the third century BC (see Ch. 3, §1.1) The first direct attestation of Sanskrit comes from around the beginning of the present era. The first extensive inscription is that of the ruler Rudradāman *c.* AD 150 at Girnar in western India; the first extant manuscripts, found in central Asia, date from about the same period.

The writing system found in most of the early inscriptions is *Brāhmī* (another, less widespread system, *Kharoṣṭhī*, an adaptation of Aramaic, is found in the northwest, already in the Aśokan edicts). Brāhmī seems to have been adapted from a Semitic writing system, though the exact details are unclear, as is the date of its introduction into India, a subject of much controversy. Brāhmī is the ancestor of most of the writing systems used in India.

Until the advent of printing and the regular publication of Sanskrit texts, Sanskrit manuscripts were written in various local scripts. Now Sanskrit is almost exclusively printed in a script known as *Nāgarī* or *Devanāgarī*, a medieval offshoot of Brāhmī, and perfectly adapted to the writing of Sanskrit, with a one-to-one correspondence between sound and symbol. The conventional transcription of Devanāgarī into Roman characters was established finally at the Tenth Congress of Orientalists, 1894. Transliterations in works published before often show deviations from the modern norm.

The system can be considered a modified or pseudo-syllabary in that each consonantal symbol represents a consonant with following short *a*-vowel (the commonest vowel in the language), for example, क = *ka*, ख = *kha*, ग = ga, घ = *gha* (not *k*, *kh*, *g*, *gh*); see Table 26.1. However, unlike "pure" syllabaries, a different symbol is not necessary to represent consonants followed by other vowels (e.g., *kā*, *ki*, *kī*, etc.). Instead, a set of universally applicable diacritics can be used to cancel the inherent short *a* and substitute a different following vowel: thus, का = *kā*, कि = *ki*, कु = *ku*, and so forth. There are also separate signs for independent vowels, for example, अ = *a*, ए = *e*.

Another drawback of some syllabaries, the inability to represent consonant clusters unambiguously, is overcome by the system of ligatures. Portions of each consonant in a cluster are combined into a single conventional sign, for example, त (*ta*) + क (*ka*) = त्क (*tka*). Final consonants can also be represented, by a stroke (*virāma*) under the sign, which cancels the short *a*: thus त = *ta*, but त् = *t*. Thus, the system combines the flexibility of an alphabet with some of the spatial economy of a syllabary.

Devanāgarī writing of Sanskrit lacks word divisions. Each linguistic string, regardless of morphosyntactic structure, is treated as a sequence of syllables (*akṣaras*) consisting of onset

Table 2.1 The Devanāgarī script

Vowel symbols

a	ā	i	ī	u	ū	r̥	r̥̄	l̥
अ	आ	इ	ई	उ	ऊ	ऋ	ॠ	ऌ
e	ai	o	au					
ए	ऐ	ओ	औ					

Consonant + vowel symbols

ka	kha	ga	gha	ṅa
क	ख	ग	घ	ङ
ca	cha	ja	jha	ña
च	छ	ज	झ	ञ
ṭa	ṭha	ḍa	ḍha	ṇa
ट	ठ	ड	ढ	ण
ta	tha	da	dha	na
त	थ	द	ध	न
pa	pha	ba	bha	ma
प	फ	ब	भ	म
ya	ra	la	va	
य	र	ल	व	
śa	ṣa	sa	ha	
श	ष	स	ह	

Sample vowel diacritics

kā	ki	kī	ku	kū
का	कि	की	कु	कू
kr̥	ke	kai	ko	kau
कृ	के	कै	को	कौ

consonant(s) (if present) plus vowel. Thus, a string like *tad etad rūpam*, with word divisions as given in transliteration, would obligatorily appear in Devanāgarī as *ta de ta drū pa m* त दे त द्रू प म् (though without spaces between the characters).

3. PHONOLOGY

3.1 Diachronic overview

From the point of view of reconstructed Proto-Indo-European, the most important phonological development in Sanskrit (and indeed in Indo-Iranian) is vowel-merger: short **e*, **o*, and **a* all merge as *a*; long **ē*, **ō*, **ā* (and short **o* under certain conditions) merge as *ā*. Since much of Proto-Indo-European morphology was based on alternations of vowels with **e*-timbre and those with **o*-timbre (qualitative ablaut), these mergers had major effects on the morphological system.

On the other hand, Sanskrit maintained the Proto-Indo-European consonantal system with some fidelity, only enlarging its inventory. The three series of stops – voiceless (T), voiced (D), and voiced aspirated (Dh) – traditionally reconstructed remain in Sanskrit, and a fourth was added, voiceless aspirated (Th). As in other satem languages the labiovelars merged with the plain velars. There was secondary palatalization of the resulting segments, reflected in thoroughgoing synchronic alternations within Sanskrit (see §3.4.2.2). Otherwise, the inventory of places of articulation was increased by the creation of a series of retroflex dental stops. For the comparatist an especially important retention in Sanskrit is the preservation of **y*, **w*, and **s* intervocalically, thus avoiding the loss of morphological clarity attendant on vowel contraction that bedevils the historical linguist in languages like Greek.

3.2 Vowels

The cardinal vowels *i*, *u*, *a* distinguish length; in addition, short *a* is a closer vowel than *ā*, equivalent to schwa. The mid vowels *ē* and *ō*, as monophthongizations of the Indo-Iranian diphthongs **ai* and **au* (preserved in Iranian), are inherently long and are so marked in the phonological sections of this work, though they are not usually so transcribed. The true diphthongs *āi* and *āu* (usually now transcribed simply *ai* and *au*) also count as long. The vocalic liquid *r̥* represents a merger of PIE (Proto-Indo-European) **r̥* and **l̥*. However, long *r̥̄* is an invention of the system and found in a few analogically generated morphological categories; PIE **r̥̄* has different, biphonemic outcomes in Sanskrit, as we will see. Vocalic *l̥* is even more limited, found in only one morpheme.

(1) Sanskrit vowel phonemes

monophthongs:	i / ī		u / ū	*diphthongs*:	āi	āu
	ē		ō			
		a			*vocalic liquids*: r̥ / r̥̄	l̥
		ā				

3.3 Consonants

The consonantal inventory of Sanskrit is presented in Table 2.2:

Table 2.2 The consonantal phonemes of Sanskrit

	Place of articulation					
Manner of articulation	Labial	Dental	Retroflex	Palatal	Velar	Glottal
Stops and affricates						
Voiceless	p	t	ṭ	c	k	
Voiceless aspirated	ph	th	ṭh	ch	kh	
Voiced	b	d	ḍ	j	g	
Voiced aspirated	bh	dh	ḍh	jh	gh	
Nasals	m	n	ṇ	ñ	ṅ	
	ṃ *anusvāra* (see below)					
Fricatives						
Voiceless		s	ṣ	ś		ḥ *visarga*
Voiced						h
Liquids		l	r			
Glides	v			y		

The apparent symmetry of this consonantal system conceals some failures of parallelism in distribution, often the results of historical changes:

1. The voiceless aspirated series is an addition to the system and significantly rarer than the other three. It is often found in etymologically obscure words.
2. The retroflex sibilant *ṣ* is the automatic product of dental *s* following *i, u, r*, and *k* (mnemonically "ruki"), a process also found not only in Iranian but in part in Balto-Slavic.
3. The series of retroflex stops was a creation of Indic, in most cases as a conditioned result of regressive assimilation to rukified *ṣ* and therefore distributionally limited; in particular, initial retroflexes are almost never found. The retroflex nasal is ordinarily the automatic product of dental nasal when the word contains a preceding *r* (subject to some conditions). Thus, all the retroflexes are in origin conditioned alternants of dentals, though from the beginning of the language they have a qualified independence.
4. The palatals are affricates, not stops. In the palatal row the voiced aspirate *jh* is a new and extremely rare phoneme; the phoneme patterning with the palatals as the voiced aspirate for morphophonemic purposes is glottal *h* (see §3.4.2.1).
5. The palatal nasal is a conditioned variant of *n* occurring next to palatal obstruents; the velar nasal is also ordinarily a conditioned product of *n*, found before velar stops, but further phonological developments (loss of final or cluster-internal velar stop) can allow the velar nasal an independent if marginal existence. *Anusvāra* is a conditioned alternant of postvocalic nasals, under certain sandhi conditions.
6. *Visarga* is a word-final (sometimes morpheme-final) conditioned alternant of *s* and *r* under certain sandhi conditions.
7. The glides and liquids regularly alternate with vowels: *i* ≈ *y*; *u* ≈ *v* ([w]); *r̥* ≈ *r*; *l̥* ≈ *l* (under conditions discussed below).

3.4 Phonological alternations

Sanskrit is characterized by a pervasive series of phonological alternations occurring on several different linguistic levels and displaying varying degrees of transparency. We begin with the most transparent.

3.4.1 External sandhi

The surface form of any linguistic string is subject to phonological rules of combination (*sandhi* or "putting together"). In other words, phenomena of the English *gonna* (from *going* + *to*) type apply to any two words in contact within a sentence, and even between sentences in a discourse. Most sandhi rules involve regressive assimilation, especially in voicing: for example, (with underlying *tad*) *ta**d bh**avati but ta**t ph**alam*. Assimilation in manner of articulation is also met with (e.g., *ta**n m**anas*). Like vowels coalesce into a single long vowel (e.g., *vad**a*** + ***a**gne* ⇒ *vad**ā**gne*), and unlike vowels undergo diphthongization or glide-formation (e.g., *vad**a o**ṣadhe* ⇒ *vad**au**ṣadhe*; *ast**i a**gniḥ* ⇒ *ast**y a**gniḥ*). Despite the simplicity of the principles, the details of sandhi rules are sometimes opaque. For example, though the change of final *-as* to *-o* before voiced sounds historically involves regressive voicing assimilation, this process is not synchronically transparent. The rules of external sandhi ordinarily apply also at compound seams, and many but not all of the same rules at morpheme boundaries.

External sandhi in Vedic is more variable than in Classical Sanskrit, not only in the form of the rules but also in their application (or nonapplication). Sandhi in Middle Indic occurs only under conditions of close syntactic nexus. Given these facts, it seems likely that the pervasive system of obligatory sandhi characteristic of Classical Sanskrit involved an artificial imposition of an originally more flexible set of processes linking words within syntactically defined phrases.

3.4.2 Internal consonantal alternations

The rest of this section presupposes the concept of the *root* and the canonical structure of the Sanskrit word presented in §4.1.

3.4.2.1 Voicing and aspiration

The voiceless, voiced, and voiced aspirated obstruents of a positional series regularly alternate with each other ($p \approx b \approx bh$; $t \approx d \approx dh$, etc.; note, however, $c \approx j \approx$ ***h***), such that, for example, a morpheme with an underlying voiced aspirate final may show alternants with all three stops under differing internal sandhi conditions: thus, √*budh* "be aware" – ***budh**-yate*, *bu**d**-dha-*, *bho**t**-syate.*

Clusters containing unaspirated stops show regressive assimilation (e.g., *chi**t**-**t**i-* from **chi**d** + **t**i-*). But in those containing voiced aspirates the resulting cluster is both voiced and aspirated whatever the position of the aspirate in the underlying cluster (hence *bu**ddh**a-* from *bu**dh**-**t**a-*) – the change known as *Bartholomae's Law*. In summary,

(2)

A. $T + T$ ⇒ T-T	B. $T + D$ ⇒ D-D	C. $Dh + T$
$D + T$	$D + D$	$Dh + D \Rightarrow D$-Dh
		$Dh + Dh$

Before *s* all stops become voiceless; hence *bho**t**-**s**yate* above. This same form illustrates another, sporadic alternation: when roots with underlying final aspirates lose that aspiration, the initial consonant often acquires aspiration (hence ***bhot**-syate*, but ***budh**-yate*). This represents a reconfiguring or reversal of a historical development – *Grassmann's Law*, whereby di-aspirate roots dissimilated the first aspirated stop.

3.4.2.2 Velars and palatals

The velar series (*k, g, gh*) regularly alternates with the palatal series (*c, j, h*). In particular, velar-initial roots reduplicate with palatals (e.g., √*kr̥*: ***c**a-**k**āra*; √*gam*: ***j**a-**g**āma*); and preobstruent velars alternate with palatals in other phonological positions (e.g., √*muc*: *mu**k**-ta*, but *muc-yate*). This alternation is the historical result of a pan-Indo-Iranian palatalization of velars by following front vowels (and *y*), the conditioning of which was obscured by the subsequent merger of **e* with **a* and **o* noted above.

3.4.2.3 Palatals and retroflexes

The structural position of the palatal series was further complicated by a different merger. Though Sanskrit *c* can only be the product of an old palatalized velar (*$k^{(w)}e$, etc.), both *j* and *h* have two sources: (i) not only palatalized velars (*$g^{(w)}e$, $g^{(w)h}e$, etc.); (ii) but also PIE palatal stops (*$\hat{g}$ and *$\hat{g}^h$), whose voiceless equivalent (*$\hat{k}$) yields Sanskrit *ś*. These underlying palatals enter into a set of synchronic alternations different from that of the old velars: palatals followed by dentals produce a retroflex cluster, for example, √*sr̥j* "emit": *sr̥j* + *ta* ⇒ *sr̥ṣ-ṭa*. Thus, though the phonetic inventory of the language contains only a single palatal series, morphological alternations define two morphophonemically distinct series: (3A) *ś, j, h*; and (3B) *c, j, h*.

(3)

A. *palatals* (≈ *retroflexes*)	B. *palatalized velars* (≈ *velars*)
ś (e.g., viś : viṣ-ṭa)	c (e.g., muc: muk-ta)
j (e.g., sr̥j : sr̥ṣ-ṭa)	j (e.g., bhaj: bhak-ta)
h (e.g., ruh : rū-ḍha)	h (e.g., snih: snig-dha)

(By Bartholomae's Law, a compensatorily lengthened vowel plus retroflex *ḍh* is the regular outcome in *rūḍha.*)

The distinction between these two series is neutralized before *s*, where both series (and all three manners) show *k*: for example, both *ruruk-ṣati* (√*ruh*) and *sisnik-ṣati* (√*snih*).

3.4.3 Internal vocalic alternations

The Sanskrit morphological system is pervaded by vocalic alternations, conveniently considered as the "strengthening" of an underlying vocalic element by two successive additions of the vowel *a* (*V* / *a*+ *V* / *a*+ *aV*). The preconsonantal versions of these strengthenings are known by the indigenous terms *guṇa* and *vr̥ddhi*, but it is useful to consider these in conjunction with their prevocalic alternants as well. In terms familiar from Indo-European descriptive grammars, the unstrengthened state corresponds to *zero-grade*, guṇa to *full-* (or *normal-*) grade, and vr̥ddhi to *extended-* (or *lengthened-*) grade. Though Proto-Indo-European *qualitative* ablaut essentially disappeared in Indo-Iranian with the merger of **e* and **o*, *quantitative* ablaut is transparently continued by the Sanskrit system of vowel strengthening. Alternations between zero-grade and full-grade are prominent in the morphological system; vr̥ddhi is especially important in the derivation of adjectives of origin and appurtenance (*vr̥ddhi derivatives*).

The alternations between consonantal and vocalic versions of glides and liquids are also relevant here, and the system is in fact clearest with these segments, especially *r̥*, where the successive additions of *a* are easily discerned (N.B. for ease of exposition, *ī* and *ū* are not included here, but will be discussed below):

(4)

	Zero-grade		*Full-grade*		*Extended-grade*	
Vowel	*PreC.*	*PreV.*	*PreC. (guṇa)*	*PreV.*	*PreC. (vr̥ddhi)*	*PreV.*
r̥	r̥	r	ar	ar	ār	ār
i	i	y	ē	ay	āi	āy
u	u	v	ō	av	āu	āv
a	a		a		ā	
ā	ā		ā		ā	

As can be seen, with the simple vowels *a* and *ā*, the progressive addition of *a* is not so clear; moreover, prevocalic position is subject to complications.

Though Sanskrit does not have surface syllabic nasals (*m̥ and *n̥) as reconstructed for Proto-Indo-European, the parallelism of morphological alternations compels us to posit such underlying vowels, which fit into the vowel gradation system as follows:

(5)

	Zero-grade		*Full-grade*		*Extended-grade*	
Vowel	*PreC.*	*PreV.*	*PreC. (guṇa)*	*PreV.*	*PreC. (vr̥ddhi)*	*PreV.*
*m̥	a	m	am	am	ām	ām
*n̥	a	n	an	an	ān	ān

The following chart gives an example of a root with each vocalism (save for the *a*-vowels), with representative forms from the various categories:

(6)

		r̥	*i*	*u*	**m̥*	**n̥*
		kr̥	ji	su	gam	han
		"do, make"	"conquer"	"press"	"go"	"smash"
Zero:	*PreC.*	k**r̥**-ta	j**i**-ta	s**u**-ta	g**a**-ta	h**a**-ta
	PreV.	cak**r**-ur	jig**y**-ur	suṣ**v**-āna	jag**m**-ur	jagh**n**-ur
Full:	*PreC.*	k**ar**-tum	j**ē**-tum	s**ō**-tum	g**an**-tum	h**an**-tum
	PreV.	ak**ar**-am	j**ay**-ati	asūṣ**av**-at	ag**am**-am	ah**an**-am
Ext.:	*PreC.*	k**ār**-ya	aj**āi**-s	as**āu**-ṣīt	—	—
	PreV.	cak**ār**-a	aj**āy**-i	as**āv**-i	jag**ām**-a	jagh**ān**-a

3.5 Syllable structure and phonotaxis

There are few constraints on syllable structure. Syllables may both begin and end with vowels, single consonants, or consonant clusters; and internal vowels may be of any weight, even before coda consonants. In Vedic, however, some traces of phonological processes (*Sievers–Edgerton Law*) seemingly function to avoid overlong syllables: some suffixes containing *y* or *v* must be read as *iy* and *uv* after heavy syllables, but *y* and *v* after light syllables. But this is a morphologically limited phenomenon, not a pervasive phonological rule.

There are constraints on word-final consonants, which apply before external sandhi rules operate. Final clusters are not allowed (though monomorphemic *r*+ obstruent is rarely retained), and certain classes of sounds, such as aspirates and palatals, are not permitted finally.

3.6 Accent

Vedic Sanskrit has a pitch accent system, described also by Pāṇini, but accent has disappeared in Classical Sanskrit. The Vedic accent can fall anywhere in the word and, as it is not phonologically predictable, the position of the accent often conveys morphological and syntactic information.

Most Vedic words possess one accent. A few loosely bound compounds keep accent on both members, and a number of linguistic forms lack accent: some particles, some pronouns, and, most interestingly, noninitial vocatives and noninitial finite verbs in main (but not subordinate) clauses.

For ease of exposition, accent will in many instances not be marked in the ensuing discussions.

3.7 Diachronic developments

As in most early Indo-European languages, the loss of the so-called *laryngeal* consonants (cover-symbol **H*) of Proto-Indo-European had major effects on Sanskrit phonology and morphology. The phonological alternations originally caused by these segments have been morphologized in various ways, especially visible in the variant forms of roots.

1. *seṭ vs. aniṭ roots*: In many obstruent-final roots, an *i* (from vocalized **H*) surfaces in preconsonantal position, with no counterpart prevocalically. Such roots are known as *seṭ* ("with an *i*"), and contrast with apparently parallel *aniṭ* ("without an *i*") roots. Compare examples of identical morphological categories:

(7)

	seṭ:	*aniṭ:*
	pat "fly"	cit "think"
PreC.	pati-ta	cit-ta
PreV.	pat-ati	cet-ati

Because the distinction is neutralized in prevocalic position and because the interposition of the *i* helps to avoid the often awkward sandhi of consonant clusters, this *i* spreads beyond its original historical boundaries. Indeed, many suffixes and endings are reinterpreted as having an initial *i* (or at least an alternate form with initial *i*).

2. *Roots in *R̥H*: Sonorants (or resonants; i.e., *i*, *u*; *r̥*, (*l̥*); **m̥*, **n̥*) followed by a laryngeal in Proto-Indo-European yield so-called *long sonorants*, having root-final alternation patterns as follows:

(8)

	Zero-grade		*Full-grade*		*Extended-grade*	
Vowel	*PreC.*	*PreV.*	*PreC. (guṇa)*	*PreV.*	*PreC. (vr̥ddhi)*	*PreV.*
*r̥H	īr/ūr	ir/ur	ari	ar	āri	ār
*iH	ī	(i)y	ayi (> ē)	ay	āyi	āy
*uH	ū	(u)v	avi	av	āvi	āv
*m̥H	āṃ	(a)m	ami	am	āmi	ām
*n̥H	ā	(a)n	ani	an	āni	ān

Consider the following examples:

(9)

		**r̥H*	**iH*	**uH*	**m̥H*	**n̥H*
		tr̥̄	nī	bhū	kram	jan
		"cross"	"lead"	"become"	"stride"	"be born"
Zero:	*PreC.*	**tīr**-ṇa	n**ī**-ta	bh**ū**-ta	kr**āṃ**-ta	j**ā**-ta
	PreV.	**tir**-ati	nin(**i**)**y**-ur	bh**uv**-āni	cak**ram**-ur	ja**jñ**-ur
Full:	*PreC.*	**tari**-ṣyati	**nayi**-tum	bh**avi**-tum	kr**ami**-ṣyati	j**ani**-tum
	PreV.	**tar**-ati	n**ay**-ati	bh**av**-ati	kr**am**-ate	j**an**-ati

The distribution of *īr/ūr* and *ir/ur* forms in **r̥h* roots was originally conditioned by the quality of the preceding consonant, with *u*-forms following labials (e.g., √*pr̥̄* "fill," with *pūrṇa*).

3. *Roots in ā*: Such roots show an extremely anomalous set of alternations in comparison with the patterns set by other root types. As was first recognized by F. de Saussure in the 1870s, the anomalies can be explained by positing the same structure and alternations as in *seṭ* roots; in other words, by rewriting (in modern terms) *ā* as **VH* and its unstrengthened form as **H*, yielding *i* before consonant and zero before vowel:

(10)

	Zero-grade		*Full-grade*
	PreC.	*PreV.*	*PreC. (guṇa)*
(*VH) > ā	(*H) > i	ø	ā
for example,			
sthā "stand"	sth**i**-ta	tasth-ur	asth**ā**-**t**

4. MORPHOLOGY

4.1 Word formation

The basis of Sanskrit morphology is the *root*, a morpheme bearing lexical meaning. Through the vowel-gradation processes described above and through the addition of affixes, verbal and nominal *stems* are derived from this root. The grammatical and syntactic identity of a stem in context is then fixed by the addition of an *ending*. In other words, the three major formal elements of the morphology are (i) root, (ii) affix, and (iii) ending; and they are roughly responsible for (i) lexical meaning, (ii) derivation, and (iii) inflection respectively. A (noncompound) word ordinarily contains only one root and one ending, but may have a theoretically unlimited number of affixes. Both ending and affix may also be represented as zero. The canonical structure of a Sanskrit word is thus:

(11) Root – Affix $_{0\text{-}n}$ – Ending $_{0\text{-}1}$

Numerous examples of roots and their alternants were given above. There are some phonological constraints on root structure, the most important being that no root can end in short *a*, though affixes and endings commonly do, and all roots are monosyllabic (not counting the *i* of *seṭ* roots; see §3.7). There are also some restrictions on co-occurrence of consonants: for example, roots do not contain two aspirates (the historical result of Grassmann's Law) or stops from the same positional series in onset and coda.

Affixes are almost entirely suffixes. There is one infix, alternating *-na/n-* found in a single verbal present class, and one clear prefix, the so-called *augment*, an *a-* prefixed to past tense verb forms in the imperfect and aorist tenses. In addition, the class of *preverbs* mimic prefixes, because they precede a verb (and its nominal derivatives) and modify it semantically (e.g., *ud* "up," *pra* "forth"). In the earliest language, however, the status of these elements is not clear, or rather it fluctuates, as both their position and their accentuation show. In the *Rig-veda* preverbs regularly occur in tmesis, in other words, separated from the finite verb. Even when immediately preceding the verb, they maintain their own accent, except in subordinate clauses. This last context is the only one in which they clearly form a part of the phonological word of the finite verb. Preverbs always precede the one undeniable prefix, the augment. With nonfinite forms of the verb and with nominal derivatives thereof, preverbs show much clearer univerbation in Vedic, both by position and by accent, and by Classical Sanskrit tmesis is no longer possible even with finite forms.

In nominal morphology three elements, *a(n)-* "un," *su-* "well," and *dus-* "ill," function like prefixes, though technically forming compounds, both determinative and possessive.

Besides these few exceptions, suffixes are the rule in affixation. Though there are few absolute phonological constraints on suffixes, most are monosyllabic (though sometimes with the old laryngeal *i* attached, see above) and have relatively simple structure: CV is a common shape. The same is true of endings.

Reduplication is a common morphological process in the verbal system. Although the details cannot be examined, several of the phonological alternation processes discussed above are exemplified in reduplication: dissimilation of aspirates (√*dhā*: ***da-dhā***-), alternation of palatals and velars (√*kr̥*: ***ca-kr***-).

Some words do not conform to the canonical structure. A few forms lack both inflection and root and do not ordinarily serve as derivational bases: for example, the negatives *ná* and *mā́*, particles of various functions like *sú* and *hí*, and conjunctions like *ca* and *vā* (some are tonic, some not). Preverbs can be classified here at least originally.

Moreover, a much larger number of words are inflected (and can enter into derivation) but lack a recognizable root. These include many terms of basic vocabulary – kinship terms (e.g., *mātar-* "mother"), body parts (e.g., *nas-* "nose"), flora and fauna (e.g., *śvan-* "dog") – but are not limited to such semantic categories. Pronouns might be usefully classified here. Numerals also lack roots; some are inflected, some not.

Sanskrit morphology is conveniently divided into two fundamental categories, namely nominal forms and verbal forms, formally distinguished by the types of endings they take and the grammatical categories these endings mark. Adjectives and participles derived from verbs are not formally distinct from nouns; pronouns share the same grammatical categories with nouns, though they may deviate somewhat in inflection. "Adverbs" are usually frozen case forms of adjectives, and nonfinite verbal forms such as infinitives and gerunds also clearly show frozen nominal case endings.

Before discussing nominal and verbal forms separately, we should note certain features and processes they share. Perhaps the most important is the distinction in each between *thematic* and *athematic* inflection. Any *stem*, nominal or verbal, that ends in short *a* (i.e., ends with a suffix consisting of or containing short *a* as final vowel) is thematic. All thematic stems show fixed form throughout their inflection, modified only by the addition of endings. There are no stem alternants and there is no accent shift in the paradigm. Any stem not ending in short *a* is athematic and ordinarily will show stem alternants (as generated by the vowel strengthening patterns discussed above) and often movable accent. For example, the noun stem *deva-* "god" is thematic and maintains this form throughout, whereas *rājan-* "king" is athematic, with the following stem alternants: "strong" *rājān-* (/*rājā-*), "middle" *rājan-*, "weak" *rājñ-* (/*rāja-*). Similarly in verbs, a nonalternating thematic present stem like *bhava-* "become" contrasts with athematic *kr̥ṇó-* / *kr̥ṇu-* (with accent shifted to the ending) "make." Given the relative simplicity of the former and the frequent morphophonemic complications of the latter, thematic inflection spreads at the expense of athematic inflection during the history of Sanskrit.

Two of the facts noted above – that affixes can be athematic (and alternating) as well as thematic, and that Sanskrit words can contain more than one affix – interact with each other. With very rare exceptions, only one element in any Sanskrit word will alternate within a single paradigm; all the rest will remain frozen in a nonalternating, usually weak form. Whenever a suffix (thematic or athematic) is added to a stem, all preceding elements become frozen. For example, the root √*kr̥* alternates within its root aorist paradigm: *ákar-am* "I have made" versus *ákr-an* "they have made." However, when the present-stem alternating suffix *-nó/nu-* is added, the root syllable *kr̥* is fixed in zero-grade: *kr̥-ṇó-/kr̥-ṇu-*. In turn, with the optative suffix *-yā́/ī-* added to that, the present stem is frozen in weak form: *kr̥ṇu-yā́-/kr̥ṇv-ī-*.

4.2 Nominal morphology

The grammatical categories of Sanskrit nominal forms are gender, number, and case.

4.2.1 Gender

Three genders exist: masculine, neuter, and feminine. Nouns have inherent gender; personal pronouns have no gender, though demonstrative and anaphoric pronouns do. The formal expression is not parallel among the three genders. The feminine is primarily expressed by *derivation*: there are two important feminine-forming suffixes, *-ā- and -ī-*. By contrast, the difference between masculine and neuter is primarily *inflectional.* For the most part the same suffixes form both masculine and neuter nouns, and different case endings signal the different genders. Most stems formally encode masculine versus neuter only in nominative and accusative. A few stem-types (especially *i*-stems) form feminines as well as masculines and neuters, where the feminine is distinguished by different case endings and by the form of modifying adjectives.

4.2.2 Number

Three numbers occur: singular, dual, and plural. The dual is a fully functioning category, used not merely for naturally paired objects, like eyes, but for any collection of two. Notable in Vedic is the "elliptical" dual, with a noun in the dual signalling a conventional paired opposition: for example, *dyāvā*, literally "the two heavens," for "heaven and earth"; *mātarā*, literally "the two mothers," for "mother and father." Number is entirely an inflectional category, except in the personal pronoun.

4.2.3 Case

Sanskrit has eight cases: nominative, accusative, instrumental, dative, ablative, genitive, locative, vocative, though no stems make all eight distinctions in all three numbers. In all stems the dual shows only three distinctions: (i) nominative, accusative, and vocative merge; as do (ii) instrumental, dative, ablative; and (iii) genitive, locative. In all nominal stems the plural collapses nominative and vocative, as well as dative and ablative; only the personal pronouns distinguish dative and ablative in the plural. Even in the singular most stems conflate ablative and genitive; only one nominal stem-type (though the most common, the short *a*-stem) and the pronouns distinguish ablative and genitive singular. Thus, since pronouns lack vocatives, only one stem-type (*a*-stem) has eight distinct case forms in any number. Case function is discussed in §5.

Case is marked inflectionally, by endings, and by stem-form alternations. In alternating paradigms some cases regularly pattern together, in other words, show the same stem alternants. Normally (i) nominative/accusative singular, (ii) nominative/vocative plural and (iii) nominative/accusative/vocative dual (the so-called *strong* cases) operate in opposition to the other, *weak cases* (the terms *direct* versus *oblique* have almost the same range of reference, but are syntactic not formal designations; moreover, the accusative plural is also a direct case).

4.2.4 Nominal stem-classes

Unlike a language such as Latin or Greek, Sanskrit has no closed set of conventionally denoted *noun declensions*. Instead, there is a fairly large set of stem-types, some of which share features of patterning, as well as a sizable group of exceptional stems (not treated here). The first major division is between *root nouns* and *derived nouns*. As the name implies, root nouns combine the bare root, without suffixes, with endings, while derived nouns interpose suffix(es) between root and ending.

4.2.4.1 Vowel stems

The major division in derived nouns is between vowel stems and consonant stems, distinguished by the patterning of stem alternants and to some extent by endings. Among vowel stems we can differentiate three types:

1. The short *a* thematic type, the commonest stem-type in the language, forming masculines (e.g., *deva-* "god") and neuters (e.g., *phala-* "fruit"). Besides its invariant stem, it is distinguished by somewhat aberrant endings and by the fact that it alone has eight distinct forms in the singular.
2. The *ā* and *ī* feminine stems (e.g., *senā-* "army," *devī-* "goddess"). In addition to their gender, these stems share a distinctive set of endings in the singular oblique cases.
3. The stems in short *i* and *u*, forming nouns of all three genders (e.g., masc. *agni-* "fire," fem. *mati-* "thought," neut. *vāri-* "water"; masc. *paśu-* "cow," fem. *dhenu-* "milk-cow," neut. *vasu-* "wealth"). In early Vedic the inflection of all three genders is essentially the same (save for the neuter endings of the direct cases), with weak forms of the stem in the singular direct cases (*agni-*) and strong forms in the singular oblique (*agnay-*). Gradually all three genders develop separate singular oblique forms. The feminine stems become more like the stems of type **2**.

4.2.4.2 *Consonant stems*

A number of varieties occur (*an-*, *ar-*, *ant-*, *vas-*, and *as-*stems, among others), forming primarily masculine and neuter nouns. Most consonant stems share a general patterning tendency: strong forms of the stem occur in the "strong" cases, weak in the "weak" cases (e.g., *rā́jān-* vs. *rā́jñ-*; *kartár-* vs. *kartr-*; *sánt-* vs. *sat-*, etc.), in direct opposition to the patterning of the short vowel stems just discussed. A few stem-types show no significant stem alternation (*in-*stems, neuter *s-*stems). Note also that *ar-*stems are often classified as vowel stems (i.e., as *r̥-*stems), and several of their cases have indeed adopted vowel-stem forms (especially acc. pl., gen. pl.). But the patterning of their stem alternants clearly classifies them with consonant stems, especially *an-*stems.

4.2.5 Endings

Though no scheme of endings is applicable to all stems and all periods of the language, the following chart gives the most common patterns. When there are significant differences, both consonant and vowel-stem endings are given, as well as some feminine alternants.

(12)

	Singular				*Dual*		*Plural*		
	Cons.	*Vow.*	*Fem.*	*Neut.*	*Cons.*	*Neut.*	*Cons.*	*Vow.*	*Neut.*
Nom.	ø	-s		ø	-au	-ī	-as		-V̄ni
Acc.	-am	-m		[=nom.]	[=nom.]		-as	-V̄n	[=nom.]
Instr.	-ā	-nā	-ā		-bhyām			-bhis	
Dat.	-ē	-ē	-āi		[=instr.]			-bhyas	
Abl.	-as	-s	-ās		[=instr.]			[=dat.]	
Gen.		[=abl.]			-os		-ām	-V̄nām	
Loc.	-i	*var.*	-ām		[=gen.]			-su	
Voc.	ø	*var.*	*var.*		[=nom.]			[=nom.]	

4.2.6 Comparison of adjectives

There are two different patterns for producing comparatives and superlatives, one primary, that is, by direct attachment to the root, not to a derived adjective (comp. *-īyas-*, splv. *-iṣṭha-*); the other secondary, by attachment to an existing adjective (*-tara-*, *-tama-*). An example of each follows:

(13)	*primary*	urú- "wide"	várīyas- "wider"	váriṣṭha- "widest"
	secondary	priyá- "dear"	priyátara- "dearer"	priyátama- "dearest"

In Vedic the secondary suffixes are used rather freely, for example, in compounds like *somapātama-* "most soma-drinking" (i.e., "best drinker of soma"); *vr̥trahantama-* "most Vr̥tra-smashing" (i.e., "best smasher of Vr̥tra").

4.2.7 Pronouns

The major division within this category is between (i) the personal pronouns of the first and second persons, unmarked for gender, and (ii) a larger number of gender-distinguishing demonstrative/deictic/anaphoric pronouns and adjectives.

4.2.7.1 Personal pronouns

The cases of these pronouns were noted above, as was the occurrence of a different stem in each number. The number of stems is in fact still greater, in that the first singular and plural and the second plural use a different form for the nominative than for the rest of the paradigm:

(14)		*1st sg.*	*1st pl.*	*2nd pl.*
	Nom.	ahám	vayám	yūyám
	Elsewhere	m-	asm-	yuṣm-

The other stem formants are 1st dual *āv-*, 2nd. sg. *tu-*, 2nd dual *yuv-*. There also exist enclitic oblique forms, often with yet a different stem (e.g., 1st. pl. *nas*, 2nd pl. *vas*). The endings of the personal pronouns are in part unique to them.

4.2.7.2 Gender-marking pronouns

Such pronouns are characterized by a number of different paradigms and partial paradigms, with different functions sometimes changing over time. Most can be used both as pronouns proper and as demonstrative adjectives. We will mention only the most important and widespread stems, beginning with the strong deictics, nearer *ayám* "this here," farther *asáu* "that yonder." Both have rather aberrant inflection, with an assortment of stems collected from different sources.

The most common pronominal stem is *sá/tám*, with a wide range of uses. While it serves as the anaphoric pronominal par excellence, it also shows traces in early Vedic of deictic usage. Moreover, it is the closest element Sanskrit possesses to both a third-person pronoun and to a definite article. It is also sometimes used with both second- and first-person reference. Its inflection shows archaic inherited features, with initial *s-* in nominative singular (masc. *sá* and fem. *sā́*), versus *t-* elsewhere (replicated by Greek masc. *ho*, fem. *hē* [with *h-* < **s-*] but neut. *tó*; see *WAL* Ch. 24, §4.1.3.4), and with an endingless nominative singular masculine (under certain sandhi conditions).

This stem also shows some peculiarities of inflection, some of which are found also in the stems of the interrogative (*ká-*), the relative (*yá-*), and a class of "pronominal adjectives" such as "other" (*anyá-*), "all" (*víśva-*, replaced by *sárva-*), "one/some" (*éka-*).

4.3 Verbal morphology

Like nouns, verbs are either thematic or athematic. Athematic verbs regularly alternate strong (guṇa) forms in the active singular, weak in the rest of the inflection.

The grammatical categories of finite verbs are person, number, voice, tense/aspect, and mood. In general, person/number/voice are expressed by a portmanteau morpheme, the ending; tense/aspect by suffixes, morphological processes directly affecting the root, and/or endings; and mood by suffixes (or endings) following the tense/aspect markers. The canonical shape of a verb is thus:

(15) Root – (Tense/Aspect suffix) – (Mood suffix) – Per./Num./Voice ending

4.3.1 Person and number

These categories index the subject of the verb. There are three persons, first, second, and third (in Western grammatical terminology); and three numbers, singular, dual, and plural. As in the noun, the dual is fully functioning, not limited to subjects naturally occurring in pairs. The nine-member grid defined by these two parameters is the basic building block of the Sanskrit verbal system, the paradigm. Each person/number pair is marked by a separate ending.

4.3.2 Voice

The approach to this topic will differ depending on whether formal or functional aspects are emphasized. Formally, many Sanskrit nine-member paradigms come in matched pairs, in two different voices – with identical stems but different endings. The two voices are *active* and *middle* (or *mediopassive*), or, in the more perspicuous Sanskrit terms, *parasmaipada* "word for another" and *ātmanepada* "word for oneself." A typical formal configuration, the endings of the present, active, and middle, is given below:

(16)

	Active			*Middle*		
	Singular	*Dual*	*Plural*	*Singular*	*Dual*	*Plural*
1st	-mi	-vas	-mas	-e	-vahe	-mahe
2nd	-si	-thas	-tha	-se	-āthe	-dhve
3rd	-ti	-tas	-anti	-te	-āte	-ante

The function of the separate voices is harder to define. Though there exist contrasting pairs such as act. *yajati* "sacrifices (on another's behalf)" : mid. *yajate* "sacrifices (for one's own benefit)," which illustrate the Sanskrit terminology, there are other active : middle functional relations: for example, transitive : intransitive, act. *vardhati* "increases X" : mid. *vardhate* "X increases." Some middles are simply passive in value, though lacking overt passive suffix, and an even greater number have no obvious functional correlate: for example, the numerous *deponents* (to use the Latin term) inflected only in the middle (e.g., *āste* "sits"). The distinction between active and middle is, in the main, a purely formal one synchronically; not surprisingly, the distinction becomes attenuated in the development of the language.

There is, however, an important functional distinction in voice, with various formal encodings: that between active and passive. As just noted, the formal middle sometimes functions as a passive. One particular present-stem type, the suffix-accented *-yá*-present with middle endings, also becomes specialized as a passive (e.g., *ucyate* "is spoken"); and the aorist system contains a third singular of peculiar formation (heavy root syllable and mysterious ending *-i*; type *avāci* "was spoken"), the so-called aorist passive. Passive value is also expressed by several verbal adjectives, the gerundive ("future passive participle") in *-ya-* and *-tavya-*, and especially the past passive participle in *-ta-* (/*-na-*). The latter often substitutes for a finite verb as sentential predicate.

4.3.3 Tense-aspect

The backbone of the tense-aspect system is the three-way contrast between the *present* system, the *aorist* system, and the *perfect* system. Each of these stems produces one or more tenses, as well as (in the early language) moods and participles. The present system has two tenses, the present and the imperfect. In post-Rig-vedic Sanskrit both the aorist and the perfect have only one, though in the *Rig-veda* there is a marginal pluperfect beside the perfect. All three systems can be inflected in either voice:

(17)

Stem		*Tense*
present	{	present
		imperfect
aorist	—	aorist
perfect	{	perfect
		(pluperfect)

Like voice, the tense-aspect system is an elaborate formal edifice whose functional motivations have essentially broken down. Though the system inherited from Proto-Indo-European was an aspectual one, aspect is no longer a clear category even in early Vedic, and only relics of the inherited system can be discerned in the *Rig-veda*. From the Sanskrit point of view, the salient functional distinction is *tense*: present (expressed by the present tense) versus past (expressed by three competing preterital forms, imperfect, aorist, and perfect, as well as by certain nonfinite forms used predicatively).

The old perfect was a stative present functionally; a few Vedic perfects maintain this function, but most already express simple past. The original distinction between the present and aorist systems was probably durative versus punctual, but this can no longer be discerned. Insofar as the aorist can be distinguished from the imperfect in Sanskrit, it expresses immediate past time. The loss of functional distinction among the three past tenses set the stage for the loss of those formal categories in later Indo-Aryan.

4.3.4 Perfect stem morphology

Formally, the perfect is characterized by special endings and, except for one widespread old form (*veda* "knows"), by reduplication. It is built directly to the root, without affixes, and shows ordinary strong/weak stem alternation (type *cakā́r-a*/*cakr-úr*). There is only one type of perfect stem formation (except for the "periphrastic perfect" of derivative presents; see §4.3.6).

4.3.5 Primary and secondary endings

The formal distinction between present and aorist systems is less well marked. The endings of the imperfect tense and the aorist are identical (the so-called *secondary* endings), and the endings of the present tense (the *primary* endings) closely resemble these. Compare, for example, the primary and secondary endings of the active singular, and contrast them with the corresponding perfect endings:

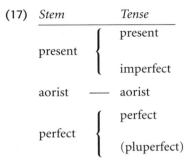

(18)

	Primary	*Secondary*	*Perfect*
1st	-mi	-m	-a
2nd	-si	-s	-tha
3rd	-ti	-t	-a

Unlike the perfect both imperfect and aorist prefix the augment, regularly in Classical Sanskrit and optionally (but commonly) in Vedic. Moreover, several types of stem formation are common to both present and aorist.

4.3.6 Present stem morphology

The indigenous grammarians distinguish ten present classes, which can be conveniently divided into thematic and athematic types. Four thematic classes occur, with the following suffixes added to the root: *-a-* (Class I); *- á-* (VI); *-ya-* (IV); and *-áya-* (X). The six athematic classes are as follows: simple root presents (endings added directly to the alternating root, Class II); reduplicated presents (III); and four classes continuing (directly or indirectly) nasal affixes – nasal infix (VII), and suffixed *-nó/nu-* (V), *-ó/u-* (VIII), and *-nā́/nī-* (IX). Examples of each follow; thematic forms (with nonalternating stems) are given in the third singular active present, athematic forms in both third singular and third plural active, to display both stem alternants:

(19) Sanskrit present tense classes

I	*simple thematic*	√bhū "become"	bháva-ti
II	*root*	√as "be"	ás-ti, s-ánti
III	*reduplicated*	√hu "pour"	juhó-ti, juhv-áti
IV	*-ya-*	√paś "see"	páśya-ti
V	*-nó/nu-*	√su "press"	sunó-ti, sunv-ánti
VI	*-á-*	√viś "enter"	viśá-ti
VII	*nasal-infix*	√yuj "yoke"	yunák-ti, yuñj-ánti
VIII	*-ó/u-*	√tan "spread"	tanó-ti, tanv-ánti
IX	*-nā́/nī-*	√krī "buy"	krīṇā́-ti, krīṇ-ánti
X	*-áya-*	√cint "think"	cintáya-ti

There is no longer any clear distinction in function among these various present classes, though again traces of prehistoric distinctions can occasionally be discerned.

Besides the above ten classes, several other formations are formally presents, but are classified separately because they have clear functional correlates.

The *future* is formed with the thematic suffix *-syá-* (or *-iṣyá-* originally proper to seṭ roots) (e.g., *kariṣyáti* "will do": √*kṛ*). There is also a periphrastic future, formed from a noun stem with the *-tar-* agent suffix.

The so-called secondary conjugations:

1. *Passive*, formed with accented *-yá-* and middle endings, for example, *nīyáte* "is led": √*nī* "lead." In Classical Sanskrit with the loss of accent the passive cannot be formally distinguished from a middle Class IV present.
2. *Intensive*, formed with heavy reduplication (sometimes disyllabic) and, in later Sanskrit, a *-yá-* suffix with middle endings. The intensive expresses repeated or intensively performed action, for example, *mármarj-*, *marmṛjyáte* "wipe repeatedly, groom": √*mṛj* "wipe."

3. *Desiderative*, formed with reduplication in *-i-* and a *-sa-* suffix. The desiderative expresses action desired, intended, or about to take place, for example, *pípāsati* "desires, intends, is about to drink": √*pā* "drink."
4. *Causative*, formed with a heavy root syllable and a suffix *-áya-*. Formally not distinguishable from Class X presents, except sometimes in the shape of the root syllable. In the earlier language the causative is ordinarily formed only to intransitive verbs, for example, *pādáyati* "cause to fall": √*pad* "fall."

In addition to present stems built to verbal roots, nouns and adjectives can form *denominative* presents by the addition of the suffix *-yá-*, for example, *áśva-* "horse": *aśvayáti* "seek horses."

The above derivative present stems can form a secondary periphrastic perfect, with a feminine accusative singular generated to the present stem, plus the perfect of √*kr̥* (in the earlier language), √*bhū* or √*as* (in the later language), of the type *pādayā́ṃ cakāra/āsa* "caused to fall." The periphrastic perfect is especially common with causatives.

4.3.7 Aorist stem morphology

The aorist shares certain stem-types with the present system. The root aorist (e.g., *ábhūt*: √*bhū* "become") and thematic aorist (*ávidat*: √*vid* "find") resemble Class II and VI presents. Class III presents somewhat resemble the reduplicated aorist, though the aorist has certain formal characteristics (heavy *ī-* reduplication, thematic vowel) and a functional connection with the causative (type *ápīpadat* "caused to fall," parallel to *pādáyati* "causes to fall") that set it apart.

Proper to the aorist, however, are a variety of sigmatic formations. The *s*-aorist and *iṣ*-aorist were originally identically built, with *s*-suffix, to aniṭ and seṭ roots respectively. Especially notable in these formations is the consistent vr̥ddhi of the root in the entire active voice, an unusual distribution of grades (e.g., *s*-aor. *ájai-s-* "he conquered": √*ji* "conquer"; *ápāvi-ṣ-* "purified": √*pū* "purify"). Analogic extensions of these two aorist types led to the creation of the marginal types, *siṣ*-aorist and *sa*-aorist.

The passive aorist was noted in §4.3.2.

4.3.8 Mood

There are four clear moods in early Sanskrit: indicative, imperative, optative, and subjunctive. In addition, the so-called injunctive of early Vedic is considered a mood by some, and the precative, a subtype of the optative, develops in the course of Vedic. This system is reduced by Classical Sanskrit. One global change is the virtual restriction of nonindicative moods to the present stem; in Vedic, aorists and perfects displayed broader modality. Furthermore, the subjunctive is effectively lost, and the injunctive, insofar as it is a mood, becomes restricted in usage.

4.3.8.1 Indicative

The indicative is the unmarked mood, used for statements, questions, etc.

4.3.8.2 Imperative

The imperative expresses command and is marked by special endings on the appropriate tense stem. In Vedic the imperative has a defective paradigm, being found only in second and third persons, but as the subjunctive is lost as a functional category, its first-person forms are incorporated into the imperative. The negative imperative (i.e., prohibitive) is expressed not by the formal imperative mood, but by the injunctive with a special form of the negative, namely *mā́* (not *ná*).

There is also a rare second imperative formation, the so-called *future imperative*, made by adding *-tāt* to the tense stem, expressing a command to be executed after the action of an intervening verb. Its value is usually second singular.

4.3.8.3 Optative

The optative expresses possibility ("might," "could"), necessity ("should," "ought to"), and will/desire ("would"), and is marked by a suffix added to the tense stem. For athematic stems, the suffix is *-yā́-* in the active, *-ī-* in the middle, added to the weak stem form (e.g., *s-yā́-* to root pres. *as-ti*, *s-anti*: √*as*; *kr̥ṇu-yā́-*, *kr̥ṇv-ī-* to *kr̥ṇóti* : √*kr̥*). For thematic stems, *-ē-* is substituted for the thematic vowel *-a-* throughout (e.g., *bhávē-* to thematic pres. *bháva-*: √*bhū*). Both suffixes take secondary endings, with some special details.

The precative is a supercharged optative, primarily expressing desire. It is formed by interposing an *-s-* between the optative suffix and the ending. Thus, the ordinary athematic optative first singular ends in *-yā́m*, that of the precative in *-yā́sam*; that of the first plural optative in *-yā́ma*, the precative in *-yā́sma*.

4.3.8.4 Subjunctive

This mood has disappeared (except for its formal representatives in the imperative) by Classical Sanskrit. It is formed by adding a suffix *-a-* (identical to the thematic vowel) to the tense stem; in thematic verbs this produces a contracted suffix *-ā-* (e.g., *bhávā-* to *bháva-ti*). Athematic verbs add the *-a-* to their strong forms (e.g., *ás-a-* to *ás-ti*; *kr̥ṇáv-a-* to *kr̥ṇó-ti*). The subjunctive stem can take either primary or secondary endings (*ásati*, *ásat*, etc.); in addition, the typical final vowel of primary middle endings, *-e*, is usually strengthened to *-āi* after the Rig-vedic period.

The function of the subjunctive is difficult to define. It often seems to express the future, or volitional future, rather than the more strictly *modal* value its Western name implies. This interpretation fits well with the fact that the future tense is quite rare in early Vedic in finite forms; their place seems to be filled by the subjunctive.

4.3.8.5 Injunctive

Formally the term *injunctive* simply refers to unaugmented preterite forms (i.e., imperfects and aorists). Such forms are quite common in the *Rig-veda* in a variety of contexts, but only one usage persists into later Vedic and Classical Sanskrit: the conjoining of aorist injunctive and the particle *mā́* to express prohibitions. Despite the best efforts of numerous distinguished scholars, a common functional core cannot be discerned in the other Rig-vedic contexts, and it seems best to regard these forms as not belonging to a unified modal category, but rather representing a period when the prefixation of the augment was still optional in the preterite.

4.3.9 Nonfinite verbals

Sanskrit possesses a large number of verbal nouns and verbal adjectives, of common occurrence. These ordinarily show verbal syntax (objects in the accusative, for example), and many can stand as the main verb in a clause. Some are built directly to the root, some to tense stems.

4.3.9.1 *Infinitive*

Classical Sanskrit has a single infinitive, built with the suffix *-tum* added directly to the root in guṇa form (type *kar-tum*: √*kr̥*), which is much rarer in textual usage than the infinitives of other early Indo-European languages. It continues the frozen accusative singular of a nominal stem with a *tu*-suffix, and indeed in Vedic other case forms of this stem appear in infinitival usage: dative *-tave* (/*-tavā́i*), ablative-genitive *-tos*. In addition, other stem-types form infinitives or quasi-infinitives in Vedic, for example, datives to *as*-stems in *-ase*. The line between an infinitive and a simple noun can be difficult to draw in the early language.

Infinitives appear as complements to verbs such as √*śak* "be able" and are used to express purpose. They are neutral as to voice and can express either active ("to X") or passive ("to be Xed") value, usually depending on the voice of the form to which they are complement.

4.3.9.2 *Gerund*

These frozen instrumentals, common in Sanskrit of all periods, are used to express an action prior to (or just simultaneous with) that of the main verb. Standard Classical Sanskrit has two formations, formally distributed: *-tvā* (also made to the *tu*-stem noted under the infinitive, §4.3.9.1) built to an uncompounded root; and *-(t)ya* built to preverb + root (thus the type *kr̥-tvā* vs. *pra-kr̥-tya*). This formal distribution is not always adhered to in the earlier language, and several other related suffixes are also employed.

4.3.9.3 *Tense-stem participles*

As with the moods, participles tend to become restricted to the present stem in later Sanskrit, although Vedic allows participles to be built to all three tense-aspect stems. Tense-stem participles distinguish voice. The active participle suffix for present and aorist is *-ant-*; the middle suffix for all three tense-aspect stems is *-āna-* for athematic verbs, *-māna-* for thematic. The active perfect participle is made with the suffix *-vas-*, of curious inflection. Though most nonpresent participles disappear by Classical Sanskrit, the perfect participle to *véda* "knows," *vid-vás-*, survives as an adjective meaning "knowing, wise."

4.3.9.4 *Past passive participle*

This is an extremely common form, both as an attributive adjective and as a predicative verb substitute. It is built directly to the unstrengthened root with the suffixes *-tá-*, *-itá-* (originating in seṭ roots and still largely found there), *-ná-*, and, rarely, *-vá-*: types *kr̥-ta-* "made, done": √*kr̥* "make, do"; *muṣitá-* "stolen": √*muṣ(i)* "steal"; *san-ná* "seated": √*sad* "sit"; *pakvá-* "cooked, ripe": √*pac* "cook." Competing with the three finite past tense forms discussed above, the past passive participle is often the successful contestant, and is responsible for the preterites in a number of later Indo-Aryan languages.

4.3.9.5 *Past active participle*

Derived from the past passive participle by the addition of the possessive suffix *-vant-* (type *kr̥távant-* to *kr̥tá-*), it is far less successful than its base.

4.3.9.6 *Gerundive (or future passive participle)*

The gerundive is another form with passive value, but with the additional component of obligation or necessity ("to be X-ed"), often the equivalent of a passive optative (type *kartavya-* "to be done"). It is formed directly to the root by the addition of one of several suffixes, the most common being *-tavya-* and *-ya-*.

4.4 Compounds

Sanskrit has an extremely well-developed system of nominal compounding; verbal compounding hardly exists. In Vedic, though all types of nominal compounds occur and are frequently encountered, individual compounds are usually limited to two or three members. In Classical Sanskrit, compounds of dozens of members are not infrequent, especially in philosophical texts: the compounding process comes to take the place of the independent syntactic arrangement of inflected words.

4.4.1 Verbal compounds

The verb shows two types of quasi-compounding: (i) the gradual incorporation of preverbs (and functionally equivalent elements) into a verbal complex (type √*gam* "go": *ā*√*gam* "come"); (ii) the so-called *cvī* construction, which combines nouns and adjectives with both finite and nonfinite forms of the roots √*kr̥* "make" and √*bhū* "become" (meaning "make/become X"). In such cases, the nominal first member substitutes invariant -*ī*- for a stem-vowel -*a*- or -*i*-, -*ū*- for -*u*- (e.g., *stambhī-bhavati* "becomes a post": *stambha*- "post").

4.4.2 Nominal compounds

Formally, nominal compounding ordinarily involves the concatenation of uninflected words (i.e., stems), resulting in a unit with a single ending and a single accent. The stems may include nouns, adjectives (including participles), adverbs, and pronouns. Both the single ending and the single accent have exceptions in the early language. Inflected case forms may appear in prior compound members, as in *rathe-ṣṭhā́*- "standing *on* a chariot" (with the first member in the locative case). And *paral* compounds (dual dvandvas; see §4.4.2.1) with both members in the dual *and* both accented (e.g., *mitrā́-váruṇā* "Mitra [and] Varuṇa") are a well-attested feature of Rig-vedic discourse.

There are three major types of nominal compounds: copulative, determinative, and possessive, known familiarly by their Sanskrit names as *dvandva*, *tatpuruṣa*, and *bahuvrīhi* respectively.

4.4.2.1 Dvandvas

These copulative compounds conjoin two or more stems as parallel members of a series: $X + Y + Z \ldots$ (the "lions and tigers and bears" type). Formally the compound may either take the gender of its final member and be inflected as dual or plural (as appropriate), or be treated as a neuter singular collective. In either case the final member is accented (in accented texts). On the Rig-vedic dual dvandvas, with double inflection and double accent, see §4.4.2.

4.4.2.2 Tatpuruṣa

The prior member of this determinative compound limits the following member in some way. Two major subtypes can be distinguished according to the underlying case relations of the members: dependent (*tatpuruṣa* proper) and descriptive (*karmadhāraya*). In the former the prior compound member would be in a different case from that one which follows. A typical relation is genitive + head, as in *nr̥-páti*-, literally "man-lord," that is "lord *of* men"; but other relations are common, especially the limiting of a final past passive participle by an underlying instrumental agent – type *agni-taptá*-, literally "fire-heated," that is, "heated *by* fire." In karmadhārayas the prior member is either a qualifier in the same underlying case as that member which it limits (typically an adjective, i.e., the "black-bird" type) or an adverbial element (*su-* "well," *dus-* "ill," and *a(n)-* "un-" are especially common). The accentual facts of determinatives are complex, but in general the accent falls on the final syllable or the final member.

4.4.2.3 *Bahuvrīhi*

This possessive compound may be based on any of the preceding types, but adds to the concatenation the semantic feature of possession: the formal sequence $X + Y$ means not simply "X-Y" but "possessing X-Y." English has similar compounds; compare *red-head* and *Bluebeard*.

An important formal consequence of the addition of this semantic feature is that the compound, whose final member is a noun, must be transformed into an adjective, capable of inflection in all genders (hence the common designation "secondary adjective compound"). Sometimes the gender switch can be accomplished silently, as it were, as when neuter nouns in *-a-* simply take masculine endings in the nominative and accusative. Sometimes the adjustment simply requires lengthening or shortening the stem-vowel, as when masculine or neuter nouns in *-a-* become feminized as *ā*-stems or, vice versa, a feminine long *ā-* or *ī*-stem is inflected as a short *a-* or *i*-stem in the masculine or neuter. At other times more complex processes must be employed. These possessive adjectives are then often resubstantivized; bahuvrīhis are a rich source for proper names in Indic and other Indo-European languages (as *Bluebeard* demonstrates).

As with determinatives, the accentual facts are complex, but the accent generally falls on the first member. In accented texts it is thus easy to distinguish determinative compounds from bahuvrīhis, but in later Sanskrit this is not formally possible unless the bahuvrīhi has undergone gender shift.

We might note here that Sanskrit nominal morphology engages in a kind of conspiracy to express the semantic feature "possessing." When a bahuvrīhi cannot be formed, because the notion being expressed is not a compound, a variety of suffixes may be utilized, especially *-vant-* (*-mant-*) and *-in-*, and in early Vedic simple accent shift is possible (e.g., *bráhman-* "formulation" gives *brahmán-* "possessing a formulation," "priest").

4.5 Numerals

The cardinals from 1 to 10, 20, 100, and 1,000 are:

(20)	1	*éka-*
	2	*dvá-*
	3	*trí-*
	4	*catúr-*
	5	*páñca*
	6	*ṣáṣ*
	7	*saptá*
	8	*aṣṭá*
	9	*náva*
	10	*dáśa*
	20	*viṃśatí*
	100	*śatá*
	1,000	*sahásra*

The relation of most of these to numerals in other Indo-European languages should be obvious.

There are some unusual inflectional details. *Dvá-* "two" is inflected regularly as a dual in all three genders (masc. nom./acc. *dváu*; fem., neut. *dvé*, etc.). Both *trí-* "three" and *catúr-* "four" display some archaic inflectional features, especially the feminine formant *-sr-* between stem and ending; thus nom./acc. pl. *tisrás* (with dissimilation < **tri-sr-as*), *cátasras*.

Ordinals are derived from cardinals with the suffixes *-ma-* (e.g., *pañcama-* "fifth") and, rarely, *-tha-* (e.g., *ṣaṣṭha-* "sixth"). Irregular forms include

(21)	first	*prathama-*
	second	*dvitīya-*
	third	*tr̥tīya-*
	fourth	*turīya-* Vedic (< **ktur-*), also *caturtha-*

5. SYNTAX

Because of its elaborate morphology many traditionally "syntactic" phenomena take place on the level of morphosyntax in Sanskrit. In particular the case system allows the syntactic roles of nominals to be encoded without recourse to rigid word order or obligatory adpositions. Both prepositions and postpositions are rare in early Sanskrit; they become more common later, developing from old preverbs and from frozen case forms of nouns.

5.1 Case usage

Sanskrit cases and their uses are typical of an early Indo-European language: vocative (address); nominative (subject); accusative (direct object; goal of motion; a number of adverbial uses, notably duration of time); instrumental (accompaniment; instrument; agent of the passive; adverbial uses); dative (purpose; indirect object, though the genitive is more commonly used for the latter); ablative (source; cause; comparison); genitive (found in all varieties of adnominal usage; a genitive absolute is also occasionally found, cf. locative absolute); locative (location in both space and time; goal of motion). The locative is also the normal "absolute" case: a noun and modifying participle in the locative can express the time or attendant circumstances under which the action of the main clause occurs: for example, "(on) the sun having risen," "(on) the enemy fleeing."

5.2 Word order

Although the case system obviates the need for rigid word order, the order of elements in a Sanskrit sentence is not entirely free. Ordinary prose is SOV (Subject–Object–Verb), with many of the standard typological features of this ordering, such as genitives preceding heads. Poetry and artful prose, however, exploit the opportunities that the syntactic clarity of the morphological system affords, by thoroughly scrambling the order of elements for expressive or discourse purposes. Even in the most extreme examples, however, it is usually possible to formulate principles of movement from a putative underlying order parallel to simple prose.

Overt marking of the subject is not necessary; the bare verb, with person/number markings, is sufficient. First- and second-person subject pronouns are used in addition to the verb only for emphatic or contrastive value. The third-person "pronoun" *sá* is more frequent with third-person verbs, but it ordinarily serves discourse functions: anaphoric to a noun previous in the discourse or coreferent with the relative pronoun in a subordinate clause.

Not only finite verb forms but also participles, especially the past passive participle, can fill the slot V. In this case the copula normally appears only in the first and second persons, and even in those circumstances the personal pronoun can serve instead:

(22)	*gató 'smi* (with copula)	or	*ahám̥ gatáḥ* (with pronoun)	"I went"
	gató 'si (with copula)	or	*tvám̥ gatáḥ* (with pronoun)	"you went"
	but	*gataḥ*		"he [she/it] went"

Also common are nominal sentences – that is, the predication of a noun (or adjective) to a noun (or pronoun) without an overt copula.

5.3 Cliticization

As in other early Indo-European languages, sentences frequently begin with a chain of clitics attached to the initial, accented word of the sentence, occupying "Wackernagel's position." Such a chain of clitics (and pseudo-clitics – some carry accent) consists of sentential particles (often several to the sentence), conjunctions, and pronouns fronted from their underlying position in the clause; their order is determined by both syntactic class and phonological shape. Word-level conjunctions and pronominal clitics may also appear elsewhere in the clause, the latter ordinarily attached to their head. In such positions the pronoun may either precede or follow the word it is attached to, but clause-initial proclitics are not permitted: all clauses (and their metrical equivalent, verse lines) begin with an accented word. Especially common initial hosts include coordinating and subordinating conjunctions, preverbs in tmesis, and tonic demonstrative and anaphoric pronouns. Much recent work on Sanskrit syntax has concentrated on the constituents of this initial chain and their functions.

5.4 Subordination

A fully inflected relative pronoun *yá-* and a number of subordinating conjunctions built to this stem (*yadā́* "when," *yádi* "if," etc.) mark subordinate clauses. These elements are normally fronted (*wh-movement*) from wherever they originate in the clause, but as other elements (including entire constituents) can be topicalized around them, the fronting is sometimes not superficially obvious. Relative clauses either precede or follow the main clause (the former is more usual except in the case of relative clauses of purpose); there is almost no embedding.

In early Vedic, subordinate clauses are sometimes marked only by verbal accentuation, not by a subordinating conjunction; and some particles (notably *hí*) also induce verbal accentuation, presumably a mark of subordination.

Indirect discourse is quite rare, especially in Classical Sanskrit; such clauses are usually expressed by direct discourse marked by the clause-final quotative particle *iti.* For example, "he thought that he would go" would be expressed as "he thought, 'I will go.' "

Other, nonclausal types of subordination are quite common. For example, a series of gerunds with nominal complements is often completed by a single finite verb (type "having come, having asked the king for permission, having received it, he went away"). A notable feature of the syntax of the gerund is that its subject is the logical *agent* of the main clause, not necessarily the overt grammatical subject (type "having smashed [ger.] with a cudgel, the tiger [nom.] was killed by the man [instr.]", where the subject of the gerund is "the man" in the instrumental).

Participles and possessive compounds often correspond to relative clauses in other languages. Noteworthy is the use of the present participle of the verb "to be" (*sánt-*) as a concessive marker ("*although* being X, ..."). Bahuvrīhis often serve as nonrestrictive relative clauses (type "Indra, [lit.] possessing slain Vr̥tra", i.e., "who had slain Vr̥tra").

Unlike some other early Indo-European languages, Sanskrit has no elaborate rules governing the succession of moods and tenses in conditional sentences.

5.5 Agreement

The usual agreement rules of early Indo-European languages hold for Sanskrit: subjects agree with their verbs in person and number; adjectives with the nouns they modify in number, gender, and case; relative pronouns with their antecedents in number and gender.

There are a few interesting exceptions. The well-known Ancient Greek rule, whereby a neuter plural subject takes a singular verb, is preserved only in a few Vedic relics; ordinarily a plural verb is used. Vedic prose has developed a subtype of defining relative clause (type: "... the X, which is Y") in which the relative marker is always neuter singular *yád*, whatever the gender and number of X and Y. This usage is reminiscent of the Iranian *izafe* marker, which has developed from the same form, but it is not clear if the two constructions are directly related. In some other equational nominal clauses, by contrast, an anaphoric pronoun is attracted to the number and gender of its antecedent.

Though conjoined nominals ordinarily agree in case, an apparently inherited exception in Vedic involves the conjoining of vocatives by *ca* "and," where the second underlying vocative appears instead in the nominative. This phenomenon is denominated the *vā́yav índraś ca* construction after one of its principal examples ("o Vāyu [voc.] and Indra [nom.]").

5.6 Stylistic syntactic developments

One may consider the history of Sanskrit a history of style, and style in turn is linked to textual genre. Although neither the grammar nor the syntax of Sanskrit shows any significant changes after the fixation of the language by the early grammarians, the usage of these fixed elements significantly alters its balance in the Classical period. The emphasis falls heavily on the nominal system, and the complex verbal system outlined above is exploited far less. We have already noted some of the features of this change in emphasis – the efflorescence of the compounding system, the employment of nominal formations built to verbal roots in preference to finite verbs, the expansion of the adnominal case, the genitive. Sanskrit works of "high" style, court literature and philosophical discourse, take these tendencies to remarkable extremes, while technical treatises, with an eye to verbal economy, arrive at a similar nominal style from a somewhat different angle.

6. LEXICON

A very large proportion of the Sanskrit vocabulary in all periods consists of transparent Indo-European inheritances. Examples need hardly be given; but the numerals given above (§4.5), as well as kinship terms like *pitar* "father," *māter*, "mother," *sūnu* "son," *duhitar* "daughter" can serve as illustrations. Not surprisingly, however, even earliest Vedic has words without clear Indo-European correspondences. While some of these may nonetheless still continue Proto-Indo-European etyma, others doubtless were borrowed from languages with which the Sanskrit speakers came in contact. The difficulty is determining the source languages, given the fact that we have no records of likely languages from remotely the same era. Though Sanskrit speakers no doubt encountered speakers of Dravidian language(s), no Dravidian language is attested until around the beginning of the present era, and then only in South India. We do not know what a northern Dravidian language would have looked like in the second millennium BC. Our knowledge of the Muṇḍa languages (belonging to the Austro-Asiatic family) comes only from the modern era. Many scholars have proposed Dravidian and Muṇḍa sources for Sanskrit words (and indeed phonemes, syntactic constructions, and so on). It is reasonable to accept the principle, but difficult to judge the plausibility of any particular suggestion. Even when a single etymon clearly reveals itself in Sanskrit and one or more Dravidian languages, for example, borrowing may have gone in the other direction, or both families may have borrowed from a third source. Later (i.e., post-Vedic) Dravidian borrowings into Sanskrit are less controversial.

In addition to borrowing from non-Indo-Aryan languages, Sanskrit also sometimes reincorporates vocabulary showing Middle Indic phonological developments, often with some phonological hypercorrection.

7. READING LIST

The standard synchronic grammar of Sanskrit in English is Whitney 1889, which, along with its supplement, Whitney 1885, is invaluable. The standard historical grammar is the multivolume but still unfinished (lacking the verb) Wackernagel and Debrunner 1896–. The first volume, reissued in 1957, has a detailed general introduction to the language by L. Renou. Many of Renou's other works can be consulted with profit, including his short but elegant history of the language (1956). The classic work on syntax (but only of the Vedic period) is Delbrück 1888. Speijer 1886 treats the Classical language. The standard etymological dictionary is Mayrhofer 1956–1976, currently updated and significantly expanded in Mayrhofer 1986–. A general discussion of the language, though with personal views, is found in Burrow 1955. A short survey, along the same lines as this, is found in Cardona 1987. Both Bloch 1965 and Masica 1991, though concentrating on later Indo-Aryan, nonetheless treat many aspects of Sanskrit as starting points for later developments.

Bibliography

Bloch, J. 1965. *Indo-Aryan from the Vedas to Modern Times.* Translated and revised by A. Master. Paris: Adrien-Maisonneuve.

Burrow, T. 1955. *The Sanskrit Language.* London. Faber and Faber.

Cardona, G. 1987. "Sanskrit" In B. Comrie (ed.), *The World's Major Languages*, pp. 448– 469. New York: Oxford University Press.

Delbrück, B. 1888. *Altindische Syntax.* Reprint 1968, Darmstadt: Wissenschaftliche Buchgesellschaft.

Masica, C. P. 1991. *The Indo-Aryan Languages.* Cambridge: Cambridge University Press.

Mayrhofer, M. 1956–1976. *Kurzgefasstes etymologisches Wörterbuch des Altindischen.* Heidelberg: Carl Winter.

______. 1986–EWA. = *Etymologisches Wörterbuch des Altindoarischen.* Heidelberg: Carl Winter.

Renou, L. 1956. *Histoire de la langue sanskrite.* Lyon: Editions IAC.

______. 1957. *Introduction générale, Altindische Grammatik*, vol. I [see Wackernagel 1896].

Speijer, J. S. 1886. *Sanskrit Syntax.* Leiden: Brill.

Wackernagel, J. and A. Debrunner, *Altindische Grammatik.* Göttingen: Vandenhoeck and Ruprecht.
Vol. I 1896. *Lautlehre* (J. Wackernagel). Reprint 1957, with intro. by L. Renou.

Vol. II.1 1905. *Einleitung zur Wortlehre. Nominalkomposition* (J. Wackernagel). Reprint 1957.
Vol. II.2 1954. *Die Nominalsuffixe* (A. Debrunner).
Vol. III 1930. *Nominalflexion – Zahlwort – Pronomen* (A. Debrunner and J. Wackernagel).

Whitney, W. D. 1885. *The Roots, Verb-Forms and Primary Derivatives of the Sanskrit Language.* Leipzig: Breitkopf and Härtel.

———. 1889. *Sanskrit Grammar* (2nd edition). Cambridge, MA: Harvard University Press.

CHAPTER 3

Middle Indic

STEPHANIE W. JAMISON

1. HISTORICAL AND CULTURAL CONTEXTS

Middle Indic (or *Prākrit*) is the designation for a range of Indo-Aryan languages displaying characteristic phonological and grammatical developments from Old Indic (i.e., Sanskrit, see Ch. 2). Like Sanskrit they belong to the Indo-Iranian branch of the Indo-European family and are directly attested beginning in the latter part of the first millennium BC and through the first millennium AD. *Middle Indic* is not strictly a chronological term, but rather refers to logical stages of linguistic development. Some of the defining characteristics of Middle Indic phonology are found already in lexical items in the oldest Sanskrit text, the *Rig-veda*, and Middle Indic languages are attested alongside Sanskrit for all of their history. The alternate designation, *Prākrit*, means "natural, unrefined," hence "vernacular," as opposed to *saṃskṛta-* "perfected," applied to the prescriptive, rule-governed Classical Sanskrit of the grammarians. As well as sometimes designating all Middle Indic speech forms, *Prākrit* is often used in the narrow sense to refer to a subset of these languages. This latter usage will be followed here.

In the following sections, we will enumerate the various Middle Indic languages and describe the evidence for them.

1.1 Inscriptions

Though forms showing characteristic Middle Indic sound changes are found in our earliest Vedic Sanskrit text, no Middle Indic languages are directly attested until the third century BC. At this time appear the earliest inscriptional records of any Indo-Aryan languages, the inscriptions of the Buddhist Mauryan emperor Aśoka (Aś.). These consist of a number of proclamations (fourteen rock inscriptions, seven pillar edicts, etc.), each with identical texts composed in several different local dialects and distributed throughout India (there are also inscriptions in Greek and Aramaic, which fall outside the scope of this chapter). The language of the texts may be termed *Early Middle Indic*, and the local dialect features displayed allow the separate versions to be used as the basis for studying later dialect development. Most of the inscriptions are written in Brāhmī script (see Ch. 2, §2), except for those in the extreme Northwest, written in Kharoṣṭhī (both scripts were deciphered in the 1830s). After this spectacular beginning, inscriptions in Middle Indic were produced for more than a half-millennium in various parts of India, continuing to show local dialect features.

1.2 Pāli (Pā.)

The Buddha is said to have preached in the vernacular, not Sanskrit, and although we have no direct records from the time of the Buddha, early Buddhist documents are in Middle Indic. The most extensive and linguistically conservative records are found in the canon of the Theravāda school, composed in the language known as Pāli. Though the texts were preserved in Śri Lanka, they were clearly brought originally from the mainland and seem to represent a Western dialect, with some admixture of Eastern features (the Buddha himself lived in the East). The redaction of the canon probably occurred around the beginning of the present era, though the texts doubtless continue older oral traditions.

1.3 Gāndhārī Prākrit

Post-Aśokan Kharoṣṭhī inscriptions of the Northwest find, to some degree, their linguistic continuation in a large cache of third-century AD documents on wood, paper, and leather, discovered in Niya in Central Asia (the so-called Niya Documents), and in a fragmentary manuscript of the Dharmapada also found in Central Asia. The language of these texts has been denominated *Gāndhārī*, and recently announced finds of Buddhist texts appear to document its use at an earlier date than heretofore known. Not surprisingly, being a geographically marginal Indic language, it shows a number of aberrant features (and the influence of other Central Asian languages) not found in the "standard," geographically more central Middle Indic Prākrits.

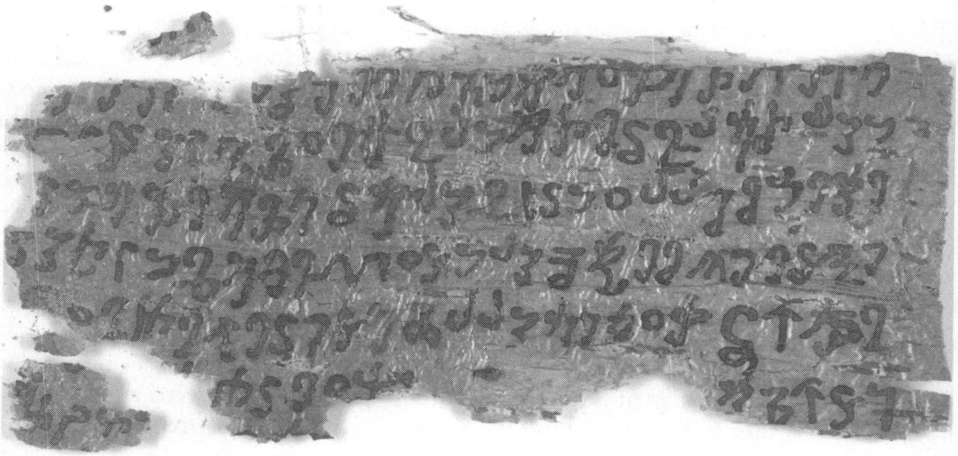

Figure 3.1 Part of scroll manuscript of the Anuvatapta-gatha or "Songs of Lake Anavatapta" in Gandhari Prakrit, c. first century AD

1.4 Prākrits "proper" (Pkt.)

This term designates a number of different linguistic systems, which no doubt began as local dialects (as their separate names imply), but which have become geographically deracinated, stylized, and deemed appropriate to different genres and expressive functions. We have two major types of textual sources for these standard Prākrits: (i) literary texts, including (a) epic and lyric poetry, and (b) the speech of most women and lower-born men in Classical Sanskrit dramas; and (ii) Jain religious texts. In addition, there is a tradition of Prākrit grammarians, paralleling that of the Sanskrit grammarians. The most common Prākrits and their usages are as follows:

1. *Māhārāṣṭrī* (M.): poetic and literary Prākrit, used also for songs in drama. Generally treated as the standard Prākrit by grammarians.
2. *Śaurasenī* (Ś.): standard dramatic prose Prākrit, spoken by high-born women and the *Vidūṣaka* (the king's buffoon, Brahmin by birth).
3. *Māgadhī* (Mg.): dramatic Prākrit, spoken by low-born men. An Eastern dialect.
4. *Ardha-Māgadhī* (AMg.): Jain Prākrit, language of the oldest parts of the canon.
5. *Jain-Śaurasenī* (JŚ.): language of the canon of the Digambara Jains.
6. *Jain-Mahārāṣṭrī* (JM.): noncanonical texts of the Śvetāmbara Jains.

In addition, snatches of other Prākrits are found in the dramas. In the earliest dramas attested, the fragments of the Buddhist author Aśvaghoṣa found in Central Asia and dated to the first–second century BC, as well as the plays attributed to Bhāsa, the distribution and linguistic form of the Prākrits are somewhat different from that encountered in Kālidāsa and later authors.

1.5 "Buddhist Hybrid Sanskrit"

Though early Buddhism was propagated in the vernacular, not in Sanskrit, as time passed various schools introduced Sanskrit or Sanskritized Prākrit. Attested texts show different degrees of this Sanskritization; the term "Buddhist Hybrid Sanskrit" is especially appropriate to certain texts of the Mahāsāṃghika-Lokottaravāda school in North India, which (to oversimplify) show Sanskritic or hyper-Sanskritic phonology, but Middle Indic morphological traits. The extent to which the language of these texts was an actual spoken medium, rather than a result of textual hypercorrection, remains a topic of discussion.

1.6 Late Prākrit (Apabhraṃśa)

Late Prākrit falls beyond the chronological limits of this volume.

While it is customary to refer to the various forms of Middle Indic as "dialects," the present treatment will ordinarily use "languages," or the more neutral but awkward "speech forms." Without appealing to mutual intelligibility or other such criteria, it seems condescending to apply the trivializing term "dialect" to linguistic systems used by such different social groups for such different purposes over a range of space and time.

2. WRITING SYSTEMS

The various Middle Indic languages are recorded using different writing systems. The inscriptions are for the most part in Brāhmī, except for those of the Northwest, where Kharoṣṭhī is found. The assemblage of speech forms denominated by the term *Gāndhārī* is also in Kharoṣṭhī. The other types of Middle Indic use various writing systems ultimately derived from Brāhmī. As noted in Chapter 2, §2, literary and religious texts were recorded in the appropriate local script, but nowadays will usually be printed in Devanāgarī, an offshoot of Northern Brāhmī.

3. PHONOLOGY

Since we are discussing not a single language, but a range of speech forms, all descended from Old Indic, we will give an overview of the characteristic Middle Indic developments from the Old Indic phonological system, rather than describing the synchronic phonological system of one (or more) Middle Indic languages. Accordingly, the Sanskrit phonological system described in Chapter 2, §3 is presupposed here.

3.1 Vowels

1. All Middle Indic languages lose *r̥*, which is replaced by *a*, *i*, or *u* (e.g., Skt. *kr̥ta-* > Pā. *kata-*). There is evidence for this change already in the *Rig-veda*, which has, for example, *śithirá-* "loose" for etymological **śr̥thirá-*.
2. The long diphthongs *āi* and *āu* develop to *ē* and *ō* respectively. This change lends obscurity to the system of vr̥ddhi derivation (see Ch. 2, §3.4.3).
3. The sequences *-aya-* (/*-ayi-*) and *-ava-* (/*-avi-*) develop to *-ē-* and *-ō-* respectively. There is evidence for this change also in the *Rig-veda*, where the well-attested imperative *bo-dhí* "become" was remade from an original *bháva*.
4. One rhythmic rule had far-reaching effects on the grammatical system, the so-called *Zwei-Moren-Gesetz* ("Two-Mora-Rule"), whereby a long vowel before two consonants is not permitted. This blanket prohibition has variant manifestations: (i) the vowel can be shortened and the consonant cluster retained; (ii) the cluster can be simplified and the long vowel retained; (iii) an anaptyptic vowel may break up the cluster and the preceding long vowel be retained. The development of Skt. *dīrgha-* to Pkt. *diggha-* and *dīha-* illustrates (i) and (ii) respectively; that of Skt. *rājñā* to Pā. *raññā* and Aś. *lājinā* illustrates (i) and (iii). This rule has introduced two new phonemes into the language: the vowels *e* and *o*, which are always long in Sanskrit, develop short versions, originally in the position before two consonants. The resulting vowel system is thus more symmetrical than that of Sanskrit:

(1)

i, ī		u, ū
e, ē		o, ō
	a, ā	

However, the backbone of the Sanskrit morphological system, the pattern of vowel gradation (see Ch. 2, §3.4.3), is seriously disturbed by these changes.

3.2 Consonants

Middle Indic developments involve both individual segments and consonant clusters (compare Ch. 2, §3.3).

1. *Sibilants*: In most Middle Indic languages the three sibilants of Sanskrit (*s*, *ṣ*, and *ś*) merge, with the usual product *s* in the West and *ś* in the East (e.g., Skt. *śata* > Pā *sataṃ*, Mg. *śada*). Gāndhārī, however, keeps the three distinct.

2. *Liquids*: The two liquids merge, with *l* the usual Eastern product, *r* the Western: compare in the West (Girnar) Aś. *rājā* with *lājā* in the East (Jaugaḍa).

3. *Glides*: Varying developments of *y* correspond roughly to chronological layers, though there are a number of aberrant changes. It is preserved in Aśoka and in Pāli, but in the

Prākrits *y* is ordinarily lost between vowels (e.g., Skt. *priya-* > Pā. *piya-*, Pkt. *pia-*) and often becomes *j* initially (Skt. *yadi* > Pā. *yadi*, Pkt. *jadi, jaï*). The change to *j* is also sometimes found between vowels, with a *Verschärfung* to *-yy-* and then *-jj-*; for example, some Prākrits have optatives in *-jja-* (from **-yā-*).

4. *Intervocalic single stops*: Pāli faithfully preserves voiceless, voiced, and voiced aspirated stops as distinct. In the Prākrits, plain voiced stops are ordinarily lost between vowels (Skt. *hr̥daya-* > *hiaa-*). The more conservative Prākrits (such as Śaurasenī) preserve some old intervocalic voiceless stops as voiced (e.g., Skt. *hita-* > Ś. *hida-*), while the more innovative (such as Māhārāṣṭrī) usually lose these too (M. *hia-*).

Old aspirates often lose their occlusion intervocalically in Prākrit (Skt. *sakhī* > Pkt. *sahī*), and in some Prākrits initially as well (Skt. *bhavati* > M. *hoi*). Again some conservative dialects voice *th* to *dh* between vowels (Skt. *atithi-* > Ś. *adidhi-*). The loss of occlusion in voiced aspirates is, of course, a sporadic feature of Sanskrit from the beginning (e.g., *hita-* past passive participle to √*dhā*).

As with many developments in the Prākrits proper, it is difficult to formulate consistent rules within a single dialect, and even within a single text, because of dialect mixture, analogy, hypercharacterization on Sanskrit models, and scribal transmission. However, the "feel" of a particular Prākrit and its stereotypical employment in literature is much affected by its treatment of intervocalic consonants. For example, the regular loss of most intervocalic consonants in Māhārāṣṭrī and the preservation of the resulting hiatus makes this speech form well adapted for its use in songs, but less suited for dialogue, due to the numerous homonyms created by these phonological changes (e.g., *maa* < Skt. *mata, mada, mr̥ta, mr̥ga*). The more conservative Śauraseni is better fit for conveying meaning in a less ambiguous function, and so for dialogue.

5. *Final consonants*: All final consonants are lost, except *anusvāra* (*ṃ*, nasal offglide; see Ch. 2, §3.3), though in formulaic close nexus, consonants may sometimes be retained (e.g., Skt. *yad asti* > AMg. *jad atthi*). In some Prākrits, final vowels (either original or produced by final-consonant loss) frequently acquire a nonetymological anusvāra (e.g., instr. sg. *-ena* > *-eṇaṃ*, instr. pl. *-ebhiḥ* > *-ehiṃ*).

6. *Final -as*: The outcome of this extremely common Sanskrit final is a shibboleth in Middle Indic: most dialects have *-o*, but Eastern Middle Indic has *-e* in the nominative singular (Aś. [Kālsī, Jaugaḍa], Mg., AMg.).

3.2.1 Consonant clusters

Probably the most conspicuous set of phonological changes spanning the Middle Indic languages involves the thoroughgoing assimilation in clusters, which significantly diminishes the transparency of the morphological system. An occasional alternative to assimilation is the insertion of an anaptyptic vowel. The assimilation rules involve a rough hierarchy of segment sonority: stops, nasals, sibilants, and (the sonorants) *l, v, y, r* – with a lower segment assimilating to a higher. When two segments belong to the same class, the first assimilates to the second.

1. *Stop + stop*: Total regressive assimilation occurs: for example, *-kt-* > *-tt-* (Skt. *mukta-* > *mutta-*), *-pt-* > *-tt-* (Skt. *sapta-* > *satta-*), *-dg-* > *-gg-* (Skt. *mudga-* > *mugga*), etc.
2. *Nasal + stop*: The nasal remains or becomes anusvāra.
3. *Stop + nasal*: The nasal assimilates (e.g., Skt. *agni-* > *aggi-*).

4. *Sibilant + stop*: The sibilant assimilates, but adds aspiration to the cluster (e.g., Skt. *asti* > *atthi*).
5. *Stop + sibilant*: The cluster *-ts-* ordinarily gives *-cch-* (e.g., Skt. *vatsa* > *vaccha*); *-kṣ-* gives either *-kkh-* or *-cch-* (e.g., Skt. *akṣi* > *akkhi/acchi*), originally distributed dialectally. A reflection of this change is probably already to be found in the *Rig-veda* in the form *akhkhalī(-kr̥tya)* (sic), from *akṣara-*.
6. *Sonorant + stop / stop + sonorant*: Total assimilation of the sonorant to the stop occurs (e.g., *r*: Skt. *artha-* > *attha-*, *cakra-* > *cakka-*; *v* : *pakva-* > *pakka-*; *y*: *vākya-* > *vakka-*. In the common combination of dental + *y*, there is palatalization of the cluster (e.g., *satya-* > *sacca-*, *adya-* > *ajja-*).
7. *Sibilant + nasal*: Ordinarily the outcome is nasal + *h*, with the aspiration also characteristic of sibilant + stop clusters (e.g., Skt. *grīṣma-* > *gimha-*).
8. *Sonorant + nasal / nasal + sonorant*: Total assimilation of the sonorant, as with stops (e.g., Skt. *anya-* > Pā. *añña-*, Pkt. *aṇṇa-*; Skt. *dharma-* > *dhamma-*).
9. *Sibilant + sonorant / sonorant + sibilant*: The sonorant assimilates to the sibilant (e.g., Skt. *aśva-* > *assa-*, *tasya-* > *tassa-*, *sahasra-* > *sahassa-*, *varṣa-* > *vassa-*).
10. *Sonorant + sonorant*: In general the lower sonorant assimilates to the higher, although there are a number of exceptions and special developments. In the hierarchy *l* prevails over the other sonorants (e.g., Skt. *durlabha-* > *dulla(b)ha-*). Next in strength is *v* (the labial glide), but clusters with *v* show some special developments. In Pāli *-rv-/-vr-* and *-vy-* become *-bb-*, as opposed to the *-vv-* prevailing in the Prākrits (e.g., Skt. *sarva-* > Pā. *sabba-*, Pkt. *savva-*; *tīvra-* > *tibba-* / *tivva-*; *-tavya-* > *-tabba-* / *-tavva-*). Finally, *r* ordinarily submits to *y*, though again with some special developments: anaptyxis is fairly common (producing *-riy-*), and *-yy-* tends to develop to *-jj-* (e.g., Skt. *arya-* > Pā. *ayya-*, but Pkt. *ajja-*).

3.3 Phonotaxis

In most Middle Indic languages only one consonant is permitted initially, two intervocalically. Cluster simplification occurs after the assimilation processes described in §3.2.1. In the case Skt. *martya-*, for example, both *r* and *y* assimilate to the medial stop, which itself has undergone palatalization before *y*. A triconsonantal **maccca-*, the expected product of assimilation, simplifies to *macca-*. Similarly, Skt. *strī* is susceptible to both *r*-assimilation and *s*-assimilation with aspiration; the resulting **ttthī* simplifies to *thī* (and, with prothetic vowel, *itthī*). As this example shows, simplified single initial consonants can alternate with intervocalic geminates; thus, when simplex verbs are compounded with preverbs, the geminate cluster resurfaces (e.g., Skt. *kramati* > *kamati*, but *upa-kramati* > *upa-kkamati*).

3.4 Accent

Just as it had disappeared in the evolution of Sanskrit, so the Vedic pitch accent system did not survive in the Middle Indic languages. For the Vedic accent, see Chapter 2, §3.6.

3.5 The Middle Indic phonological system

Despite the global nature of the changes discussed in the preceding sections, they had essentially no effect on the phonological inventory of Middle Indic. All (or almost all) of the segments occurring in the Middle Indic languages already existed in Old Indic, and very few segments or contrasts were eliminated (elimination occurred in the case of (i) the velar nasal *ṅ*; (ii) contrast between sibilants; (iii) contrast between liquids; (iv) in part, contrast between nasals; (v) the changes in the vowel system discussed above). However, the distribution of and phonotactic relations among segments have drastically changed in every Middle Indic language, and the syllable structure was entirely altered by the effects of the Two-Mora-Rule and the restrictions on length and types of clusters already discussed.

These changes also had dramatic repercussions in the morphological system. The elaborate but orderly morphophonemic alternations that pervade Sanskrit morphology (see Ch. 2, §3.4) were significantly obscured by the numerous consonantal assimilations, as well as by the loss of *r̥* and the shortening of vr̥ddhi vowels before two consonants. Some of the transparent variants of the root √*kr̥* in various morphological categories in Sanskrit and their Middle Indic equivalents provide a telling example:

(2)

Sanskrit	*Middle Indic*
kr̥ta-	kata- (kada-, kida-, kaa-)
kr̥ṇoti	kuṇadi
kr̥tya	kicca
karma-	kamma-
kartum	kātum (< expected *kattum)
kārya-	kajja- (/kayya-)
akārṣīt	akāsī
kuryāt	kujjā

4. MORPHOLOGY

4.1 Word formation

As with phonology, the development of Middle Indic from Sanskrit involves the redistribution and reduction of existing categories, rather then the creation of new ones. Again, however, the result is superficially very distinct from its source. The structure of the word is theoretically as in Sanskrit: Root–Suffix(es)–Ending (see Ch. 2, §4.1). But phonological changes have conspired to make the root less consistently recognizable (as the above example of √*kr̥* demonstrates), and the morpheme-boundaries less delimitive than in Sanskrit. Because of its loss of salience, the root plays a far less prominent role in Middle Indic morphology than in Sanskrit, and in verbal forms the *present stem* is often the base of derivation.

It is again more convenient to describe the various developments of the Middle Indic languages from Sanskrit along a continuum, rather than producing a synchronic description of one Middle Indic speech form. Hence the following discussion presupposes the description of Sanskrit morphology found in Chapter 2, §4.

We noted the pervasive distinction between *thematic* inflection (invariant stems ending in *a*) and *athematic* inflection (stems, often alternating, ending in consonants or vowels other than short *a*) in Sanskrit (see Ch. 2, §4.1). With the loss of final consonants (as well as the general obscuring of morphophonemic relations), this distinction has become irrelevant in Middle Indic. Consonant-final noun stems are found only as marginal relics, and consonant-final verb-stems are essentially nonexistent. Almost all stems are nonalternating (again, except for relics), and endings are more uniform across stem-types. The formal features that set thematic forms apart from athematic ones were generalized by all Middle Indic languages, and the formal inventory consists of different types of vocalic stems.

Middle Indic closely resembles Sanskrit with respect to affixation. Suffixation remains the dominant mode. The single true prefix of Sanskrit, the verb augment (*-a*), is still found in the past tense, but is not obligatory. The same inventory of preverbs is found as in Sanskrit with the same functions; indeed, tmesis is still possible in older Pāli. The single infix in Sanskrit (*-na/n-*) is only marginally present, frozen in the verbal inflection of a set of roots originally containing the infix.

Reduplication is no longer a functioning morphological process in Middle Indic.

4.2 Nominal morphology

The grammatical categories of Middle Indic nominal forms are gender, number, and case.

4.2.1 Gender

Three genders exist – masculine, neuter, and feminine. The differences are expressed, as in Sanskrit, primarily inflectionally between masculine and neuter, derivationally between masculine/neuter and feminine; that is to say, masculine and neuter nominals employ the same stem, but different endings (which differ only in the nominative/accusative), while the feminine is built to a different stem. In fact, this tendency has become more pronounced than in Sanskrit, in that the old short *i* and *u* feminines tend to fall together inflectionally with their long *ī* and *ū* counterparts, and become distinct from the short *i* and *u* masculine and neuter stems.

4.2.2 Number

There are only two numbers, Middle Indic having lost the dual. The plural takes its place.

4.2.3 Case

There are formally eight cases in older Middle Indic, as in Sanskrit: nominative, accusative, instrumental, dative, ablative, genitive, locative, vocative. However, the apparent identity of case systems masks a significant loss of strength in the distinctions among the cases.

As a general rule, the dative has been lost or almost lost in most Middle Indic languages. Formal expression of the dative is found only in the *a*-stem and only in Aśokan, Pāli, and a few Prākrits (notably Māhārāṣṭrī and Ardha-Māgadhī), its function primarily restricted to expressing purpose. It is otherwise replaced by the genitive. This functional restriction and replacement by genitive we also noted in Sanskrit (see Ch. 2, §5).

The conflation of cases in many stems, also noted for Sanskrit (see Ch. 2, §4.2.3), has progressed much further in Middle Indic. For example, the instrumental and ablative plural of most stems coincide; for the most part, the feminine singular oblique cases employ only a single form, and so forth. Thus, the progressively developing tendency in Middle Indic is to distinguish the direct cases (nominative and accusative) from a less differentiated oblique inflection, though nowhere does this development come to completion. There is one major countercurrent: the creation of new ablative singulars with a *-tas* adverbial suffix, found also in Sanskrit.

Case is marked primarily by endings, since stem-form alternations have generally disappeared.

4.2.4 Nominal stem-classes

The Sanskrit distinction between vowel and consonant stems has been almost entirely lost.

4.2.4.1 Consonant stems

Consonant stems exist marginally, in relic forms and incomplete declensions. Most older consonant-stem nouns have been reformed as vowel stems. This is another legacy of the loss of final consonants; once this happened, old consonant-final stems could easily fit into the appropriate vocalic category (e.g., Skt. *cakṣus-* becomes a neuter *u*-stem *cakkhu-*; *sarpis-* > *sappi-*, etc.). This reinterpretation was also favored by the ambiguity of certain common case forms. Thus, the masculine accusative singular of both consonant stems and *a*-stems ends in *-am*, allowing the abstraction of a new *a*-stem; for example, the Sanskrit *n*-stem *mūrdhan-*, with accusative singular *mūrdhānam* (= MI *muddhāṇaṃ*), can backform a Prākrit nominative singular *muddhāṇo* next to older *muddhā*.

4.2.4.2 Vowel stems

These changes leave Middle Indic with a limited set of fully functioning vowel-final stems: masculine and neuter *a*-stems; feminine *ā*- and *ī*-stems; masculine and neuter *i*- and *u*-stems, continuing their Sanskrit counterparts. As in Sanskrit, the endings of the *a*-stems are somewhat aberrant; the feminine singular has a unique set of oblique endings; and the masculine and neuter are distinguished only in nominative/accusative.

4.2.5 Endings

Because of the wide variation in endings both between and within Middle Indic languages, a generalized scheme of endings cannot be given here. Wholesale analogies and adaptations from other stems have operated in the generation of paradigms, especially when phonological change would have made the inherited ending inconvenient. A few examples show the types of rearrangements that occur:

1. The instrumental plural ending of the *a*-stems, *-ehi(ṃ)*, continues the Vedic Sanskrit alternant *-ebhis*, rather than Classical *-ais*, which would have become undercharacterized **-e*. In addition, the Vedic *a*-stem alternative nominative plural *-āsas* is attested in Pāli verse as *-āse*.
2. The accusative plural of masculine vowel stems would have fallen together with the accusative singular by regular sound change: *-am* and *-ān* > *-aṃ* (and probably *-im* / *-īn* > *-iṃ*, *-um* / *-ūn* > *uṃ*, though this is disputed). The *a*-stem has accusative plural *-e*, apparently adapted from the stem-vowel of the old oblique plurals (*-ebhis*, *-ebhyas*), though some scholars explain it as borrowed from the nominative plural of the demonstrative pronoun.
3. Short *i*- and *u*-stems show traces of stem alternation in the Pāli: nominative plural *aggayo* (< Skt. *agnayas*), stem *aggi-*; *bhikkhavo* (< Skt. *bhikṣavas*), stem *bhikkhu-*. But in the Prākrits this has largely been replaced by forms of the type *aggiṇo* (from the *in*-stems) and *aggī* (from the accusative plural, itself probably borrowed from the feminine *i*-stems).

Relics of consonant-stem inflection are most conspicuous in conservative speech forms like Pāli, and there especially in the older layers of the language. Even so, only *r*-stems (both kinship terms and agent nouns), *n*-stems (esp. *rājan-* "king," *ātman-* "self"), and *nt*-stems (pres. act. part.) preserve anything resembling a paradigm; the old *s*-stems offer relic instrumentals in *-asā*, but little else.

4.2.6 Comparison of adjectives

The two forms of comparison found in Sanskrit (see Ch. 2, §4.2.6) are still utilized in Middle Indic. The simple adjective can also function as the comparative, and the comparative in *-tara-* tends to stand in for the superlative-*tama-*, at least in Pāli.

4.2.7 Pronouns

As in Sanskrit, we can distinguish the nongender-marked personal pronouns of the first and second person and the gender-marking demonstrative/anaphoric types.

4.2.7.1 Personal pronouns

Many of the idiosyncrasies of these pronouns in Sanskrit have been maintained and indeed built upon, producing an efflorescence of analogic confections across the range of Middle Indic languages. The distinction between nominative and oblique stem-forms is ordinarily kept in the first-person singular (*ahaṃ*, or forms based on it, vs. *m-*); in the plural, the oblique stem. *amh-* has generally spread to the nominative, though Pāli has *mayam*, built to old *vayam* (nom. pl.) with the initial of the singular oblique. In the second person, the plural has adopted the initial of the singular throughout, but otherwise keeps the plural stem (Skt. *yuṣm-* replaced by *tumh-*, after *t(u)vam*, etc.). The separate enclitic forms are also generally preserved in one form or another.

4.2.7.2 Gender-marking pronouns

The Sanskrit anaphoric/demonstrative *sa, sā, ta-* also preserves many peculiarities of inflection through much of Middle Indic, including the distinctive distribution of *s-* and *t*-stems. The *ayam* and *asau* pronominal paradigms also remain alive, and the relative and interrogative stems, *ya-* and *ka-*, and the "pronominal adjectives" continue the Sanskrit forms.

4.3 Verbal morphology

The Middle Indic verbal system experienced a dramatic reduction in the formal categories which characterized the Sanskrit verb, and a consolidation of the functions of those which do remain, rather than the production of new categories. The motivations for these losses are often already to be seen in Sanskrit, where, as we noted, a number of separate formal categories were insufficiently distinguished functionally. The older Middle Indic languages often preserve relics of otherwise lost categories.

Formally alternating stems within paradigms have been virtually eliminated, and often the present stem has become the basis for all other categories.

The grammatical categories of finite verbal forms are person, number, tense, mood, and voice. There are also formal relics of distinct aspect stems in older Middle Indic, but without functional value. Generally, person and number are expressed by a portmanteau morpheme, the ending; tense by suffixes and/or endings; mood also by suffixes and/or endings; voice by a suffix.

4.3.1 Person and number

As in the noun, the dual was eliminated. The basic building block of the verbal system is thus the six-member paradigm: first, second, third person; singular and plural.

4.3.2 Voice

As discussed in Chapter 2 (§4.3.2), Old Indic had a formal voice distinction, active versus middle (*parasmaipada* vs. *ātmanepada*), the functional differentiation of which was not always clear. This distinction has essentially been lost in Middle Indic; though some Middle Indic languages can employ old middle endings, they are used indifferently with the active, and active endings far outnumber them. Only in Aśoka are there some possible traces of a distinct *middle* use of middle endings.

Sanskrit also had a functional voice distinction, active versus passive, encoded in various ways. This distinction is maintained in Middle Indic. In addition, Middle Indic ordinarily opposes a causative stem to the simple present, and so it is useful to consider the grammar as displaying a three-way contrast: active, passive, causative.

The old Sanskrit *-ya-* passive suffix, often extended to *-īya-* or *-iyya-* (*-ijja-*), is added to either the root or the present stem. Unlike the Sanskrit passive stem, that of Middle Indic ordinarily takes active endings.

Since the Sanskrit *-aya-* causative falls together phonologically with other representatives of the expanding *ē*-stem present, a new causative suffix spreads in Middle Indic, based on the Sanskrit *p*-causative to roots ending in *ā*, Pā. *-(ā)paya-*, *-(ā)pē-*, Pkt. *-(ā)vē-*.

4.3.3 Tense

As we saw in Chapter 2 (§4.3.3), Old Indic had a complex set of formal tense/aspect categories, some with low functional load. In particular, there were three competing past tenses – imperfect, aorist, perfect – as well as a possible nominal expression of past tense. From this elaborate system there emerges in Middle Indic a simple three-way expression of tense: present, future, and past. The present continues the old present and the future the old finite future. The past ordinarily continues the aorist in older Middle Indic, but the past passive participle in younger speech forms.

4.3.4 Stem formation

In verbs, as in nouns, consonant-final stems have essentially disappeared, as have alternating stems within a paradigm. Therefore, a distinction between thematic (*a*-) stems and others is less relevant than a division into different varieties of vowel stems.

4.3.5 Present stem morphology

Middle Indic present stems continue many of the Sanskrit types (see Ch. 2, §4.3.6), though transformed into invariant, vowel-final forms. However, the verb "to be" (Skt. √*as*) preserves consonant-final forms and even traces of stem alternation in many Middle Indic languages.

Compare the following Pāli forms, which differ from their Sanskrit equivalents only by regular phonological developments:

(3)

	Sanskrit	*Pāli*
1st sg.	asmi	amhi
2nd sg.	asi	asi
3rd sg.	asti	atthi
3rd pl.	santi	santi

Other old root-class (Sanskrit class II) verbs are preserved only in traces in older Middle Indic.

The most numerous present type by far is the *a*-stem (incorporating Sanskrit classes I, IV, and VI), into which were attracted many old athematic presents (e.g., root *hanti* > *hanati*; reduplicated *dadhāti* > Pāli *dahati*; nasal infix *yunakti* > Pāli *yuñjati*). Sanskrit class X (*-aya-* verbs) and causatives and denominatives with the phonologically identical suffix produce a different stem-type in contracted *-ē-*, which is also widespread in Middle Indic and attracts old athematic presents to its inflection. Other old vowel-final stems are much rarer: for example, class VIII *karoti*, class IX *jānāti*.

Rather than listing numerous old Sanskrit presents and their outcomes, it is more instructive to examine the fate of a single present in various Middle Indic languages, that of the root √*kr̥* "make, do." In early Vedic this formed a class V present, *kr̥ṇoti*, *kr̥ṇute*, soon replaced by the prevailing Sanskrit class VIII *karoti*, *kurute*. Traces of both these present types are found in Middle Indic: *kr̥ṇo-/ṇu-* in Pkt. *kuṇa-* (reformed according to the *a*-class); the strong stem *karo-* in Pā. *karoti*, the weak stem *kuru-* in Pā., Pkt. *kubba-/kuvva-* (< prevocalic *kurv-*, with *a*-stem inflection). In addition, Pāli and Prākrit regularly inflect the simple root as an *a*-stem (*kara-*), and Prākrit also as an *ē*-stem (*karē-*). Here and in many other cases, Middle Indic absorbed the leftovers of the formally diverse Sanskrit present system and redistributed them in a very few classes.

The productive future is built to the present stem, with the continuation of the Sanskrit future suffix which is proper to seṭ roots, Skt. *-iṣya-* > *-issa-*, though in older Middle Indic we find some examples of old *-sya-* added directly to roots.

4.3.6 Preterite stem morphology

The preterite in older Middle Indic (esp. Aśoka, Pāli, also more rarely in Ardha-Māgadhī, etc.) ordinarily continues an aorist form, though there are occasional traces of the other competing Sanskrit preterites. The old imperfect is preserved in *āsī* (Pāli and some Prākrits, < *āsīt*) to the root √*as* "be" (which did not form an aorist in Sanskrit); and a few relics of the perfect remain, notably Aś., Pā., Pkt *āhu(ṃ)* to the root √*ah* "say," Pā. *vidu(ṃ)* to √*vid* "know."

Otherwise, forms of the old sigmatic aorists prevail, though reformed, redistributed, and usually attached to the present stem. Present stems ending in short vowels add *-i*, derived from the *-iṣ*-aorist (Pā. *pucchati* "asks": *pucchi* "asked"), while those in long vowels add *-si*, from the *s*-aorist (Pā. *kathēti* "tells": *kathēsi* "told"). Relics of other aorist types are also found (e.g., root aorist, Skt. *adāt* > Pā. *adā*).

The Sanskrit augment, which marked both imperfect and aorist (optionally in Vedic, obligatorily in Classical Sanskrit), is also found optionally in Middle Indic and seems especially utilized in shorter forms. The preterite is characterized by endings ultimately derived from the old Sanskrit secondary endings.

Finite forms of the preterite survive only as relics in Prākrit, where the standard means of expressing past tense is the predicated past passive participle (with or without the copula), a periphrastic method commonly found already in Sanskrit and older Middle Indic.

4.3.7 Mood

Middle Indic attests three moods: indicative, imperative, and optative, all built to the present stem. These continue their Sanskrit counterparts both formally and functionally. The subjunctive has been lost (as in Classical Sanskrit), except for a few possible relics in early Middle Indic.

4.3.7.1 Imperative

The imperative is marked entirely by special endings on the present stem. As in Sanskrit, the negative imperative is expressed with the special negation *mā* and the unaugmented preterite in older Middle Indic speech forms.

4.3.7.2 Optative

The Middle Indic optative is ordinarily built to the present stem with the suffix *-eyy(a)-* (Pkt. *-ejja-*), most likely derived from the Sanskrit thematic optative (in prevocalic position: e.g., 1st. sg. *bhavey-am*). Traces of athematic optatives (note esp. Aś., Pā., AMg. *siyā* < Skt. *s(i)yāt*, √*as* "be") and of preconsonantal thematic forms are also found.

4.3.8 Verb endings

The entire range of endings found in Middle Indic cannot be treated here, but a few general facts can be noted. The primary active endings are the major set retained from Old Indic. These are used for the present (including the passive and causative) and the future and have been preserved with remarkable fidelity:

(4)

	Sanskrit	*Pāli*	*Prākrit*
1st sg.	-mi	-mi	-mi
2nd sg.	-si	-si	-si
3rd sg.	-ti	-ti	-di (Ś.), -i (M.)
1st pl.	-mas	-ma	-mo
2nd pl.	-tha	-tha	-dha (Ś.), -ha (M.)
3rd pl.	-(a)nti	-(a)nti	-(a)nti

As noted before, middle (primary) endings are encountered sporadically, without distinctive function. The Sanskrit secondary endings (of imperfect and aorist) are continued, though less transparently and systematically, in the endings of the aorist and optative (the fact that they ended in consonants for the most part contributed to their transformation). The endings of the Sanskrit imperative are also rather well preserved, especially the distinctive third person *-(n)tu*.

4.3.9 Nonfinite verbals

Like Sanskrit, Middle Indic deploys a number of verbal nouns and adjectives, some built directly to the root, some to tense stems. They display verbal case-syntax and often can serve as predicates. In the case of the verbal nouns, the formal connection between the formants of these frozen nominals and synchronic case endings is not as clear as in Sanskrit.

4.3.9.1 *Infinitive*

Middle Indic knows continuators of *-tum* and Vedic *-tave*. The former can be built to the present stem as well as to the root.

4.3.9.2 *Gerund*

This is a very well-developed formation in Middle Indic, with a number of suffixes, some continuing Sanskrit *-tvā* and *-(t)ya*. Again, these can be built to present stems as well as roots. The Classical Sanskrit rules for the distribution of *-tvā* and *-(t)ya* do not rigidly hold in Middle Indic.

4.3.9.3 *Tense-stem participles*

The active present participle suffix of Sanskrit, consonant stem *-ant-*, is common in Middle Indic to all types of present stems (including the passive). It is regularly thematized as an *a*-stem (yielding *-anta-*), though abundant relics of the old athematic paradigm are found in older Middle Indic. The Sanskrit middle present participle suffix *-māna-* is also widely attested, built to originally active stems and with an "active" meaning. The old perfect participle *vid-vas-* "wise" (weak stem *vid-us-*) survives in the Pāli *u*-stem adjective *vidū-*.

4.3.9.4 *Past passive participle*

As in Sanskrit, this is an extremely common form and, as noted, the basis for the preterite tense in younger Middle Indic. Its suffixes continue *-ta-*, *-ita-*, and *-na-*, and it is the part of the verbal system that most successfully resists the tendency to substitute the present stem for the root, though past passive participles built on tense stems are also quite common. Numerous Middle Indic past passive participles are historically identical to their Sanskrit counterparts, with regular phonological developments.

4.3.9.5 *Past active participle*

This verbal (Skt. *-tavant-*) is also found in Middle Indic, though less commonly.

4.3.9.6 *Gerundive*

The Middle Indic gerundive occurs commonly, with continuators of Sanskrit *-tavya-*, *-anīya-*, and *-ya-*. It too can be formed to the present stem as well as to the root.

4.4 Compounds

Middle Indic displays the same varieties of compounds as Sanskrit and employs them regularly and productively.

As in Sanskrit, verbs incorporate preverbs into both finite and nonfinite forms. In addition the *cvī*-formation (compounding of noun or adjective with forms of √*kr̥* "make" or √*bhū* "become") continues (e.g., Pā. *udakī-bhū-* "consist of water": *udaka-* "water").

The three major types of Sanskrit nominal compounds – copulative, determinative, and possessive (dvandva, tatpuruṣa, and bahuvrīhi) – are present in Middle Indic, though the baroque exuberance of Classical Sanskrit multiple compounding is restrained.

4.5 Numerals

The numerals ordinarily continue the Sanskrit forms, with appropriate sound changes:

(5) The Pāli cardinals

1	*eka-*
2	*d(v)i-*
3	*ti-*
4	*catur-*
5	*pañca*
6	*cha*
7	*satta*
8	*aṭṭha*
9	*nava*
10	*dasa*
20	*vīsati*
100	*sata-*
1,000	*sahassa-*

Prākrit cardinals correspond to the above for the most part.

In Pāli both *ti-* ("three") and *catur-* ("four") maintain the archaic inflectional features found in Sanskrit, including distinction between strong and weak cases (Pā. masc. nom./acc. pl. *tayo*, gen. *tiṇṇaṃ*; *cattāro*, *catunnaṃ*) and the unusual feminine formant *-ss-* between stem and ending (thus Pā. fem. nom./acc. pl. *tisso*, *catasso*). Continuators of these forms are found in the Prākrits, although not usually distributed systematically in a paradigm.

Ordinals are derived from cardinals as in Sanskrit, with the irregular forms preserved:

(6) The Pāli ordinals

1st	*paṭhama-*
2nd	*dutiya-*
3rd	*titiya-*

5. SYNTAX

Most observations made regarding Sanskrit syntax are equally applicable to Middle Indic, especially in its older layers. Certain stylistic devices are especially well developed; for example, the piling up of numerous nonfinite clauses, each typically containing a final gerund, completed by a final verb having the same subject as the preceding clauses, is especially characteristic of Middle Indic prose style. On the other hand, the excessively nominal style of later Classical Sanskrit is usually avoided, except in genres founded directly on Sanskrit models.

In the younger layers of Middle Indic the most important syntactic development is the replacement of the old preterite(s) with forms of the past passive participle. Since the agent of the preterite is then expressed in the instrumental case and the patient in the nominative (as opposed to the active syntax – nominative agent, accusative patient – of the present and future tenses), the stage is set for the *split ergative* systems that arise in many modern Indo-Aryan languages. It also goes without saying that this originally participial form agrees with the grammatical subject in number and gender and takes nominal rather than verbal endings. As in Sanskrit, the copula with the third person is optional and, in fact, rare.

6. LEXICON

The majority of the Middle Indic lexicon is derived from Sanskrit. In addition to words inherited from Sanskrit, and therefore undergoing regular phonological development, other words were borrowed directly from Sanskrit, which has served as a cultural word-hoard for all Indian languages (Dravidian as well as Indo-Aryan) through their histories. This distinction between actual inheritances and internal borrowings is similar, though not identical, to that made by the Prākrit grammarians between *tadbhavas* and *tatsamas*. The latter ("same as that") refers to words that are identical to their Sanskrit counterparts; this includes not only internal borrowings, but also inherited words, like *bhara*, *nāma*, etc., that have the same form in both Sanskrit and Middle Indic because no sound laws have applied. *Tadbhavas* ("arisen from that") are Middle Indic words that show Sanskrit elements modified by normal sound change.

A third class of words is identified by the grammarians as *deśya* (/*deśī*), "belonging to the country, provincial" – words that do not have obvious Sanskrit equivalents. Etymologically these no doubt include numerous inherited Indo-Aryan words that lack Old Indic counterparts, as well as words borrowed from non-Indo-Aryan languages. Here, as with Sanskrit, identifying the source in a particular case is often difficult; though, especially in Northwest Prākrit loanwords from Iranian, Greek, and Central Asian languages are identifiable.

The Middle Indic languages used primarily for religious texts, Buddhist or Jain, also have large stocks of technical religious terms. Though many of these terms are Sanskrit in origin, they have developed senses not found in their Sanskrit sources. At the opposite extreme are the dramatic Prākrits, which can often be rendered, morpheme by morpheme, into intelligible Sanskrit simply by reversing the sound laws. In fact, most dramas have been provided with such translations, known as *chāyās* ("shadows"), much used by students.

7. READING LIST

Invaluable is the up-to-date, comprehensive, and detailed historical survey of von Hinüber a 2001. Also useful are the surveys of Bloch (1965) and Masica (1991), though both are more concerned with modern Indo-Aryan. Cardona 1987 gives a necessarily brief sketch of Middle Indic developments. There is no general dictionary of Middle Indic, but Turner 1966–1969 is often useful.

For individual languages, the standard work on Pāli is Geiger 1916, revised and edited by K.R. Norman (1994) and a useful introduction is provided by Warder 1963. For the Prākrits, Pischel 1900 is standard, but difficult to use. The English translation (1981) provides a much needed *index verborum* (but omits the table of contents). A brief but well-organized introduction is provided by Woolner 1928. For Buddhist Hybrid Sanskrit the standard work is Edgerton 1953.

Bibliography

Bloch, J. 1965. *Indo-Aryan from the Vedas to Modern Times*. Translated and revised by A. Master. Paris: Adrien-Maisonneuve.

Cardona, G. 1987. "Indo-Aryan languages." In B. Comrie (ed.), *The World's Major Languages*, pp. 440–447. New York: Oxford University Press.
Edgerton, F. 1953. *Buddhist Hybrid Sanskrit Grammar and Dictionary*. New Haven: Yale University Press.
Geiger, W. 1916. *Pāli Literatur und Sprache*. Strasburg: Trübner. Translated into English by B. Ghosh, 1943; revised and edited by K. R. Norman, 1994 as *Pāli Grammar*. Oxford: Pali Text Society.
Hinüber, O. Von 2002. *Das ältere Mittelindisch im Überblick* (2nd expanded edition). Vienna: Österreichische Akademie des Wissenschaft.
Masica, C. P. 1991. *The Indo-Aryan Languages*. Cambridge: Cambridge University Press.
Pischel, R. 1900. *Grammatik der Prakrit-Sprachen*. Strasburg: Trübner. Translated into English by S. Jha, Delhi: Motilal Banarsidass, 1981.
Turner, R. L. 1966–1969. *A Comparative Dictionary of the Indo-Aryan Languages*. London: Oxford University Press.
Warder, A. K. 1963. *Introduction to Pali*. Oxford: Pali Text Society.
Woolner, A. C. 1928. *Introduction to Prakrit* (2nd edition). Reprint, Delhi: Motilal Banarsidass.

CHAPTER 4

Old Tamil

SANFORD B. STEEVER

1. HISTORICAL AND CULTURAL CONTEXTS

Old Tamil stands alongside Sanskrit as one of India's two classical languages. First attested about 254 BC, Old Tamil is the oldest recorded member of the Dravidian languages, a family which today encompasses twenty-four distinct languages. Old Tamil belongs to the southern branch of this family, which includes Malayalam, Irula, Kota, Toda, Kannada, Badaga, Kodagu, and Tulu, as well as Modern Tamil (see Steever 1987).

The era of Old Tamil extends until roughly the seventh century AD, a period of transition to Medieval Tamil. Medieval Tamil differs from Old Tamil in several respects: Old Tamil has two simple tenses – past and non-past – while Medieval Tamil has three: past, present, and future. Old Tamil has relatively few Indo-Aryan lexical borrowings, while Medieval Tamil admits many. During the fourteenth century AD, Medieval Tamil develops into Modern Tamil, a language spoken by nearly 50 million people today. All three periods of Tamil possess a rich literature.

Old Tamil was spoken throughout southern India, in what are now the states of Kerala and Tamil Nadu, as well as in northern Śri Lanka. It is the immediate predecessor of not only Medieval Tamil, but also Malayalam. The western dialects of Late Old Tamil or Early Medieval Tamil, geographically separated from the others by the Western Ghats, developed into Malayalam. Malayalam lost rules of subject–verb agreement so that finite verbs in the modern language lack personal endings. Malayalam also acquired so many Sanskritic loans that aspirated stops now contrast with nonaspirated counterparts. The Old Tamil dialects of Tamil Nadu and northern Śri Lanka developed into Medieval, then Modern Tamil. Late Old Tamil or Medieval Tamil is also likely the predecessor of Irula, a nonliterary language spoken on the slopes of the Nilgiri Mountains in western Tamil Nadu.

Śri Lankan Tamil is more conservative than Continental Tamil, preserving the three-way deictic distinction between *proximal* (*ivaṉ* "this man"), *medial* (*uvaṉ* "the man in between") and *distal* (*avaṉ* "that man") of Old and Medieval Tamil. Modern Continental Tamil has reduced the contrast to two by eliminating the medial degree. Śri Lankan Tamil has a synthetic present perfect tense which appears to preserve an Old Tamil present perfect (Steever 1993). Nevertheless, the modern dialects of Śri Lankan and Continental Tamil retain a degree of mutual intelligibility.

Old Tamil exists in three varieties, distinguished by source. *Epigraphic Tamil* is known from rock edicts, cave carvings, and similar inscriptions written in several varieties of Asokan Brahmi script; the earliest of these date to 254 BC. *Mixed Tamil*, also recorded in lithic inscriptions, consists of a mixture of Old Tamil and Sanskrit, which prefigures the medieval code-mixing style called *maṇippiravāḷam* (lit. "gems and pearls"). Although neither of these varieties is extensively attested, enough survives to date them as contemporaneous with the third type, known today as *caṅka.t tamiḻ "Tamil of the Academy."* It is richly attested in a large literary corpus and is the variety treated herein. These texts have come down to us through rote memory and on palm-leaf manuscripts (*ōlai*), copied and recopied over the centuries.

Lehmann (1994) divides Old Tamil into three stages – Early, Middle, and Late. Early Old Tamil (250 BC to AD 100) is represented by the grammar *Tolkāppiyam*, and probably by some poems from the anthology *Puṟanāṉūru* (Four hundred poems on heroism). Middle Old Tamil is the language of bardic poems on themes of love and war (AD 100 to 400) represented in the two collections, *Ettuttokai* (The eight anthologies) and *Pattupāṭṭu* (Ten long songs). Late Old Tamil (AD 400 to 700) is preserved in the twin epics, *Cilappatikāram* and *Maṇimēkalai*, didactic and religious texts, and certain other poems ascribed to that stage. Middle Old Tamil will be the focus of this chapter.

The majority of Old Tamil texts, along with their medieval commentaries, lay forgotten for centuries, resurfacing only during the latter half of the nineteenth century. The medieval period witnessed religious struggles among Hindus, Buddhists, and Jains. When the Hindus ultimately prevailed, they anathematized as irreligious all secular and heterodox texts, destroying them outright or withholding them from copyists. As a result, only a single Buddhist text, the epic *Maṇimēkalai*, survives from the late classical period. Jain texts fared much better because of the ritual of *sastradaṉam* which enjoins rich patrons to commission new copies of old texts to present to scholars at such auspicious occasions as weddings. The *Caṅkam* texts are largely secular, containing poems of love and war; many are informed by a Jain sensibility. Hindu devotional texts such as *Paripāṭal* appear during the Late Old Tamil period. In any event, the classical texts were never known to a wide audience before the modern era. Many were composed for a specific patron and transmitted from teacher to student. When finally committed to writing, the copies were jealously guarded. Frail palm-leaf manuscripts suffered from the extremes of the Indian climate: some crumbled when the leaves were untied, others were thrown into rivers following the death of their owner, and others still probably ended as kindling for cooking fires.

It is only with such Indian scholars as U. V. Caminata Aiyar (1855–1937) that the slow, laborious collecting and editing of these texts began. This paralleled the rediscovery, cataloging, and decipherment of Old Tamil inscriptions by British surveyors and scholars. There is a real sense in which Old Tamil is still being discovered, even among Tamilians. We lack, for example, critical editions of texts (in the Western sense), although we do have editions that may be considered authoritative. Tamil has its own linguistic tradition, anchored in the ancient grammar *Tolkāppiyam* (On ancient composition); but even this text is not fully understood. The linguistic analysis of Old Tamil is still in its infancy, so much so that scholars can still debate the number of cases or tense forms in the language.

2. WRITING SYSTEM

Old Tamil was earliest recorded utilizing three different writing systems (see Lehmann 1994). All of these are syllabic scripts that developed from the southern branch of the Ashokan Brāhmī writing system (see Ch. 2, §2). By convention, Old Tamil texts are now transcribed in the modern form of *Tamiḻ Eḻuttu.*

Table 4.1 The Tamil syllabary

VOWEL		<u>k</u>	k	ṅ	c	ñ	ṭ	ṇ	t	n
a	அ		க	ங	ச	ஞ	ட	ண	த	ந
ā	ஆ		கா	ஙா	சா	ஞா	டா	ணா	தா	நா
i	இ		கி	ஙி	சி	ஞி	டி	ணி	தி	நி
ī	ஈ		கீ	ஙீ	சீ	ஞீ	டீ	ணீ	தீ	நீ
u	உ		கு	ஙு	சு	ஞு	டு	ணு	து	நு
ū	ஊ		கூ	ஙூ	சூ	ஞூ	டூ	ணூ	தூ	நூ
e	எ		கெ	ஙெ	செ	ஞெ	டெ	ணெ	தெ	நெ
ē	ஏ		கே	ஙே	சே	ஞே	டே	ணே	தே	நே
ai	ஐ		கை	ஙை	சை	ஞை	டை	ணை	தை	நை
o	ஒ		கொ	ஙொ	சொ	ஞொ	டொ	ணொ	தொ	நொ
ō	ஓ		கோ	ஙோ	சோ	ஞோ	டோ	ணோ	தோ	நோ
au	ஔ		கௌ	ஙௌ	சௌ	ஞௌ	ளட	ணௌ	தௌ	நௌ
None		ஃ	க்	ங்	ச்	ஞ்	ட்	ண்	த்	ந்

VOWEL	p	m	y	r	l	v	ẓ	ḷ	ṟ	ṉ
a	ப	ம	ய	ர	ல	வ	ழ	ள	ற	ன
ā	பா	மா	யா	ரா	லா	வா	ழா	ளா	றா	னா
i	பி	மி	யி	ரி	லி	வி	ழி	ளி	றி	னி
ī	பீ	மீ	யீ	ரீ	லீ	வீ	ழீ	ளீ	றீ	னீ
u	பு	மு	யு	ரு	லு	வு	ழு	ளு	று	னு
ū	பூ	மூ	யூ	ரூ	லூ	வூ	ழூ	ளூ	றூ	னூ
e	பெ	மெ	யெ	ரெ	லெ	வெ	ழெ	ளெ	றெ	னெ
ē	பே	மே	யே	ரே	லே	வே	ழே	ளே	றே	னே
ai	பை	மை	யை	ரை	லை	வை	ழை	ளை	றை	னை
o	பொ	மொ	யொ	ரொ	லொ	வொ	ழொ	ளொ	றொ	னொ
ō	போ	மோ	யோ	ரோ	லோ	வோ	ழோ	ளோ	றோ	னோ
au	பௌ	மௌ	யௌ	ரௌ	லௌ	வௌ	ழௌ	NA	றௌ	னௌ
None	ப்	ம்	ய்	ர்	ல்	வ்	ழ்	ள்	ற்	ன்

While preserving the fundamental principles of the syllabic systems descended from Brāhmī, the Tamil orthographic system, *Tamiẓ Eẓuttu* "Tamil letter," has continued to evolve. In Tamiẓ Eẓuttu, as in related syllabaries, each graph represents a *vowel* or a sequence of *consonant + vowel*. Vowels (*uyir* "breath, soul") are represented by two main allographs: (i) one for initial position; and (ii) one, or more, used in combination with a consonant graph. Consonant (*mey* "body") graphs have a so-called basic form with the syllabic value *consonant* + *a*. This basic form is graphically modified to express other vowel values by adding diacritics above it or below it, or to its left or right. To represent consonant clusters, the basic graph is modified by adding a *pulli*, a small circle, above the basic sign of all but the last graph of the cluster. The *aytam*, symbol for k̲, lacks an inherent vowel component and never occurs with a vowel diacritic.

For further discussion and illustration of the Brahmi and Tamil writing systems, see Daniels and Bright 1996.

3. PHONOLOGY

3.1 Consonants

The seventeen consonants of Tamil are as follows:

(1) Tamil consonant phones

	Labial	*Dental*	*Alveolar*	*Retroflex*	*Palatal*	*Velar*	*Glottal*
Stop	p	t	r̲	ṭ	c	g	
Nasal	m	n	n̲	ṇ	ñ	(ŋ)	
Lateral		l		ḷ			
Tap		r					
Approximant					ẓ		
Glide	v				y		(h)

All sounds are phonemically distinct except those placed within parentheses, which are allophones having a distinct graphemic representation. With the notable exception of /yaŋŋan̲am/ "what manner," the velar nasal [ŋ], transcribed as ṅ, appears to occur as an allophone of other nasals, occuring only before the velar stop /k/. The fricative [h], called *aytam* and transcribed as k̲, occurs only between a short vowel and a stop (e.g., /ahtu/ "it, that"). As such, it may be regarded as an allophone of /v/ since /v/ is the only consonant that does not occur in this context.

3.2 Vowels

Old Tamil has ten vowels, five short and five long:

(2)

i, ī		u, ū
e, ē		o, ō
	a, ā	

Diphthongs /ai/ and /au/ also occur.

For metrical purposes, the long vowels and the diphthong /ai/ may be lengthened (through, in effect, the addition of a short vowel). This lengthening may then be repeated; in other words, an already elongated vowel may itself be lengthened. Consider, for example, /cir̲ār/ "small ones" (*Pari* 3.6) becoming /cir̲āar/ (*Aka* 107.17) and further /cir̲āaar/ (*Pur̲a* 291.2).

3.3 Morphophonemic variation

When morphemes combine and compound words are formed, several kinds of morphophonemic changes (*sandhi*) may occur. Among the more common are the following:

1. Loss of a final segment: *pāṭṭu* "song" + *-āl* instrumental case > *pāṭṭ-āl* "by song"; *maram* "wood" + *vīṭu* "house" > *mara-vīṭu* "wooden house"
2. Assimilation: *kaṇ-* "eye" + *-ku* dative case > *kaṭ-ku* "to the eye"
3. Consonant insertion: *kal* + *āl* > *kal.l-āl* "with stone"; *pacu* "fresh" + *īṟa* "shrimp" > *pac.c-īṟa* "fresh shrimp")
4. Glide insertion: *katti* + *āl* > *katti.y-āl* "with a knife"

This chapter adopts Lehmann's (1994) convention of placing a period before a segment that is automatically inserted by phonological rule in order to clarify morphemic identity. Such processes are obligatory with a bound morpheme, less frequent between members of a compound and least frequent elsewhere.

3.4 Phonotaxis

All vowels and the diphthong /au/ may occur in word-initial position. All vowels and diphthongs occur after all consonants except /n/ and *k̲*. There is only a single occurrence of /a/ after /ŋ/: /yaŋŋaṉam/ "in which way" (*Aka* 27.12). All vowels and /au/ may appear in word-final position. Only the nine consonants /p/, /t/, /c/, /k/, /m/, /n/, /ñ/, /y/, and /v/ appear in word-initial position. Word-finally, ten consonants, all of them nonobstruents, are permitted: /m/, /n/, /ṉ/, /ṇ/, /l/, /ḷ/, /y/, /w/, /r/, and /ẕ/. Consonant clusters are limited in scope.

3.5 Prosody

Old Tamil is a quantitative language: quantitative units called *acai* "morae" fall at regular intervals. These units are combined into feet, and the feet into meters. Rajam 1992 outlines the prosodic system, particularly as it involves poetic composition.

4. MORPHOLOGY

4.1 Word formation and word classes

Old Tamil morphology is predominantly agglutinating, with a one-to-one correspondence between morpheme and morph. Despite what appear to be exceptions, it is exclusively suffixal. There also occur some instances of fusion.

Old Tamil has two major, formally distinct parts of speech – noun and verb. Most lexical stems belong to one of these two classes; some stems have a double categorial status: for example, *col* can be the verb stem meaning "say," or the noun stem meaning "word." Beyond this, consensus as to the number and identity of parts of speech breaks down. A small number of words fail to exhibit all the properties nouns and verbs typically exhibit: some scholars assign them to two minor classes, adjectives and adverbs; others treat them as defective nouns and verbs.

Distinct from the parts of speech is a set of clitic particles which combine with their host to form a phonological word, but which may syntactically combine with an entire clause. Clitics are herein identified by the boundary marker =, and include quantifiers, discourse particles, and emphatic markers.

4.2 Nominal morphology

Nominals in Old Tamil include common nouns, numerals, proper names, pronouns, and certain other forms. Nominals are primarily inflected for case and number, and secondarily for gender and person. Nominal stems may be simple or complex. Complex stems include all derivatives. The complex noun *āṇ-mai* "manliness, strength" (*Pati* 70.20; a complete list of abbreviations and texts cited is to be found at the end of the chapter) consists of the noun *āḷ* "man" and the abstract suffix *-mai*; while the complex noun *kaḷv-i* "female thief" consists of the stem *kaḷ-* "theft" and the feminine suffix *-i*.

4.2.1 Gender

In Old Tamil gender is largely natural. There are two basic genders, *uyartiṇai* "animate" (lit. "high-class") and *akr̲iṇai* "inanimate" (lit. "non-class"), which determine, *inter alia*, the choice of plural marker and pronouns.

4.2.2 Number

In Old Tamil, singular number is unmarked. The plural has three basic markers: *-kaḷ*, *-ar*, *-ir*. The first occurs with inanimate nouns, the second and third, with animate. Examples include the following: (i) *kaṇ* "eye" ~ *kaṇ-kaḷ* "eyes" (*Kali* 39.42); *iyam* "musical instrument" ~ *iyaṅ-kaḷ* "musical instruments" (*Malai* 277); *vaẓi* "path" ~ *vaẓi-kaḷ* "paths" (*Aka* 8.1); (ii) *arivai* "woman" ~ *arivai.y-ar* "women" (Pati 68.19); *koṭicci* "young girl" ~ *koṭicci.y-ar* "young girls" (*Kali* 40.11); *kēḷ* "relative" ~ *kēḷ-ir* "relatives" (*Kali* 61.3); (iii) *peṇṭu* "woman" ~ *peṇṭ-ir* "women" (*Aiṅk* 271.3). Certain other plural suffixes, such as *-mār*, are also attested: for example, *tōẓi* "girlfriend" ~ *tōẓi-mār* "girlfriends" (*Aka* 15.9). Even when a finite verb bears a plural suffix, the subject need not appear marked as a plural: thus, *paṭāa em kaṇ* "my$_2$ eyes$_3$ do.not.sleep$_1$" (*Aka* 218.9).

4.2.3 Stem-forms

Old Tamil nouns may have an oblique stem that differs from the nominative. There are two basic kinds of oblique stems. For neuter nouns ending in *-am*, the oblique replaces the final *-m* with *-ttu*: for example, the nominative form *paẓam* "fruit" has the oblique stem *paẓa-ttu-* (*Aka* 292.14). Nouns that end in *-tu* or *-r̲u* double the consonant in the oblique: thus, nominative *nāṭu* "country" has the oblique stem *nāṭ.ṭu-* (*Aiṅk* 203.2). The oblique is the form to which non-nominative case markers and postpositions are added (3A, B); the form that appears when a case ending is elided (3C, D); and the form that serves as an appositive attribute (3E, F). It is, in short, the combining form of the noun.

(3) A. man̲a-tt-ōṭu
mind-OBL.-SOC.
"With the mind" (*Kali* 47.17)

B. kaḷir̲.-r̲-ōṭu
elephant-OBL.-SOC.
"With the elephant" (*Pati* 66.7)

C. aṭuka-ttu aruvi viẓa
cliff-OBL. waterfall-NOM. fall-INF.
"As the waterfall descends from the cliff" (*Kali* 44.2)

D. nāṭṭu.c cell-al
country-OBL. go-NEG.-IMPV.
"Don't return to [your] country" (*Aiṅk* 233.4)

E. vēẓa-ttu.k kōṭu
elephant-OBL. tusk
"The elephant tusk" (*Kuṟu* 100.4)

F. nāṭṭu.k kuṉṟam
country-OBL. hill-NOM.
"The hills of the country" (*Kuṟu* 249.3–4)

With the oblique case forms, compare the euphonic suffixes *-iṉ-* and *-aṉ-*, which may appear between a noun stem and a case-marker. Traditional accounts suggest these forms are inserted for metrical purposes. Examples include the accusative form *kulai.y-iṉ-ai* "a bunch" (*Kali* 45.3) and the dative *naṭp-iṟ-ku* "for friendship" (*Puṟa* 236.6)

4.2.4 Case

The *Tolkāppiyam* identifies eight cases in all: nominative, accusative, dative, instrumental, equative, genitive, locative, and vocative. Case-markers are added to the singular or plural stem of the noun; however, only rarely are plural inanimate nouns marked for case. Postpositions extend the case system.

4.2.4.1 Nominative

The nominative is the unmarked case, and has several functions. It serves as the subject of a clause (4) and as predicate nominative (5), among other functions.

(4) A. yāṉ vantaṉeṉ
I-NOM. come-PST-1ST PER. SG.
"I have come" (*Naṟṟ* 267.8)

B. yāṉ=um nī.y=um e.v-vaẓi aṟitum
I-NOM.=and you-NOM.=and what.path meet-PST-1ST PER. PL.
"Where did you and I meet?" (*Kuṟu* 40.3)

(5) A. ivar pāri makaḷ-ir
these.ones-NOM. Pari daughter-PL.-NOM.
"These are the daughters of Pari" (*Puṟa* 202.14–5)

B. yāt=um ūr=ē, yāvar=uṅ
which one-NOM.=and town-NOM.=and whoever-NOM.=and
kēḷir
relation-PL.-NOM.
"Any [town] is [our] town, all people are [our] kinfolk" (*Puṟa* 192.1)

Owing to the common elision of case-markers, many nouns, particularly inanimates, appear in the nominative even though the semantics of the clause would require some other case-marker. In (5A), for example, the proper name *Pari* "Pari" functions as a genitive, but appears in the nominative.

4.2.4.2 Accusative

The accusative typically marks an animate direct (6A, B) or indirect (6C) object. The Old Tamil corpus, however, contains some examples of inanimate objects marked as accusative (6D).

(6) A. en̲ tōẓi.y-ai nōkki
my friend-ACC. look.at-CF
"[You are] looking at my friend" (*Kali* 50.8)

B. orūupa nin̲.n̲-ai
shun-NPST-3RD PER. PL. you-ACC.
"They shun you" (*Pati* 34.1)

C. nin̲.n̲-ai ampuli kāṭṭal in̲itu
you-ACC. moon-NOM. show-VN sweet-NOM.
"It is nice to show the moon to you" (*Kali* 80.18–19)

D. upp-ai mār̲i vennel tarīiya
salt-ACC. trade-CF white.paddy-NOM. bring-INF.
"In order to obtain white paddy by trading salt" (*Kur̲u* 269.5)

4.2.4.3 *Dative*

The dative typically marks indirect object, (7A, B), direction (7C), or causality (7D, E):

(7) A. an̲n̲ai-kku moẓi.y-um vēlan̲
mother-DAT. speak-NPST-3RD PER. SG. priest-NOM.
"The priest speaks to the mother" (*Aiṅk* 249.1–2)

B. nin̲.a-kku on̲ru kur̲uvam kēḷ in̲i
you-DAT. one.thing tell-NPST-1ST PER. PL. listen-IMPV. now
"Listen now to what I (lit. we) have to say to you" (*Kali* 55.5)

C. ūru-kku.p pōvōy
village-DAT go-NPST-2ND PER.SG.
"You will go to your village" (*Nar̲r̲* 200.7)

D. poruṭ-ku ir̲atti
wealth-DAT. depart-CF
"Departing for riches" (*Kali* 10.12)

E. vaṇ peyar̲-ku aviẓnta paiṅkoṭai mullai
heavy rain-DAT. unfold-PST-ADN. fresh.vine jasmine
"The fresh jasmine on the vine which blossomed because of the heavy rain" (*Aka* 124.11)

Old Tamil also has some structures which, in the light of modern Dravidian structures, could be interpreted as dative-subject constructions:

(8) A. nin̲.a-kk=ō ar̲iyunal neñc=ē
you-DAT.=INTERR. know-VN-3RD SG. FEM. heart=VOC.
"Is she someone known to you, O my heart?" (*Nar̲r̲* 44.5) meaning: "Do you know her, O my heart?"

B. emakku il
we-DAT. not.be
"There is nothing for us" (*Pati* 39.2) meaning: "We have nothing"

4.2.4.4 *Instrumental*

The instrumental case may be signaled by the morphs *ān̲* and *-āl*. The suffix expresses the relations of instrument, association and location. Due to sandhi, it is sometimes difficult to identify which morph is used (as in 9C).

(9) A. nī munṉ-att-āṉ kāṭṭ-iṉ-ai
you-SG.-NOM. sign-OBL.-INSTR. show-PST-2ND PER. SG.
"You showed with a sign" (*Kali* 61.7)

B. aṭi.y-ai talai.y-iṉ-āl toṭṭu
foot-ACC. head-OBL.-INSTR. touch-CF
"Touching [his] foot with [my] head" (*Kali* 1108.55–56)

C. niṉ kaṇṇ-ār kaṇpēṉ yāṉ
you-OBL. eye-INSTR. see-NPST-1ST PER. SG. I-NOM.
"I see with your eyes" (*Kali* 39.43)

4.2.4.5 *Sociative*

The sociative is marked by the suffixes *-oṭu* and *-ōṭu.* It signals accompaniment or instrumentality:

(10) A. kaḷiṟṟu.t toẓuti.y-ōṭu vantu
elephant-OBL. driver-SOC. come-CF
"[He] came with a mahout" (*Pati* 62.1–5)

B. ivaḷ-ōṭu vāẓiya
she-SOC. live-OPT.
"May you live/prosper with her" (*Pati* 21.37–8)

C. vitt-ōṭu ceṉṟa vatti paṟpala mīṉ-ōṭu peyarum
seed-SOC. go-PST-ADN. basket many many fish-SOC. return-NPST-3RD PER.SG.
"The basket which left with seeds returns with many kinds of fish" (*Naṟṟ* 210.3–4)

4.2.4.6 *Equative*

The equative case marks an object of comparison with the suffix *-iṉ.* Its subsidiary nuances include locatival, instrumental and causal. This case no longer exists in Modern Tamil, having been replaced by the postposition *viṭa* "than" (e.g. *avaṉ-ai viṭa* "than$_2$ that.man$_1$"):

(11) A. tokai aṇi maṭantai.y-iṉ tōṉṟ-um
peacock-NOM. decoration-NOM. girl-EQ. appear-NPST-3RD PER. NEUT.
"The peacock looks like a decorated young girl" (*Aiṅk* 294.1–2)

B. ciṟṟil kāl-iṉ cītai.y-a
small.house foot-EQ. trample-CF
"[We] trample the hut with [our] feet" (*Kali* 51.2)

C. irav-iṉ var-al
night-EQ. come-NEG.IMPV.
"Do not come at night" (*Kali* 49.23)

4.2.4.7 *Genitive*

The genitive, signaled by *-atu* and *a*, is adnominal: it marks such relations as possession between two noun phrases:

(12) A. eṉ toẓi.y-atu kaviṉ
I-OBL. friend-FEM.-GEN. beauty
"My girlfriend's beauty" (*Kali* 50.24)

B. avar-a kayam
those.people-GEN. pool
"Their pools [of water]" (*Puṟa* 15.9–10)

4.2.4.8 *Locative*

The locative case, one of the most unstable in Dravidian, is marked by a case formant and no less than nineteen postpositions (*Tolkāppiyam, collatikāram*, 82). The case-marker *-il*, the inanimate locative case-marker in Modern Tamil, is attested in Old Tamil (13A, B). However, locative postpositions with specific meanings are more commonly encountered: *uḻai* "place" (13C), *vayiṉ* "area" (13D). These typically combine with the oblique stem of the preceding noun. The oblique stem itself, unmodified by any case-marker, often conveys the sense of the locative (13E):

(13) A. cilamp-il tuñcum kavari
hillside-LOC. sleep-NPST-ADN. antelope
"The antelope that sleeps on the hillside" (*Pati* 11.21)

B. eḻḻ-iṉ-il peyartal
dusk-LOC. leave-VN
"Leaving at dusk" (*Aka* 100.4)

C. NP[kēḷir N[uḻai.c]N]NP ceṉṟu
relative-PL.-OBL. place go-CF
"going to one's relatives" (*Kali* 61.3)

D. kiḷavi NP[nam N[vayiṉ]N]NP vantaṉṟu
word-NOM. we-OBL. place come-PST-3RD PER.NEUT.
"Word has come to us" (*Kuru* 106.3–4)

E. nal nāṭ.ṭu.c celkam
good land-OBL. go-NPST-3RD SG.MASC.
"He is going to his beautiful country" (*Aiṅk* 236.4)

4.2.4.9 *Vocative*

The vocative, used in address, is formed in several ways. Nouns that end in *-aṉ* delete the final nasal: for example, *marukaṉ* "son," *marukā* "O son" (*Pati* 63.16). Certain nouns form the vocative by lengthening the final vowel of the last syllable: for example, *nutal* "forehead," *nutāl* "O [one with the broad] forehead" (*Kali* 37.12); *aṉṉai* "mother," *aṉṉāy* "O mother" (*Aiṅk* 201.1). In other instances, usually with inanimates, the clitic =*ē* is added: thus, *nāṭu* "country," *nāṭ*= *ē* "O (my) country" (*Aiṅk* 221.4).

(14) aṉṉāy vāḻi ventaṉṉai
mother-VOC. live-OPT. listen-PST-2ND PER.SG.
"Bless you, my friend [lit. mother]. You must listen" (*Aiṅk* 203.1)

4.2.4.10 *Absence of case-marking*

Lehmann (1994: 52ff.) observes that case-markers in Old Tamil are often omitted in contexts that one would expect to trigger their presence. For example, the transitive verb *uḷ-* "think" ordinarily requires direct objects in the accusative case. Note that in (15A) the object in the first conjunct appears in the nominative case, the object in the second in the oblique stem. The result of this elision is that Old Tamil contains many phrases that resemble large compounds consisting of nominal stems, as in (15B).

(15) A. cuṟṟam=um em.m=um uḷḷ-al
companions-NOM.=and we-OBL.=and think-NEG.-3RD PER.FEM.
"She doesn't think of us (=me) and our companions" (*Aka* 17.6)

B. [[kaya vāy] [peru.ṅ kai] yān̲ai]
[[great mouth] [big trunk] elephant]
"The elephant with a great maul and a large trunk" (*Aka* 118.7–8)

4.2.5 Person

Old Tamil nouns may also mark person by suffixing personal endings that agree with a subject; these are the so-called *appellative nouns* of the literature. Lehmann (1994: 61ff.) shows these forms to be the result of a syntactic, not a morphological, process. Appellative nouns in Old Tamil are generally predicate nominals (16A–E) or vocatives. In Medieval Tamil they may take such non-nominative case forms as the accusative (16F), while they are absent in the modern language

(16) A. tōl-ēn̲
shoulder-1ST PER.SG.
"I, with [broad] shoulders" (*Aka* 82.18)

B. peṇṭ-ir-ēm all-ēm
woman-PL.-1ST PER.PL. become-NEG.-1ST PER.PL.
"We are not women" (*Pur̲a* 246.10)

C. nall-āy
good.one-2ND PER.SG.
"You, who are good" (*Kali* 39.30)

D. eyir̲.r̲-āḷ
tooth-3RD SG.FEM.
"She, with [shining] teeth" (*Aiṅk* 256.3)

E. niẓal-ōr
shadow-3RD PER.PL.
"Those who are in the shadow" (*Pati* 68.20)

F. aṭi.y-ēn̲-ai.k kaṇṭān̲
devotee-1ST PER.SG.-ACC. see-PST-3RD SG.MASC.
"He saw me, a devotee"

4.2.6 Pronouns

Old Tamil has personal as well as demonstrative and interrogative pronouns.

4.2.6.1 Personal pronouns

The personal pronouns of Old Tamil are shown in (17). The nominative forms are followed by their oblique forms in parentheses. Note that Old Tamil distinguishes between an *inclusive* and an *exclusive* plural. The dramatis personae of Old Tamil poems often use first-person plural inclusive where the first-person singular might be expected; this convention persists in Modern Tamil when a speaker engages in musing or soliloquy.

(17)

	Singular		*Plural*
First	yān̲ (en̲(n̲), en̲a)	*Exclusive*:	yām (yām(m), yama)
		Inclusive:	nām (nām(m), nama)
Second	nī (nin̲(n̲), nin̲a		nīr, nīyir (num(m), num)
Third	tān̲ (tan̲(n̲), tan̲a		tām (tam(m), tama)

4.2.6.2 *Demonstrative and interrogative pronouns*

Old Tamil also has a series of demonstrative and interrogative pronouns. Forms in *i-* are proximal, *u-* medial, *a-* distal, and *e-/ya-* interrogative. The medial series is not fully attested in the old language: the forms **uḵtu* "this one in-between" and **uvai* "these in-between" are not attested in the corpus. The series is lost in the modern continental dialects. Members of the distal series frequently serve as general-purpose third-person pronouns.

(18)

		Proximal	*Medial*	*Distal*	*Interrogative*
Singular	*Masculine*	ivaṉ	uvaṉ	avaṉ	yāvaṉ
	Feminine	ivaḷ	uvaḷ	avaḷ	yāvaḷ
	Neuter	itu/iḵtu	utu/NA	atu/aḵtu	yātu/yāvatu
Plural	*Animate*	ivar	uvar	avar	yār
	Inanimate	ivai	NA	avai	yāvai/yā

4.3 Verbal morphology

Verbs in Old Tamil mark such categories as illocutionary force, tense, mood, negative polarity, and subject–verb agreement. Verbs are formally distinguished as finite verbs and nonfinite verbs.

4.3.1 Stem-forms

A majority of Tamil verb-bases may form two related stems, one weak, the other strong. This morphophonemic distinction corresponds to a voice distinction, *affective* voice versus *effective* voice (Paramasivam 1979). Certain stems have distinct variants for the negative conjugation: for example, positive *kaṇ-* "see" versus negative *kāṇ-*. Two important verbs, *āka* "become" and *iru* "be (located)," have the suppletive variants *al-* "not become" and *il-* "not be," respectively, in the negative conjugation.

4.3.2 Verbal conjugations

Old Tamil has seven conjugation classes, based on the allomorphs of the suffixes they take. Once the voice and the phonological shape of the stem are taken into account, it may be possible to reduce the number of conjugations.

4.3.2 Nonindicative moods

In addition to the indicative (see §4.3.3) Old Tamil finite verbs can occur in the imperative and optative moods. All finite verbs mark subject–verb agreement.

4.3.2.1 *Imperative*

Imperatives convey an order, request, and so forth, and encode second-person agreement. The simple verb-stem often functions as the singular imperative (19), although there exist exceptions: thus, the verb-stem *taru-* "give to you or me" has the imperative form *tā* "give (to me)."

(19) A. aṅku iṟa
there go-IMPV.
"Go there" (*Kali* 63.9)

B. kēḷ avan̲ nilaiy=ē
listen-IMPV. he-GEN. condition=PCL.
"Listen to his condition" (*Peru* 38)

The negative singular imperative has two forms. One adds the ending *-ati* to the verb stem (20A). The other is a compound verb: the verb appears in its stem-form and is followed by the auxiliary verb *al* "not become" inflected for the imperative (20B):

(20) A. varunt-ati
grieve-NEG.-IMPV.
"Don't grieve" (*Kali* 107.30)

B. an̲pin̲ V[VS[aẓ]VS AUX[al]AUX]V
love-EQ cry-STEM not.become-IMPV.
"Do not cry from love" (*Nar̲r̲* 309.3–4)

The plural imperative consists of a verb-stem and one of several suffixes: *-mati*, *-min̲*, or *-m*:

(21) A. ivar-ai koṇ-mati
this.man-ACC. take-IMPV.-PL.
"Take this man" (*Pur̲a* 201.16)

B. avar̲-ku ar̲iya urai-min̲
he-DAT. understand-INF. speak-IMPV.-PL.
"Speak so that he understands" (*Nar̲r̲* 376.9)

C. yāvar=um varu-ka ēn̲ōr=um tā-m
who=and come-OPT. others=and bring-IMPV.-PL.
"Let everyone [of you] come. Bring others, too" (*Matu* 747)

The negative plural imperative is periphrastic, consisting of the verb-stem and the auxiliary verb *al* "not become" (*an̲-* by sandhi) inflected for the imperative with *-min̲*:

(22) evvam V[VS[patar]VS AUX[an̲-min̲]AUX]V
distress suffer-STEM not.become-IMPV.-2
"Don't suffer in distress" (*Kali* 9.22)

4.3.2.2 Optative

The optative is marked by several suffixes, the most common of which is *-k(k)a*. Lehmann's (1994:76) examples show that unlike the imperative, which is restricted to second-person subjects, the optative occurs with all persons.

(23) A. peṇṭu yān̲ āku-ka
woman-NOM. I-NOM. become-OPT.
"May I become a woman"; "Would that I were a woman" (*Aka* 203.18)

B. oṇ kuẓ-āy cel-ka
shining earring-2ND PER. SG. go-OPT.
"May you, with the shining earrings, go" (*Kali* 37.21)

C. yāy ar̲intu uṇar-ka
my.mother know-CF understand-OPT.
"May my mother know and understand [it]" (*Aka* 203.2)

The negative optative is an auxiliary compound verb consisting of the verb-stem of the main verb and *al* "not become" (*an̲*- by sandhi), inflected for the optative suffix:

(24) aiyam V[VS[koḷ̣]VS AUX.[an̲-min̲]AUX.]V ar-ar̲ival-ir
doubt hold-STEM not.become-OPT. full-knowledge-2ND PER.PL.
"May you, who are full of knowledge, have no doubts" (*Pur̲a* 216.5)

Old Tamil has additional suffixes and constructions used to convey the imperative and optative modes. Second-person indicative verbs often serve as imperatives or optatives.

4.3.3 Indicative mood

Indicative finite verbs consist of a (i) verb-stem, (ii) tense marker, and (iii) personal ending (though see below). In the negative, they consist of a (i) verb-stem, (ii) negative marker, and (iii) personal ending. In the positive, there are two tenses – past and non-past. Steever (1993) suggests that what have been treated as allomorphs of the past tense are actually markers of a present perfect tense which is cognate with present perfect forms in other Dravidian languages and which survives in Śri Lankan Tamil. There is, in the negative, a single paradigm corresponding to the past and non-past positive paradigms (see [30] below).

The positive indicative forms exhibit some variation in their morphological composition. The majority consist simply of a verb-stem, tense marker, and personal ending that marks subject–verb agreement (25A). Some insert a euphonic increment between the stem and tense marker, while others place the increment between the tense marker and the personal ending (25B). Such euphonic increments may represent the historical residue of earlier tense suffixes (25C). In still other indicative forms, the tense marker and agreement-marker have fused into a portmanteau morph incapable of segmentation (25D). Lehmann (1994:79) presents these four possibilities with the verb *cey*- "do, make":

(25) A. cey-t-ān̲
do-PST-3RD SG.MASC.
"(He) did" (*Kali* 51.16)
B. cey-t-an̲-ai
do-PST-EUPH-2ND PER.SG.
"(You) did" (*Aiṅk* 294.3)
C. cey-ku-v-am
do-EUPH.-NPST-1ST PER.PL.
"(We) do" (*Aiṅk* 288.2)
D. cey.y-um
do-NPST+3RD PER.PL.
"(They) do" (*Aiṅk* 244.4)

4.3.3.1 *Tense markers*

The past tense morpheme has the following allomorphs: *-t-*, *-nt-*, *-tt-*, *-i-*, *-in̲-*, and gemination of the stem-final consonant (marked -CC- in [26]). The non-past morpheme has the allomorphs *-v-*, *-p-*, *-pp-*. They are distributed according to the seven conjugational classes of Old Tamil as follows.

(26) Old Tamil conjugational classes

Class	*Past*		*Non-past*	
I	-t-	cey-t-ēn̲ "I did" (*Kali* 37.12)	-v-	cey-v-ēn̲ "I do" (*Kali* 62.12)
II	-nt-	ar̲i-nt-ēn̲ "I knew" (*Kali* 47.3)	-v-	ar̲i-v-ēn̲ "I know" (*Aiṅk* 247.1)
III	-in̲-/-i-	añc-in̲-ān̲ "he feared" (*Kali* 65.20)	-v-	añcu-v-aḷ "she fears" (*Kali* 48.22)
IV	-CC-	per̲.r̲-an̲-ar "they got" (*Pur̲a* 10.4)	-v-	per̲u-v-ai "you get" (*Kali* 49.25)
V	-t-	kaṇ-ṭ-ai "you saw" (*Kali* 64.6)	-p-	kaṇ-p-ēn̲ "I see" (*Kali* 39.43)
VI	-tt-	urai-tt-al "she spoke" (*Kali* 39.21)	-pp-	urai-pp-atu "it speaks" (*Kali* 48.19)
VII	-nt-	ira-nt-an̲-an̲ "he asked" (*Aiṅk* 257.2)	-pp-	ira-pp-ān̲ "he asks" (*Kali* 62.12)

4.3.3.2 Personal endings

The personal endings illustrated in (27) may be added to the past stem, the non-past stem, or the negative stem of a verb. They are the most general in the language, and give rise to the personal endings of the modern language.

(27) Old Tamil personal endings I

	Singular		*Plural*
First	-ēn̲, -en̲, -al, -an̲-		-ām, -am, -ēm, -em
Second	-ai, -āy, -ōy		-īr, -ir
Third			
Masculine	-ān, -an, -on̲	*Epicene*	-ār, -ar, -or
Feminine	-āḷ, -aḷ, -ōḷ		
Neuter	-tu, -ttu, -atu		-a

The personal endings of (28) are added directly to the verb-stem; these are portmanteau forms that encode not merely person, number, and gender but also non-past tense. This structure, presented in (29B), is contrasted with the more general structure in (29A). Only the third-person neuter singular form *-um* survives into Modern Tamil; the loss of the portmanteau forms represents a reassertion of the general agglutinative character of Tamil morphology which discourages fusional forms.

(28) Old Tamil personal endings II

	Singular	*Plural*
First	-ku/-kku	-tum, -kum, -kam
Second	-ti, -tti	-tir
Third		
Neuter	-um	-um
Epicene		-pa, -mār

(29) A. ira-pp-ān̲
ask-NPST-3RD SG.MASC.
"He asks" (*Kali* 62.12)

B. ira-kku
ask-NPST+1ST PER.SG.
"I ask" (*Pati* 61.11)

Corresponding to the past and non-past indicative paradigms is a single negative indicative paradigm. It consists of the verb-stem, negative marker, and personal ending (with a long vowel), as already seen in the negative imperative and optative forms. The negative marker is often realized by a zero morph, although its operation can sometimes be inferred from a change of vowel quantity in the verb-stem: for example, *kaṇpēṉ* "I see" versus *kāṇāḷ* "she didn't/doesn't see."

(30) A. cel.l-ēṉ cel.l-ēṉ piṟar mukam
go-NEG.-1ST PER.SG. go-NEG.-1ST PER.SG. other-GEN. face-NOM.
nōk.k-ēṉ
look.at-NEG.-1ST PER.SG.
"I won't go. I won't go. I won't look at the faces of others" (*Puṟa* 399:14)

B. ivaṉ-ai.p poy-ppa vıṭ-ēem
he-ACC. tell-lies-INF. let-NEG.-1ST PER.PL.
"We won't let him tell lies" (*Kali* 89.13)

C. aṉṟu nam aṟi.y-āy
then we-OBL. know-NEG.-2ND PER.SG.
"You did not know us then" (*Aka* 33.18)

D. pāṇaṉ cūṭ-āṉ pāṭiṉi aṇi.y-aḷ
bard-NOM. wear-NEG.-3RD SG.MASC. bard's.wife-NOM. decorate-NEG.-3RD SG.FEM.
"The bard doesn't wear [the jasmine], his wife doesn't decorate herself [with it]" (*Puṟa* 139.1)

4.3.4 Periphrastic constructions

Old Tamil also has several periphrastic forms that simultaneously express tense and negation. One variety uses a serial verb construction (Steever 1988) that combines the past or non-past affirmative form of the main verb with the negative auxiliary *al-* "not become"; both are inflected for congruent personal endings.

(31) A. cel-v-ēm all-ēm
go-NPST-1ST PER. PL. become.not-1ST PER. PL.
"We will not go" (*Puṟa* 31.11)

B. aṟi-nt-aṉ-aḷ all-aḷ
know-PST-EUPH-3RD SG.FEM. become.not-3RD SG.FEM.
"She did not know" (*Aka* 98.6)

Such constructions alternate with another in which the auxiliary verb *al-* "not.become" combines with the bare root of the main verb, rather than any inflected form. The compound verb *maṟavaleṉ* "I will not forget" in (26A) consists of the root of the main verb *maṟa* "forget" and *aleṉ* "I do not become."

(32) A. maṟa.v-al-eṉ
forget-not.become-1ST PER.SG.
"I will not forget" (*Puṟa* 395.32)

B. vāẓ-al-aḷ
live-not.become-3RD SG.FEM.
"She will not live" (*Aka* 12.14)

Other auxiliary verbs occur in similar constructions: for example, when the auxiliary *tara* "give to you or me" combines with the bare root of the main verb, it indicates that the action is oriented toward the speaker or addressee in the speech event.

(33) pō-tara
go-give.to.you.or.me
"to come" (*Kali* 56.31)

Such constructions fell into disuse by the medieval period, being replaced by auxiliary verb constructions in which the main verb appears in an inflected, nonfinite form. Thus, while the bare verb root could function as a free form in Old Tamil, it no longer does so in Modern Tamil.

4.3.5 Nonfinite verbals

Old Tamil has three sets of nonfinite verbals: (i) primary forms, (ii) secondary forms, and (iii) verbal nouns. The primary forms directly add a suffix to the verb-stem or, rarely, to the tensed stem. Secondary nonfinite forms add a clitic to a primary form. Verbal nouns are nominalized forms which may be inflected for case. As the number and distribution of finite predicates is greatly limited in the Old Tamil sentence (see Steever 1988, Lehmann 1994), nonfinite forms figure prominently in complex syntactic structures.

4.3.5.1 Primary forms

There are four primary nonfinite verb forms: (i) the conjunctive, (ii) the infinitive, (iii) the conditional and (iv) the adnominal. The suffixes for the conjunctive and the conditional have several allomorphs in free variation. The infinitive entails five subtypes with various semantic functions. The adnominal form has two tensed and two negative forms. Nonfinite verbals are illustrated in (34), (38), and (40) with forms of the verb *oḷir-* "shine."

(34) Primary nonfinite verbals

Conjunctive	oḷir-ā, oḷirū, oḷir-ntu, oḷir-pu
Negative conjunctive	oḷir-ā, oḷir-ā-tu, oḷir-ā-mal, oḷir-ā-mai
Infinitive	oḷir-a, oḷir-iya, oḷir-iyar, oḷir-mār, oḷir-vāṉ
Conditional	oḷir-iṉ, oḷir-nt-āl
Adnominal	
Past	oḷir-nt-a
Non-past	oḷir-um
Negative adnominal	oḷir-a, oḷir-a-ta

The *infinitive* in its varieties is the most general of the nonfinite forms in Old Tamil, conveying such notions as circumstance, result, and purpose:

(35) A. $_S$[mēṉi nalam tolai.y-a]$_S$ tuyaram cey-t-ōṉ
body beauty lose-INF. distress-NOM. do-PST-3RD SG.MASC.
"He brought distress, and [her] body lost its beauty" (*Aka* 278.13–14)

B. paru-ntu icai niṟ-ka.p pāṭ-iṉ-aṉ
spread-CF renown-NOM. remain-INF. sing-PST-3RD SG.MASC.
"He sang to spread [your] renown and [make] it remain" (*Puṟa* 126.13)

The various *conditional* verb forms mark the protasis of a conditional sentence. The simple conditional verb forms do not differentiate all of the verbal categories that finite verbs do; they do not distinguish, for example, between past and non-past tense. A periphrastic construction may also be used in which the conditional form *āka* "become" combines with a finite verb to mark a protasis.

(36) A. [ayar emar] ā<u>n</u>-āl aytti.y-ēm
cowherd-NOM. our.kin-NOM. become-CND. cowherd+FEM.-NOM.-1ST PER.PL.
yām
1ST PER.PL.INC-NOM.
"If our kin are cowherds, we are cowherdesses" (*Kali* 108.9)

B. [ni<u>n</u> marpu muyaṅk-ēm āy-i<u>n</u>] yām
you-OBL. breast-OBL. embrace-NEG.-1ST PER.PL. become-CND. we-NOM.
cāytum
swoon-NPST-1ST PER.PL.
"If we (=I) did not embrace your breast, we would swoon" (*Aka* 218.15–17)

The *adnominal* forms (called *adjectival* or *relative participles* in the literature) are nonfinite verbals that co-occur with a following nominal, with or without intervening material. Adnominal forms typically subordinate a clause to the following nominal: in (37A) it subordinates a relative clause to a head noun; in (37B) it subordinates a sentential complement to a noun; and in (37C) it helps form a complex adverbial expression.

(37) A. ${}_{NP}$[S[t_1 ni<u>r</u>am pāy-nt-a]$_S$ kaṇai$_1$]$_{NP}$
breast-NOM. pierce-PST-ADN. arrow
"The arrow that pierced [his] breast" (*Kali* 57.14)

B. ${}_S$[tiram=um vaiyai.y=um cēr-ki<u>n</u><u>r</u>-a]$_S$ kaṇ kavi<u>n</u>
riverbank-NOM.=and Vaiyai-NOM.=and join-NPST-ADN. eye captivation-NOM.
"The eye-captivating beauty of the [river] Vaiyai joining the riverbank" (*Pari* 22.35)

C. ${}_S$[nī iravu va-nta.k]$_S$ kāl
you-NOM. night-NOM. come-PST-ADN. time
"The time that you came by night" (*Kali* 38.14)

4.3.5.2 *Secondary forms*

The four secondary nonfinite forms combine a primary form with an independent word or a suffix: (i) the causal (< conjunctive in *-ntu* + *e<u>n</u>a*); (ii) the equative (< conjunctive in *-ntu* + *āṅku*); (iii) the concessive conditional (< conditional + =*um*); and (iv) the factive concessive (< infinitive + = *um*).

(38) Secondary nonfinite verbals

Causal	oḷir-nt-e<u>n</u>a
Equative	oḷir-nt-āṅku
Concessive conditional	oḷir-i<u>n</u>-um, oḷir-nt-āl-um
Factive concessive	oḷir-a.v-um

Consider the factive concessive as an example of a secondary finite verb. It consists of a verb form in the infinitive and the clitic = *um* "and, even," and is translated as "even though V."

(39) [nāṭa<u>n</u> var-a.v=um] ivaḷ mē<u>n</u>i paca-pp-atu eva<u>n</u>
land-3RD SG.MASC. come-INF.=and she-GEN. body-NOM. be.pale-VN why
"Why is it that, even though her chief had come, her body is pale?" (*Aiṅk* 217.3–4)

4.3.5.3 *Verbal nouns*

Nominalized verb forms or verbal nouns are divided into tensed and tenseless verbal nouns. The latter group has five variant forms. Some verbal nouns, such as those with *-pu*, never mark case.

(40) **Verbal nouns**

Tenseless verbal noun	oḷir-al, oḷir-kai, oḷir-tal, oḷir-pu, oḷir-vu
Tensed verbal noun	
Past	oḷir-nt-ā-mai, oḷir-nt-atu
Non-past	oḷir-v-atu
Negative verbal noun	oḷir-ā-mai

At one level of generalization, some verbal nouns may be analyzed as combinations of an adnominal form and an abstract pronominal head noun. This construction is transparent in some instances, but is obscured by fusional morphology in others.

(41) A. [niṟ kaṇ-ṭ-ar-kku] aṇanku ākum
you-OBL. see-PST+ADN.-3RD PER.PL.-DAT. awe-NOM. become-NPST-3RD SG.NEUT.
"Those who saw you were struck with awe" (*Kali* 56.21)

B. [kuvalai malar-tal] ari-tu
kuvalai-flower bloom-VN rare.thing-3RD SG.NEUT.
"It is rare for the kuvalai flower to bloom" (*Aiṅk* 299.2–4)

4.3.5.4 *Nonfinite verbal constructs*

Nonfinite verb forms dominate the formation of complex structures: compound verbs and complex clauses. The *conjunctive* form (also, *adverbial participle*) *vantu* "coming" functions as a main verb in the compound verb construction of (42A), and as a form that conjoins two clauses in (42B). Note also that the tenseless verbal noun *ayar-tal* "accomplish" in (42B) embeds a complement beneath a verb of wishing.

(42) A. va-ntu ilar
come-CF not.be-3RD PER.PL.
"They did not come" (*Pari* 9.25)

B. vaikaṟai va-ntu vatuvai ayartal vēṇṭu-v-al
daybreak come-CF marriage accomplish-VN wish-NPST-1ST PER. SG.
"I want you to come at daybreak and marry [me]" (*Kali* 52.22–23)

4.4 Adjectives and adverbs

Old Tamil has two "minor parts of speech": adjectives and adverbs. These differ grammatically from nouns and verbs; each set has few members.

4.4.1 Adjectives

Adjectives include *aru* "difficult," *nal* "good," *putu* "new," and *peru* "big," as well as words denoting color. They are morphologically invariant, lacking inflections: the comparative and superlative degrees are marked syntactically. Adjectives do not behave like nouns to the extent that they occur neither as subject nor as object; they do not behave like verbs in that they neither subcategorize verbal arguments nor assign case. They occur only as adnominal attributes with an adjectival function. Adjectives such as *nal* "good" could, however, be treated as defective nouns, specifically ones that lack case inflection. They can therefore occur in compound nouns, but never as the head. They may also participate in noun derivation: like nouns, *nal* may take the abstract derivative suffix *-mai*, yielding *naṉ-mai* "goodness" or *-tu*, yielding *naṉ-ṟu* "that which is good, a good thing."

4.4.2 Adverbs

Adverbs constitute an even smaller set of uninflected words. They occur only as attributes of verbs, nouns, and adjectives. Words such as *uṟu*, *naṉi*, and *tava*, all meaning "much," are examples of adverbs. These appear to be verb roots that have become frozen in an idiomatic function. Some inflected word forms are grammaticalized as adverbs with a particular lexical meaning: for example, the conjunctive form *aẓi-ttu* from *aẓi* "finish" idiomatically means "again." The paucity of adjectives and adverbs in Old Tamil reflects the transparent, agglutinative morphological character of the language, which tends to discourage extensive morphophonemic variation and defective morphology alike.

5. SYNTAX

5.1 Word order

Like other South Dravidian languages, Old Tamil is a head-final, SOV language. In simple clauses, the unmarked order of the major constituents is Subject–Object–Verb. While explicit case-marking allows for the permutation of noun phrases within the clause, the verb firmly remains at the right clause boundary and is displaced from that position only under marked circumstances. The direct object tends to occur just before the verb, while other oblique arguments occur before the direct object but after the subject. The texts include departures from this expected SOV template, leading some (Rajam 1992) to doubt that the language is indeed SOV. In (43), for example, the object follows the verb rather than precedes it.

(43) orūupa   niṉ.ṉ-ai
shun-NPST-3RD PER.PL.   you-ACC.
"They shun you" (*Pati* 34.1)

It must be borne in mind, however, that the Old Tamil corpus consists almost exclusively of poetic discourse. To accommodate their poetic designs, the bards permuted constituents and so departed from canonic SOV patterns. However, just below the surface lie robust SOV syntactic patterns. In harmony with an overall SOV framework, genitives in Old Tamil always precede their heads, main verbs always precede auxiliaries, and relative clauses always precede their head nominals.

5.2 Sentence structure

The simple sentence in Old Tamil consists of a subject and predicate. While the great majority of texts cast the subject in the nominative case, a few examples appear to cast it in the dative (44E), a phenomenon well documented in other South Dravidian languages. The predicate of a simple sentence may be a finite verb (44A, C, E) or a predicate nominal (44B, D) without any copula:

(44) A. nī munṉ-att-āṉ kāṭṭ-iṉ-ai
you sign-OBL.-INSTR. show-PST-2ND PER.SG.
"You showed with a sign" (*Kali* 61.7)

B. entai.y=um nuntai=um emmuṟai kẹ̄lir
my.father-NOM.=and your.father-NOM.=and what.degree kin-PL.-NOM.
"What kin are your father and mine?" (*Kuṟu* 40.2)

C. yāṉ=um nī.y=um evvaẓi aṟitum
I-NOM.=and you-NOM.=and what.path-NOM. know-NPST+1ST PER.PL.
"On what path would you and I meet?" (*Kuṟu* 40.3)

D. tōl-ēṉ
shoulder-1ST PER. SG.
"I, with [broad] shoulders" (*Aka* 82.18)

E. niṉ.a-kk=ō aṟiyunaḷ neñc=ē
you-DAT.=INTERR. know-VN-3RD SG.FEM. heart=VOC.
"Is she someone known to you, O my heart?" (*Naṟr* 44.5)
meaning: "Do you know her, O my heart?"

5.3 Agreement

In simple sentences, predicates agree in person, number, and gender with subjects in the nominative case; agreement is marked by personal endings on the predicate. While predicate nominals in Old Tamil carried personal endings to mark agreement with their subjects (44B, E), their counterparts in Modern Tamil no longer do so.

5.4 Pro-drop

The use of personal endings on finite predicates allows for the omission of a subject noun phrase; consequently, Old Tamil is a pro-drop language. However, subject pronouns are seldom dropped when they occur in an extended usage (Steever 1981:80ff.). When, for example, the second-person plural pronoun is used honorifically for a singular referent, it is rarely dropped; nor is the first-person inclusive plural pronoun *yām* "we and you" absent when it is used to denote the speaker in soliloquy. Other arguments may be omitted as well. No South Dravidian language, including Old Tamil, has a verb phrase constituent, with the result that verbs need not overtly mark their objects to show their valence.

5.5 Clitics

Old Tamil has several clitics which may be added to noun and verbal forms, but not to adjectives. Although they combine morphologically with a noun or verb, their scope is the entire phrase or clause, whose head is that noun or verb. The clitic =*um* "and" coordinates noun phrases and nonfinite clauses; =*ō* and =*kol* mark a clause as being interrogative; and =*ē* "even" indicates emphasis.

5.6 Compound and complex clauses

The examples of (44B) and (44C) reveal that the subject of a simple sentence may be a coordinate structure; the quantifier =*um* "and, all," morphologically a clitic, is added to each constituent of the conjunct. Predicates, however, may not be baldly conjoined in this way to form complex sentence structures; instead, a variety of morphological and lexical devices are used to create complex structures with multiple clauses.

Lacking a distinct morphological category of *conjunction*, Old Tamil deploys its nonfinite verb forms (see §4.3.5) to join one clause to the next in the formation of subordinate and coordinate clauses. As a rule, there can be only one finite predicate per sentence; it generally occurs rightmost in the sentence and c-commands all other verbs in the sentence. All other predicates are nonfinite (see Steever 1988, Lehmann 1994). In (45A) the nonfinite conjunctive form *ar̲intu* "knowing" conjoins the two clauses "my mother knows" and "my mother understands" to form a coordinate sentence; in (45B), the nonfinite infinitive form *tolaiya* "lose" subordinates a result clause to the following main clause.

(45) A. $_{S0}$[$_{S1}$[yāy$_1$ ar̲intu]$_{S1}$ $_{S2}$[t_1 uṇar-ka]$_{S2}$]$_{S0}$
my.mother know-CF understand-OPT.
"May my mother know and understand [it]" (*Aka* 203.2)

B. $_{S0}$[$_{S1}$[mēn̲i nalam tolai.y-a]$_{S1}$ tuyarm cey-t-ōn]$_{S0}$
body beauty lose-INF. distress-NOM. do-PST-3RD SG.MASC.
"He brought distress, and/so that [her] body lost its beauty" (*Aka* 278.13–14)

The constraint against multiple finite predicates prevents any predicate nominal from appearing in a subordinate clause or a nonfinal conjunct *tout court*. In ruling out finite predicates in such contexts, it would also prevent the possibility of direct discourse. While Old Tamil texts do contain some examples of asyndetic parataxis, the language has three verbs that permit a finite predicate to be embedded in a complex sentence. The verbs *āka* "become," *en̲a* "say" and *pōla* "resemble" may take as their objects expressions of any category without imposing any morphological change on those objects; they may consequently embed finite predicates. In this capacity, these verbs contribute no lexical meaning to the structure. But as verbs, they may occur in nonfinite forms and thus be embedded in the larger structure. The infinitival form *en̲a* "say" in (46A) embeds the finite verb *uḷan̲* "he is" – it acts as a complementizer to mark direct discourse. The conditional form *ān̲āl* "if become" in (46B) embeds the predicate nominal *emar* "our kin" in the protasis of a conditional. On occasion, other verbs of communication or perception, such as *kēḷ* "hear" (46C), may also embed finite predicates.

(46) A. $_{S0}$[$_{S1}$[nin̲ makan̲ yāṇṭ(u) uḷan̲=ō]$_{S1}$ en̲a
your son-NOM. where-NOM. be-NPST-3RD.SG.MASC.=INTERR. say-INF.
vin̲avuti]$_{S0}$
ask-NPST+2ND PER.SG.
"You ask (saying), 'Where is your son?' " (*Pur̲a* 40.1–2)

B. [ayar emar] ān̲-āl aytti.y-ēm
cowherd-NOM. our.kin-NOM. become-CND. cowherd+FEM.-NOM.-1ST PER.PL.
yām
we^{inc}-NOM.
"If [it is the case that] our kin are cowherds, we are cowherdesses" (*Kali* 108.9)

C. $_{S0}$[$_{S1}$[nin̲.a-kku on̲ru kur̲uvam]$_{S1}$ kēḷ in̲i]$_{S0}$
you-DAT. one.thing tell-NPST-1ST PER.PL. listen-IMPV. now
"Listen now to what I have to say to you" (*Kali* 55.5)

Finally, Old Tamil permits finite verb forms to occur where nonfinite forms might otherwise be expected. The language has a structure called *mur̲r̲eccam* in the traditional grammatical literature – a finite form that functions as a nonfinite form (Steever 1988: 45–52). The negative compound verbs in (31) above provide examples. Consider (47), where the finite past tense forms *āṭiṉir pāṭiṉir* "you celebrated" (lit. "you sang and danced') occur where nonfinite conjunctive forms *āṭ-i pāṭ-i* "celebrating" (lit. "singing and dancing") are expected:

(47)	āṭi-iṉ-ir	pāṭ-iṉ-ir	cel-iṉ=ē
	dance-PST-3RD PER.PL.	sing-PST-3RD PER.PL.	go-CND.=EMP.-PCL.

"If you go celebrating (lit. singing and dancing)" (*Puṟa* 198.10)

This construction occurs in many other Dravidian languages (Steever 1988), but has dropped out of Modern Tamil.

6. LEXICON

The vocabulary of Old Tamil significantly reflects its Dravidian lexical heritage; however, even in the earliest stages of the language we find borrowings from Indo-Aryan languages, principally Sanskrit and the Prakrits. Sanskrit proper names appear in early texts: for example, in *Pura* 161.6, *Kaṅkai* "Ganges" renders the Sanskrit *Gaṃga.* Further examples of borrowings include (i) Prakrit *pāhuḍa* "gift," which was borrowed into Old Tamil as *pākuṭam* with appropriate adjustments and rephonemicization to the Tamil sound system; (ii) Sanskrit *nagara* "town," which became Tamil *nakar* (*Puṟa* 6.18); (iii) Prakrit *khavaṇa* "eject." which gave Tamil *kavaṇai* "sling" (*Kali* 23.2).

In Old Tamil, the set of verbal bases was closed so that all borrowed words were nouns (note *kavaṇai* "sling" above). In the medieval language, the set of verbal bases was slightly expanded through borrowing; for example, *yōci-kka* "to think, ponder" comes from the Sanskrit root *yuj-*. However, this set became closed again with the advent of the modern language. In general, verbs from other languages are borrowed into Tamil as nouns that may then be compounded with native Tamil verbal bases.

Despite travel abroad and contacts with traders from the classical Mediterranean world in the Tamil coastal emporia (where spices and other luxury goods were traded for Roman gold coins), Tamilians appear not to have borrowed words from Western sources in antiquity. Attempts to assign particular words to Greek or Latin sources are uncertain – based perhaps more on fancy than on careful philological and etymological analysis. In the medieval and modern periods, however, Tamil has borrowed from a wide array of source languages – Indo-Aryan, Persian, Arabic, Portuguese, and English, among others.

7. DISCOURSE

Two poems are presented to illustrate connected discourse in Old Tamil. The language is represented by a fixed corpus; specifically, Middle Old Tamil is attested in two anthologies, which consist of 2,381 poems that range in length from 3 to 782 lines, totaling approximately 32,000 lines. It is only during the medieval period that this corpus came to be known as the *caṅkam* "academy, community" literature or *cāṉṟor ceyyuḷ* "poetry of the nobles."

The Old Tamil corpus consists primarily of poetic compositions. Ramanujan (1985:xi) observes that the poems of the two major anthologies are both "classical," i.e., ancient, early, and "classics", i.e., they have withstood the test of time. As many as 475 bards composed these poems for their patrons, who were usually kings or chieftains. The poetry of the two anthologies treats two principal themes: love and war. While Tamil literature later grows to include didactic verse, epics and other literary forms, the poems of the two anthologies inform much of the later Tamil canon, as evidenced in medieval devotional (*bhakti*) literature.

Kailasapathy (1968) characterizes this corpus as bardic: the poetry was orally composed and transmitted, as various figures and tropes attest. Further, the poems form a highly coherent literary body: the many poets appealed to a shared set of conventions treating composition, leading to the name *caṅkam* "academy, community." According to tradition, the first book in Old Tamil is the grammar, *Tolkāppiyam* "On ancient composition." Its first two books treat phonology and morphology but the third, *Poruḷatikāram* "chapter on content," discusses what constitutes a well-formed poem.

The *Poruḷatikāram* and later commentaries enumerate such poetic elements as appropriate themes, characters, landscapes, figures and meter. Poems belong to one of two main groups: *akam* "interior" and *pur̲am* "exterior" The *akam* poems treat the different phases of love. These poems are general; the characters in them are not historical persons, but actors in an interior drama. The *pur̲am* poems detail various acts of heroism such as valor in war or daring in cattle raids.

These poems are dramatic in two senses. First, they distill an experience – that is, an insight gained from action – and give it shape through poetic figures. Second, the colophons of the poems observe that each poem is spoken by a particular character in a drama: one might stipulate that a heroine is addressing her confidante over the delayed return of her lover. The poet thus stands at a remove, reinforcing the often anonymous nature of the composition.

The first poem, number 86 in the anthology *pur̲anānūr̲u* "Four hundred verses on heroism," is a *pur̲am* poem. The colophon observes that it is uttered by the mother of a warrior.

What his mother said:

cir̲.r̲-il	*nar̲r̲ūṇ*	*par̲r̲-i*	*nin̲*	*makan̲*		
small.house	pillar-NOM.	grasp-cf	you-OBL.	son-NOM.		
yāṇṭ(u)	*uḷan̲=ō*	*en̲a*	*vin̲avuti*	*en̲*	*makan̲*	
where-NOM.	be-NPST-3LD MASC.=INT	say-INF.	ask-NPST+2ND SG.	I-OBL.	son-NOM.	
yāṇṭ(u)	*uḷan̲*	*ā.y-in̲=um*	*ar̲i.y-ēn̲*	*ōrum*		
where-NOM.	be-NPST-3RD SG.MASC.	become-CND.=AND	know-NEG.+1ST SG.	once		
puli	*cērntu*	*pōkiya*	*kal*	*alai*	*pōla*	
tiger-NOM.	join-CF	go-ADN.	stone-NOM.	cave-NOM.	resemble-INF.	
īn̲ra	*vayir̲=ō*	*itu.v=ē*				
give.birth-PST-ADN.	womb-NOM.=INTERR.	this.one=EVEN				
tōn̲ravan̲	*mātō*	*pōrkal̤l̤a.t*	*tān̲=ē*			
appear-VN-3RD SG.. NEUT.	indeed	battlefield-OBL.	indeed=EVEN			

"You grasp the pillar of my hut and ask:
'Where is your son?' Wherever my son might be,
I don't know.
Though this womb, that gave him birth,
was once a den for that tiger,
Now he appears only on battlefields."

The second poem belongs to the *akam* genre, and comes from the anthology *kur̲untokai* "Collection of short poems" (40).

What he said to her:

yāy=um	*ñāy=um*	*yār*	*āk-ir=ō*
my.mother-NOM.=AND	your.mother-NOM.=AND	who-NOM.	become-NPST-3RD PL=INTERR.
entai.y=um	*nuntai=um*	*emmur̲ai*	*kēḷir*
my.father-NOM.=AND	your.father-NOM.=AND	what.degree	kin-NOM.
yān̲=um	*nī.y=um*	*evvaẓi*	*ar̲itum*
I-NOM.=AND	you-NOM.=AND	what.path-OBL.	know-NPST+1ST PL.

cem-pola.p-peya-nīr	*pōla*
red-earth-rain-water	resemble-INF.

an̲p-uṭai	*neñcam*	*tāṅ*	*kala-nt-an̲a.v=ē*
love-have	heart-NOM.	indeed	mix-PST-3RD PL.=EVEN

'What is my mother to yours?
What kin are your father and mine?
And on what path could you and I have met?
'But, with love, our hearts have mingled
Like the red earth and pouring rain.'

Abbreviations

adn.	adnominal form
cf	conjunctive form
cnd.	conditional
euph.	euphonic particle
npst	non-past tense
pst	past tense
vn	verbal noun
vs	verb-stem
=	clitic boundary
–	simple morpheme boundary
+	portmanteau form

Texts cited

Aka	Akanān̲ūr̲u	*Pati*	Patir̲r̲upattu
Aiṅk	Aiṅkur̲unūr̲u	*Peru*	Perupaṇār̲r̲uppaṭai
Kali	Kalittokai	*Pur̲a*	Pur̲anān̲ūru
Kur̲u	Kur̲untokai	*Malai*	Malaipaṭukaṭam
Nar̲r̲	Nar̲r̲iṇai	*Matu*	Maturaikkañci
Pari	Paripāṭal		

Bibliography

Akattiyaliṅkam, C. 1983. *Caṅkat Tamiẓ I, II, III*. Annamalainagar: An̲aittintiyat Tamiẓ Moẓiyiar̲ Kaẓakam.

Andronov, M. 1969. *A Standard Reference Grammar of Modern and Classical Tamil*. Madras: New Century Book House.

Camin̲ataiyar, U. 1950. *En̲ Carittiram*. Madras: Daktar U. Ve. Camin̲ataiyar Nūl Nilaiyam.

Daniels, P. and W. Bright (eds.). 1996. *The World's Writing Systems.* Oxford: Oxford University Press.
Kailasapathy, K. 1968. *Tamil Heroic Poetry.* London: Oxford University Press.
Lehmann, T. 1994. *Grammatik des Alttamil.* Stuttgart: Steiner.
Paramasivam, K. 1979. *Effectivity and Causativity in Tamil.* Trivandrum: Dravidian Linguistics Association.
Rajam, V. 1992. *A Reference Grammar of Classical Tamil Poetry.* Philadelphia: American Philosophical Society.
Ramanujan, A. 1985. *Poems of Love and War.* New York: Columbia University Press.
Steever, S. 1981. *Selected Papers in Tamil and Dravidian Linguistics.* Maturai: Muttu Patippakam.
_______. 1987. "Tamil and the Dravidian languages." In B. Comrie (ed.), *The World's Major Languages*, pp. 725–746. London: Croom Helm.
_______. 1988. *The Serial Verb Formation in the Dravidian Languages.* Delhi: Motilal Banarsidas.
_______. 1993. *Analysis to Synthesis: The Development of Complex Verb Morphology in the Dravidian Languages.* New York: Oxford University Press.
_______. 1996. "Tamil writing." In Daniels and Bright 1996, pp. 426–428.
Zvelebil, K. 1967. (The language of Perunkunrur Kilar). In K. Zvelebil, J. Glazov, and M. Andronov (eds.), *Introduction to the Historical Grammar of the Tamil Language.* Moscow: Nauka.
_______. 1973. *The Smile of Murugan: On Tamil Literature of South Asia.* Leiden: Brill.
_______. 1974. *Tamil Literature.* Wiesbaden: Otto Harrassowitz.

CHAPTER 5

Old Persian

RÜDIGER SCHMITT

1. HISTORICAL AND CULTURAL CONTEXTS

Old Persian is one of two Old Iranian languages which are attested in the Achaemenid royal inscriptions (see below), members of that branch of the Indo-European language family called Indo-Iranian, or Aryan (the Persians designate themselves and their language by the term *ariya-*). The Iranian languages began to take shape when the ancestors of the Indo-Aryans left the common homeland in the steppes of Central Asia in the first half of the second millennium BC. The Western Iranian peoples, the Medes who settled in Media and the Persians in Fārs (speaking a Northwestern and Southwestern Iranian dialect respectively), step into the light of history in the ninth century BC, when Median names are first attested in Assyrian documents.

While "Old Persian" was certainly the language of Fārs, the variety which is attested in the Achaemenid inscriptions appears to be a rather artificial idiom, peppered with dialectal and archaic words, unlike any dialect actually spoken (characteristics of a distinct spoken Old Persian may be discerned from certain spontaneous phonetic developments, and from Old Persian words and names as rendered in other languages). The language called Old Persian was thus restricted to royal usage (as was the cuneiform script in which Old Persian was recorded). Even so, Old Persian was neither the lingua franca nor the administrative language of the Achaemenid Empire, roles fulfilled by Aramaic and, to a limited extent, various regional languages spoken within the empire. As a consequence, the linguistic situation of the empire was a quite complex one; and epigraphical Old Persian was itself influenced by these other languages, particularly in its vocabulary and even syntax (e.g., in the occurrence of a postpositive genitive, as in *xšāyaϑiya xšāyaϑiyānām* "king of kings" or *vašnā Auramazdāha* "by the favor of Auramazdā").

The language of the Old Persian inscriptions is dialectologically homogeneous in principle. Only some lexical items (technical terms, etc.) prove to be borrowed from other Iranian languages, mainly the Northwestern Iranian dialect of the Medes (see §6), the political predecessors of the Persian Achaemenids.

The only direct and authentic sources available for the Old Persian language are the cuneiform inscriptions on durable objects (rock, stone, metal, rarely clay tablets) ranging over the period from Darius I (522–486 BC) to Artaxerxes III (359/8–338/7 BC), but dating in the main from the reigns of Darius I and Xerxes I (486–465 BC). In this short period the inscriptions, for the most part, are trilingual (in Old Persian, Elamite, and Babylonian), but even the oldest text, the one of the Bīsutūn monument of Darius I (see below), has sections which are only in Old Persian, or in Old Persian and Elamite. With Artaxerxes I

(465–425/4 BC) the number, size, and significance of the texts begin to decrease rapidly, and they consist almost exclusively of stereotyped formulae, which, in part, seem to have been poorly understood at the time of composition. On the other hand, however, apart from their trilingualism, it is just this monotonous stereotyped style of the texts, along with the great number of parallel texts with their often-repeated invocations of the supreme god and with the regularly quoted royal titles, that has facilitated an understanding of the language and texts and which has allowed reconstruction of fragmentary texts. The abbreviatory system of citing texts is presented at the end of the chapter.

The decreasing number of Old Persian texts after the reign of Xerxes I may be attributed to a loss of fluency with the royal language. By that period, spoken Persian had evolved into a somewhat different form, so discrepancies between everyday speech and the traditional language of inscriptions had arisen. Only upon that basis can the serious grammatical faults which appear in the texts of later Achaemenid kings (mainly of Artaxerxes II and III) be understood.

Most of those "corrupt" forms (incorrect endings, hybrid genitive forms, etc.) can be found in the monolingual inscription A^3Pa of Artaxerxes III; but they also occur in most of the inscriptions of Artaxerxes II and in the monolingual texts claiming to have been composed by Ariaramnes and Arsames in the sixth century BC (that these texts were produced under Artaxerxes III instead, is suggested by the fact that among the later Achaemenids it is only this king who derives his lineage from Arsames, and not only from Darius' father Hystaspes). The use of a form like *būmām* in lieu of the expected accusative singular feminine *būmīm* "earth" can best be explained by positing an actually spoken monosyllabic [bu:m] (like Middle Persian *būm*) and a scribal attempt to "transform" the spoken form into an Old Persian one (an attempt which was rendered detectable by its lack of success, as it used the *ā*-stems as the normal class of feminine nouns). A similar archaizing process is seen in the pseudo-Old Persian accusative singular *šāyatām* for expected *šiyātim* "happiness," where the later form *šāt* has been changed into *šāyat-* by reversing the regular sound change of Old Persian *āya* to Middle Persian *ā* (though being inappropriate here) and adding again the ending *-ām* of the feminine *ā*-stems.

2. WRITING SYSTEM

2.1 Graphemic shape and inventory

Old Persian texts are recorded only in a cuneiform script. This script does not, however, directly continue the Mesopotamian cuneiform tradition (see *WAL* Ch. 8, §2), being similar to the other cuneiform systems only in the employment of "wedge-shaped" characters. In other words, the Old Persian script is not the result of an evolution of the Mesopotamian system, but a deliberate creation of the sixth century BC. It remains unclear why the Persians did not take over the Mesopotamian system in earlier times, as the Elamites and other peoples of the Near East had, and, for that matter, why the Persians did not adopt the Aramaic consonantal script (Aramaic being the lingua franca of the Persian Empire; see §1).

Old Persian cuneiform was used only by the Achaemenid kings for two centuries and only for their own language – that is, the rather artificial literary language of their royal inscriptions. The use of this script was thus in effect a royal privilege. It was a splendid and imposing script best suited for hard surfaces, and apparently used neither for poetic texts nor for administrative nor historical writings.

Table 5.1 The Old Persian cuneiform script

Syllabic symbols

𐎠	𐎡	𐎢								
a	i	u								
𐎲	𐎨	𐏂	𐎭	𐎳	𐎥	𐏃	𐎩	𐎣	𐎾	𐎶
$b^{(a)}$	$c^{(a)}$	$ç^{(a)}$	$d^{(a)}$	$f^{(a)}$	$g^{(a)}$	$h^{(a)}$	$j^{(a)}$	$k^{(a)}$	$l^{(a)}$	$m^{(a)}$
𐎴	𐎱	𐎼	𐎿	𐏁	𐎫	𐎰	𐎺	𐎧	𐎹	𐏀
$n^{(a)}$	$p^{(a)}$	$r^{(a)}$	$s^{(a)}$	$š^{(a)}$	$t^{(a)}$	$ϑ^{(a)}$	$v^{(a)}$	$x^{(a)}$	$y^{(a)}$	$z^{(a)}$
𐎮	𐎪	𐎷	𐎻							
d^i	j^i	m^i	v^i							
𐎯	𐎦	𐎤	𐎸	𐎵	𐎽	𐎬				
d^u	g^u	k^u	m^u	n^u	r^u	t^u				

Logograms

𐏋	𐏌	𐏍	𐏎	𐏏
XŠ	DH_1	DH_2	BG	BU
xšāyaϑiya-	dahyu-	dahyu-	baga-	būmĭ-
"king"	"land"	"land"	"god"	"earth"
𐏈	𐏉	𐏊		
AM_1	AM_2	AMha		
Auramazdā	Auramazdā	Auramazdāha (genitive singular)		

The total number of phonetic characters (which consist of two to five single elements) is thirty-six. These are naturally divided into four groups:

(1) A. Three pure vowel (V) characters: *a, i, u*

B. Twenty-two syllabic characters whose vowel component is *a* (C^a), but which can also be used to represent a consonant occurring before another consonant or in word-final position (C): $b^{(a)}$, $c^{(a)}$, $ç^{(a)}$, $d^{(a)}$, $f^{(a)}$, $g^{(a)}$, $h^{(a)}$, $j^{(a)}$, $k^{(a)}$, $l^{(a)}$, $m^{(a)}$, $n^{(a)}$, $p^{(a)}$, $r^{(a)}$, $s^{(a)}$, $š^{(a)}$, $t^{(a)}$, $ϑ^{(a)}$, $v^{(a)}$, $x^{(a)}$, $y^{(a)}$, $z^{(a)}$

C. Four syllabic characters with inherent *i* vowel (C^i): d^i, j^i, m^i, v^i

D. Seven syllabic characters with inherent *u* vowel (C^u): d^u, g^u, k^u, m^u, n^u, r^u, t^u

In addition, there are eight logograms for commonly used words such as "king," "god" or "land"; these are not obligatory and are not used consistently. The logograms are of a more complex shape, contain up to twelve elements and even show angles placed above angles (as is the case with the numerals). Further, a word-divider is used as well as number symbols (vertical wedges for the units, angles for the tens, and a special symbol for 100 (found in a single inscription).

One of the remarkable stylistic features of Old Persian cuneiform is that the wedges and angles which make up the cuneiform symbols never cross. The attested characters (excluding the numerals and the word-divider) are presented in Table 5.1.

Within the relatively short period of its use this writing system shows a few changes in character shapes – an attempted standardization of the height of those wedges which at first (i.e., in the Bīsutūn text) took up only half the height of the line. However, the mechanics of the writing system (see below), with all its "imperfections," remain unchanged.

2.2 Orthographic conventions

As the set of CV characters with inherent *i* or *u* vowel shows, the inventory as a whole is inconsistent and asymmetric in its structure, for no ascertained reason (phonetic or otherwise):

(2)	d^a	g^a	j^a	k^a	m^a	n^a	r^a	t^a	v^a
	d^i		j^i		m^i				v^i
	d^u	g^u		k^u	m^u	n^u	r^u	t^u	

Beyond this, there are no C^i and C^u characters of the form $b^{i/u}$, $c^{i/u}$, $ç^{i/u}$, $f^{i/u}$, $h^{i/u}$, $l^{i/u}$, $p^{i/u}$, $s^{i/u}$, $š^{i/u}$, $\vartheta^{i/u}$, $x^{i/u}$, $y^{i/u}$, $z^{i/u}$. Even if the writing system were not plagued by such omissions, the ambiguity of many spellings would not be eliminated; the entire group of C^a graphemes has its own affiliated spelling difficulties, which reveal that this writing system is neither phonemic nor phonetic.

As a consequence of the preceding graphemic problems, a number of *orthographic conventions* had to be employed when particular phonemic sequences are written. The most important of these "rules" (to the extent that they can be identified with certainty) are the following:

1. Long vowels are not distinguished from short ones except for *ā* in medial position.
2. Proto-Iranian final *-*a* is written with an additional <a> (i.e., as <-C^a-a>), though in all probability this indicates an actual lengthening of the vowel.
3. The vowels *ī̆* and *ū̆* are written with the vocalic characters <i> and <u>, and medially with an additional preceding <C^i> or <C^u> sign (when available, otherwise <C^a> is used).
4. Final -*ī̆* and -*ū̆* are written with an additional semivowel as <-i-y> and <-u-v> respectively.
5. The "short" diphthongs *ai* and *au* are written <-C^a-i->, <-C^a-u-> (in final position extended by <-y>, <-v>) and therefore can be only partially distinguished from simple vowels (namely, <d^a-i> = *dai*, but <d^i-i> = *di* or *dī*, whereas <t^a-i> = *tai* and *ti* or *tī*).
6. The so-called "long" diphthongs *āi* and *āu* are written <-C^a-a-i->, <-C^a-a-u-> and are thus unambiguous (except in initial position according to **1**).
7. Syllabic *r̥*, which in all probability was pronounced as [ər], is written with consonantal <r> as <C^a-r-C^x> (= *Cr̥C*) in medial position, and as <a-r-> (= *r̥*-) word-initially (where it cannot be distinguished from *ar*- and *ār*-).
8. The nasal consonants *m* and *n* are written before consonants only in special cases, like *mn* in <k^a-m-n^a-> = *kamna*- "few"; otherwise they are not written, so that <b^a-r^a-t-i-y> spells *baranti* "they bear" as well as *barati* "(s)he bears."
9. In word-final position the only consonants which appear are -*m*, -*r*, and -*š*. Thus, while final -*m* is commonly written, as in <a-b^a-r^a-m> = *abaram* "I brought," final -*n* (from Proto-Iranian *-*n* and ultimately from *-*nt*) is omitted: <a-b^a-r^a> = *abaran* "they brought."
10. The postconsonantal glides *y* and *w* are usually written <-i-y-> and <-u-v-> (with <-$C^{i/a}$-i-y-> spelling [Ciy]).

11. Early Iranian **h* (from Indo-Iranian **s*) is omitted in writing before Old Persian *ū̆*, *m*, and *r* (cf. <a-u-r-> = *Aura-*, equivalent to Avestan *ahura-* "lord"), apparently reflecting its phonetic status in the particular Old Persian dialect, on which the inscriptional language is based.
12. The Early Iranian cluster **hw* is likewise spelled as Old Persian <u-v> (by **10** and **11**).
13. The vowel *ī̆* is commonly omitted after the *h* sign, though not without exception, as in <h-i-d^{u}-u-š> = *Hinduš* "Indus."

Given the cumbersome nature of the writing system, clear, one-to-one correspondences between graphs and phonemes do not exist. Some of the above spelling rules result in critical morphology being hidden, particularly rule **5** (e.g., the absence of a distinction between *tai* and *ti* means that third singular, indicative present endings, active *-ti* and mediopassive *-tai* cannot be distinguished) and rule **8** (the omission of preconsonantal *n* blurs, for example, the distinction between the third-person singular and plural endings *-ti*, *-tu* and *-nti*, *-ntu*).

The ambiguous nature of Old Persian spelling means that there is normally some set of possible interpretations of a word. In any particular case then a correct reading is dependent upon careful philological and linguistic (in particular, etymological) analysis – chiefly by comparison with cognate languages (Avestan, Vedic, etc.) or with later Persian developments. In the case of names and technical terms, the forms which they take in Elamite and Babylonian versions of an Old Persian inscription plays a decisive role. For example, the Old Persian spelling <a-s$^{(a)}$-t$^{(a)}$-i-y$^{(a)}$> "is" has, according to the above rules, seventy-two possible readings. Only from Avestan *asti*, Vedic *ásti*, Middle and Modern Persian *ast*, and so forth, does it become clear that the correct interpretation of this sequence is *a-s-t-i-y*, that is, *asti*. That the geographical name spelled <k$^{(a)}$-p$^{(a)}$-d$^{(a)}$> is to be read *Kampanda* (with two nasals omitted in the spelling by rule **8** above) can be ascertained by the Elamite rendering *Ka-um-pan-taš*. Things are not, however, always so simple; a great number of uncertain readings remain unresolved, among them, for example, the second syllable of King Cambyses' Persian name.

It is important to distinguish sharply between graphic and phonemic (and eventually phonetic) units in the publication of Old Persian inscriptions and discussion of lexical or grammatical problems. Most of the existing manuals (text editions, grammars, etc.) use a "normalizing" interpretation – a kind of blend of the graphic and the phonemic which often is determined by the views about Old Persian held by the particular scholar, her/his scholarly tradition, or her/his time.

2.3 Origin of the script

The problems of the origin of the Old Persian cuneiform script, of the date and process of its introduction, have been treated again and again without general agreement having yet been reached concerning the controversial issues. There are several factors that one must take into account:

1. The passage DB IV 88–92, in which a new "form of writing" (Old Persian *dipiciçam*) is mentioned that Darius has made and is said to be *ariyā* "in Aryan."
2. A number of archeological and stylistic observations regarding the Bīsutūn monument, by which several subsequent stages in its genesis may be established.
3. Those Old Persian inscriptions that are supposed or claimed to predate Darius I.
4. The structural analysis of the script itself.

Though the oldest attested inscriptions in Old Persian language are the Bīsutūn texts (first the minor captions, then the major inscription), the creation of a new type of writing for recording the king's mother tongue seems to have begun already under Cyrus II. This assumption is based not least on the observation that the characters k^u and r^u needed for writing the royal name *Kuruš* must belong to some initial set of characters, for their shapes have a quite simple pattern, even though the phonemic sequences expressed by them are not very common. A similar observation reveals that this writing system was created for the Old Persian language and not for some other Iranian dialect like Median: the fricative *ç*, which is the Old Persian reflex of Proto-Iranian **ϑr* and which was foreign to Median, likewise is represented by one of the simplest characters, which must have been among the earliest of signs created.

A number of striking features appear to suggest that the *invention* of the script indeed began under Cyrus, but that Darius was the first to employ it. An original strategy seems to have aimed at a consistent and unambiguous system of marking short and long vowels and diphthongs by means of a complete set of three CV characters – for each consonant – used in conjunction with three V signs; for example:

(3)	*<b^{a}> = *ba*	*<b^{i}> = *bi*	*<b^{u}> = *bu*
	*<b^{a}-a> = *bā*	*<b^{i}-i> = *bī*	*<b^{u}-u> = *bū*
	*<b^{a}-i> = *bai*		
	*<b^{a}-a-i> = *bāi*		
	*<b^{a}-u> = *bau*		
	*<b^{a}-a-u> = *bāu*		

But this concept (which would have required a total of sixty-nine symbols) must have been abandoned at some point in favor of the attested system with its many ambiguities. As can be seen from the system's inconsistent structure (see [2]), the reorganization of the original system must have been regulated by extralinguistic (formal and stylistic) considerations – for example, the tendency to avoid complex signs with crossed wedges or with more than five elements. In any event, the principle of "Occam's razor" was not employed in devising the Old Persian spelling practices to the extent that many spellings are quite uneconomical (e.g., that of final *-i*, *-u*, etc.).

It is the history and genesis of the Bīsutūn monument itself which strongly suggests that the Old Persian script was introduced in connection with these texts. The Old Persian captions of the figures represented in the relief and likewise the Old Persian text of the major inscription do not belong to the original design of the monument, but were added only later to the Elamite and Babylonian versions. That the mother tongue of the kings had been at first neglected on this monument certainly suggests that the Old Persian language had not been previously set to writing.

2.4 Decipherment

Because Old Persian cuneiform fell into disuse with the fall of the Achaemenid Empire, and thus knowledge of that script and of the values of its individual characters was lost already in antiquity, this writing system had to be deciphered in the modern era. Old Persian texts first came to the attention of the West during the seventeenth century. A solid basis for the decipherment was laid by C. Niebuhr, who in 1778 published the first precise copies of Achaemenid trilingual texts and who recognized that the first and most simple system was written from left to right. Following the identification of the word-divider and the attribution of the texts to the Achaemenids, G. F. Grotefend, in 1802, began the process of decipherment. By assuming that the inscriptions were records of the ancient Persians and might therefore contain the names, titles, and genealogies of some of their kings, he succeeded in determining the approximate phonetic values of about ten signs.

From this starting point, other scholars, progressing step by step, brought the decipherment to its conclusion. In 1826 R. Rask identified the $n^{(a)}$ and $m^{(a)}$ signs in the genitive plural ending *-ānām* (corresponding to Avestan *-anąm*) and thus produced the first evidence for a close relationship with the Avestan language. In 1836 E. Burnouf and C. Lassen undertook a more systematic comparison with Avestan. Lassen, in 1845, made the very important discovery that the consonant characters of the Old Persian script could have an inherent vowel, as in the ancient Indian scripts. The work was completed in 1846/1847 by H. C. Rawlinson with his publication, translation, and interpretation of the entire DB text. A final touch was added in 1851 by J. Oppert, who established the value of the last (and most rarely used) of the phonetic signs, $l^{(a)}$, which even now is attested only in four foreign names for the marginal phoneme /l/ (not belonging to Old Persian proper).

3. PHONOLOGY

3.1 Phonemic inventory

Identifying the complete system of Old Persian phonemes is a rather difficult task, since only a minimal set of phonemes is revealed by the attested graphemes. In order to advance beyond that set, the data must be analyzed and evaluated on a language-internal basis and by methods of historical-comparative linguistic analysis.

3.1.1 Consonants

The following consonantal phonemes can be confidently identified for Old Persian:

(4)

	Bilabial	*Labiodental*	*Interdental*	*Dental*	*Velar*
Stop					
Voiceless	p			t	k
Voiced	b			d	g
Fricative		f	ϑ		x
Nasal	m			n	

(the velar nasal [ŋ] is only a positional variant with allophonic status). In addition, Old Persian possesses two so-called "palatal" affricates *c* and *j*, which in all probability were palato-alveolar /č/ and /ǰ/. There also occur six fricatives – /s/, /z/, /ç/, /š/, /ž/, and /h/, the liquids /r/ and /l/, and the glides /y/ and /w/.

The actual pronunciation of those phonemes is not as secure as is suggested by the conventional representation. Thus, regarding the voiced stops /b, d, g/, it has been hypothesized that they were – at least in intervocalic position (if not more generally) – voiced fricatives [β, ð, ɣ]. The sibilant /ž/, which is not represented graphically by a separate character, but is written with the *j* sign, must be postulated for reasons of historical phonology: DB II 64 *n-i-j-a-y-m* = [niž-āyam] "I departed, went off" presents evidence for the Proto-Aryan verbal root **ay* + prefix **niš-/niž-* (with a *j* sign denoting the reflex not of Proto-Aryan **ǰ*, but of **ž*, the voiced counterpart of **š* in the position before a voiced sound). For the time being, however, the question of whether *ž* and *ǰ* are two distinct phonemes or only allophones of one and the same archiphoneme remains unresolved.

The fricative phoneme identified as the palatal /ç/ is the Old Persian reflex of the Proto-Iranian cluster **ϑr* (which is preserved in [nearly] all other Old Iranian dialects). Its phonetic realization remains unclear, however. It can be said with certainty only that the sound was pronounced as a voiceless sibilant (certainly not as a palato-alveolar sibilant [š] and not as an affricate [č]); in Middle Persian its reflex has merged with that of Old Persian /s/.

Old Persian has a syllabic [r̥], which is only a contextually conditioned allophone of the liquid /r/ (between stops), however, and not an independent phoneme. The lateral /l/ has a marginal position in the phonemic inventory of Old Persian, since it is attested only in four foreign names.

3.1.2 Vowels

Old Persian possesses three short and three long vowel phonemes, presented in Figure 5.1:

	FRONT	*CENTRAL*	*BACK*
HIGH	ī / i		ū / u
LOW		ā / a	

Figure 5.1 Old Persian vowels

Whether the long vowels are somewhat lower than the short ones cannot be established. In addition, there are two "short" and two "long" diphthongs, which are not phonemes, but only biphonematic combinations of the short or long low-central vowel with a subsequent short high-front or back vowel; since the first is the syllable nucleus, those diphthongs result in

(5)

Short diphthongs	*Long diphthongs*
ai	āi
au	āu

Those four diphthongs, inherited from Proto-Iranian, are preserved in Old Persian as such at the time of the origin of the Old Persian cuneiform script and during the reign of Darius I and Xerxes I, as can be deduced from their regular orthographic representation (see §2). From a later period, there is evidence of a monophthongization of *ai* and *au* to *ē* and *ō* respectively – seen in the development from Old to Middle Persian and revealed by transcriptions of Persian words in other languages (the "collateral" tradition; see §6). The only transcription evidence of any linguistic weight for Old Persian proper is provided by the Elamite language, which has no diphthongs itself (see *WAL* Ch. 3, §3.2). The Elamite script therefore lacks a regular means of spelling such sounds and so offers little possibility of documenting an early (pre-460 BC) monophthongization. Even so there are, in fact, unmistakable Elamite attempts to render Old Persian diphthongs: for example, *ti-ig-ra-ka-u-da* for Old Persian *tigra-xauda-* "with pointed caps."

It should be noted that not every graphic sequence seemingly pointing to *ai* and *au* actually records a diphthong. Spellings like *a-i-š-t-t-a* "he stood" (from Proto-Iranian **a-hišta°*), the theonym *a-u-r-m-z-d-a* (from Proto-Iranian **Ahura Mazdā*) or the country name *h-r-u-v-t-i-š* (from Eastern Iranian **Harahwatī-* "Arachosia") record sequences of two syllables, [-a$i-] and [-a$u-] (i.e., *A-uramazdā*, not *Au-ramazdā*, etc.).

3.2 Phonotaxis

Vowels and diphthongs are not subject to any phonotactic restrictions, and likewise all single consonants appear in initial and intervocalic position. For the final position, however, only single consonants (neither geminate consonants nor any other consonant clusters) are found, and only *-m*, *-r*, and *-š* are written. Those final consonants which are omitted in writing were perhaps still pronounced but in some manner phonetically reduced. Note that original Proto-Iranian **-a* is written as Old Persian <-a> (i.e., [-a:]), but original **-an* or **-ad* is written as -<C^a> (i.e., [-a]).

Even if Old Persian shows a certain preference for open syllables (see §3.3; suggested also by historical developments like that of the Proto-Iranian clusters **Cy*, **Cw* to *Ciy*, *Cuw*), consonant clusters appear in great number, especially biconsonantal clusters, and particularly in word-internal position. More complex clusters with three (*xšn-*, *-xšn-*, *-xtr-*, *-ršn-*, *-nst-*) or even four elements (only non-native *-xštr-*) are rare. Because of the very limited corpus of Old Persian texts, only a small subset of all clusters possible is actually attested. The most commonly occurring of the attested clusters are (i) those of the form *Cr* and *rC*; (ii) those having an initial sibilant (*sk*, *st*, *zd*, *zb*, *zm*, *šk*, *št*, etc.); and (iii) those having an initial nasal (though not written; *nk*, *ng*, *nt*, *nd*, *mp*, *mb*, etc.).

3.3 Syllable structure

It is difficult to make specific observations about the syllable structure of Old Persian. Most syllables appear to be open: [\$(C)V]; more rarely [$\$C_1C_2V\$$] (e.g., *xša-ça-* "kingdom") or even [$\$C_1C_2C_3V\$$] (e.g., *xšnā-sā-ti* "he may know"). In the case of consonant clusters the syllable boundary may fall within the cluster or before it; the position of the boundary may depend on various criteria: the relative sonority of the particular elements of the cluster; the presence and position of a morpheme boundary; whether or not the cluster concerned is permissible in word-initial position; and so forth. Syllables also occur with the structure [\$VC\$], [\$CVC\$], and [$\$C_1C_2VC\$$] (e.g., *u-fraš-ta-* "well punished"), and perhaps also those with two consonants following the syllabic nucleus (e.g., *ϑans-ta-nai* "to say").

3.4 Accent

Accent is not marked in the Old Persian writing system; consequently both the nature and the position of the accent are quite uncertain. In the development from Old to Middle Persian, final syllables disappear, suggesting that the accent was fixed in the manner of Classical Latin or later Old Indo-Aryan. There may be (indirect) evidence for the hypothesis that the inherited free accent (perhaps a pitch or tonal accent), of which there are traces in Avestan and in modern Iranian languages (especially Pashto), survived until the reign of Darius I.

3.5 Diachronic developments

In this section, only the most interesting and significant diachronic phonological developments will be presented (and only vis-à-vis Proto-Iranian).

3.5.1 Consonants

Among consonantal developments, the most distinctive concerns the Old Persian reflexes of the Proto-Iranian continuants (presumably affricates *t^s and *d^z), which are themselves reflexes of the Proto-Indo-European palatals *$\hat{k}$, *$\hat{g}$, *$\hat{g}^h$: in contrast to the other Iranian languages Old Persian shows *ϑ* in, for example, *viϑ-* "house, royal house" = Avestan *vīs-* = Vedic *víś-* from Proto-Aryan **wíć-*, and *d* (if not [ð]; see §3.1.1) both in, for example, *yad-* "to worship" = Avestan *yaz-* = Vedic *yaj-* from Proto-Aryan **yaȷ́-*, and in *adam* "I" = Avestan *azəm* = Vedic *ahám* from Proto-Aryan *$a\acute{j}^h$*ám*.

There are also certain distinctive Old Persian consonantal changes of a conditioned or syntagmatic type. These changes show an Old Persian development which has progressed beyond that seen in the other Old Iranian languages. Thus, the Proto-Iranian cluster **ϑr* develops into Old Persian *ç* in, for example, *puça-* "son" = Avestan *puϑra-* = Vedic *putrá-*. That this change is of a rather late date is suggested by the fact that Proto-Persian **ϑr*, where *ϑ* is a reflex of Proto-Indo-European *$\hat{k}$, Proto-Iranian *t^s, has also undergone the change: thus, one finds Old Persian *ni-çāraya-* "to restore" = Avestan *ni-srāraiia-* from Proto-Aryan **ćrai-* and Proto-Indo-European *$\hat{k}$*lei-*.

Before **n* or **y* Proto-Iranian **ϑ* became Old Persian *š*: for example, *a-r-š-n-i-* ([arašni-]) "cubit" from Proto-Iranian **araϑni-* = Vedic *aratní-*; *h-š-i-y-* ([hašiya-]) "true" = Avestan *ha^{i}ϑiia-* from Proto-Iranian **haϑya-* = Vedic *satyá-*.

Old Persian *šiy* develops from Proto-Iranian **čy* (i.e., from a Proto-Indo-European *k^w that was palatalized before **y*): for example, *š-i-y-a-t-i-* ([šiya:ti-]) "happiness" = Avestan *šā^{i}ti-* from Proto-Aryan **čyāti-* = Latin *quiēti-*, nominative *quiēs*.

A completely independent development of Old Persian, setting it apart from all the other Iranian languages (and thus one of its chief innovative characteristics), is the simplification of the Proto-Iranian clusters *$t^s v$ and *$d^z v$, producing Old Persian *s* and *z* (not *sp* and *zb*): for example, *a-s-* ([asa-]) "horse" = Avestan *aspa-* = Vedic *áśva-*; *v^i-i-s-* ([visa-]) "all" = Avestan *vīspa-* = Vedic *víśva-*; *h-z-a-n-m* (acc. sg. [hiza:nam]) "tongue" (for the spelling *h-z-* see §2.2, **13**), evolving from Proto-Iranian **hid^{z}vā^o* as do Avestan *hizuuā-* or Parthian *ʿzbʾn* ([izβa:n]) from earlier **hizbān^o*.

3.5.2 Vowels

The vowels and diphthongs of Proto-Iranian remained unchanged in Old Persian at least until the period of Darius I and Xerxes I (on the later monophthongization of the short diphthongs see §3.1.2). The reflex of Proto-Iranian word-final short *-*a* is usually written as <-C^a-a> = *-ā*, as in *u-t-a* ([uta:]) "and" (Avestan *uta*, Vedic *utá*); it appears probable that this lengthening was a linguistic reality and not only a graphic phenomenon. Vowel contraction seems to play a minor role in Old Persian. The most obvious example is that of *-*iya-* producing *-ī-*, as in *n-i-š-a-d-y-m* ([ni:ša:dayam]) from uncontracted **ni-a-šādayam* "I have put down" (cf. the alternative form *n-i-y-š-a-d-y-m*), and in *m-r-i-k-* ([mari:ka-]) "young man" from **mariyaka-* (with a secondary *-Ciya-* from*-*Cya-*, from Proto-Aryan **maryaka-* (= Vedic *maryaká-*).

Proto-Iranian sonorants, **m*, **n*, **y*, **w*, and **r* (including Proto-Iranian **ar* from Proto-Aryan **r̥H* as in *darga-* "long" = Old Avestan *dar^{ə}ga-* = Vedic *dīrghá-*, etc.), remain unchanged in Old Persian. Proto-Aryan **Cy* and **Cw* developed into Old Persian *Ciy* and *Cuw* respectively, regularly written as <C$^{i/a}$-i-y> and <C$^{u/a}$-u-v>: for example, *a-n-i-y-* ([aniya-]) "other" = Avestan *a^{i}niia-* = Vedic *anyá-*; *h-r^u-u-v-* ([haruva-]) "all" = Avestan *ha^{u}ruua-* = Vedic *sárva-*.

Syllabic **r̥* as an allophone of consonantal **r* occurring between consonants (C__C) and word-initially before a consonant (#__C) likewise is preserved in Old Persian and probably was pronounced as [ər]. Since in Old Persian orthography this [ər] can be rendered only in a makeshift fashion (like the sequence [ar]) by <(C)a-r-C>, other unambiguous evidence is required to confirm the value [ər] – either morphological (e.g., *k-r-t-* "made, done" = [kərta-] with the zero-grade of the root like Avestan *kər*^{ə}*ta-* and Vedic *kr̥tá-*), or etymological (e.g., *a-r-š-t-i-* "spear" = [əršti-], revealed by Vedic *r̥ṣṭí-*). A special case is the development of Proto-Iranian **r̥* to Old Persian *u* in the present and aorist stems of the root *kar* "to do" (e.g., *k*^{u}*-u-n-u-t-i-y* [kunauti] "he does" = Avestan *kər*^{ə}*nao*^{i}*ti* = Vedic *kr̥ṇóti*); these are usually explained as allegro forms originating in (and spreading from) the imperative.

Two phonetic phenomena, which have given such a strange appearance to many Avestan words (see Ch. 6, §§3.3; 3.4.2; 3.4.10), are without significance for Old Persian. Epenthesis (i.e., the insertion of *i* or *u* into an existing syllable) is completely foreign to Old Persian, and anaptyxis (i.e., the development of a vowel between two consonants) is nearly unknown. The Avestan epenthesis, which is triggered by an ensuing *i/y* or *u/w* (as in Avestan *ha*^{i}*ϑiia-* "true" from **haϑya-*, see §3.5.1), is not attested in Old Persian inscriptions (transcription of Old Persian words in other languages may reveal that a late process of this sort characterized colloquial Old Persian). Anaptyxis is found only in the case of the clusters *dr* and *gd* when followed by *u*: for example, one finds *d*^{u}*-u-r*^{u}*-u-v-* ([duruva-]) "firm" = Avestan *druua-* ([druwa-]) = Vedic *dhruvá-*; present tense stem *d*^{u}*-u-r*^{u}*-u-j*^{i}*-i-y-* ([durujiya-]) "to lie" = Vedic *drúhya-*; *s-u-g*^{u}*-u-d-* ([Suguda-]), as well as *s-u-g-d-* ([Sugda-]), "Sogdiana."

4. MORPHOLOGY

4.1 Morphological type

Typical of ancient Indo-European, Old Persian is an inflectional language with synthetic morphological patterns. Owing to lack of evidence, both the nominal and pronominal and, still more, the verbal paradigms are known only partially in most instances. Therefore it is not possible to give a fully formed account of the formation, function, and actual use of nominal, pronominal, and verbal forms. The same is true, by and large, with regard to nominal and verbal stem formation.

4.2 Nominal morphology

The grammatical categories marked on the Old Persian noun are case (seven), gender (three), and number (three). Whereas the three genders (masculine, feminine, and neuter) and the three numbers (singular, dual, and plural) inherited from Proto-Indo-European have preserved their usual significance and function, the case system has been reduced by one in Old Persian. Likewise gender and number show the expected and customary grammatical agreement (see §5.6), though there are some instances in which two singular subjects occur not (as would be expected) with a dual, but with a plural form of the verb.

The seven attested nominal cases are the following: (i) nominative (for subject); (ii) vocative (for direct address); (iii) accusative (for direct object and direction); (iv) genitive (used as possessive, subjective, objective, and partitive genitive); (v) locative (for indication of place or goal); (vi) instrumental (for indication of means, cause, and extension); and (vii) ablative (only combined with prepositions). The functions of the Proto-Indo-European dative (as the case of the indirect object) have been absorbed by the Old Persian genitive (e.g., *haya šiyātim adā martiyahyā* "who created happiness for man"). Moreover, the case system has also been reduced and simplified by abandoning formal distinctions; thus, for example, there are only three separate forms in the singular of the *ā*-stems: nom., voc. *-ā*; acc. *-ām*; gen.(-dat.), abl., loc., instr. *-āyā*.

4.2.1 Stem formation

Old Persian has inherited from Proto-Indo-European its two chief means of nominal stem formation: (i) *derivation* (by means of primary or secondary suffixes attached to the underlying [verbal] root itself or to an already derived nominal stem), and (ii) *composition* of two word stems (with or without a particular [compositional] suffix). Also playing a role in stem formation are *ablaut* (see *WAL* Ch. 17, §3.2) and, for derivation, the vowel-lengthening process known as *vr̥ddhi*. Only some subset of the numerous inherited nominal suffixes of Old Persian can be treated here, since the scanty evidence available does not allow one to judge whether some particular formation is only a traditional relic within Old Persian or actually remains a living and productive process.

One of the productive suffixes is undoubtedly the "locatival" suffix *-iya-*, forming adjectives, especially ethnics such as *Armin-iya-* "Armenian" (from *Armina-*), *Ūj-iya-* "Elamite" (from *Ūja-*), *Mac-iya-* "inhabitant of Makrān" (from *Maka-*), and so forth. The Proto-Iranian suffix **-hwa-/*-šwa-* forming fractions (see §4.6) seems to be similarly productive.

A distinctive phenomenon of derivation which Old Persian has inherited and which, as several indisputable examples show, is still productive in this language, is the lengthening of the first vowel of a word, a process traditionally called *vr̥ddhi* (a term coined by the ancient Indian grammarians). The clearest examples attested are the ethnic *Māргava-* "inhabitant of Margiana," derived from *Margu-* "Marv, Margiana"; and the month name *Bāgayādi-*, based on **baga-yāda-* "worship of the gods." Other apparent cases are not without problems: for example, the month name *Θāigraci-*; a form which – could *vr̥ddhi* be confirmed – would be essential for settling the question of whether Old Persian derivatives of words with *i* or *u* vowels have the *vr̥ddhi* form *āi* and *āu* like Old Indo-Aryan or the short diphthong *ai*, and *au*, as it is found in Avestan.

4.2.2 Nominal declension

Old Persian nouns have been traditionally grouped into declensional classes, though with regard to the origin of the nominal system at an earlier stage of the Indo-European parent language, a number of other criteria are of relevance, chiefly accent placement and ablaut variation and their distribution over the root, the (optional) suffix, and the ending (see *WAL* Ch. 24, §4.1.1.3). Old Persian evidence is available for stems ending in *-a-*, *-ā-*, *-i-*, *-ī-*, *-ī/yā-*, *-u-*, *-ū-*, *-h-* or *-š-*, *-r-*, *-n-* and in several stops and fricatives. The only productive stems, however, are those ending in vowels, and in particular those of the *a*-class, as those lexemes suggest which show forms of different declensions side by side: most clearly *tunuvant-* "strong" (in nom. sg. *tunuvā*) versus *tunuvanta-* (in gen. sg. *tunuvantahyā*); compare the "bridge" accusative singular *tunuvantam*.

The only paradigms which are known somewhat extensively are those of the stems in *a-* and *ā-*; their singular and plural forms may be given in (6) and (7) (for the dual see below); all other case forms and declensional patterns are presented only in the larger summary of (8) and (9):

(6) The Old Persian *a*-stems

	Singular		*Plural*	
	Example	*Ending*	*Example*	*Ending*
Animate				
Nom.	martiya "man"	-ø < *-s	martiyā	-ā < *-ās
			bagāha "god"	-āha < *-āsas
Voc.	martiyā	*-ø	—	
Acc.	martiyam	-m	martiyā	-ā < *-āns
Gen.	martiyahyā	-hyā	martiyānām	-ānām
Abl.	Pārsā	-ā < *-āt	Sakaibiš	=instr.
Instr.	kārā "army"	-ā	martiyaibiš	-aibiš
Loc.	Pārsai	-i	Mādaišuvā	-aišu + -ā
	dastay-ā "hand"	-i + -ā		
Neuter				
Nom.-acc.	xšaçam "kingdom"	-m	āyadanā "place of worship"	-ā < *-ā

(7) The Old Persian *ā*-stems

	Singular		*Plural*	
	Example	*Ending*	*Example*	*Ending*
Animate				
Nom.	taumā "family"	-ø	stūnā "column"	-ā < *-ās
Voc.	—		—	
Acc.	taumām	-m	[hamiçi]yā "rebellious"	-ā < *-āns
Gen.	taumāyā	-yā < *-yās	°zanānām "with . . . races"	-ānām
Abl.	Same as genitive		—	
Instr.	framānāyā "order"	-yā	—	
Loc.	Aϑurāyā	-i + ā	maškāuvā "skin"	-u < *-su + -ā

The set of case endings attested in Old Persian may be summarized in (8) and (9) without differentiating them by declensional class and without a detailed historical-comparative interpretation:

(8) Summary of Old Persian singular case endings

Animate	
Nom.	-ø, -š from *-s; -ø from *-ø
Voc.	-ø from *-ø
Acc.	-m, -am from *-m, -m̥
Gen.	-a from *-as; -ø, -š from *-s; -hyā from *-sya; -yā from *-yās
Abl.	-ā from *-āt; -ø from *-t; or identical to the genitive
Instr.	-ā from *-ā; -yā from *-yā
Loc.	-i from *-i; -ø from *-ø, both with or without postpositive -ā
Neuter	
Nom.-acc.	-m from *-m; -ø from *-ø

(9) Summary of Old Persian plural case endings

Animate	
Nom.	-a from *-as; -ā from *-ās; -āha from *-āsas
Voc.	Identical to the nominative, but not attested
Acc.	-ā from *-āns; -ø, -š from *-ns
Gen.	-ānām, -ūnām from *-V̄nām
Abl.	Identical to the instrumental
Instr.	-biš, -aibiš from *-biš
Loc.	-aišuvā, -šuvā from *-šw-ā; -uvā from *-sw-ā, attested only with postpositive -ā
Neuter	
Nom.-acc.	-ā from *-ā

Several dual forms are securely attested in Old Persian texts, such as nom. *u-b-a* ([uba:]) "both"; acc. *g-u-š-a* ([gauša:]) "both ears"; gen. *g-u-š-a-y-a* ([gauša:ya:]); instr. *d-s-t-i-b-i-y-a* ([dastaibiya:]) "with both hands," all belonging to stems in *-a-*. In addition, the following occur: nom. *u-š-i-y* ([uši:]), as well as *u-š-i-y-a* ([ušiya:]), three times each, and instr. *u-š-i-b-i-y-a* ([uši:biya:]), from neuter *uši-* "intelligence" (literally "ear" and therefore in dual number).

Adjectives behave like the nouns with regard to stem formation and declension. The comparative is formed by means of the Proto-Indo-European suffix **-yes-/-yos-* and the superlative by **-is-to-*. As examples, consider Old Persian nom. masc. sg. *t-u-v*^{i}*-i-y-a* ([taviya:]), from **tau-yah-* "stronger," and *m-ϑ-i-š-t* ([maθišta]) "greatest."

4.3 Pronominal morphology

A variety of pronouns is attested in Old Persian: (i) personal pronouns (including the so-called anaphoric pronoun); (ii) several demonstrative pronouns; (iii) relative; and (iv) interrogative-indefinite pronouns.

4.3.1 Personal pronouns

The personal pronouns are characterized (i) by an absence of grammatical gender; (ii) by a remarkable heteroclisis between the nominative and oblique cases; and (iii) by the existence of frequently used enclitic forms. All these characteristics have Proto-Indo-European ancestry. The following personal pronouns are attested in Old Persian:

(10)

	Accented forms		
	First	*Second*	*First Plural*
Nominative	adam	tuvam	vayam
Accusative	mām	ϑuvām	—
Genitive	manā	—	amāxam
Ablative	-ma	—	—
	Enclitic forms		
Accusative	-mā	—	—
Genitive	-mai	-tai	—

The dual forms are not attested at all; the genitive has taken over the function of the dative. Ablative *-ma*, though being attested only in combination with the preposition "by," *h-c-a-m* ([hacā-ma]) "by me," is not enclitic (demonstrated by accented Vedic *mát*).

The anaphoric pronouns "he, she, it" share the characteristic features of the personal pronouns, though there are no nominative forms and no heteroclisis. Old Persian exhibits enclitic forms built from the stems *-ša-*/*-ši-* and *-di-*: acc. sg.*-šim* "him," gen. *-šai* "his," acc. pl. *-šiš* "them," gen. *-šām* "their"; acc. sg. *-dim* "him" and acc. pl. *-diš* "them."

4.3.2 Demonstrative pronouns

Other pronominal stems exhibit grammatical gender distinctions and, in part, are characterized by a declension differing from that of nominal stems in *-a-* and *-ā-*. Included in this group are three demonstrative pronouns. The pronoun *iyam* (nom. sg. masc./fem.) "this" combines forms of the stems *i-*, *ima-*, and *a-*: for example, *ima* (nom.-acc. sg. neut.), *anā* (instr. sg. masc.), *ahyāyā* (loc. sg. fem.). The remaining two are *aita-* "this here" (more emphatic), and *hau-* (nom. sg. masc./fem.) "that"; the paradigm of the latter is supplemented in the oblique cases by the stem *ava-*: for example, *ava* (nom.-acc. sg. neut.), *avai* (nom.-acc. pl. masc.), *avaišām* (gen. pl. masc.), *av[ā]* (nom. dual masc.).

4.3.3 Relative and interrogative pronouns

The relative pronoun, which has also acquired the function of an article (see §5.5), is an Old Persian innovation. Its stems *haya-* (nom. sg. masc./fem.) and *taya-* (elsewhere) "who, which" emerged from the fusion of the Proto-Aryan correlating demonstrative and relative pronouns **sá-*/**tá-* + **yá-* "the one, who." The interrogative pronoun is not attested in Old Persian texts and can be recovered only from the indefinite pronouns *kaš-ci* (nom. sg. masc.) "somebody," *ciš-ci* (neut.) "something," which are derived by means of the generalizing particle *-ci*, as in *ya-ci* (nom.-acc. sg. neut.) "whatever."

4.3.4 Pronominal adjectives

The declension of certain adjectives, which are semantically close to the pronouns, shares also the special declensional forms of pronouns. Old Persian attests only *aniya-* "other" (e.g., nom.-acc. sg. neut. *aniya*, abl. sg. masc. *aniyanā*); *haruva-* "all" (e.g., loc. sg. fem. *haruvahyāyā*); and *hama-* "the same" (in gen. sg. fem. *hamahyāyā*).

4.4 Verbal morphology

The grammatical categories of the Old Persian verbal system were inherited from Proto-Aryan, the consequent and consistent structure of which can still plainly be observed in the earliest Vedic texts. But with regard to both function and form, a great number of fundamental innovations and reorganizations have occurred which leave the distinct impression that Old Persian, like Young Avestan (see Ch. 6, §1), has begun to part company with the Proto-Aryan system and already represents a kind of transitional stage from Old to Middle Iranian. This is revealed by phonetic developments and innovations in nominal morphology, but especially by changes in the system of verbal morphology: (i) the aspectual opposition of aorist versus imperfect has been lost; (ii) aorist and perfect tense forms are attested only rarely; (iii) a periphrastic "neo-perfect" has emerged (see §4.4.6); and (iv) present stems in *-aya-* begin to gain prominence.

Old Persian verbal forms are marked for tense (originally aspect), voice, mood, and the usual three persons and three numbers. The Old Persian evidence is, however, rather unbalanced, owing to the nature of the contents of the inscriptions: thus, for example, the only dual form found in the texts is the third plural imperfect active *ajīvatam* "they both (still) lived." Together with the three persons and numbers, two of the three voices (i.e., active and middle) find expression in two sets of personal endings: the so-called *primary* endings in the present indicative (which alone denotes a real present time) and subjunctive (which may do the same, at least in the speaker's view), and the *secondary* endings otherwise, apart from the imperative, which has distinctive endings.

4.4.1 Voice

The voices usually have their customary functions (inherited from the Indo-European parent language). A particularly striking exception is provided by certain third plural middle forms which lack middle function and are to be interpreted as having arisen only to avoid ambiguity. Passive morphology is more innovative, with the following attested: (i) forms built from the passive stem in *-ya-* (e.g., imperfect *a-ϑanh-ya* "it has been said"), common to Indo-Iranian for the present stem; (ii) middle forms like *a-naya-tā* "he was led"; and (iii) phrases consisting of a verbal adjective in *-ta-* plus the copula (which usually is omitted, however, in the third person: see §4.4.6).

4.4.2 Mood

The five moods attested in Old Persian are indicative, subjunctive, optative, imperative, and, as an Indo-European relic, injunctive (see below). Typical of Iranian is both the use of the perfect optative for the irrealis of the past, and (even more so) the use of the present optative with the temporal augment *a-* (thus looking like an imperfect optative) to express a repeated action of the past (e.g., *avājaniyā* from **ava-a-jan-yā-t* "he used to slay").

The Old Persian moods exhibit the same functions as their counterparts in Young Avestan. The *indicative* is used to express factual statements – present indicative (formed with the primary endings) for those in present time, and imperfect indicative (the augment *a-* and secondary endings being added to the present stem) for those in past time. The *subjunctive* expresses the eventual or potential realization of actions in the present or future; the present subjunctive is formed with primary endings, which are added to the present stem enlarged by *-a-* (e.g., *ah-a-ti* "it may be"). The *optative* is used for wishes and prayers and is formed with a stem in *-iyā-* (in the athematic singular) or *-ī-* (otherwise) – suffixes descended from Proto-Indo-European **-yeh$_1$-*/**-ih$_1$-*; the optative takes secondary endings (e.g., 2nd sg. mid. *yadaišā* "you may worship"). The *imperative* is the mood of command and prayer and makes use of distinctive imperative endings which are added to the present or aorist stem.

The *injunctive* (with secondary endings) is found in Old Persian only in prohibitive constructions introduced by the particle *mā* "not!" but even in preventive clauses never combined with forms of the aorist tense stem. Together with the loss of the aorist (see §4.4.3) Old Persian obviously has lost the inherited distinction between the inhibitive present injunctive and the preventive aorist injunctive. Moreover, if combined with the optative present, the prohibitive particle *mā* denotes a corrective notion with regard to a present action: for example, *daivā mā yadiyaiša* "the Daivas shall not be worshiped any longer!"

4.4.3 Tense

The tenses find expression in stem formations which had originally been used to distinguish aspect (imperfective vs. perfective) and still did so in Proto-Aryan and Proto-Iranian. Several doublets of such forms make it clear, however, that the imperfect (which is built on the present stem and thus expressed the imperfective aspect of a past action) and the aorist (being the counterpart in the perfective aspect) are used in Old Persian without any obvious difference in function, suggesting that aspectual distinctions were no longer being productively made. The "sigmatic" aorist *adarši* "I took possession of" (1st sg. indic. aor. middle of the root *dar-*) alone seems to point to a living use of the aorist indicative (i.e., for conveying the perfective aspect of an action). The one perfect form attested is an optative expressing past irrealis, *caxriyā* "he might have done." Regarding perfect morphology, therefore, all that can be said is that Old Persian inherited stem reduplication (*ca-xr-* from Proto-Aryan **ča-kr-* and Proto-Indo-European *k^we-k^wr-*), but nothing can be discerned about the particular endings of the perfect indicative active.

4.4.4 Verbal stems

The stem formations occurring in Old Persian are essentially those inherited from Proto-Aryan and in the end often from Proto-Indo-European. This includes the inherited distinction between the *thematic* and the *athematic* stems marked by the presence or absence of the thematic vowel *-a-* (from Proto-Indo-European **-e/o-*; see *WAL* Ch. 17, §3.4) preceding the personal endings (e.g., athematic *as-ti* "he is," but thematic *bav-a-ti* "he becomes"). The present and aorist stems (and likewise the only perfect stem attested; see §4.4.3) are formed either from the verbal root to which one of a set of suffixes is attached, or from the unsuffixed root itself (root presents and root aorists). Most numerous and to a certain degree productive are the present stems in *-aya-* like *tāvaya-* "to be able," *mānaya-* "to wait, expect," and so forth. Ancestral formations of Proto-Indo-European origin are the stems in *-sa-* (= Avestan *-sa-*) like *pr̥sa-* "to ask, interrogate" (= Avestan *pərᵊsa-*), *tr̥sa-* "to be afraid" (= Avestan *tərᵊsa-*), *xšnāsa-* "to know."

4.4.5 Verbal endings

The various sets of verbal endings are only partially attested in Old Persian; these are presented in (11)–(16) together with their Proto-Aryan preforms:

(11) The Old Persian primary endings: active

	Singular
First	-mi from *-mi (also in the thematic verbs); -ni from *-ni (subjunctive)
Second	-hi from *-si (attested only in subjunctive)
Third	-ti from *-ti
	Plural
First	-mahi from *-masi
Second	—
Third	-nti from *-nti

(12) The Old Persian primary endings: middle

	Singular
First	-ai from *-ai; -nai from Proto-Iranian *-nai (subjunctive)
Second	-hai from *-sai
Third	-tai from *-tai
	Plural
	Not attested

(13) The Old Persian secondary endings: active

	Singular
First	-m from *-m; -am (athematic) from Proto-Aryan *-am replacing Proto-Indo-European *-m̥
Second	-ø from *-s
Third	-ø from *-t; -š after ai, au (in imperfect and optative forms like *akunauš* "he did" = Avestan *akər*^{ə}*naot̰*)
	Dual
Third	-tam = Avestan -təm (see §4.4)
	Plural
First	-mā from *-ma
Second	—
Third	-ø from *-nt; -h after a and -š after ai (in imperfect and optative forms like *abaraha* "they brought" or *yadiyaiša* "they shall not be worshiped") from *-s

(14) The Old Persian secondary endings: middle

	Singular
First	-i from *-i
Second	-šā from *-sa
Third	-tā from *-ta
	Plural
First	—
Second	—
Third	-ntā from *-nta

(15) The Old Persian imperative endings: active

	Singular
Second	-ā from *-a (thematic) and -di from *-d^{h}i (athematic)
Third	-tu from *-tu
	Plural
Second	-tā from *-ta
Third	-ntu from *-ntu

(16) The Old Persian imperative endings: middle

	Singular
Second	-uvā and -šuvā from *-swa
Third	-tām from *- tām
	Plural
	Not attested

4.4.6 Nonfinite verbal forms

Old Persian exhibits only one type of infinitive: a construction with the formant *-t-n-i-y* ([-tanai] or [-tani]?), being an oblique case, dative (or locative) singular, of an action noun in *-tan-*, and built on the full-grade verb root: for example, *cartanai* "to do"; *bartanai* "to bear;"

ϑanstanai "to say." In the case of *kantanai* "to dig" and *nipaištanai* "to engrave, write," the passive interpretation "to be dug," "to be engraved" cannot be ruled out.

The only reliably attested active participles are *tunuvant-* "strong" (literally "being able"; nom. sg. masc. *tunuvā*, from **-wānt-s*) and *yaudant-* "being in turmoil" (only acc. sg. fem. *y-u-d-[t-i]-m* ([yaudant-i(:)m]). Present middle participles are formed by means of the suffix *-mna-* = Avestan *-mna-*, as in *xšaya-mna-* "being in control of."

The commonly occurring verbal adjective or perfect passive participle in *-ta-* is inherited from the Proto-Indo-European formation in **-to-*, which usually is added to the zero-grade verbal root: for example, *kr̥ta-* "done, made"; *jata-* "slain"; *pāta-* "protected"; but also *basta-* "bound" like Young Avestan *basta-* (in contrast to Vedic *baddhá-*) and the like. In addition, there are also some formations in *-ata-* (like *ϑak-ata-* "passed" or *han-gm-ata-* "assembled"; cf. Avestan *gmata-*) which go back to Proto-Indo-European **-eto-*.

The verbal adjective in *-ta-* is used in Old Persian particularly for creating the new periphrastic perfect of the type *manā kr̥tam* "(it was) done by me" (cf. Middle Persian *man kard*) replacing the inherited Proto-Aryan active perfect for expressing an accomplished action and/or a situation achieved by it. In origin this "neo-perfect" was formed by combining the copula "to be" with the *-ta*-adjective, though the third singular *asti* "she/he/it is" normally has been deleted. Moreover, the agent of transitive verbs is expressed in the genitive case (though the sense of the construction is not a possessive). Examples include the following: *ima, taya manā kr̥tam* "this [is], what [has been] done by me"; *taya Br̥diya avajata* "that Smerdis [had been] slain"; *yadi kāra Pārsa pāta ahati* "if the Persian people shall be protected."

4.5 Compounds

In principle, Old Persian exhibits all the types of compounds known from the other ancient Aryan languages (see Ch. 2, §4.4.2) and inherited from Proto-Indo-European (see *WAL* Ch. 17, §3.5.1). Compounds contain two elements, the last of which is inflected. Attested are *determinative* and *possessive* compounds (including those which have an inseparable prefix like *a(n)-* "without, un-"; *u-* "well-"; or *duš-* "mis-, dis-" as first element), but no *copulative* compounds are attested as yet. Especially remarkable are the compounds having a verbal stem as the first element; Old Persian exhibits a number of such formations in anthroponomastics: for example, the throne names of Darius and Xerxes, *Dāraya-vauš* "holding the good" and *Xšaya-r̥šan-* "having command of heroes." These forms reveal that Old Persian does not share in the Aryan recasting of the first element as a participial form in *-at-*, as one finds in Avestan and Old Indo-Aryan (cf. Avestan *Dāraiiaṭ.raϑa-* "holding the chariot," *xšaiiaṭ.vac-* "having (a good) command of speech"; Vedic *dhārayát-kṣiti-* "sustaining the creatures," *kṣayád-vīra-* "having command of heroes").

4.6 Numerals

Since the cardinals are normally indicated by numeral signs and not written phonetically, hardly anything can be said about them. The number 1 is *aiwa-*, which like Avestan *aēuua-* goes back to Proto-Indo-European **oi-wo-* "one, alone" (= Greek *oî(w)os* (οἶ(Ϝ)ος)). One hundred must have been **ϑata-* (= Avestan *satəm* = Vedic *śatám*) and in all probability is attested in the name of the province Sattagydia, *Θata-gu-*. Other cardinals are reflected in the "collateral" linguistic traditions (see §6), especially in Elamite garb, in compounded titles like **daϑa-pati-* (Elamite *da-sa-bat-ti-iš*) "chief of ten, decurion" or **ϑata-pati-* (Elamite *sa-ad-da-bat-ti-iš*) "chief of hundred, centurion."

Of the ordinals there are attested in the Old Persian inscriptions: *fratama-* "first" = Avestan *fratəma-*; *duvitīya-* "second" = Old Avestan *d^aibitiia-*, Young Avestan *bitiia-* (= Vedic *dvitī́ya-*); *çitīya-* "third" = Avestan *θritiia-*; *navama-* "ninth" = Avestan *naoma-* (from **nawəma-*).

A quite interesting Iranian innovation is found in the fractions formed by addition of the Proto-Iranian suffix *-*swa-* (realized as Avestan -*huua-* or -*šuua-*). The Old Persian reflexes are attested in Elamite renderings only and can be reconstructed as **çišuva-* "one-third" (Elamite ši-iš-maš; cf. Avestan *θrišuua-*); **caçušuva-* and (with haplology) **caçuva-* "one-quarter" (Elamite *za-aš-maš, za-iš-šu-maš, za-iš-šu-iš-maš*; cf. Avestan *caθrušuua-*); **pancauva-* "one-fifth" (Elamite *pan-su-ma-iš*; cf. Avestan *paŋtaŋhuua-*); **aštauva-* "one-eighth" (Elamite *aš-du-maš*; cf. Avestan *aštahuua-*); **navauva-* "one-ninth" (Elamite *nu-ma-u-maš*); **daθauva-* "one-tenth" (Elamite *da-sa-maš*) and **vīstauva-* "one-twentieth" (Elamite *mi-iš-du-ma-kaš*, with an additional *ka*-suffix).

5. SYNTAX

5.1 Word order

The word order found in the Old Persian inscriptions is on the whole rather free, as is common among the ancient Indo-Iranian languages. The "unmarked" order, however, is Subject–Object–Verb (SOV):

(17) Auramazdā-mai upastām abara
Auramazdā-me aid he brought
"Auramazdā brought me aid"

For enclitic -*mai*, see §5.3. Other complements, especially those indicating place, may follow the verb. There are attested, however, a number of cases showing varying order of the sentence constituents: for example, (i) of copula and predicate noun (cf. DNb 42f. *θanuvaniya uθanuvaniya ami* "as a bowman I am a good bowman" vs. DNb 44 *r̥̊štika ami uvr̥̊štika* "as a spearman I am a good spearman"); or (ii) of two coordinated constituents (DB IV 72f. *yadi imām dipim vaināhi imaivā patikarā* "if you shall look at this inscription or these sculptures" vs. DB IV 77 *yadi imām dipim imaivā patikarā vaināhi*).

Nevertheless some peculiarities of word order must be noted, mainly "marked" sentence-initial or sentence-final position of words for reasons of emphasis. Here belong, for example, the initial position of the object (OSV) when expressed by a deictic pronoun

(18) ima hadiš adam akunavam
this palace I I have built
"I have built this palace"

or the nonfinal (medial) position of verbs expressing an urgent plea. Notable is also the uncommon initial position of the verb in the formulaic expression *θāti NN xšāyaθiya* "proclaims NN, the king."

When two or more coordinated elements form the subject or the object of a sentence, only the first element is placed before the verb, and the remaining elements follow, for example:

(19) mām Auramazdā pātu utamai xšaçam
me Auramazdā may he protect and my kingdom
"May Auramazdā protect me and my kingdom!"

Within phrases the word order is more fixed. A noun or pronoun (in the genitive case) which is dependent upon a noun precedes that noun: for example, *Kurauš puça* "son of Cyrus"; *manā pitā* "my father." Exceptions which are attested in royal titles (cf. *xšāyaϑiya xšāyaϑiyānām* "king of kings" in contrast to Middle Persian *šāhān šāh*) or religious formulae (*vašnā Auramazdāha* "by the favor of Auramazdā") are caused by foreign influence.

5.2 Topicalization

A striking feature of Old Persian syntax and stylistics is the frequent use of a sentence-initial (so-called) *casus pendens* (usually an absolute nominative), which is resumed by a demonstrative pronoun (20A) or adverb (20B):

(20) A.

Vištāspa	manā	pitā,	hau	Parϑavai	āha
Hystaspes	my	father	that one	in Parthia	he was

"Hystaspes my father, he was in Parthia"

B.

Pr̥ga	nāma	kaufa,	avadā . . .
Pr̥ga	by name	mountain	there

"There is a mountain, Pr̥ga by name, there . . . "

This phenomenon is often combined with another stylistic peculiarity found in the Old Persian inscriptions, the origin of which must be sought, as Vedic parallels in prose texts show convincingly, in colloquial Proto-Aryan and not, as has been previously presumed, in Aramaic influence. This concerns parenthetical (more exactly, prosthothetical) constructions taking the form of nominal (i.e., verbless) clauses which introduce less common personal or geographical names: for example, *Dādr̥šiš nāma Arminiya, manā bandaka, avam* . . . "[There is] an Armenian, Dādr̥ši by name, my vassal, him . . . "

It should be noted that nominal sentences are very frequently used in Old Persian, mainly because the third singular form of the copula is normally omitted; consider DB I 27:

(21)

ima,	taya	manā	kr̥tam
this	what	by me	done

"This [is], what [has been] done by me"

with relevant examples in both the main and relative clauses.

5.3 Clitics

Old Persian attests a number of enclitics (atonic lexemes which in Old Persian form a graphic unity with the preceding word); chiefly the following: (i) the oblique cases of the personal pronouns (including the anaphoric pronoun); (ii) the copulative and disjunctive conjunctions (*-cā* "and," *-vā* "or"); and (iii) various emphatic particles. According to *Wackernagel's Law* the enclitics are attached to the first accented word of the sentence or clause in Old Persian, as in Proto-Aryan and, still earlier, in Proto-Indo-European. This becomes particularly clear from examples like (17), *Auramazdā-mai upastām abara* "Auramazdā brought me aid," when contrasted with

(22)

pasāva-mai	Auramazdā	upastām	abara
afterwards-me	Auramazdā	aid	he brought

"Afterwards Auramazdā brought me aid"

Enclitics which are construed with single words only and not with an entire sentence do not follow Wackernagel's Law, but are attached to that particular word: for example, *yaϑā paruvam-ci* "just as [it was] previously." For a special treatment of enclisis see Schmitt 1995.

5.4 Coordination and subordination

In the Old Persian inscriptions both coordination and subordination are used for expressing complex statements. It is not uncommon to find short simple sentences following one another, either accompanied by a connector (a coordinating conjunction like *utā* "and" or a temporal adverb like *pasāva* "afterwards, then"), or without such (asyndeton). In other cases (and, in part, in closely parallel passages), subordinate clauses occur introduced by a relative pronoun or by some appropriate conjunction. Most conjunctions used in Old Persian are derived from the (original) stem of the relative pronoun (as is the case in the cognate languages, too): for example, *yaϑā* (often correlated with *avaϑā* "thus") "when, after, so that" (introducing temporal, modal, and consecutive clauses); *yadi* "if" (normally with a subjunctive verb), "when" (with an indicative; introducing temporal and conditional clauses). While both of these are inherited, *yātā* "until, when, as long as" is a new formation, as is *taya* "that, so that" (acc. sg. neut. of the relative pronoun) which introduces causal, explicative clauses, indirectly reported speech, and so forth. Relative clauses are commonly attested, positioned both before and after the main clause.

There are also some passages that show a subordinate infinitive. Typical is that construction after a main clause containing verbs like "to order," "to be able," "to dare" (e.g., *adam nīštāyam imām dipim nipaištanai* "I ordered to engrave this inscription"); another likewise typical use of an infinitive construction is that expressing purpose after verbs like "to go," "to send" (e.g., *paraitā patiš Dādr̥šim hamaranam cartanai* "went forth against Dādr̥ši to fight a battle").

5.5 Relative constructions

The relative pronoun *haya-/taya-* functions as a definite article in expressions indicating various attributive complements to nouns, with case attraction if appropriate; for example:

(23) A. Gaumāta haya maguš (nominative)
Gaumātam tayam magum (accusative)
"Gaumāta the magus"
B. kāram tayam Mādam (accusative)
"The Median army"
C. viϑam tayām amāxam (genitive plural)
"Our [royal] house"
D. xšaçam taya Bābirau (locative)
"The kingship in Babylonia"

Those constructions have similar counterparts in Avestan, but have spread considerably in Middle Persian and are ultimately the source of the Modern Persian *iẓāfat* construction.

5.6 Agreement

Grammatical agreement in Old Persian is of the sort common to the older Indo-European languages: (i) appositive and attributive adjectives and nouns agree in gender, number, and case; (ii) predicate nouns and adjectives agree at least in case, but now and then there are particular conditions for gender and number; (iii) relative, resumptive, and anaphoric pronouns agree in gender and number, whereas their case is dependent upon their syntactic use (examples of case attraction not being attested); (iv) verbs agree with their subject in person and number. The existence in Old Persian of the Proto-Indo-European use of a singular verb with a neuter plural subject cannot be demonstrated, both for lack of evidence and for orthographic reasons. The only evidence is found in the usual dating formulae (see §6), and there the copula *āha* (with *ϑakatā* nom. pl. neut.) may be third-person singular as well as plural.

5.7 Stylistics

A comprehensive and systematic study of the stylistic features that may be detected in the Old Persian inscriptions (which show clear traces of stylization), is an urgent desideratum. There is found evidence for the stylistic figures of the asyndeton, of chiasmus, parallelism, and so forth; see the discussion in Kent 1953 (pp. 99f. §§ 316–317 in the relevant paragraphs). Some additional stylistic features can be briefly noted here. Epiphora (repetition of the same words at the end of each of a set of sentences) occurs several times: for example, in DPd 22 and 24 *hadā visaibiš bagaibiš* "with all the gods." Examples of personification are attested: for example, with *dahyu-* "land" (which "does not fear anybody else") or *dušiyāra-* "crop failure" (which "may not come"). But attempts to demonstrate rhyming phrases in Old Persian texts or to detect metrical passages (especially in DB) are not convincing in this author's view.

6. LEXICON

The Old Persian vocabulary is known only in part owing to the limited corpus of the texts and to their stereotyped character. On the whole it corresponds closely to the vocabulary of the other attested ancient Aryan languages, Avestan and Old Indo-Aryan (especially Vedic). A striking characteristic feature of Old Persian is the considerable quantity of foreign words and names which it uses. Such foreign influences, however, are only to be expected in such a multinational state as that of the Persian Empire. Among those foreign elements, borrowings from the Median language take a special place, and they can be justified historically without difficulty. The fact that particular terms are of Median origin can sometimes be established by phonetic criteria, even if the non-Persian phonetic developments observed are not unique to the Median language, but also belong to other Old Iranian dialects. Medisms occur more frequently among royal titles and among terms of the chancellery, military, and judicial affairs (*vazr̥ka-* "great," *zūra-* "evil," *zūrakara-* "evil-doer," etc.); they are found not least in the official characterizations of the empire and its countries (*uvaspa-* "with good horses," *vispazana-* "with all races," etc.).

From a dialectological perspective, one notes some peculiar developments. Particularly striking is the case of the verb "to say, speak"; Old Persian continues neither Proto-Iranian **wač-* nor **mrau-*, both of which are attested in Avestan, but has *gaub-*. A similar case is found with "to hear": Old Persian has lost Proto-Iranian **srau-* (Avestan *srauu-*), and has instead the root *ā-xšnau-* (literally "to grasp, understand").

In addition to the shared isogloss of Old Persian *gaub-* "to say, speak" and Sogdian *γwβ-* ([ɣoːβ-]) "to praise," there are a number of remarkable features common to Old Persian (Southwest Iranian) and Sogdian (East Iranian). For example, to both belong **kun-* "to do" (from Proto-Iranian **kar-*, pres. **kr̥nau-*) in Old Persian *kunau-* = Sogdian *kwn-* ([kun-]). Both share the meaning "to have" for the Iranian root **dar-* "to hold, keep" (Old Persian *dar-*, pres. *dāraya-*), and the dating formulae of the type Old Persian *NN māhyā X raucabiš ϑakatā* *āha* "in the month NN X days had passed" and Sogdian *pr 'tδrtyk YRH' pr 10 sγth* "in the third month at/after ten passed [days]."

In other cases, borrowings from some East Iranian language have been assumed: for example, *kāsaka-* "semiprecious stone." In addition, the influence of the other languages spoken by the indigenous peoples of the Ancient Near East can be detected in the Old Persian lexicon. Thus, the Persians seem to have acquired *dipi-* "inscription" from Elamite, *maškā-* "[raft of] skin" from some Semitic language, and *pīru-* "ivory" likewise from some Near Eastern source.

A considerable portion of the Old Persian lexicon has simply not survived (because of the nature of the texts). However, the possibility exists of reconstructing Old Persian lexemes, provided they are inherited from Proto-Aryan (and from Proto-Indo-European), by comparing the Proto-Aryan vocabulary (which can be reconstructed from the very rich records available in Old Indo-Aryan) with Middle and Modern Persian words, since such later attested lexemes necessarily must have passed through an Old Persian stage.

In addition, a great many Old Persian lexemes, including proper names, are preserved in a borrowed form in non-Persian languages – the so-called "collateral" tradition of Old Persian (within or outside the Achaemenid Empire). The main sources of that tradition are Elamite (especially the Persepolis tablets), Late Babylonian (with numerous administrative texts), Aramaic (as the lingua franca of the official imperial administration), Hebrew, Egyptian, and Greek authors (from Aeschylus and Herodotus) and inscriptions. It must be borne in mind, however, that not every purported Old Iranian form attested in this manner is an actual lexeme of Old Persian. Thus, for example, the title "satrap," best known in its Greek form σατράπης, in fact mirrors Median **xšaϑra-pā-*, whereas the first element of the Old Persian form was *xšaça-* and the form attested epigraphically is *xšaça-pā-van-*. A collection of the complete material attested in the various branches of the collateral tradition is not available; Hinz 1975 offers the most comprehensive collection, though is far from being complete (e.g., by omitting even Median **xšaϑra-pā-*) and is often unreliable.

7. READING LIST

The most comprehensive treatment of Old Persian (containing a full descriptive as well as historical grammar, the transcribed texts with English translation, and a lexicon with full references) is found in Kent 1953; for a traditional grammar see also Meillet and Benveniste 1931. A more structured outline of morphology and an etymological lexicon (including, in part, the collateral tradition) is presented by Mayrhofer in Brandenstein and Mayrhofer 1964 (pp. 55–82 and 99–157). Mayrhofer 1979: II (pp. 11–32) provides a special treatment of the personal names attested in the inscriptions. A brief account of the Old Persian language (with the most essential bibliography) is also presented in Schmitt 1989.

A complete corpus of all Old Persian Achaemenid inscriptions is not available; there are only partial collections outdated by later discoveries or limited to certain groups or types of texts. The Old Persian texts alone can be found in Kent 1953: 107–157 (with an English translation); this has been supplemented by Mayrhofer 1978, who also provides a full inventory list of the Old Persian texts (pp. 37–47); though even this list is not up to date.

Abbreviations

The most important Old Persian texts are listed below. Texts are usually cited utilizing a system of abbreviations, in which the king's name normally appears first (D = Darius I, X = Xerxes I, A^{1-3} = Artaxerxes I–III, etc.), followed by the place of origin (B = Bīsutūn,

P = Persepolis, N = Naqš-i Rustam, S = Susa, etc.). Several texts by the same king at the same place are distinguished by additional small letters:

DB: the major inscription of Darius I at the rock of Mt. Bīsutūn, the most extensive and most important trilingual inscription, with five columns and 414 lines of Old Persian text (newly edited by Schmitt 1991).

DNa, DNb: two major trilingual inscriptions at the tomb of Darius I at Naqš-i Rustam, the lower text DNb being some kind of guide for the ideal ruler (new edition by Schmitt 2000:23–44).

DPd, DPe: two monolingual Old Persian inscriptions which form part of an ensemble of texts at the southern wall of the Persepolis terrace and in all probability are the oldest Persepolitan inscriptions (new edition by Schmitt 2000:56–62).

DSab: the trilingual cuneiform text on the Egyptian-made statue of Darius I excavated in Susa in 1972.

DSe, DSf: two major trilingual building inscriptions from the palace of Susa, which are preserved, however, only in a great number of fragments.

DZc: the longest of the cuneiform inscriptions from the Suez Canal.

XPf: a bilingual (Old Persian and Babylonian) foundation document of Xerxes from Persepolis, which is of special historical importance owing to some details reported about the king's succession.

XPh: the trilingual, so-called Daiva-inscription describing a revolt and praising the cult of Auramazdā (rather than the Daivas).

XPl: an Old Persian text on a stone tablet, which is essentially parallel to DNb, but associated with the name of Xerxes I.

Bibliography

Brandenstein, W. and M. Mayrhofer. 1964. *Handbuch des Altpersischen.* Wiesbaden: Otto Harrassowitz.

Hinz, W. 1975. *Altiranisches Sprachgut der Nebenüberlieferungen.* Wiesbaden: Otto Harrassowitz.

Kent, R. G. 1953. *Old Persian: Grammar, Texts, Lexicon* (2nd edition). New Haven: American Oriental Society.

Mayrhofer, M. 1978. *Supplement zur Sammlung der altpersischen Inschriften.* Vienna: Österreichische Akademie der Wissenschaften.

———. 1979. *Iranisches Personennamenbuch.* Vol. I. Vienna: Österreichische Akademie der Wissenschaften.

Meillet, A. and E. Benveniste. 1931. *Grammaire du vieux-perse* (2nd edition). Paris: Édouard Champion.

Schmitt, R. 1989. "Altpersisch." In R. Schmitt (ed.), *Compendium Linguarum Iranicarum*, pp. 56–85. Wiesbaden: Dr. Ludwig Reichert.

———. 1991. *The Bisitun Inscriptions of Darius the Great: Old Persian Text.* London: School of Oriental and African Studies.

———. 1995. "Zur Enklise im Altpersischen." In H. Hettrich, W. Hock, P. Mumm, *et al.* (eds.), *Verba et Structurae: Festschrift für Klaus Strunk*, pp. 285–301. Innsbruck: Institut für Sprachwissenschaft der Universität Innsbruck.

———. 2000. *The Old Persian Inscriptions of Naqsh-i Rustam and Persepolis.* London: School of Oriental and African Studies.

CHAPTER 6

Avestan

MARK HALE

1. HISTORICAL AND CULTURAL CONTEXTS

Avestan is a member of the Indo-European language family. It is the most richly attested ancient member of the Iranian branch of the Indo-Iranian subgroup of that family. As such, it is closely related to the Sanskrit language (which represents the most archaic member of the Indic subgroup of Indo-Iranian; see Ch. 2). For those who hold that the centum–satem division (fundamentally an east/west bifurcation in the Indo-European language family) is a matter of subgrouping, Indo-Iranian (and therefore Avestan) is a member of the satem group (indeed, it is the Avestan word for "100," *satəm*, which gives that group its name).

There are uncertainties regarding both the dating and the geographical provenance of the surviving Avestan texts. The oldest manuscript is quite young (manuscript K7a, dating from AD 1278) and therefore of little assistance in resolving these matters. The issue of chronology is usually linked to the problems surrounding the dates of the founder of Zoroastrianism, the prophet Zarathuštra. Current scholarly consensus places his life considerably earlier than the traditional Zoroastrian sources are thought to, favoring a birth date before 1000 BC. Since the Gāθās are recognized as being the work of Zarathuštra, these Old Avestan texts appear to date from around that time. Precise dating of the Young Avestan texts, many of which appear to have a long oral transmission history, is in most cases impossible. Regarding geography, the Avestan language itself is now widely believed to be an Eastern Iranian language, though it cannot be directly connected to any known group of ancient Iranian speakers, thus greater geographical precision is not at this time possible. For the most recent and more coherent consideration of these complex issues, the interested reader is referred to the introduction to the first volume of Humbach *et al.* (1991). The Avestan texts continue to be used in ritual and other hieratic contexts in Zoroastrian communities.

Although Avestan is quite conservative in several crucial respects both phonologically and morphologically, many (though not all) of its archaisms are also found in the better-attested, better-preserved, and generally more widely studied Sanskrit language, leading to a certain degree of neglect of Avestan in Western scholarship. This has been rectified to some extent in the postwar era of Indo-European studies, during which the type of philological problems posed by the Avestan records have captured the attention of many prominent Indo-Europeanists.

It is traditional to refer to the two major dialects of Avestan as *Old* (or *Gāthic*) *Avestan* and *Young Avestan*. Nevertheless, it is apparent that the relationship between the two dialects is not strictly a chronological one (i.e., Young Avestan is not a direct descendant of Old Avestan). These labels may accurately reflect the relative chronology of the respective corpora, although the matter is complicated by the fact, noted above, that many of the Young Avestan texts appear to be originally oral compositions with a potentially long transmission history before becoming fixed canonical texts.

The Avestan language is transmitted almost exclusively through the surviving text of the *Avesta*, a collection of Zoroastrian religious and legal texts. Unfortunately, the transmission history of these texts involves several serious disruptions, leading to loss of a large number of texts (the contents of which can be in part gleaned from a surviving Pahlavi, i.e., Middle Persian, summary) and challenging philological problems for those texts which do survive. Excluding a number of minor texts, there are three major sections of the surviving Avesta: (i) the *Yasnas* (Y.), containing prayers, hymns, and liturgical works; (ii) the *Yašts* (Yt.), containing invocations of specific holy figures and concepts; (iii) the *Vidēvdāt* (V.), containing "legal" texts, broadly construed. All of the Old Avestan texts are contained within the Yasnas. These texts include the *Gāθās* (metrical hymns the composition of which is attributed to the prophet Zarathuštra), the prose liturgy of the *Yasna Haptaŋhāiti*, and a set of short prayers, the most sacred in Zoroastrianism.

Many of the Yašts are rather poorly preserved, or were not originally native-speaker compositions. One usually distinguishes between the best-transmitted Yašts – the so-called *Great Yašts* – and the lesser works. The Great Yašts represent the high points of Young Avestan literature. Included among them are Yt. 5 (in honor of Arəduuī, the personification of a mythic river); Yt. 8 (in honor of Tištriia, the personification of the star Sirius); Yt. 10 (in honor of Miθra, the personification of the contract); Yt. 13 (in honor of the Frauuaṣ̌is – protective spirits of the faithful); Yt. 14 (in honor of Vərəθraγna, the personification of victory); Yt. 17 (in honor of Aṣ̌i Vaŋuhī, the personification of the reward of the pious); Yt. 19 (in honor of X^{v}arənah, the personification of royal power/glory); and two Yašts preserved in the Yasna section of the Avesta: Y.9–Y.11.8 (in honor of Haoma, the Avestan cognate of Sanskrit *soma*, a ritualistic intoxicant) and Y.57 (in honor of Sraoša, the personification of obedience to divine will).

Finally, the Vidēvdāt, while containing some significant mythological material, focuses the bulk of its attention on matters of purity and pollution, of crime and of punishment. It is of great significance for our understanding of the history of Zoroastrian doctrine and practice.

As noted above in the discussion of the chronology of Avestan, the two major dialects are in part chronological and in part almost certainly geographical variants of one another. They are sufficiently distinct – although the bulk of the identified contrasts are in the phonological domain – that I have chosen to focus on the more extensively transmitted variant, that of Young Avestan, in what follows. I will not, however, hesitate to cite Gāthic forms where appropriate or necessary, noting the forms as such. Young Avestan itself does not appear to have been uniform, though the study of its variants faces a number of philological difficulties. The differences between Young Avestan dialects are, at any rate, too minor to be of concern in a survey of this type.

The texts themselves show clear evidence of indigenous scholarly redaction, much like the *pada*-texts of the Vedic Sanskrit tradition. For example, in the transmitted text of the Avesta, sandhi – phonological variation conditioned by the context in which a word is placed – has been for the most part eliminated through the generalization of a single sandhi variant for each final sequence. Clear evidence of redactorial intervention in the text can be seen in the orthographic repetition, in Gāthic Avestan, of preverbs which are separated from their verbs (i.e., in *tmesis*, much like German separable prefixes) in a position immediately preceding the verb itself. Thus, Yasna 32.14 transmits *nī . . . nī.dadaṯ* "they put down," where the meter assures us that the intended reading is *nī . . . dadaṯ*. The doubling of the "preverb" *nī* before the verb *dadaṯ* appears to represent an indigenous analytical hypothesis about the syntactic dependency between the preverb in tmesis (i.e., separated from the verb) and the verb itself. This tells us that the text we have shows the effects of grammatical analysis by an indigenous tradition.

2. WRITING SYSTEM

Avestan is transmitted in an alphabetic writing system specifically designed to preserve relatively low-level phonetic details of hieratic recitation. The writing system itself is based on Pahlavi script, greatly enlarged in inventory by the use of diacritic modifications of the symbols of that orthography. The Pahlavi writing system itself is derived from a greatly simplified cursive version of the Aramaic script. The full set of characters, not all of which are found in all manuscript traditions, can be seen in Table 6.1.

Table 6.1 The Avestan writing system (from Hoffmann and Forssman 1996:41)

1	𐬀	*a*
2	𐬁	*ā*
3	𐬂	*å*
4	𐬃	*ā̊*
5	𐬄	*ą*
6	𐬅	*ą̇*
7	𐬆	*ə*
8	𐬇	*ə̄*
9	𐬈	*e*
10	𐬉	*ē*
11	𐬊	*o*
12	𐬋	*ō*
13	𐬌	*i*
14	𐬍	*ī*
15	𐬎	*u*
16	𐬏	*ū*
17	𐬐	*k*
18	𐬑	*x*
19	𐬒	*x́*
20	𐬓	*xᵛ*
21	𐬔	*g*
22	𐬕	*ġ*
23	𐬖	*γ*
24	𐬗	*c*
25	𐬘	*j*
26	𐬙	*t*
27	𐬚	*ϑ*
28	𐬛	*d*
29	𐬜	*δ*
30	𐬝	*t̰*
31	𐬞	*p*
32	𐬟	*f*
33	𐬠	*b*
34	𐬡	*β*
35	𐬢	*ŋ*
36	𐬣	*ŋ́*
37	𐬤	*ŋᵛ*
38	𐬥	*n*
39	𐬦	*ń*
40	𐬧	*ṇ*
41	𐬨	*m*
42	𐬩	*m̨*
43	𐬪	*ẏ*
44	𐬫	*y*
45	𐬬	*v*
46	𐬭	*r*
47	𐬯	*s*
48	𐬰	*z*
49	𐬱	*š*
50	𐬲	*ž*
51	𐬳	*š́*
52	𐬴	*ṣ̌*
53	𐬵	*h*

The transliteration given in Table 6.1 for each character is now the standard, but differs in some details from prominent earlier work on Avestan (such as Reichelt's 1909 grammar and Bartholomae's 1904 dictionary). The principal differences are as follows:

(1) å (3) was formerly transliterated å̄, thus identically to (4)
ą̇ (6) was formerly transliterated ą, thus identically to (5)
x́ (19) was formerly transliterated ḣ
ġ (22) was formerly transliterated g, thus identically to (21)
c (24) was formerly transliterated č
j (25) was formerly transliterated ǰ
β (34) was formerly transliterated w
ŋ^{v} (37) was generally transliterated ŋu
ń (39) and ṇ (40) were formerly transliterated n, thus identically to (38)
m̨ (42) was formerly transliterated hm
ẏ(43), as well as ii sequences, were formerly transliterated y, thus identically to (44)
uu sequences were formerly transliterated v, thus identically to (45)
ś (51) and ṣ̌ (52) were formerly transliterated š, thus identically to (49)

In many of these cases the underdifferentiation of characters extends to Western books printed in Avestan characters, including Geldner's (1886–1896) extensive critical edition of the bulk of the Avestan corpus. Character 6 (*ą̇*), for example, is generally not used in Geldner's edition, even in the critical apparatus. Moreover, some of these distinctions are lacking in certain Avestan manuscripts or manuscript traditions (for example, the *y* : *ẏ* contrast is generally, though not universally, absent from Indian manuscripts).

The phonetic value of some of these characters, especially some of the "minor" ones which were earlier not distinguished, is not particularly clear, though there is published speculation on virtually all of them. In general, however, we can be fairly confident about the values assigned to the vast majority of symbols.

3. PHONOLOGY

3.1 Phonemic status

Determining the precise phonemic inventory of Avestan is problematic, though further research may allow us to resolve some or all of the outstanding issues. The writing system, designed to capture the nuances of hieratic recitation, is closer to the phonetic level. The principal difficulties arise from the fact that some relevant aspects of the sound system of Avestan are not explicitly indicated in the writing system. For example, there are no direct encodings of the position of stress (though some aspects of stress placement can probably be safely inferred), nor of syllable boundaries (which appear to be relevant to the determination of the phonemic status of some segments). In addition, as pointed out above (see §1), the final sandhi variants which were certainly present in the language (as indicated by their rare preservation in fixed phrases, for example) have been for the most part leveled out in the transmitted text.

3.2 Consonants

The approximate phonetic values of the consonant symbols are generally not in dispute. The uncontroversial stops, fricatives, affricates, and nasals of Avestan are presented in Table 6.2.

Table 6.2 Consonantal sounds of Avestan

Manner of articulation	Place of articulation: Labial	Inter-dental	Dental/ Alveolar	Palato-alveolar	Palatal	Retro-flex	Front velar	Round velar	Plain velar
Stop									
Voiceless	p		t						k
Voiced	b		d						g
Fricative									
Voiceless	f	θ	s	š	ś	ṣ̌	x́	xᵛ	x
Voiced	β	ð	z	ž					γ
Affricate									
Voiceless					c				
Voiced					j				
Nasal									
Voiceless	m̥								
Voiced	m		n		ń		ŋ́	ŋᵛ	ŋ

In addition, it is generally recognized that the symbol *ṯ* represents an "unreleased" voiceless dental stop – it is extremely limited in distribution, being regularly found only in word-final position and before certain obstruents. The phonetic nature of *ŋ̣* is taken by Hoffmann to be a "postuvular nasal" without oral occlusion of any type.

The values of the symbols which represent liquids and glides present only minor difficulties of detail. There appears to be a voicing contrast in the liquids between *r* and the digraph *hr*, the latter being voiceless. The symbol *v* appears to differ from *β* by the former being round, the latter not. While the symbol *h* is uncontroversially held to be a glottal approximant, there is some speculation that the symbol transliterated as *y* originally represented *ž*, contrasting therefore with the voiced palatal glide (which was represented by the symbol *ẏ*). As noted, the contrast is not observed in all manuscripts nor by the earlier Western scholarly tradition. A detailed study of the distribution of these two symbols in manuscripts which use both of them remains a desideratum.

3.3 Vowels

The confidently identified vowel symbols may be approximately distributed in the vowel space as in Figure 6.1:

	FRONT		*CENTRAL*		*BACK*
HIGH	ī / i				ū / u
MID		ē / e	ə̄ / ə	ō / o	
LOW			ā / a		å̄

Figure 6.1 Avestan vowels

A macron indicates vowel length; however, it seems likely, and is now generally accepted, that the original length contrast has become a qualitative one, either as well as or instead of a purely quantitative one. It must be noted in this regard that the manuscripts do not, in general, do a particularly good job of distinguishing length contrasts in the high vowels *ĭ* and *ŭ*. The vowel *ą* represents nasalized *a* as well as nasalized *ā*. In addition to these simple vowels, Avestan has a number of diphthongs, including the so-called short diphthongs *aē*, *ōi*, and *ao* and the long diphthongs *āi* and *āu* (see §3.4.9).

One of the most salient differences between Gāthic and Young Avestan concerns vowel quantities in absolute word-final position. In Gāthic Avestan all such vowels are long, whereas in Young Avestan final vowels are long only in monosyllables (discounting a few sandhi forms, on which more below). The fact that monosyllables are treated differently in this regard than polysyllables in Young Avestan allows one to determine certain otherwise somewhat obscure facts about the syllabification of Young Avestan word forms. For example, the instrumental singular of the word for "earth" (*zam-*) is transmitted as *zəmā*, which must, given the rule just stated concerning final vowel quantities, represent a monosyllable. The epenthesis is thus phonologically irrelevant (either postdating the rule regulating final vowel quantities or too low-level phonetic to be of concern, or both). It is, as it turns out, also metrically irrelevant, the phonological facts thus supporting the analysis of the meter nicely. This case can be contrasted with that of the nominative singular of the word for "bowstring," *jiia*, Sanskrit *jyā̀*, which must be disyllabic in Avestan given its short final vowel, as it originally was in Sanskrit.

3.4 Diachronic developments

3.4.1 Proto-Indo-Iranian

Avestan, being an Indo-Iranian language, shares with Sanskrit the phonological developments of Proto-Indo-Iranian (PIIr.). The most salient of these are (i) the merger of the labiovelar and velar stop series (definitional of satem languages); (ii) the development of the syllabic nasals to PIIr. **a*; (iii) the RUKI-inducing backing of PIE **s* (in Avestan to *š*); (iv) the merger of PIE **e*, **a*, and **o* into PIIr. **a*, and that of PIE **ē*, **ā*, and **ō* into PIIr. **ā*. In keeping with *Brugmann's Law*, short **o* in open syllables shows up in Avestan as *ā*, rather than the expected *ă* (examples include *dāuru* "wood" < PIE **doru* and *srāuuaiia-*, the causative stem of *sru* "to hear" < PIE **k̂loweye-*). The palatalization of the Proto-Indo-European velars (and the Proto-Indo-European labiovelars which had fallen together with this set of stops) before front vowels and **y* preceded the merger of the vowels.

Avestan provides key evidence for the status of PIE **T^sT* (< **TT*, where *T* is any dental stop) in Proto-Indo-Iranian: whereas Sanskrit shows *TT* as the outcome of this sequence (*vittá-* "found" < PIE **vit^s tó-*, morphologically **vid* + *-*tó*), Avestan has *ST* (thus *vista-* "found"). The evidence of these two major branches of Indo-Iranian points to preservation in Proto-Indo-Iranian of PIE **T^sT*, thus suggesting the reconstruction of an affricate-formation rule for Proto-Indo-European phonology.

3.4.2 Indo-European laryngeals

In the matter of the laryngeals of Proto-Indo-European (see *WAL* Ch. 17, §2.1.3), Avestan provides only limited direct phonological evidence. In virtually all positions, the laryngeals have disappeared without a trace. There are, however, two exceptions to this statement. First, in Old Avestan the hiatus left by intervocalic laryngeal loss is generally preserved, as indicated by the syllable-counting meter of the Gāthas. Thus, the apparently disyllabic *zrazdā̊*, the nominative plural of *zrazdā-* "having faith," the second compound member of which comes from PIE *$d^h eH_1 es$, scans as a trisyllable in Old Avestan (*$d^h eH_1 es$ having become PIIr. *$d^h aHas$ and then pre-Avestan **daas*, with two syllables). Unfortunately, our lack of a firm understanding of Young Avestan meter, coupled with, and in part deriving from, the flawed transmission of the relevant metrical texts, does not permit us to determine conclusively whether such scansions were also attested in this language.

Secondly, in a few instances interconsonantal laryngeals appear to have "vocalized" to *i* in Avestan, much as in Sanskrit. This is particularly clear in the paradigm of "father," PIE *$pH_2 ter$-, which shows laryngeal vocalization in the nominative singular (*pitā*, Skt. *pitā́*), accusative singular (*pitarəm*, Skt. *pitáram*), and dative singular (*piθre*, Skt. *pitré*). This development must be seen as dialectal, since Avestan also shows forms of this paradigm without traces of the vocalized laryngeal, including Old Avestan nominative singulars *ptā* and *tā*, Old Avestan dative singular *fəδrōi*, and the Young Avestan accusative plural *fəδrō* (the schwas in the last two forms are the result of a late epenthesis process – they do not count for purposes of the meter, and thus were apparently not there at the time of composition; such epenthetic schwas will not be explicitly pointed out in the discussion which follows). One may also contrast Avestan *duɣδar-* "daughter" both with Sanskrit *duhitár-* (where the *i* represents the vocalized laryngeal) and with Greek *tʰugátēr* (where the laryngeal is represented by *a*), all three from PIE *$d^h ugH_2 ter$-. These forms make it impossible to see laryngeal vocalization to *i* as a property of Proto-Indo-Iranian itself in spite of the fact that only Sanskrit and, in some instances, Avestan, appear to show such a development within the Indo-European family.

Indirect evidence of the prior presence of the laryngeals is, by contrast, quite easy to come by. The sequence of syllabic nasal + laryngeal yields Avestan *ā*, giving rise to alternations of the type *zan-* "give birth" (< PIIr. **ȷ́an* < PIE *$\hat{g}enH_1$-, Skt. *jan*) : *zāta-* "born" (< PIIr. **ȷ́āta-* < PIE *$\hat{g}\d{n}H_1 to$-, Skt. *jātá-*). More interesting is the divergence between Avestan and Sanskrit in the treatment of pre-laryngeal syllabic liquids (PIE **r̥H* and **l̥H*). Whereas Sanskrit regularly shows *ī̆r* from such sequences, the Avestan reflex is *ar*: for example, *darəɣa-* "long" < PIE *$d\d{l}H_1 g^h o$- (Skt. *dīrghá-*); *starəta-* "strewn" < PIE *$st\d{r}H_3 to$- (cf. Skt. *stīrṇá-*), *taró* "across" < PIE *$t\d{r}H_2 es$ (Skt. *tiráḥ*). The best reconstruction for the Proto-Indo-Iranian reflex of these sequences is not at all clear given the Avestan and Sanskrit developments.

3.4.3 Stops

A number of distinctive phonological developments in the consonant system give Avestan a quite different "look" from that of Sanskrit. Quite salient among these is the development of the Proto-Indo-European palatal stops (**k̂*, **ĝ*, and *$\hat{g}^h$). In the first instance, these stops develop into palatal fricatives in Proto-Indo-Iranian, usually designated **ć*, **ȷ́*, and **ȷ́h*, respectively (and thus distinguished from the outcome of the palatalization of the Proto-Indo-European plain and rounded velar stops, which became the affricates **č*, **ǰ*, and **ǰh*). The place of articulation of these fricatives then shifts to the dental region, and we find *s* as the regular reflex of **ć*, and *z* as the regular outcome of both **ȷ́* and **ȷ́h* (with the regular Avestan loss of distinctive aspiration of the voiced aspirates). Examples include *satəm* "100" < PIIr. **ćatam* < PIE **k̂m̥tom* (Skt. *śatám*); *zan-* "beget" < PIIr. **ȷ́an-* < PIE *$\hat{g}enH_1$- (Skt. *jan-*); *zari-* "yellow" < PIIr. *$ȷ́^h ali$- < PIE *$\hat{g}^h eli$- (Skt. *hári-*).

The voiceless unaspirated stops of Proto-Indo-Iranian have been generally preserved. However, they have developed into voiceless fricatives preconsonantally (excepting **p* before **t*, which remains unchanged): for example, Av. *xratu-* "insight" < PIIr. **kratu-* (Skt. *krátu-*); Av. *friia-* "beloved" < PIIr. **priHa* (Skt. *priyá-*). Contrast Av. *hapta* "seven" < PIIr. **sapta*

(Skt. *saptá*). This development does not take place if the stop in question is preceded by PIIr. **s* (or its RUKI-variant, **š*): thus, *vastra-* "clothing" < PIIr. **wastra-* (Skt. *vástra-*); *uštra-* "camel" (cf. Skt. *úṣṭra-*), with preserved **t*.

The voiceless aspirated stops of Proto-Indo-European have become corresponding voiceless fricatives: for example, Av. *haxāii-* "companion" < PIIr. **sak*^{h}*āy-* (Skt. *sákhāy-*); Av. *kafa-* "foam" < PIIr. **kap*^{h}*a-* (Skt. *kapha-*). Avestan preserves better than Sanskrit the paradigm-internal effects of aspiration arising from an ensuing *H_2 in the Proto-Indo-Iranian word for "path," which has the nominative singular paṇtā̊ < PIIr. **pantaH*$_2$*- s* (contrast Skt. *pánthāḥ*, with generalized aspiration), genitive singular *paθō* < **pn̥tH*$_2$*as* (Skt. *patháḥ*).

The voiced aspirated stops of Indo-European (and Indo-Iranian) have merged, via loss of aspiration, with corresponding simple voiced stops in Avestan (and Iranian generally). The resulting voiced stops are generally preserved as such in Old Avestan, but have lenited (or "weakened") to voiced fricatives in all but a few positions in Young Avestan. They are generally preserved as stops only in word-initial position (except in a few word-initial consonant clusters) and after nasals and fricatives. These developments can be seen in the following examples, sorted by place of articulation:

1. *Iranian *b (< PIE *b, *b*^{h} *) >*
   (i) Avestan *b*: *brātā* "brother" < PIIr. **b*^{h}*rātā* (Skt. *bhrā́tā*); Avestan *xumba-* "pot" < PIIr. **k*^{h}*umb*^{h}*a-* (cf. Skt. *kumbhá-*).
   (ii) Avestan *β*: *aiβi* "toward" (Old Avestan *aibī*) < PIIr. **ab*^{h}*i* (Skt. *abhí*).
2. *Iranian *d (< PIE *d, *d*^{h}*)>*
   (i) Avestan *d*: *dasa* "ten" < PIIr. **daća* (Skt. *dáśa*); *viṇdəṇti* "they find" < PIIr. **windanti* (Skt. *vindánti*).
   (ii) Avestan *δ*: *maδa-* "intoxicating drink" (Old Avestan *mada-*) < PIIr. **mada-* (Skt. *máda-*).
3. *Iranian *g (< PIE unpalatalized *g, *g*^{w}*, *g*^{h}*, *g*^{wh} *) >*
   (i) Avestan *g*: *garəma-* "warm" < PIIr. **g*^{h}*arma-* (Skt. *gharmá-*); *zaṇga-* "ankle" < PIIr. **ǰang*^{h}*a-* (cf. Skt. *jáṅghā-* "shin"); *mazga-* "marrow" (cf. Skt. *majján-*).
   (ii) Avestan *ɣ*: *darəɣa-* "long" (Old Avestan *darəga-*) < PIIr. **dl̥H*$_1$*g*^{h}*a-* (Skt. *dīrghá-*); *uɣra-* "strong" (Old Avestan *ugra-*) < PIIr. **ugra-* (Skt. *ugrá-*).
4. *Iranian *ǰ (PIE palatalized *g, *g*^{w}*, *g*^{h}*, *g*^{wh} *) >*
   (i) Avestan *j*: *jani-* "woman" < PIIr. **ǰani-* (Skt. *jáni-*); *rəṇja-* "move quickly" < PIIr. **ranǰ*^{h}*a-* (Skt. *raṁha-* "run").
   (ii) Avestan *ž*: *aži-* "serpent" < PIIr. **aǰ*^{h}*i-* (Skt. *áhi-*); *dažaiti* "he burns" (transitive) < PIIr. **daǰ*^{h}*ati* (Skt. *dáhati*).

Exceptions to the Young Avestan lenition processes evidenced above are attested. While some exceptional forms appear to represent the borrowing of religious vocabulary from the Gāthic dialect, others seem to require the assumption of dialectal developments within Young Avestan itself. Finally, in a number of cases, analogical restructuring appears to be at work. For example, in a reduplicated form such as *dadāθa* "you give," built to the verbal root *dā*, the transparency of the reduplicative morphology has allowed the medial *d* to avoid lenition (or, more likely, to be remade to *d* after undergoing lenition). Similarly, in a number of transparent compounds the first member of which ends in a vowel and the second member of which begins with a voiced stop (e.g., *hu-baoδi-* "having a good fragrance"), lenition of the morpheme-initial voiced stop is lacking. Analogy to the uncompounded form (*baoδi-* "fragrance") is clearly at work. Note that, in the example cited, the presence of lenition on the dental stop of *hubaoδi-* makes a dialectal explanation for the lack of lenition on the labial stop unlikely.

In spite of the general loss of aspiration on voiced stops treated above, Avestan does preserve some morphological traces of the original aspiration through the workings of *Bartholomae's Law*. This law states that the direction of voicing assimilation in obstruent clusters (usually regressive) is reversed just in the cases in which the first obstruent is a voiced aspirate. In addition, the aspiration originally present on the first obstruent is shifted to the second. A Sanskrit example will make this clear: when the *-ta-* participial suffix is added to the verbal root *vr̥dh* "grow," Bartholomae's Law triggers the following development: *vr̥dh* + *ta-*> *vr̥ddha-* "grown." The corresponding Avestan form, with the *ST* treatment of the dental cluster, as expected, is *vərəzda-* "grown." Although the aspiration is no longer present, its earlier existence is reflected in the rightward spread of voicing. The effects of Bartholomae's Law are well preserved in Old Avestan, but frequently Young Avestan has analogically recreated the forms, applying the much more general regressive voicing assimilation to the cluster created in the remaking. Thus, corresponding to the Old Avestan third singular *aogədā* "he spoke," from the verbal root *aog* (cf. Skt. *ohate*) + *-ta*, the ending of the third singular middle, Young Avestan generally has *aoxta*.

3.4.4 Fricatives

Avestan shares with Greek (though independently, of course) the development of Proto-Indo-European presonorant **s* to *h*. This Proto-Iranian **h* underwent a number of conditioned changes in Avestan, of which the principal ones are as follows:

1. **h*> *ŋh* between low vowels (Av. *aŋhaiti* "he would be" < PIIr. **asati*, Skt. *asati*) – contrast the preservation of **h* before non-low vowels (Av. *ahi* "you are" < PIIr. **asi*, Skt. *asi*). Correspondingly, **ăhwă* > *ăŋ*^{u}*hă*, **ăhyă* > *ăŋ́hă* (*pərəsaŋ*^{v} *ha* "ask for your own benefit" < **pr̥ćšćaswa*, Skt. *pr̥cchasva*; *vaŋ́hō* "better" [nom. sg. neut.] < PIIr. **wasyas*, Skt. *vásyaḥ*)
2. Initial **hw-* > *x*^{v}*-* (Av. *x*^{v}*afna-* "sleep" < PIIr. **swapna-*, Skt. *svápna-*).
3. Initial **hm-* > *m-* (Av. *mahi* "we are" < PIIr. **smasi*, Skt. *smasi*), contrast preservation of this sequence word-internally (Av. *ahmi* "I am" < PIIr. **asmi*, Skt. *asmi*).
4. Final **-ah* > *ō* (*-ō* nom. sg. masc. ending of thematic nouns < PIIr. **-as* < PIE **-os*), compare the Sanskrit sandhi of final *-aḥ* > *-o* before voiced segments.
5. Final **-āh* > *-ā̊* (*m ā̊* nom. sg. masc. "moon" < PIIr. **maas* < PIE **meHn̥s*).

An exception to the development of Proto-Indo-Iranian **s* to Avestan *h* is provided by so-called RUKI contexts (i.e., when the **s* immediately followed any type of *r*, *ŭ̆*, *ĭ̆*, velar stop, or palatal affricate). In such a context, PIIr. **s* and **z* show up as Avestan *š* and *ž*, respectively. Examples include: *vīša-* "poison" (Skt. *viṣá-*), *mīžda-* "payment" (Skt. *mīḍhá-*). Interestingly, in Avestan (though not in Sanskrit), we find the same development after labials: *drafša-* "banner" < PIIr. **drapsa-* (Skt. *drapsá-*), *vaβ ža-ka-* "wasp" < PIIr. **wabz*^{h}*a-* < PIE **wob*^{h}*-so-*.

3.4.5 Liquids

Proto-Indo-European **l* and **r* have merged as Avestan *r*, which is generally preserved as such. Interestingly, however, an *r* following a low vowel in the coda of a stressed syllable is devoiced before a following voiceless stop, the voiceless *r* being indicated by the digraph <hr>. In the case of *p* and *k*, nothing further befalls these segments: thus, *vəhrka-* "wolf" < PIIr. *wŕ̥̥ka-* (Skt. *vŕ̥̥ka-*); *kəhrpa-* "body" < PIIr. **kŕ̥̥pa-* (Skt. *kŕ̥̥pa-*). When the following voiceless stop was *t*, however, the sequence *hrt* became *ṣ̌*: *maṣ̌iia-* "man" < PIIr.

**mártiya-* (Skt. *mártya-*); *pəṣ̌anā-* "battle" < PIIr. **pṛ̥tanā-* (Skt. *pṛ́tanā-*). Particularly instructive is the pair *mərəta-* "dead" (< PIIr. **mṛ̥tá-*, Skt. *mṛtá-*), aməša- "immortal" (< PIIr. **a-mṛ́ta-*, Skt. *amṛ́ta-*).

3.4.6 Nasals

The nasals have developed into *ṇ* before stops and affricates: for example, *aṇtarə* "beside" (Skt. *antár*); *paṇca* "five" (Skt. *pañca*). The sequence *an* becomes *ą* before fricatives: *mąθra-* "mantra" < **mantra-* (Skt. *mántra-*). In most other positions PIIr nasals have been preserved.

It is worth pointing out that although in general the syllabic nasals have developed into PIIr. **a*, before glides we find instead that PIE **n̥* > *an* (Av. *janiiāṯ* "he would smite" [with an analogical initial palatal] < PIIr. **gʰanyāt* < PIE **gʷʰn̥-yeH-t*, Skt. *hanyāt*) and PIE **m̥* > *am* (*jamiiā̊* "you would go" [also with an analogical palatal] < PIIr. **gamyās* < PIE **gʷm̥-yeH-s*, Skt. *gamyāḥ*).

3.4.7 Glides

The glide **w* shows a number of conditioned developments in Avestan. After the Proto-Indo-European palatal stops, this glide becomes a labial stop (voiceless after the Proto-Indo-European voiceless palatal stop, voiced after the Proto-Indo-European voiced and voiced aspirated palatal stops): for example, *aspa-* "horse" < PIE **Hek̂wo-* (Skt. *áśva-*); *zbaiia-* present stem of "call" < PIIr. *ǰʰwaya-* (Skt. *hváya-*). After the dental stops, it becomes a voiced labial fricative: *θβąm* "you" (acc. sg.) < PIIr. **twām* (Skt. *tvā́m*); *caθβārō* < PIE **kʷetwores* (Skt. *catvā́raḥ*); *aδβan-* "way" (Skt. *ádhvan-*).

3.4.8 Vowels

The vowels of Avestan have in general undergone fewer modifications than the consonants, the exception being the short low vowel *a*. This vowel shows a number of conditioned changes, some of them apparently dialectal (and thus "sporadic" in our text), some of them quite regular. One of the more significant of the regular changes, because of its interaction with other phonological rules of Avestan, is the raising of *a* to ə before word-final nasals (and, dialectally, before word-internal nasals as well). The effects of this process are seen in nearly every line of the Avesta, producing forms such as the accusative singular of *a*-stems in *-əm* (thus *narəm* "man" [acc. sg.], Sanskrit *náram*) as well as forms such as *satəm* "100" (Sanskrit *śatám*).

This schwa is itself subject to further raising to *i* under the influence of a preceding palatal (*y*, *c*, *j*, or *ž*). Thus, the accusative singular masculine of the relative pronoun, corresponding precisely to Sanskrit *yám*, has undergone the following stages of development: **yam* > **yəm* > *yim*. Similarly, the accusative singular of the word for "deceit," *druj-*, corresponding to Sanskrit *drúham*, is *drujim* (< earlier **drujəm*).

Moreover, when the prenasal raising to schwa took place in the environment of a preceding consonant + glide sequence, the development went even further, with *-Cyə-* sequences becoming *-Cī̆-*, and *-Cwə-* sequences becoming *-Cū̆-* (the lack of clarity about high vowel quantity is the result of the general problem of the transmission of quantities in the case of these vowels alluded to above). Examples include *haiθīm* "truth" < **haθyəm* < **satyam* (Skt. *satyám*) and *haurum* "whole" < **harwəm* < **sarwam* (Skt. *sárvam*).

The sequences *-ayə-* and *-awə-* show a corresponding assimilation of the ə to the preceding glide with subsequent loss of the glide. The end result of this development is the appropriate Avestan diphthong (see §3.4.9), as can be seen in the following examples: (i) **wayam* "we" (Skt. *vayám*) > **vayəm* > **vayim* > **vaim* > *vaēm*; (ii) **awam* "that" > **awəm* > **awum* > **aum* > *aom*. Glide + ə sequences show precisely parallel developments after *ā*, giving rise to the "long" diphthongs *āi* and *āu*.

3.4.9 Diphthongs

The development of the Proto-Indo-Iranian diphthong **ai* is dependent upon both position in the word (nonfinal vs. final) and syllable structure (open vs. closed) in Avestan. Turning first to the development of nonfinal **ai*, we find development to Avestan *aē* in open syllables – *aēiti* "he goes" < PIIr. **aiti* (Skt. *éti*) – but to Avestan *ōi* in closed syllables: *kauuōiš* "of the singer" (gen. sg. of *kauui-* "singer") < PIIr. **kawaiš* (Skt. *kaveḥ*).

In word-final position, the usual development of PIIr. **ai* is to Young Avestan *-ĕ* (the length determined by syllable count, as always in Young Avestan), Old Avestan *-ōi*: for example, *naire* "man" (dat. sg.) < PIIr. **narai* (Skt. *náre*, compare Gāthic *narōi*). After glides, however, the development is different, PIIr. **-wai* becoming *-uiie* (*aŋhuiie* "life," dat. sg. of *ahu-*, < **ahwai*), PIIr. **-yai* becoming *-iiōi* (*maiδiiōi* "in the middle," loc. sg. of *maiδiia-* < PIIr. **mad^h yai*, Skt. *mádhye*; *yōi*, nom. pl. of the relative pronoun *ya-*, < **yai*, Skt. *yé*).

Proto-Indo-Iranian **au* does not show such a syllable-structure set of developments in Young Avestan, becoming *ao* in nonfinal position across the board: thus, *aojah-* "strength" < PIIr. **auǰas-* (Skt. *ójas*); *gaoš* "of the cow" (gen. sg. of *gauu-*) < **gauš* (Skt. *góḥ*).

In final position, PIIr. **au* becomes Avestan *-uuō* (compare the *-iie* development of **ai* after glides): for example, *huuō* "that" < **sau* (Old Persian *hauv*, cf. Sanskrit *asáu*); *ərəzuuō* "O righteous one" (voc. sg. of *ərəzu-* "straight, correct, righteous") < **r̥ǰvau*.

The so-called long diphthongs of Indo-Iranian, **āi* and **āu*, become Avestan *āi* and *āu*, respectively. Examples include the following: the dative singular of Avestan *a*-stems (PIE *o*-stems) such as (unattested) *aspāi*, dative singular of *aspa-* "horse" < PIE **Heḱwōi* (compare Greek *-ōi*, but contrast Skt. *-āya*); the nominative singular of the word *gauu-* "cow," which has the form *gāuš* < PIIr. **gāus* (Skt. *gáuḥ*).

3.4.10 Epenthesis

Avestan shows the effects of a relatively recent process of *i*-epenthesis. It is important to note that this epenthesis has no metrical effects and thus may postdate the time of the composition of the texts. There are two distinct versions of *i*-epenthesis – one word-initial, the other word-internal. The word-initial version is quite restricted, affecting only initial **ri-* and **θy-* (itself from **ty-*), as seen in *irišta-* "damaged" (Skt. *riṣṭa-*) and *iθiiejah-* "abandonment" (Skt. *tyájas-*). Both of these forms are disyllabic in Avestan. The word-internal version is much more general, occurring before dental and labial stops and fricatives as well as before *n*, *n̥t*, *r*, and *rm* if a front vowel or palatal glide follows. The phenomenon is quite common and can be seen in examples such as *baraiti* "he carries" (Sanskrit *bhárati*) and *aiβi* "towards" (Sanskrit *abhí*).

Interestingly, this epenthesis appears to be an ongoing synchronic process. As such, it tells us something significant about the accentual system of Avestan at the stage during which *i*-epenthesis took place. The addition of the enclitic conjunction *-ca* "and" regularly undoes the effects of *i*-epenthesis in penultimate syllables (i.e., penultimate before the cliticization of *-ca*). Thus, we find *baēšaziiatica* "and he heals" for what would appear without *-ca* as *baēšaziiaiti*, or *varəδatica* "and it increases" next to *varəδaiti*. The standard explanation for such alternations is that the cliticization of *-ca* gave rise to an accent shift from the original penult to the syllable immediately preceding the *-ca*. Such shifts are characteristic of stress-based, rather than pitch-accent type accentual systems, indicating that unlike Sanskrit, the Avestan accentual system was of the former type. The *-ca* induced alternation also indicates that internal *i*-epenthesis should be expected only in stressed syllables.

Somewhat parallel to *i*-epenthesis, though much more restricted, is the phenomenon of *u*-epenthesis. Like *i*-epenthesis, the latter process is metrically irrelevant and thus would appear to be rather late. The phenomenon of *u*-epenthesis is essentially restricted to *ru* and *ruu* sequences. Standard examples include *uruuata-* "duty" (< **rwata-*, which shows an Avestan metathesis of the initial cluster when compared to Skt. *vratá*) and *hauruua-* "whole" (< PIIr. **sarwa-*, Skt. *sárva-*). Further evidence that this is a late process can be seen from the fact that in cases in which, dialectally, Young Avestan *ß* has become *uu* (i.e., /w/) after *r*, the *u*-epenthesis is still triggered – thus *gəuruuaiia-* "seize" (< PIIr. **gr̥bʰāya-*).

4. MORPHOLOGY

4.1 Morphological type

Avestan is a highly inflected language, much like other Indo-European languages of very early attestation, making use of a rich set of derivational suffixes and inflectional endings in both the nominal and verbal systems.

4.2 Nominal morphology

The standard Indo-European cases, genders, and numbers are preserved in Avestan, where they serve to inflect nouns and adjectives, as well as pronouns. There are eight cases (nominative, accusative, instrumental, dative, ablative, genitive, locative, and vocative – generally cited in this order). There are three genders (masculine, feminine, and neuter), distributed in the usual archaic Indo-European manner (i.e., the masculine and neuter differ only in the nominative, vocative, and accusative, which are not distinguished from one another in the neuter). Finally, there are three numbers (singular, dual, and plural). Adjectives agree with their head nouns in case, number, and gender. The nominal inflection system appears quite robust throughout the period of attestation, although some breakdown in the understanding of the case system is evident in very late compositions.

The nominal paradigms may be roughly divided between *vocalic stems*, the descendants of PIE **-o* and **-eH₂* stems, and *consonant stems*, continuing Proto-Indo-European consonant stems (see *WAL* Ch. 17, §3.5). The latter frequently show ablaut variations in their suffixal (or occasionally root) syllables (on Indo-European ablaut, see *WAL* Ch. 17, §3.2). For ablauting stems, it is often useful to distinguish between the so-called *strong cases* (nominative, accusative, locative, and vocative singular; nominative and accusative dual; and nominative plural) – characterized by full- or lengthened-grade ablaut before the ending – and *weak cases*, which show by contrast zero-grade ablaut. The paradigm of Indo-European thematic (*o*-stem) nouns, generally masculine or neuter, shows up in Avestan as follows (using **Hek̑wo-* "horse" > Avestan *aspa-* as an example, unattested cases of this particular lexeme being marked with an asterisk):

(2)

	Singular	Dual	Plural
Nominative	aspō	aspa*	aspåŋhō / aspa
Accusative	aspəm	aspa*	aspą*
Instrumental	aspa*	aspaēibiia	aspāiš*
Dative	aspāi*	aspaēibiia	aspaēibiiō*
Ablative	aspāṯ*	aspaēibiia	aspaēibiiō*
Genitive	aspahe	aspaiiå*	aspanąm
Locative	aspe*	aspaiiō*	aspaēšu
Vocative	aspa*	aspa*	aspåŋhō / aspa*

Indo-European stems in *-eH_2, generally feminines, inflect like Avestan *daēnā-* "religion":

(3)

	Singular	Dual	Plural
Nominative	daēna	daēne*	daēnå
Accusative	daēnąm	daēnå	daēnå
Instrumental	daēna	daēnābiia*	daēnābiš
Dative	daēnaiia / daēna	daēnāibiia*	aspaēibiiō
Ablative	daēnaiiāṯ	daēnāibiia*	daēnāibiiō
Genitive	daēnaiiå	daēnaiiå*	daēnanąm*
Locative	daēnaiia*	daēnaiiå*	daēnāhu
Vocative	daēne*/daēna	daēne*	daēnå*

It is not practical in the present survey to list fully the many variants of consonant-stem inflection attested in Avestan. However, two representative paradigms will be presented: that of the Avestan masculine *r*-stem *nar-* "man" (PIE *H_2*ner-*)

(4)

	Singular	Dual	Plural
Nominative	nā	nara	narō
Accusative	narəm		nərəuš
Instrumental	nara		
Dative	naire	nərəbiia	nərəbiiō
Ablative	nərəṯ		nərəbiiō
Genitive	narš	narå	narąm
Locative	nairi		
Vocative	narə		

and that of the Avestan neuter *s*-stem *manas-* "thought" (PIE **mene/os-*):

(5)

	Singular	Plural
Nominative	manō	manå
Accusative	manō	manå
Instrumental	manaŋhā	manə̄bīš
Dative	manaŋhe	
Ablative	manaŋhaṯ	
Genitive	manaŋhō	-manaŋhąm
Locative	(manahi)	

Readers are referred to the more comprehensive grammars of Avestan (Hoffmann and Forssman 1996 or Reichelt 1909) for more details concerning the many classes of noun inflection.

4.3 Pronominal morphology

4.3.1 Personal pronouns

The personal pronouns have singular, dual, and plural forms, though there are many gaps in attestation. For the accusative and some oblique cases, one must distinguish between tonic and enclitic forms, as elsewhere in Indo-European. The pronouns for the third person are generally supplied by demonstratives (see §4.3.2). Attested Young Avestan forms for the first and second persons are presented in Table 6.3; forms in parenthesis are Gāthic, provided when the Young Avestan form is unattested:

Table 6.3 First- and second-person personal pronouns of Avestan

	First person		Second person	
	Tonic	Enclitic	Tonic	Enclitic
Singular				
Nominative	azəm		tūm	
Accusative	mąm	mā	θβąm	θβā
Instrumental			θβā	
Dative	māuuōiia	mē	(taibiiā)	tē
Ablative	(mat̰)		θβat̰	
Genitive	mana	mē	tauua	tē
Dual				
Nominative	(vā)			
Accusative	(ə̄əāuuā)			
Genitive		(nā)	yauuākəm	
Plural				
Nominative	vaēm		yūžəm	
Accusative	ahma	nō		vō
Instrumental	(ə̄hmā)		(xšmā)	
Dative	(ahmaibiiā)	nō	yūšmaoiiō xšmāuuōiia	vō
Ablative	(ahmat̰)		yūšmat̰	
Genitive	ahmākəm	nō	yūšmākəm	vō

A special set of enclitic forms of the third-person pronoun is also attested. It does not distinguish between masculine and feminine, but has distinct neuter forms. It is found only for the accusative, except in the singular, where a dative-genitive form is also found:

(6)

	Masc./Fem.	*Neuter*
Acc. singular	īm, hī, dim	it̰, dit̰
Dat./Gen. singular	hē	hē
Acc. dual	(ī)	
Acc. plural	hīš, dīš	ī, dī

4.3.2 Demonstrative pronouns

An example of the inflection of demonstrative pronouns (usually referred to as the "pronominal inflection") is presented in Table 6.4; the table shows the forms of Avestan *ta-* "this"

Table 6.4 Demonstrative pronouns of Avestan

	Masculine	Neuter	Feminine
Singular			
Nominative	hō / hā	tat̰	hā
Accusative	təm	tat̰	tąm
Instrumental	tā	tā	aētaiia
Dative	aētahmāi	aētahmāi	
Ablative	aētahmāt̰	aētahmāt̰	
Genitive	aētahe	aētahe	aētaŋ́ha / aētaiiå
Locative	aētahmi	aētahmi	
Dual			
Nom./Acc.	tā	tē	
Genitive	aētaiiå	aētaiiå	
Plural			
Nominative	tē	tā	tå
Accusative	tə̄ / tą	tā	ta
Instrumental	(tāiš)	(tāiš)	
Dative	aētaēibiiō	aētaēibiiō	aētābiiō
Genitive	aētaēšąm	aētaēšąm	aētaŋhąm
Locative	aētaēšu	aētaēšu	

(fem. *tā-*), compare Sanskrit *tá-*. As in Sanskrit, the nominative singular masculine and feminine of this pronoun is formed from PIE **se/o-*, rather than **te/o-*. For cases in which the relevant form of *ta-* is not attested, but a form of the similarly inflected pronoun *aēta-* (likewise "this," compare Sanskrit *etá-*) is attested, the *aēta-* form is provided.

4.4 Verbal morphology

The Avestan verbal system, like that of Proto-Indo-European, is built around the verbal root. From such a root may be derived a set of tense-aspect stems (though not all roots are found in all tense categories), including the present stem, the aorist stem, and the perfect stem. To these stems are built the moods of Avestan, which continue more or less directly the like-named Proto-Indo-European mood categories. Not all tense stems form the basis for all moods. The moods include the indicative, the injunctive, the subjunctive, the optative, and the imperative. Finally, the endings are added to the mood-stem. The endings encode person, number, and voice – in addition, they play a role in the encoding of some moods. The Avestan categories indicated by the endings are much like those of Proto-Indo-European itself – person (first, second, third), number (singular, dual, plural), voice (active and middle, perhaps also stative and passive).

The endings themselves fall into four well-defined sets, each used in the expression of one or more tense/aspect categories: (i) primary endings (used in the indicative present, indicative future, and in part in the subjunctive); (ii) secondary endings (used in the indicative imperfect, indicative aorist, indicative pluperfect, injunctive, optative, and in part in the subjunctive); (iii) imperative endings (used in the imperative); and (iv) perfect endings (used in the indicative perfect). In the active, these endings have the forms which are presented in (7) (absence of a form indicates lack of attestation; — indicates that no form is expected):

(7)

	Primary	*Secondary*	*Imperative*	*Perfect*
Singular				
First	-mi, (-a)	-(a)m	—	-a
Second	-hi	-h	-Ø, di	-θa
Third	-ti	-t, -t	-tu	-a
Dual				
First	(-uuahī)	(-uuā)	—	
Second				
Third	-tō, -θō	-təm		-atarə
Plural				
First	-mahi	-ma	—	-ma
Second	-θa	-ta	-ta	
Third	-n̩ti, -ati -ain̩ti	-n, -at, -ārə, -ārəš	-n̩tu, -ən̩tu, -an̩tu	-arə, -ərəš

Using the verb *bar* "carry" as an example of a simple thematic present, the expected forms of the present indicative active would be as follows:

(8)

	Singular	*Dual*	*Plural*
First	barāmi	barāuuahi	barāmahi
Second	barahi	baratō	baraθa
Third	baraiti	baratō	barən̩ti

In Gāthic Avestan, the first singular ending *-mi* is found only with athematic stems. Thematic stems such as *bara-* show the archaic ending *-ā* instead.

The injunctive present active of *bar*, which is identical to the imperfect except for the absence of the so-called *augment* (an *a-* prefix), is presented below

(9)

	Singular	*Dual*	*Plural*
First	barəm	barāuua	barāma
Second	barō	baratəm	barata
Third	barat̰	baratəm	barən

The subjunctive present active, which shows some variation as to whether or not it takes primary or secondary endings in some persons, is illustrated in (10):

(10)

	Singular	*Dual*	*Plural*
First	barāni	—	barāmahi
Second	barāhi	barātō	barāθa
Third	barāiti / barāt̰	barātō	barā̊n̩ti / baran̨

The optative active present of *bar* is as follows (the duals are not attested):

(11)

	Singular	*Plural*
First	—	baraēma
Second	barōiš	baraēta
Third	barōit̰	baraiiən

Avestan attests a large number of present stem classes and several different types of aorist and perfect. Again, readers are referred to the standard grammars of Avestan for further details.

Avestan, like Sanskrit, presents well-known difficulties in distinguishing between infinitivals and case forms (usually "datives") of verbal abstracts. The only infinitival form not directly traceable to a nominal case-form origin is the infinitive in *-diiāi*/*-δiiāi* (compare Sanskrit *-dhyai*), which may be built either to the verbal root (as in Gāthic *dərəidiiāi* "to hold" < *dar*) or to a present tense stem (as in Young Avestan *vazadiiāi* "to drive" < *vaz*, present tense stem *vaza-*). The bulk of the remaining infinitives of Avestan represent descendants of Proto-Indo-European "directives" in **-ay* built to a variety of verbal abstracts, including (i) root nouns (*buiie* "to become" < **b^{h}uH$_2$-ai*; Skt. *bhuvé*), built on the Avestan verbal root *bū*; (ii) *t*-abstracts (*stē* "to be" < **H$_1$s-t-ai*, built on the root *ah*; and (iii) *s*-abstracts (Gāthic *srāuuaiieŋhē* "to recite," as if from **k̂loweyes-ai*, built on the present causative stem *srāuuaiia-* of *sru-* "hear." Infinitives built on other abstracts (*men*-stems, *wen*-stems, and *ti*-stems, for example) are also attested.

The participle system is quite robustly attested. The present and aorist systems show participles in *-n̥t-/-at-* (added to the tense stem), continuing PIE **-ent-/-ont-/-n̥t-* participles. In the perfect system, the suffix is *-uuāh-* in the strong cases, and *-uš-* in the weak cases (cf. Skt. *-vāṁs-/-uṣ-*).

The PIE **-to*-participle (and its variant in **-no-*) is also well attested in Avestan, showing up normally with the zero-grade of the verbal root. It has a "passive" meaning with inherently transitive verbal roots and an active meaning with inherently intransitive ones, thus *kərəta-* "made" < *kar* "make" and *gata-* "gone" from *gam* "go". Proto-Indo-European **-no-* is found, for example, in *pərəna-* "filled" (i.e., "full") from **pl̥h$_1$no-* (with a root vocalism analogical to the nasal-infix present), built on the Avestan root *par* "fill" (cf. Skt. *pūrṇa-*).

4.5 Numerals

As in other archaic Indo-European languages, the numerals 1 to 4 are inflected for case and number (1 being invariably singular, 2 invariably dual, 3 and 4 invariably plural), while higher numerals up to 19 are not. The Young Avestan numbers 1–10 are as follows:

(12)	*1*	aēuua-	*6*	xšuuaš
	2	duua-	*7*	hapta
	3	θraii-, tišr- (fem.)	*8*	ašta
	4	caθβar-/ catur-, cataŋra- (fem.)	*9*	nauua
	5	paṇca	*10*	dasa

For the teens, compounds are used, much as in English. The second element of these compounds is *dasa*, thus 12 is *duua.dasa* and 15 is *paṇca.dasa*.

The decads 20 to 90 show a variety of formations and are generally inflected. The Young Avestan decads, with some revealing case forms provided, are presented below (see Hoffmann and Forssman 1996:175):

(13)	*20*	vīsąs, vīsaiti	*60*	xšuuašti-
	30	θrisąs, θrisatəm; θrisatanąm	*70*	haptāiti-
	40	caθβarəsatəm	*80*	aštāiti-
	50	paṇcāsatəm, paṇcāsatbīš-ca	*90*	nauuaiti-

Finally, the numerals 100 and 1,000 are inflected as regular *a*-stems, their stem-forms being: *sata-* 100 and *hazaŋra-* 1,000. A noninflecting numeral for 10,000, *baēuuarə*, is also found.

5. SYNTAX

5.1 Word order

The study of word order in Avestan reveals a typical archaic Indo-Iranian system, the "basic" order of which can be clearly determined only by a detailed investigation of a number of technical details. Such an investigation has not been fully undertaken for Avestan at this time. It is apparent that the placement of major nominal arguments of the verb – when they are not clitic pronouns or so-called WH-words (i.e., interrogatives and relatives) – is determined by a variety of pragmatic systems (topic, focus), rather than by the role of the argument in the clause (subject, object, etc.). While such systems are sometimes referred to as "free word order," it would be a mistake to take such a label too literally. Many restrictions on word order do in fact exist, one of the best known of which is *Wackernagel's Law* (see §5.2). Another, less well-known restriction, concerns the placement of WH-elements, relative pronouns, and complementizers. These elements always occur either sentence-initially, or with a single focused constituent to their left. The latter construction can be seen in the Old Avestan example (*Yasna* 28.1):

(14) vaŋhə̄uš xratūm manaŋhō yā xšnəuuīšā
good-GEN.SG. insight-ACC.SG. thought-GEN.SG. which-INSTR.SG. you may satisfy
gə̄uščā uruuąnəm
cow-GEN.SG.=and soul-ACC.SG.
"With which you may satisfy the insight of good thought and the soul of the cow"

In this example the noun phrase *vaŋhə̄uš xratūm manaŋhō* "the insight of good thought" has been fronted into sentence-initial position around the relative pronoun (*yā*) as a focusing process. Such constructions are much more rare in Iranian than in Indic, and are virtually limited, within Avestan, to Old Avestan texts. Nevertheless, their widespread occurrence in a wide variety of archaic Indo-European languages allows us to see these Old Avestan examples as a valuable syntactic archaism.

Given the highly restricted placement possibilities for WH-elements, it seems most profitable to posit that such items always occupy the same position in the clause (the so-called *complementizer* slot). They sometimes occur after a single focused constituent as a consequence of the fronting of that constituent for emphasis. Thus, like the Wackernagel's Law clitics, WH-elements are rigidly fixed in place. Word order is thus obviously not "free" in any meaningful sense.

5.2 Clitics

It is necessary to distinguish between three classes of clitic elements in archaic Indo-European languages, including Avestan (Hale 1987a and b). *Sentential clitics* include sentence-level connectives (the conjunction "and," Avestan *ca*, and the disjunction "or," Avestan *vā*) and adverbial particles. *Emphatic clitics*, such as Avestan *zī*, indicate focus on the element to which they attach. Finally, *pronominal clitics* are stressless versions of the personal pronouns, usually found in a limited number of case forms. A listing is provided in the discussion of pronominal morphology above. Each of these types of clitics is normally found in so-called second position. The observation that these elements show such a restricted distribution is credited to Bartholomae, who demonstrated the relevant phenomenon using Avestan data in his *Arische Forschungen* (1886). Wackernagel (1892) expanded the data set used by Bartholomae to include extensive materials from Sanskrit and Greek. From his study the phenomenon of second-position placement of clitics has come to be called Wackernagel's Law.

Each of the clitic types identified above occupies second position for rather different reasons and through distinct mechanisms, such that the definition of "second" turns out to vary somewhat with the class of clitic under discussion (Hale 1987b). Wackernagel's Law is thus the epiphenomenal by-product of a diverse set of processes. Crucial with respect to several of these processes is one overarching principle – that clitic elements, being prosodically deficient through their stresslessness, must not occur at the left edge of a (prosodic) constituent. If the syntax places the clitic in such a position, the prosodic phonology repositions the clitic rightward until it has an appropriately stressed host on its left. We can see the effects of this operation quite clearly in the case of conjunctive clitics like Avestan *ca* "and." Examine the following conjoined sentences, for example (from *Yašt* 19.51):

(15) A. ā.dim haθra haṇgəuruuaiiat̰ apąm napå̄ auruuat̰.aspō
preverb.him at once grabbed Apam Napat quick-horsed
"Quick-horsed Apam Napat grabbed at him at once"
B. tat̰.ca iziieiti apąm napå̄ auruuat̰.aspō
it.and desired Apam Napat quick-horsed
"and quick-horsed Apam Napat desired it"

It is clear that the sentence of (15) represents the conjunction of two clauses, the first one being *ā.dim haθra haṇgəuruuaiiat̰ apąm napå̄ auruuat̰.aspō*, the second *tat̰ iziieiti apąm napå̄ auruuat̰.aspō*. The conjunction itself (*ca*) is not part of the content of the second clause, but rather the link between the two (though of course it is related to the second clause, indicating that that clause is conjoined to what precedes). Thus, syntactically, we might identify the basic (i.e., underlying) structure of (15) as being something like the following:

(16) ā.dim haθra haṇgəuruuaiiat̰ apąm napå̄ auruuat̰.aspō [ca [tat̰ iziieiti apąm napå̄ auruuat̰.aspō]]

The syntactic structure gives rise to the following problem: a clause cannot begin with a clitic, which requires a host on its left, yet the second conjunct in (16) is a clause which begins with the clitic *ca*. The clitic thus is shifted phonologically rightward to the first available position which would give it an appropriate host – in this case to the spot immediately after *tat̰*. The result is the Wackernagel's Law placement of *ca* seen in (15B). This phonological process has been referred to as a "prosodic flip" (Halpern 1992).

In the case of emphatic clitics in Wackernagel's Law position, the facts are somewhat different. Avestan, like other archaic Indo-European languages, provides a number of mechanisms for emphasizing a particular constituent of the sentence. These include adding a particle, such as Avestan *cit̰* (Skt. *cit*), to the constituent, as in the following example (from *Yašt* 5.86):

(17) θβąm nara-cit̰ yōi taxma jaiδiiåṇte ...
you men-EMPHATIC.PARTICLE REL. bold entreat ...
"Even bold men entreat you ..."

The subject (*nara yōi taxma* "bold men") has been given a degree of emphasis by the addition of the particle *cit̰* (which takes second position within the subject noun phrase by the same "prosodic flip" processes described above). However, in this same sentence the direct object (*θβąm* "you" [acc. sg.]) has also been focused, in this case syntactically, by being fronted into clause-initial position. The pragmatics of the two processes of focusing can be somewhat distinct, as can be seen from the English translation of (17). However, since both addition of a particle and syntactic fronting encode emphasis, it is not surprising to find that sometimes both forms of emphasis are placed on the same element, which is then both accompanied by an emphatic particle and fronted into sentence-initial position. Indeed, the pragmatic force of some emphatic particles is such that they are only appropriately used when the element to which they attach is fronted. Such is the case with the Avestan emphatic particle *zī* (cognate with Sanskrit *hí*). An example of the use of this particle can be seen in the recurrent Avestan formula in (18):

(18) aēte	zī	vācō . . .	ahurō	mazdā̊	frāmraot̰	zaraθuštrāi
these	EMPHATIC.PARTICLE	words . . .	Ahura	Mazdā	spoke to	Zarathustra

"Ahura Mazdā spoke *these words* to Zarathustra"

The placement of an emphatic clitic such as *zī* works in the same ways as the placement of *cit̰* in (17) – such emphatic clitics take second position within the constituent being emphasized. In the case of the sentence in (18), that constituent is *aēte vācō* "these words" and second position within that constituent is the position immediately following *aēte*. When the entire constituent is fronted into clause-initial position, as is appropriate given the type of emphasis indicated by *zī*, it is clear that the emphatic clitic will end up – accidentally, as it were – in second position in the clause. The emphatic clitics thus appear to occupy the same position as the sentential clitics, when in fact somewhat different processes lie behind their placement.

The precise mechanism whereby pronominal clitics come to occupy second position is again somewhat different, though the details are far too complex and theory-dependent to warrant full treatment in the present discussion (see the essays in Halpern and Zwicky 1996 for interesting speculations on this matter). What is of relevance here, however, is that there are only rarely exceptions to second position placement of such pronominals in Avestan. Just as in Sanskrit, where the number of such exceptions steadily decreases between the earliest Rig-vedic hymns and the later Vedic Prose texts, Old Avestan offers a greater – though still small – number of exceptions to Wackernagel's Law positioning of pronominal clitics than does Young Avestan. The surviving exceptions in Young Avestan clearly represent archaisms and are themselves systematic – they involve cliticization to the verb, rather than the clause. A formulaic and often cited example, involving the first-person singular dative clitic *mē*, is given in (19):

(19) auuat̰	āiiaptəm	dazdi	mē
this	boon	grant	me

"Grant me this boon!"

Given these exceptions, Avestan will offer very real contributions to the much needed study of the diachronic development of the processes which underlie Wackernagel's Law in the archaic Indo-European languages. This domain has already proven to be one of the most productive for the study of Indo-European diachronic syntax.

6. LEXICON

One of the more interesting features of the Avestan lexicon is the split in a number of common vocabulary items between *daēuuic* and *ahurian* terms. The term *daēuua-* has come to refer to demonic beings in Avestan, in sharp contrast to the use in Sanskrit of the cognate word *deva-* to refer to the gods. It is of some interest to note in this context that the Sanskrit term *asura-*, clearly the cognate of Avestan *ahura-*, which forms part of the name of Ahura Mazdā "the Wise Lord," who is the god of the Zoroastrians, came, during the Vedic period, to refer to a set of demonic enemies of the gods (*deva-*; for a discussion of these interesting inversions, see Humbach 1991:21ff.). Daēuuic vocabulary items are used when reference is being made to the properties (usually body parts) or actions of manifestations of evil, the ahurian terms being used when referring to manifestations of good (the creations of Ahura Mazdā). Examples include the following:

(20)

Daēuuic term	*Ahurian term*	*Gloss*
duuar-	i-	"go"
gah-	x^var-	"eat"
aš(i)-	dōiθra-	"eye"
karəna-	gaoša-	"ear"

The fundamental role of dualism as a guiding principle of Zoroastrian thought is clearly evidenced by such lexical splits.

7. READING LIST

The most up-to-date and comprehensive grammar of Avestan is that of Hoffmann and Forssman 1996; the earlier grammar of Reichelt 1909, however, contains a detailed discussion of syntax and other matters not handled by later grammars. Beekes 1988 presents an idiosyncratic "interpretation" of the Old Avestan texts and should be used only by those familiar enough with Avestan philology to appreciate fully the implications of such an approach. All work on Avestan before that of Karl Hoffmann tends to misinterpret linguistically relevant phenomena as a superficial matter of orthographic convention. Hoffmann and Narten 1989 represents the most valuable work on the nature of the textual transmission of the Avesta. The only dictionary making any claim to completeness is Bartholomae 1904. Schlerath 1966, in spite of its name, is not a dictionary, but a set of tools for the study of textual repetitions and parallels, including Vedic parallels, as well as a passage-linked bibliography.

Geldner 1886–1896 is the standard edition of the core Avestan corpus, being based on a large number of valuable manuscripts since gone astray. There are a few texts which were excluded from Geldner's edition, including the *Aogəmadaēcā*, of which JamaspAsa 1982 provides an edition and translation. Translations of the Gāθās include Humbach *et al.* 1991, Insler 1975, and Kellens and Pirart 1988. An excellent overview of the difficulties involved in interpreting the Gāθās can be gained from the detailed treatment by three Iranists of a single hymn, *Yasna* 33, in Schmidt 1985. For Young Avestan texts, Gershevitch 1967 presents one of the Great Yašts (*Yašt* 10). Wolff 1960 presents the translation of the entire corpus which is contained in Bartholomae's (1904) dictionary – arranged in text order (rather than by keyword). Finally, Reichelt 1911 provides a number of Old and Young Avestan texts, with glossary and notes.

The texts represent the founding documents of Zoroastrianism, and it is therefore of considerable assistance to familiarize oneself with the fundamental doctrines and history of that religion before attempting to tackle them. Boyce 1979 provides a detailed survey of current practices.

Bibliography

Bartholomae, C. 1886. *Arische Forschungen*, vol. II. Halle: Niemeyer.

______. 1904. *Altiranishces Wörterbuch*. Strasburg: Trübner. Reprint (as a single volume together with Bartholomae's 1906 *Zum altiranischen Wörterbuch*) 1979. Berlin/New York.

Beekes, R. 1988. *A Grammar of Gatha-Avestan*. Leiden: Brill.

Boyce, M. 1979. *Zoroastrians: Their Religious Beliefs and Practices*. London: Routledge and Kegan Paul.

Geldner, K. 1886–1896. *Avesta: The Sacred Books of the Parsis*. Stuttgart: Kohlhammer.

Gershevitch, I. 1967. *The Avestan Hymn to Mithra*. Cambridge: Cambridge University Press.

Hale, M. 1987a. "Wackernagel's Law and the language of the Rigveda." In C. Watkins (ed.), *Studies in Memory of Warren Cowgill*. Berlin: de Gruyter.

______. 1987b. "Studies in the comparative syntax of the oldest Indo-Iranian Languages." Ph.D. dissertation, Harvard University.

Halpern, A. 1992. "Topics in the placement and morphology of clitics." Ph.D. dissertation, Stanford University.

Halpern, A. and A. Zwicky (eds.). 1996. *Approaching Second: Second Position Clitics and Related Phenomena*. Stanford: CSLI Publications.

Hoffmann, K. 1975–1976. *Aufsätze zur Indoiranistik* (2 vols.). Wiesbaden: Dr. Ludwig Reichert.

Hoffmann, K. and B. Forssman. 1996. *Avestische Laut- und Flexionslehre*. Innsbruck: Innsbrucker Beiträge zur Sprachwissenschaft.

Hoffmann, K. and J. Narten. 1989. *Der Sasanidische Archetypus*. Wiesbaden: Dr. Ludwig Reichert.

Humbach, H. (with J. Elfenbein and P. Skjaervø). 1991. *The Gāthās of Zarathustra* (2 vols.). Heidelberg: Carl Winter.

Insler, S. 1975. *The Gāthās of Zarathustra*. Leiden: Brill.

JamaspAsa, K. 1982. *Aogəmadaēcā: A Zoroastrian Liturgy*. Vienna: Austrian Academy of Sciences.

Kellens, J. 1984. *Le verbe avestique*. Wiesbaden: Dr. Ludwig Reichert.

Kellens, J. and E. Pirart. 1988. *Les textes vieil-avestiques*. Wiesbaden: Dr. Ludwig Reichert.

Kuiper, F. 1978. *On Zarathustra's Language*. Amsterdam: Noord-Hallandsche.

Mayrhofer, M. 1986ff. *Etymologisches Wörterbuch des Altindoarischen*. Heidelberg: Carl Winter.

Narten, J. 1986. *Der Yasna Haptaŋhāiti*. Wiesbaden: Dr. Ludwig Reichert.

Reichelt, H. 1909. *Awestisches Elementarbuch*. Heidelberg: Carl Winter.

______. 1911. *Avestan Reader*. Strasburg: Trübner. Reprint 1968. Berlin: de Gruyter.

Schlerath, B. 1966. *Awesta-Wörterbuch: Vorarbeiten I–II*. Wiesbaden: Otto Harrassowitz.

Schmidt, H-P. (with contributions by W. Lentz and S. Insler). 1985. *Form and Meaning of Yasna 33*. New Haven: American Oriental Society.

Schmitt, R. (ed.). 1989. *Compendium Linguarum Iranicarum*. Wiesbaden: Dr. Ludwig Reichert.

Tavadia, J. 1956. *Die Mittelpersische Sprach und Literatur der Zarathustrier*. Leipzig: Otto Harrassowitz.

Wackernagel, J. 1892. "Über ein Gesetz der indogermanischen Wortstellung." *Indogermanische Forschungen* 1:333–436.

Wolff, F. 1960. *Avesta: Die heiligen Bücher der Parsen, Übersetz auf der Grundlage von Chr. Bartholomae's Altiranischem Wörterbuch*. Berlin: de Gruyter.

CHAPTER 7

Pahlavi

MARK HALE

1. HISTORICAL AND CULTURAL CONTEXTS

The term *Pahlavi* is used to describe a variety of closely related Middle Iranian languages, including a more archaic variety – the language of early inscriptions – and a more innovative one, so-called *Book Pahlavi.* Given the sparseness of attestation of the earliest varieties of Pahlavi, this sketch will focus on Book Pahlavi, which is in fact quite richly attested. Book Pahlavi is the name generally used to designate that particular variety of Western Middle Iranian used in Zoroastrian writings. Its use in this function covers both a long temporal span (the third century BC to the eighth/ninth century AD) and a broad geographic area. Given this spatio-temporal range, it can be safely assumed that the language showed considerable variation, particularly in the phonological domain. However, the archaizing writing system in which virtually all of our Pahlavi records survive remained quite stable throughout this period and in these diverse regions. Many details of the interpretation of the Pahlavi records thus remain somewhat speculative, our sketches doubtless (inadvertently, of course) combining features of diverse temporal (and perhaps geographical) strata.

The "golden age" of Pahlavi was almost certainly the third to seventh centuries AD, during which time it served as the "standard" language of the Sasanian realms, both for government and for commerce. The Pahlavi corpus includes texts from an impressively broad range of genres, including (but not limited to) royal inscriptions, encyclopedia-like collections (e.g., the *Bundahišn*), texts of religious instruction and worship, legal documents (both laws and instruments), historical texts, and translations.

2. WRITING SYSTEM

The Pahlavi writing system is derived from a cursive Aramaic script. Like Aramaic, the script runs right to left and vowels are not written. As noted in Chapter 6 (see §2), the Pahlavi script formed the basis for the Avestan script, which represents an elaboration of the earlier writing system for the purposes of capturing details of hieratic recitation. The Pahlavi writing system includes a number of symbols which carry multiple values (e.g., a single symbol is used to represent *w*, *n*, and *r*; similarly, a single symbol stands for *g*, *d*, and *y*); moreover, many of the combined forms of individual signs are identical in shape to either simplex or combined forms of other signs. When coupled with the lack of vowel symbols, these factors make the orthography highly ambiguous. In practice, remarkably, the many ambiguities rarely impede interpretation.

Table 7.1 The Pahlavi script

		Transliteration		
	Character	Segmental Pahlavi	Aramaic-based logogram	"Corrupt"
1	ىد	ʾ	A, H	—
2	ـد	b	B	ḡ, d̲, ȳ
3	د د	g, d, y	G, D, Y	b̲, z̲, k̲, B̲, Z̲, K̲
4	ﻌ	—	E	—
5	١	w, n, r, ʿ	W, N, O, R, ʿ	—
6	S	z	Z	G̲, D̲, Y̲
7	ﺩ	k	K	—
8	٢	(ɣ)	K	—
9	ﻜ ﺩ	l	L	—
10	ٮ	(ɫ)	Ł	—
11	ـ٤	m	M, Q	—
12	ىد ـى	s	S	—
13	ى	p	P	—
14	ﻪ ﻉ	c	C	P̲, p̄
15	ـىد	š	Š	—
16	٢ ﻌ	t	T	D̲, R̲

The symbols used in Pahlavi writing, including both those used in the regular Iranian vocabulary and those used in Aramaic-derived logograms (on which see below), can be found in Table 7.1. On occasion (usually in specific lexical items), a "reduced" form of certain letters is used – MacKenzie (1971) calls these *corrupt.* They are transliterated by the addition of a bar to the letter used to transliterate the nonreduced glyph.

To understand the Pahlavi script, it is necessary to distinguish carefully between a *transliteration* and a *transcription.* Because of the great ambiguities present in the Pahlavi writing system, both of these representations involve an interpretation, rather than simple remapping, of the graphic sequence. In the case of a *transliteration,* the number of symbols in the transliterated string is the same as the number of symbols in the Pahlavi string – but the mapping is not one-to-one. Since, as mentioned above, in some cases an individual Pahlavi character may represent any of a number of segments, the scholar responsible for the transliteration must make a decision about which of these segments is being represented. By contrast, in the case of a *transcription,* the word itself is interpreted phonemically. A standard target "stage" in the historical development of Pahlavi is used to establish this phonemic representation (usually the third century AD) – the vowels are inserted and the archaizing practices of the script are "corrected for" such that the representation reaches the form believed to be an accurate phonemic representation for this historical stage.

An example will make this clearer. The Pahlavi orthographic sequence [ﻪ١د] consists of character 3 from Table 7.1, followed by character 5, followed by character 14. Since character 3 can represent either Pahlavi *g*, *d*, or *y* (ignoring its use in so-called "corrupt" characters), and character 5 can represent, in this position in the word, either *w*, *n*, or *r*, a number of distinct *transliterations* are available for this sequence, including, for example, *dwc*, *gnc*, *gwc*, and *ywc*. Each of these transliterations (which will henceforth be represented in square brackets; care should be taken to distinguish between square brackets in this use and their use for representing allophones in the phonological discussions of §3) can then be interpreted in light of current hypotheses regarding the phonemic system of Pahlavi and what is known about the phonology of the lexeme in question, giving, in these cases, the following *transcriptions* respectively (see MacKenzie 1971): *duz* [*dwc*] "thief," *ganǰ* [*gnc*] "treasure," *gōz* [*gwc*] "walnut," and *yōz* [*ywc*] "cheetah." One should not, therefore, confuse the transliteration of Pahlavi with the usual transliteration of, for example, ancient Greek into Roman characters. The latter involves a fixed mapping between individual characters in the Greek writing system and individual characters in the Roman alphabet (with added diacritics). Such transliterations are purely mechanical and can be handled by individuals (or computers) with no knowledge of Greek. Pahlavi transliteration is a more interpretive procedure, not at all mechanical. Words frequently cannot be transliterated in isolation from their textual context.

The writing system reached a relatively fixed state at what appears to be quite an early date – perhaps by the third century BC, almost certainly by the second. Since many of the surviving texts were composed well after this date, the script may be, and has been, labeled "archaizing," in other words reflective of a much earlier pronunciation than that in use at the time of writing (as is the case, for example, with the present writing system of English). Moreover, since words written for the first time in the later period are made to fit the "archaic" patterns established for earlier vocabulary, the writing system is frequently "pseudo-archaizing," giving the words a historical shape which they, in fact, never had.

Pahlavi scribes frequently used Aramaic-based logograms in place of Iranian lexical items, particularly for verbs and a number of "function" words. That these masks were purely a feature of the orthography – standing in for Iranian words much as Hittite scribes used Akkadian and Sumerian graphic sequences to stand in for Hittite words – and not, for example, loanwords is made quite clear by the utter absence of Aramaic loanwords in Middle Iranian texts transmitted in other scripts (including Manichean Middle Persian, Parthian, and Pazend), as well as by manuscript variants (some of which contain the native Iranian word, others the Aramaic "mask"). These logograms are transliterated in all capital letters, thus the logogramic representation of Pahlavi *duxt* [dwht′] "daughter" is transliterated BRTE (from Aramaic *brt-h*). The logograms representing verb forms are regularly accompanied by the appropriate Pahlavi inflectional ending, giving a mixed orthographic representation: for example, YB̲LWN-*yt′*, with the logogram YB̲LWN "carry" (from Aramaic *ybl*) and the Pahlavi third singular present indicative ending, the entire written form standing for Pahlavi *barēd* "he carries."

3. PHONOLOGY

3.1 Phonemic inventory

The phonemic inventory for Pahlavi of roughly the third century AD is, in its general outlines, not highly controversial.

3.1.1 Consonants

The consonant phonemes are presented in Table 7.2; of these, phonemic ɣ and ž are limited to what appear to be learned loanwords, for the most part from Avestan.

The voiced stops and affricates (/b/, /d/, /ǰ/, and /g/) in the table are generally assumed to have had voiced fricative allophones ([β], [ð], [ž], and [ɣ], respectively). The precise

Table 7.2 Consonantal sounds of Pahlavi

	Place of articulation					
Manner of articulation	Labial	Dental/ Alveolar	Palato-alveolar	Palatal	Velar	Glottal
Stop						
Voiceless	p	t			k	
Voiced	b	d			g	
Fricative						
Voiceless	f	s	š		x	h
Voiced		z	ž		ɣ	
Affricate						
Voiceless			č			
Voiced			ǰ			
Nasal	m	n				
Liquid		l, r				
Glide	w			y		

conditioning of these allophones clearly varied somewhat over time, it being generally accepted that this spirantization took place in the first instance in postvocalic, preconsonantal position (V_C): for example, in a word like *abd* [*'p̄d*] "wonderful" (the square brackets here marking a *transliteration*; see §2), which is taken to have been pronounced with a medial [β]. The voiced fricative allophones were eventually, perhaps by the third or fourth century AD, the usual realization of the voiced stops in all postvocalic positions.

3.1.2 Vowels

The vowels include the following:

	FRONT	*CENTRAL*	*BACK*
HIGH	i, ī		u, u¯
MID	(e), ē		(o), ō
LOW		a, ā	

Figure 7.1 Pahlavi vowels

As indicated by the parentheses in the figure above, the phonemic status of the short mid vowels is not at present entirely clear.

3.2 Interesting and significant diachronic developments

The Iranian voiceless unaspirated stops are generally preserved as such in word-initial position (PIIr. is Proto-Indo-Iranian; PIr. is Proto-Iranian):

(1) pid [AB′, p(y)t′] "father" < PIIr. *pətā (Av. pitā)
tār [t'l] "darkness" < PIr. *tantra- (Av. tąθra-)
kōf [kwp] "hill" < PIr. *kaufa- (Av. kaofa-)

as well as in word-internal position when following a voiceless fricative:

(2) asp [SWSYA, ʼsp̄] "horse" < PIr. *aspa- < PIIr. *aću̯a- (Av. aspa-)
hušk [hwšk′] "dry" < PIr. *huška- (Av. huška-)

After *r* and the vowels, the voiceless stops have become voiced:

(3) kirb [klp] "body, form" < PIIr. *kr̥pa- (Av. kəhrpa-)
nab [np] "grandson" < PIIr. *napāt- (Av. napāt-)
sard [slt′] "cold" < PIIr. *ćarta- (Av. sarəta-)
pad [PWN] "to, at, in" < PIIr. *pati (Av. paiti)
gurg [gwlg] "wolf" < PIIr. *wr̥ka- (Av. vəhrka-)

Following nasals the voiceless stops have become voiced as well, though it is of some interest to note that the Pahlavi orthography actually writes the postnasal stops as voiced, while, as the examples above show, in its characteristically archaizing style, it writes the postvocalic and post-*r* stops as voiceless: *frazand* [*przn̲d*] "child" (cf. Av. *frazaiṇti-*). This has generally been taken as evidence that the voicing after nasals was earlier than that in other positions.

The Indo-Iranian affricate **č* (< PIE *k, *k^w in palatalizing environments) shows similar developments. Preserved in word-initial position (*čarm* [*clm*] "leather," cf. Av. carəman-), it is voiced after nasals (*panǰ* [*pnc*] "five," cf. Av. *paṇca*). However, it becomes /z/ after vowels and after *r*:

(4) az [MN, hc] "from" (Av. haca)
rōz [rwc] "day" < PIr. *raučah- (Av. raocah-)

The Indo-Iranian affricate **ć* (for PIE *$\hat{k}$) is reflected in Pahlavi, as in Avestan, as *s*:

(5) sad [100] "hundred" < PIIr. *ćata- (Av. sata-)
suxr [swhl] "red" < *PIIr. *ćukra- (Av. suxra-)

In general, the Iranian voiced stops are preserved, though as pointed out above they had fricative allophones in a variety of positions:

(6) baxt [bht′] "fate, fortune" < PIr. *baxta- (Av. baxta-)
abr [ʻbl,ʼpl] "cloud" < PIr. *abra- (Av. aβra-)
dēn [dyn′] "religion" < PIr. *dainā- (Av. daēnā-)
nazd [nzd] "near" < PIr. *nazda- (cf. Av. nazdišta- 'nearest')
garm [glm] "warm" < PIr. *garma- (Av. garəma-)
mazg [mzg] "marrow, brain" < PIr. *mazga- (Av. mazga-)

Proto-Iranian **b* is lenited to Pahlavi *w* when originally intervocalic (OP is Old Persian):

(7) nēw [nyw′] "good, brave" < PIr. *naiba- (OP naiba-)
aswār [ʼswbʼl, ʼspwʼl] "rider" < PIr. *aspa-bāra- "horse-born"

Additionally, Proto-Iranian **g* is weakened to *w* when intervocalic (even if **r* precedes):

(8) murw [mwlw′] "bird" < PIr. *mr̥ga- (Av. ᴍərəɣa-)
mowbēd [mgwpt′] "Mazdean priest" < PIr. *magu-pati- (cf. OP magu- "priest")

The Indo-Iranian voiced affricates **ǰ* (from palatalized voiced velars) and **ȷ́* (from PIE voiced palatal stops) are both realized as *z* in Pahlavi:

(9) zan [NYŠE, zn'] "woman, wife" < PIIr. *ǰani- (Av. jani-)
zofr [zwpl] "deep" < PIIr. *ǰafra- (Av. jafra-)
zand [znd] "district" < PIIr. *ǰantu- (Av. zaṇtu-)
zrēh [zlyh] "sea" < PIIr. *ǰrayah- (Av. zraiiah-)

The vowel developments from Proto-Iranian to Pahlavi are quite straightforward. Iranian *a and *ā are generally preserved as such:

(10) ast ['st'] "bone" < PIr. *ast- (Av. ast-)
tan [tn'] "body" < PIr. *tanū- (Av. tanū-)
kām [k'm] "desire" < PIr. *kāma- (Av. kāma-)
āb ['p'] "water" < PIr. *āp- (Av. āp-)

As part of certain consonant cluster simplifications Proto-Iranian *a shows compensatory lengthening to Pahlavi *ā*:

(11) hazār [hc'l] "thousand" < PIr. *hazahra- (Av. hazaŋra-)
sāl [s'l] "year" < PIr. *sard- (Av. sarəd-)
māl- [m'l-] "rub, sweep" < PIr. *marz- (Av. marəz-)

A number of sequences involving intervocalic glides lose their glides and show vowel coalescence such that Pahlavi *ā* results:

(12) *āwa: srāy- [sl'd-] "sing" < PIr. *srāwaya- (causative of sru "hear")
*awā: bād [b't'] "may be" < *bawāti (Av. bauuāiti)
Pretonic *āwi: āškārag ['šk'lk'] "obvious, evident" < PIr. *āwiš-kāra-ka- "made manifest"

The high vowels as well are generally preserved as such, both long and short:

(13) *i: tigr [tgl] "arrow" < PIr. *tigra- (Av. tiɣra-)
*ī: wīr [wyl] "hero" < PIr. *wīra- (Av. vīra-)
*u: pus [pws] "son" < PIr. *puθra- (Av. Puθra-)
*ū: stūn [stwn'] "column" < PIr. *stūna- (Av. stūna-)

The Proto-Iranian diphthong *ai gives Pahlavi *ē*:

(14) ēw [1] "one" < PIr. *aiwa- (Av. aēuua-)
wēn- [wyn-] "see" < PIr. *waina- (Av. vaēna-)

In addition, several sequences involving the palatal glide result in Pahlavi *ē* as well:

(15) *aya: sē [3] "three" < PIr. *θraya-
-ēd 3rd sg. pres. tense verbal ending < PIr. *-ayati
*ahya: kē [MNW] "who" < PIr. *kahya "whose" (O.Av. kahiiā, Y.Av. kahe)
*arya: ēr ['yl] "noble" < PIr. arya- (Av. airiia-)

In a strongly parallel manner, the Proto-Iranian diphthong *au and the sequence *awa yield Pahlavi *ō*:

(16) gōš [gwš] "ear" < PIr. *gauša- (Av. gaoša-)
nōg [nwk'] "new" < PIr. *nawa-ka- (cf. Av. nauua- "new")

Finally, Proto-Iranian *r̥ is reflected in the majority of cases by Pahlavi *ur* (though occasionally Pahlavi *ir* is found):

(17) purs- [pwrs-] "ask" < PIr. *pr̥sa- (Av. pərəsa-)
wazurg [wzlg] "big" < PIr. *wazr̥ka- (OP vazarka-)
buland [bwlnd] "high" < PIr. *br̥zant- (Av. bərəzaṇt-)

It should be apparent from the above examples that Pahlavi has suffered serious "erosion from the right" – the final syllables (or at least their codas) having more or less uniformly disappeared. The set of developments which gave rise to this loss – a function of the development of strong dynamic stress – are clearly implicated in the massive morphological (and syntactic) restructuring which Pahlavi has undergone.

4. MORPHOLOGY

4.1 Morphological type

Not surprisingly, given the extensive erosion from the right that words have suffered in the phonological history of Middle Iranian, Pahlavi is much more isolating than its Indo-European inflectional forebears, virtually nothing but traces remaining of the elaborate nominal (case, gender, number) and verbal (tense, aspect, mood) morphological systems of Proto-Indo-Iranian.

4.2 Nominal morphology

The nominal inflection system of Old Iranian, with numerous distinct stem-types each showing a somewhat different pattern of inflection, was clearly eliminated in the early stages of Middle Iranian. It is generally held that this system was reduced to two cases, usually called the *casus rectus* (deriving from the earlier nominative) and the *casus obliquus* (from the earlier genitive), and two numbers (a singular and plural, the dual having vanished). The inflection of nominals, with generalization of the *a*-stem endings to the other stem-classes of Iranian, thus took the following form:

(18)

	Singular	*Plural*
Casus rectus	asp < PIr. *aspah (nom. sg.)	asp < PIr. *aspāh (nom. pl.)
Casus obliquus	aspē < PIr. *aspahya (gen. sg.)	aspān < PIr. *aspānām (gen. pl)

The distinctive oblique case-marker in the singular was apparently lost early, with a merger of the rectus/obliquus contrast in the singular. The -*ān* plural subsequently came to be used in both cases in the plural, though both forms (those with -ø and those with -*ān*) are found in both cases in most Pahlavi texts. Various factors appear to favor explicit marking of plurality, including animacy (animate nouns are more likely to have explicitly marked plurals) and whether or not the verb form in the clause unambiguously indicates the number of its subject.

In general, the surviving nominal stem-form in Pahlavi looks like the old oblique without its case ending in -*ē*. In a few cases, however, mostly involving Old Iranian *r*-stem kinship terms, Pahlavi shows both a reflex of the earlier rectus and a reflex of the earlier oblique. For example, the word for "father" is attested both in a form which must have originally been the rectus case (*pid* [*AB'*, *p(y)t'*] < PIr. **pitā*, nom. sg.) and in a form which must have originally been the oblique (*pidar* [*ABYtl*, *pytl*], ultimately – after morphological elimination of the oblique -*ē* case ending – from PIr. **pitarahya*, genitive singular, with the ending generalized from the *a*-stems). The stem-doublets do not appear to be distributed systematically in the bulk of the surviving Book Pahlavi texts, though detailed philological work in this area remains a desideratum. Additional examples include the following:

(19) mād [AM] next to mādar [AMYtl, m'tl] "mother"
brād [AH, bl't'] next to brādar [bl'tl] "brother"
xwah [AHTE] next to xwahar [AHTEl, hw'hl] "sister"
duxt [BRTE, dwht'] next to duxtar [dwhtl] "daughter"

In other cases, it is clear that the old nominative case form (rather than the old oblique) is the one that survives in Pahlavi. This usually involves what were originally neuter *r*/*n*-stems. Examples include the following:

(20) A. kišwar [kyšwl] "region" (Av. nom. sg. karšuuarə, weak cases made to the stem karšuuan-)
B. zafar [zpl] "mouth" (daevic only) (Av. nom. sg. zafarə, oblique not directly attested, but doubtless an *n*-stem)
C. ǰagar [ykl] "liver" (Av. nom. sg. yākarə, oblique also not directly attested)

Since the final *-r* of the Pahlavi lexical items was originally found only in the nominative – the obliques having *-n* in its stead (in the well-known Indo-European pattern) – it must be the *casus rectus* which has been generalized in these lexemes.

4.3 Pronominal morphology

As was originally the case with nominals, the Pahlavi pronominal system showed a reduction of the rich case system of Proto-Iranian to a simple *casus rectus* : *casus obliquus* system. This system was further reduced, except in the first-person singular, to a single form. Pahlavi distinguishes between tonic and enclitic pronouns in first (oblique), second, and third person:

(21)

		Tonic	*Enclitic*
Singular	*1. Rectus*	az (?) [ANE]	—
	1. Oblique	man [L]	-m
	2	tō [LK]	-t
	3	ōy [OLE]	-š
Plural	1.	amā [LNE]	-mān
	2.	ašmā [LKWM]	-tān
	3.	awēšān [OLEš'n]	-šān

The reading of the first singular rectus form is not entirely clear, some scholars favoring *az*, others *an*. Note that the enclitic plural forms appear to be derived from the enclitic singulars (themselves corresponding more or less directly to Av. *mē*, *tē*, and the RUKI-induced [see Ch. 6, §3.4.4] *šē* realization of the third singular *hē*) by the addition of the nominal pluralizer *-ān*.

4.4 Verbal morphology

Pahlavi verbs are inflected for person, number, tense, and mood, though most of these categories are significantly reduced relative to the rich systems present in Old Iranian. With respect to number, there is no trace of the Old Iranian dual endings. The tense system has been reduced to a simple present versus preterite (past) stem (the latter built on the PIE

**to*-particle), with the loss of the imperfect, the aorist, and the perfect of Old Iranian. In Book Pahlavi, the moods (subjunctive and optative) are attested in only limited distribution, being wholly unattested for certain persons.

In general, the inflection of the present indicative is to be traced back to Old Iranian **aya*-presents, the endings being characterized by the vowel *ē* < PIr. **-aya-*. There is some debate regarding the etymological status of endings which have instead the vowels *a* or *o* – some scholars (e.g., Nyberg) believe these reflect Old Iranian simple thematic verbs, others (e.g., Tedesco, Sundermann) that they represent innovations within the history of Pahlavi.

The endings of the present indicative are as follows:

(22)

	Singular	*Plural*
First	-ēm [-ym], -am [-m], -om [-wm]	-ēm [-ym], -am [-m], -om [-wm]
Second	-ē(h) [-yd̲, -yh]	-ēd [-yt′]
Third	ēd [-yt′], -at [-t′]	-ēnd [-ynd], -and [-nd]

The inflection of the verb *būdan* [*YHWWNtn′*, *bwtn′*] "to be" shows a mixture of forms, some coming from the cognate of Avestan *bauuaiti* "is, becomes" (Pahlavi present stem *baw-*), some corresponding to Avestan *asti/hə̣nti* "is"/"are" (Pahlavi present stem *h-*). In many instances, forms from both stems are found:

Table 7.3 Pahlavi verb inflection

		STEM	
		baw-	*h-*
Indicative			
Singular	*1.*	bawam [YHWWNm]	hom [HWEwm], ham [HWEm], hēm [HWEym]
	2.	bawē [YHWWNyd̲, -yh]	hē [HWE′ybd̲, -yh]
	3.	bawēd [YHWWNyt′], bēd [byt′]	hast [′YT′]
Plural	*1.*	bawēm [YHWWNym]	hēm [HWE′ym]
	2.	bawēd [YHWWNyt′]	hēd [HWE′yt′]
	3.	bawēnd [YHWWNd]	hēnd [HWEnd]
Subjunctive			
Singular	*2.*	bawāi [bwp′y]	hāi [HWE′′y], hāh [HWE′′h], hā [HWE′′]
	3.	bawād [YHWWN(′)t′], bād [b′t′]	hād [HWE′′t′], hat [HWEt]
Plural	*2.*	bawād [YHWWN′t′]	
	3.	—	hānd [HWEnd]
Optative			
Singular	*3.*	—	hē [HWE′yd̲, HWEd]
Infinitive		būdan [YHWWNtn′, bwtn′]	
Past		būd [YHWWNt′, bwt′]	

Although there is a basic uniformity in the inflectional endings found on Pahlavi verbs, something of the richness of the Proto-Indo-Iranian verbal system can still be seen in the great diversity of formal relationships holding between the present stem and the infinitive. The Pahlavi present stem often reflects aspects of the Proto-Indo-Iranian present class of which the verbal root was a member. For example, Avestan has as the general present stem of the verbal root x^v*ap-* "sleep" (PIE **swep-*) the reflex of a Proto-Indo-European *-*s̑ke/o-* "inchoative": namely, x^v*afsa-*. This root makes a normal past participle of the Proto-Indo-European *-*to*-type: thus, x^v*apta-*. These forms correspond directly to the Pahlavi present/infinitive stem pair *xufs- : xuftan* [*hwps- : HLMWNtn′, hwptn′*], where the *s* of the present stem can only be motivated by a historical account. Analogies between the infinitival stem (generally identical to the past tense form) and the present stem are common: corresponding to the *s*-inchoative present stem *purs-* [*pwrs-*] "ask" (Av. *pərəsa-* < PIE **pr̥k̑-s̑ke/o-*) is the infinitive *pursīdan* [*pwrsytn′*], clearly analogically remade, since it contains the derivational affix -*s*, originally limited to the present system. In other cases, the present stem appears to have been analogically remade based on the infinitive (or past) stem.

Traces of a wide range of the present-tense formation categories of Old Indo-Iranian can be seen in this way in Pahlavi. Some examples include the following:

1. *Zero-grade thematic presents*: for example, *kuš- : kuštan* [*kwš- : NKSWNtn′, kwštn′*] "kill" (cf. the Avestan present stem *kuša-*)
2. *Full-grade thematic presents*: for example, *yaz- : yaštan* [*yc- : YḎBHWNtn′, yštn′*] "worship" (cf. Av. present stem *yaza-* : past participle *yašta-*)
3. *Lengthened-grade causatives*: for example, *tāz- : tāxtan* [*t'c- : t'htn′*] "cause to run" (as if from Old Iranian **tācaya-*)
4. *Reduplicated presents*: for example, *dah- : dādan* [*dh- : YHBWNtn′, d'tn′*] "give, create" (cf. Av. present stem *daδā-* : past participle *dāta-*)
5. *Nasal-infix presents*: for example, *hanǰ- : hixtan* [*hnc- : hyhtn′*] "draw [water]" (cf. Av. present stem *hiṇca-* : past participle *hixta-*)

In some cases, the present stem and infinitive came to diverge considerably, as in *ōft- : ōbastan* [*'wpt- : NPLWNstn′, 'wpstn′*] "fall"

The present stem here reflects an Iranian **awa-pta-* (cf. the Avestan present stem-forms in *pta-* for the root *pat-* "fall"), with zero-grade of the root. By contrast, the infinitive (built like the *to*-participle, as usual) shows the preconsonantal full-grade of the root, coming thus from **awa-pasta-* (**pasta-* being from **pat-ta-*, with the usual Iranian treatment of Proto-Indo-European **tt*-clusters).

In terms of synchronic morphology – rather than the traces of Iranian morphology which have become lexicalized by the time of Pahlavi – there is a productive causative suffix -*ēn*-, no doubt originally denominative, seemingly from *-*anya-*. It is added to the present stem: for example, *abzāy- : abzūdan* [*'p̄z'd- : 'p̄zwtn′*] "increase, grow" → *abzāyēnēd* [*'p̄z'dynyt′*] "makes increase, makes grow."

The preterite (or past) tense, as indicated in passing above, was built from the Proto-Indo-European **to*-participle, being used in periphrastic constructions with auxiliary verbs such as *budan* "be/become," *h-* "be," and *ēstādan* "stand." The **to*-participle had the property of being *active* in interpretation with intransitive verbs, but *passive* with transitive verbs. Using the intransitive verb *šudan* "go" and the transitive verb *kardan* "do, make" as examples, the interpretation of these various periphrases was as follows (cf. Brunner 1977:213ff.):

(23)

	Intransitive verb	*Transitive verb*
Simple preterite	šud h- "went"	kard h- "was made"
Perfect	šud ēst- "has gone"	kard ēst- "has been made"
Pluperfect	šud būd h- "had gone"	kard būd h- "had been made"

The forms of the verb *h-* "to be" were optional in this construction and not normally expressed.

Given this method of constructing preterites, the issue of how to express the past tense of a simple *active* transitive verb arises. That is, what corresponds in the past tense to the present tense clause *awēšān kušēm* "I slay them"? It seems clear that in Pahlavi the relevant construction was *man kušt hēnd* "they were slain by me," though it remains somewhat unclear whether the meaning of this construction was, for the Pahlavi speaker, passive (as I have expressed in my translation) or active (i.e., "I slew them"). Hand-in-hand with this lack of clarity as to the real interpretation of this construction is a lack of clarity as to its syntactic structure (is it an ergative-like structure or a passive one?). It seems likely that there is no one resolution to these matters for "Pahlavi" in all its temporal, geographical, and stylistic diversity.

4.5 Numerals

The Pahlavi numerals 1 to 10 are presented below:

(24) *1*	ēk ['ywk']	*6*	šaš [ŠTA]
2	dō [TLYN']	*7*	haft [hp̄t']
3	sē [TLTA]	*8*	hašt [hšt']
4	čahār [ALBA, ch'l]	*9*	nō [TŠA]
5	panǰ [pnc]	*10*	dah [ASLYA]

The decads generally reflect the diverse formations found in Proto-Indo-Iranian (and Proto-Indo-European) for this function (many of the higher numbers are represented only by digits, not spelled out, in the texts):

(25) *20*	wīst [wyst']	*70*	haftād
30	sīh	*80*	haštād
40	čehel	*90*	nawad
50	panǰā [pnc'h]	*100*	sad
60	šast	*1,000*	hazār [hc'l]

The attested ordinals include:

(26) *1st*	fradom [AWLA, pltwm]	*6th*	šašom [6wm]
2nd	dudīgar [dtykl]	*7th*	haftom [7wm]
3rd	sidīg(ar) [styk', stykl]	*8th*	haštom [8wm]
4th	čahārom [ch'lwm]	*9th*	nohom [9wm, nhwm]
5th	panǰom [5wm]	*10th*	dahom [dhwm]

5. SYNTAX

5.1 Word order

The loss of the elaborate case system of Old Iranian has, not surprisingly, led to a considerably more restrictive use of word order in Pahlavi. The "normal" order – in the sense both that it is statistically most common and that it involves no particular pragmatic focus on any element of the sentence – is *Subject–Object–Verb*. The possibility of fronting elements from within the verbal complex to sentence-initial position for emphasis of some type (not at this time explored in any great detail) certainly exists.

A regular exception to this ordering statement arises in the case of arguments expressed by the enclitic personal pronouns presented above (see §4.3). These elements tend strongly to occur in *Wackernagel's Law position* (i.e., after the first constituent of their clause) regardless of their syntactic function. When used in subject function, they are often redundant, as in (27):

(27)	guft-aš	Ohrmazd	ō	Spitāmān	Zarduxšt
	gwptš	'whrmzd	'L	spyt'm'n	zltwhšt
	spoke-he	Ohrmazd	to	Spitāmān	Zarduxšt

"Ohrmazd said to Spitāmān Zarduxšt"

This example also shows the fronting of the verb to sentence-initial position. The "unmarked" order of such a sentence, without the redundant enclitic pronominal *-aš*, would be as follows:

(28)	Ohrmazd	ō	Spitāmān	Zarduxšt	guft
	'whrmzd	'L	spyt'm'n	zltwhšt	gwpt
	Ohrmazd	to	Spitāmān	Zarduxšt	spoke

"Ohrmazd said to Spitāmān Zarduxšt"

No deep understanding of the pragmatic differences indicated by the order in (27) versus that in (28) has as yet been attained, nor is it generally understood why, in the case of this particular clause (in which the creator makes a pronouncement of religious significance to the prophet Zoroaster), the "marked" order in (27) is in fact regular.

6. READING LIST

The standard dictionary for Pahlavi, which includes the necessary tools to allow one to actually decipher the script as well, is that of MacKenzie 1971. Those attempting to read Pahlavi texts are also likely to find the glossaries in Nyberg 1964 and Boyce 1977 of considerable assistance. For inscriptions, the necessary lexical material can be found in Gignoux 1972.

There is no comprehensive grammatical description of Pahlavi, though considerable historical and descriptive information can still be usefully gleaned from Salemann 1895–1901. Beyond this, there is a grammatical sketch in Nyberg 1964, an extensive discussion of a variety of syntactic issues in Brunner 1977, and scattered observations on grammar in the various "survey" articles (Henning 1958, Sundermann 1989).

Extensive text editions from a wide range of genres with, in some cases, quite detailed notes can be found in Nyberg 1964. Boyce 1975 presents a wealth of Manichaean Middle Persian (and Parthian) texts, the basic grammatical structure of which differs only in matters of fine detail from that presented here. For specific texts see, for example, Gignoux 1984 and Humbach and Skjaervø 1978–1983. Tavadia 1956 and Boyce 1968 present useful surveys of just what types of texts are found in the corpus.

Finally, Dresden 1966 presents one of a number of Pahlavi manuscripts – this one of the very significant text known as the Denkart – which are available in facsimile. Such facsimile editions are more critical than usual in this field, where disputes about the details of the interpretation of what is written on the page are inevitable.

Bibliography

Bartholomae, C. 1904. *Altiranisches Wörterbuch.* Strasburg: Trübner. Reprint (as a single volume together with Bartholomae's 1906 *Zum altiranischen Wörterbuch*) 1979. Berlin/New York.

Boyce, M. 1958. "Middle Persian literature." In *Iranistik*, 2 Literatur, pp. 67–76. Handbuch der Orientalistik I. Leiden: Brill.

_______. 1975. *A Reader in Manichaean Middle Persian and Parthian: Texts with Notes.* Leiden: Brill.
_______. 1977. *A Word-List of Manichaean Middle Persian and Parthian.* Leiden: Brill.
Brunner, C. 1977. *A Syntax of Western Middle Iranian.* Delmar, NY: Caravan Books.
Dresden, M. 1966. *Denkart: A Pahlavi Text.* Wiesbaden: Otto Harrassowitz.
Gignoux, P. 1972. *Glossaire des inscriptions pehlevies et parthes. Corpus Inscriptionum Iranicarum* Suppl. Series, vol. I. London: Lund Humphries.
_______. 1984. *Le livre d'Arda Viraz: translittēration, transcription et traduction du texte pehlevi.* Paris: Editions Recherche sur les Civilisations.
Henning, W. 1933. "Das Verbum des Mittelpersischen der Turfanfragmente." *Zeitschrift für Indologie und Iranistik* 9:158–253.
_______. 1958. "Mitteliranisch." In *Iranistik*, 1 Linguistik, pp. 20–130. Handbuch der Orientalistik I. Leiden: Brill.
Humbach, H. and O. Skjaervø. 1978–. *The Sassanian Inscription of Paikuli.* Wiesbaden: Dr. Ludwig Reichert.
MacKenzie, D. 1971. *A Concise Pahlavi Dictionary.* London: Oxford University Press.
Nyberg, H. 1964. *A Manual of Pahlavi* (2 vols.). Wiesbaden: Otto Harrassowitz.
Salemann, C. 1895–1901. "Mittelpersisch." In W. Geiger and E. Kuhn (eds.), *Grundriss der iranischen Philologie*, vol. I, section 1, pp. 249–332. Strasburg: Trübner.
Sundermann, W. 1989. "Mittelpersisch." In R. Schmitt (ed.), *Compendium Linguarum Iranicarum.* Wiesbaden: Dr. Ludwig Reichert.
Tavadia, J. 1956. *Die mittelpersische Sprache und Literatur der Zarathustrier.* Leipzig: Otto Harrassowitz.

CHAPTER 8

Ancient Chinese

ALAIN PEYRAUBE

1. HISTORICAL AND CULTURAL CONTEXTS

1.1 Introduction

"Chinese is only one of a very few languages whose history is documented in an unbroken tradition extending back to the second millennium BC" (Norman 1988: ix). There are two main causes for this situation: (i) the unity of Chinese culture in spite of periods of political disunity; (ii) the use of a script which has been independent of any particular phonetic manifestation of the languages it represented.

Chinese is usually divided into *Ancient Chinese* (*gudai hanyu*) and *Contemporary Chinese* (*xiandai hanyu*; the pronunciation of all Chinese characters is herein given in the modern standard language *putonghua*, in the standard romanization *pinyin*). Ancient Chinese is simply defined as "the language of the writings of the past" (Wang 1979:1). It covers a very long period, from the first Chinese inscriptions known to us, dated to the fourteenth century BC, until the nineteenth century. One then distinguishes generally for Ancient Chinese three basic stages: (i) the Archaic period (*shanggu*), until the second century BC; (ii) the Middle or Medieval period (*zhonggu*), from the first century BC to the middle of the thirteenth century AD; (iii) the Modern period (*jindai*), from the middle of the thirteenth century to the middle of the nineteenth century.

It is during the Archaic period that what is known today as *Classical Chinese* (*wenyan*) is fixed. This language remained as the main written language used in literary texts until the beginning of the twentieth century, but has progressively become a dead language since the beginning of the Medieval period (playing a role like that of Latin in Europe), and the current spoken Sinitic languages have diverged from it considerably.

The Classical period proper begins with Confucius (551–479 BC), and ends around the founding of the Qin Empire in 221 BC. The attested language of the period was probably not very different from cultured speech. The gap between the written and the spoken language began to develop in the Han dynasty (206 BC–AD 220) and increased naturally with time. Before Confucius, the literary language is called *Preclassic*.

It is essentially the classical language par excellence – that of the Warring States period (475–221 BC) – that will be discussed in this chapter. Attention will, however, also be paid to the preclassic language and, above all, to the language as known after the Han dynasty, up until around AD 600.

1.2 The linguistic family of Chinese

Chinese is considered today by most specialists of the language, and also by Tibeto-Burmanists, to belong to the *Sino-Tibetan* family of languages (subdivided principally into Chinese [Sinitic] and Tibeto-Burman). Other hypotheses regarding the genetic affiliations of Chinese have been offered in very recent years. Sagart (1994) posits a Sino-Tibetan-Austronesian family (with the three subdivisions of Sinitic, Tibeto-Burman, and Austronesian). Starostin (1989) argues for a Sino-Caucasian macrofamily which includes Sino-Tibetan, Yeniseian, and North Caucasian. Pulleyblank (1995) relates Sino-Tibetan and Indo-European to one another, stressing that "the traces of shared phonological and morphological correspondences at a very deep level are hard to explain except as evidence of common origin."

1.3 Chronological stages

At present there are several possible periodizations of the Chinese language, falling into two major categories according to phonological or syntactic criteria.

The long history of Chinese phonology is divided today into the following periods: (i) *Old Chinese* (this term has replaced what Karlgren [1915–1926] called "Archaic Chinese"), representing the language of around 1000–800 BC; (ii) *Early Middle Chinese* (replacing Karlgren's "Ancient Chinese"), which represents the literary pronunciation of the sixth century AD; (iii) *Late Middle Chinese*, the language of the Late Tang (618–907) and Early Song (960–1279) periods; (iv) *Early* (or *Old*) *Mandarin*, the language of the Yuan (1279–1368) period (see Pulleyblank 1970–1971; Baxter 1992:14–15).

A different periodization is based on syntactic criteria only. It distinguishes four major stages, *Archaic* (*shanggu*), *Medieval* (*zhonggu*), *Modern* (*jindai*), and *Contemporary* (*xiandai*), which are subdivided as follows: (i) *Pre-Archaic*, the language of the oracle inscriptions on bone and shell (fourteenth–eleventh centuries BC); (ii) *Early Archaic*, bronze inscriptions and early Chinese classics (tenth–sixth BC); (iii) *Late Archaic*, the Classical Chinese par excellence, comprising such well-known texts as the *Analects of Confucius*, and *Mencius* (fifth–second BC); (iv) *Pre-Medieval*, a transitional period, which witnesses the birth and development of an attested vernacular language different from the literary one (first century BC–first century AD); (v) *Early Medieval* (second–sixth AD); (vi) *Late Medieval* (seventh–mid-thirteenth AD); (vii) *Pre-Modern*, another transitional period (mid-thirteenth–fourteenth AD); (viii) *Modern Chinese* (fifteenth–mid-nineteenth AD); (ix) *Contemporary Chinese* (mid-nineteenth century to the present; see Wang 1958:35; Chou 1963:432–438; and especially Peyraube 1988). This syntactic periodization is followed below, except for the section on phonology, which adopts the periodization based on phonological criteria.

For all these stages, inscriptions and texts have survived in great quantities.

1.4 Dialectal variation

Regional dialects surely existed in China from the most ancient period. We have an early record of dialectal words, the *Fangyan* by Yang Xiong (53 BC–AD 18), but it tells us very little about how the different words were pronounced.

The classical literary language, and also the vernacular literary language which appeared around the second century AD, apparently established norms preventing the development of any real dialectal or regional literary competitors. However, if we consider the classical period proper, corresponding to the Late Archaic Chinese of the Warring States period (fifth–third centuries BC), we do find some linguistic diversity among the texts. This is probably not merely the result of different historical phases; various regional dialects most likely were in use as the vehicles of literature in their respective areas.

Pulleyblank (1995:3) distinguishes the following four dialects: (i) a rather archaic form of literary language, based probably on a central dialect, used in historical texts; (ii) an Eastern Lu dialect used in *Lun yu* (*Analects*) and *Mengzi* (*Mencius*); (iii) a Southwestern Chu dialect; (iv) a third-century BC dialect found in philosophical texts.

By the Tang period, and probably earlier, China has acquired a standard common language (*gongtongyu*). This is clearly the case for the written language, but there are numerous indications that it is also the case for the spoken (see Mei 1994).

2. WRITING SYSTEMS

The following section is largely inspired by Norman (1988:58–82) and Qiu (1978).

2.1 The origin of Chinese writing

It can be reasonably assumed that Chinese writing begins sometime around the seventeenth century BC (see Qiu 1978). The Chinese script already appears as a fully developed writing system in the late Shang dynasty (fourteenth–eleventh centuries BC). We have for this period a great number of texts inscribed or written on tortoise-shells or bones, the script being known as *jiaguwen* ("oracle bone script").

The next phase of the Chinese script, *jinwen* ("bronze script"), used during the Western Zhou (eleventh century–771 BC), and the Spring and Autumn (770–476 BC) periods, in its basic structure and style is similar to that of the late Shang, and is clearly derived from it. Later scripts will similarly be derived in succession from the preceding form, until the appearance of the "standard script" (*kaishu*), which begins to take shape around the third century AD, and is still in use today (see §2.3).

One could therefore say that Chinese writing is characterized by continuous use of the same system since remote antiquity.

2.2 The nature of the writing system

From its very beginning, the Chinese writing system has been fundamentally morphemic, in other words, almost every graph represents a single morpheme. Since the overwhelming majority of Archaic Chinese morphemes are monosyllabic, every graph then represents a single morpheme at the phonological level.

If one excludes a very small number of early graphs, which are apparently arbitrary signs bearing no iconic or phonetic relationship to the word represented, one can claim that the Shang script contains characters of two basic types: (i) those which are semantically representational without any indication of the pronunciation of the words represented; and (ii) those which are in some fashion tied to the pronunciation of the words.

The earliest Chinese writing clearly reveals a basically pictographic origin of the characters. It is now quite difficult, however, to identify what object was originally depicted by many of the symbols; that is, after being simplified and stylized in later stages, they lost their original pictorial quality. Graphic representations were thus originally linked to the words they represented without any reference to the pronunciation of the morphemes in question (the system was iconic). However, as in all fully developed writing systems, phonetic elements were eventually introduced. These were particularly needed for representing abstract notions

Table 8.1 Development of the Chinese script

	Shang bone script	Zhou bronze script	Warring States script	Seal script	Clerical script (Han)
1. "child"	子	子	子	子	子
2. "cloud"	雲	雲	雲	雲	雲
3. "water"	水	水	水	水	水
4. "year"	年	年	年	年	年
5. "silk"	絲	絲	絲	絲	絲
6. "be born"	生	生	生	生	生
7. "eye"	目	目	目	目	目
8. "fruit"	果	果	果	果	果
9. "tripod"	鼎	鼎	鼎	鼎	鼎
10. "deer"	鹿	鹿	鹿	鹿	鹿
11. "wise"	聖	聖	聖	聖	聖
12. "buy"	買	買	買	買	買

and grammatical elements which were difficult to represent in pictorial form. Through the application of the so-called rebus principle, a pictograph or some other nonphonetic representational graph could be used for its sound value only. Many of the early graphs are derived by this "phonetic borrowing principle" – indeed, almost all functional words and grammatical elements are so represented.

One thing is certain. The individual graphs of the Shang writing system represent specific *words*, and most probably spoken words, in the Shang language. They do not directly represent *ideas*: "The notion which is sometimes encountered that Chinese characters in some Platonic fashion represent ideas rather than specific Chinese words is patently absurd" (Norman 1988: 60–61).

Later on, beginning in the Early Archaic period, another strategy for character formation is utilized which in subsequent centuries is to become increasingly important – that of phonetic compounding. A character of this type consists of a semantic element combined with a second element used to indicate the pronunciation of the new graph. About 85 percent of Chinese characters are presently of this type.

2.3 Evolution of the writing system

After the *jiaguwen* ("oracle bone script"), which already had 4,000 to 5,000 characters, and the *jinwen* ("bronze script"), another type of writing called *zhouwen* (or *dazhuan*) "large seal" appears, in conjunction with the bronze script, in the Spring and Autumn period (770–476 BC). By the end of the period, the use of this script has already spread to virtually all levels of society, leading to the development of many simplified forms – which may be called *demotic*– accelerating conventionalization and the movement away from pictographic symbols.

During the Warring States period (475–221 BC), a growing diversity among the scripts of the various states can be observed, due mainly to political fragmentation. These are called *liuguo wenzi* "scripts of the Six States." The Qin dynasty, newly established in 221 BC, undertook a script standerdization, sanctioning only two scripts – a complex form and a simplified demotic. The former, known as *zhuanshu* "seal script," also frequently referred to as *xiaozhuan* "small seal," is derived from the *jinwen* and *zhouwen* mentioned above. The latter of the reformed scripts, more important for the history of Chinese writing, is called *lishu* "clerical script." It is highly evolved in its graphic form and represents a much simplified version of the standard seal script. All attempts to preserve the pictorial nature of graphs are abandoned, and convenience becomes the overriding principle.

Around the end of the first century BC, the demotic clerical script becomes the official form of writing employed for all purposes, and the use of the ancient script comes almost to an end. By the end of the Han period (*c.* third century AD), when approximately 10,000 characters exist (the *Shuo wen jie zi* [*Explanation of Graphs and Analysis of Characters*], compiled by Xu Shen around the second century AD, lists 9,353 different characters), the standard form of the script called *kaishu* begins to take shape. It represents a further evolution toward a more regular and convenient form of writing in which the wave-like strokes of the clerical script are replaced by more linear strokes. By the fifth century AD, *kaishu* becomes the standard form of Chinese script for all ordinary purposes, and it is still widely used at the present time.

3. PHONOLOGY

The earliest important analyses of Chinese historical phonology owe a great deal to the Swedish sinologist Karlgren, who was the first to apply the methods of European historical linguistics to Chinese. Karlgren provided two complete reconstructions: (i) one which he called Ancient Chinese (now Middle Chinese), based on the *Qieyun* (AD 601) by Lu Fayan, a dictionary of Chinese characters arranged by tone and rhyme, and (ii) the other which he called Archaic Chinese (now Old Chinese), based on the rhymes of the *Shi jing* (*Classic of Poetry*), a collection of 305 poems completed about 600 BC (see Karlgren 1957 for their almost definitive versions).

The hypotheses of Karlgren, after being modified by Jaxontov (1960 [1983]), Pulleyblank (1962, 1984, 1991), Li (1971), Bodman (1980), and Baxter (1980, 1992), have become obsolete today. At present, the most developed systems of reconstruction are those of Pulleyblank (1991) for Middle Chinese, and Baxter (1992) for Old Chinese.

3.1 Reconstruction of Middle Chinese phonology

The source of Middle Chinese is the *Qieyun* dictionary. It represents most probably a single, coherent form of the Chinese language, namely the elite standard which was common to educated speakers from both north and south around the sixth century AD.

3.1.1 Consonants and vowels

The Chinese syllable can be divided into two parts: (i) an initial (*shengmu*), the consonantal onset; and (ii) a final (*yunmu*), further divided into (a) a medial glide (*yuntou*), (b) a main vowel (*yunfu*), and (c) a coda (*yunwei*). Upon the basis of this structure, the inventory of phonetic segments for Early Middle Chinese in Baxter's (1992:45–61) transcriptions of the traditional categories is presented below. Aspiration of stops and affricates is indicated by superscript ^{h}; *r* does not represent a separate segment, but a retroflex articulation of the preceding consonant; ^{y} indicates a palatal articulation of the preceding consonant. The velar nasal [ŋ] is represented by *ng*. Initial *h*- represents a voiced guttural fricative (probably pharyngeal [ɦ] or velar [ɣ]), in contrast to *x*-, which is voiceless:

(1) Middle Chinese initials

Labials	p	p^h	b	m			
Dentals	t	t^h	d	n			
Lateral						l	
Dental stridents	ts	ts^h	dz		s	z	
Retroflex stops	tr	tr^h	dr	nr			
Retroflex stridents	tsr	tsr^h	dzr		sr	zr	
Palatals	ts^y	ts^{yh}	dz^y	n^y	s^y	z^y	y
Velars	k	k^h	g	ng			
Laryngeals	ʔ				x	h	

A *final* includes at least a main vowel, which may be followed by a coda, or may be preceded by one or more medials. The basic medials are the glides -*y*- and -*w*-.

The Middle Chinese main vowels are as follows:

(2) Middle Chinese main vowels

i	ɨ	u
e		o
ɛ		
æ	a	

These main vowels may be followed by the codas of (3):

(3) Middle Chinese codas

	w		y	ɨ
ng	wng	m	n	
k	wk	p	t	

The combinations -*wng* and -*wk* may be taken literally, or interpreted as labiovelars /$ŋ^w$/ and /k^w/.

3.1.2 Tones

Middle Chinese has a system of four tones which, according to Chinese tradition, was first identified and named by Shen Yue in the fifth century: the tones are called *ping* "level," *shang* "rising," *qu* "departing," and *ru* "entering." Every Chinese syllable is marked by one of these four tonal categories. The entering tone occurs on all syllables which end in one of the three stops *p*, *t*, and *k*. Scholars have also argued that particular voice qualities are associated with the rising and departing tones (Mei 1970, Pulleyblank 1978, Sagart 1986).

3.2 Reconstruction of Old Chinese phonology

The reconstruction of an Old Chinese phase is much more problematic than Middle Chinese, since available evidence is more fragmentary. Such a reconstruction is based on two types of evidence: Old Chinese rhyming as reflected in *Shi jing*; and the phonetic series. Only the phonetic series gives us information on the initial consonants or groups of consonants.

3.2.1 Consonants and vowels

The Old Chinese syllable is also analyzed as being composed of an *initial* and a *final* (cf. §3.1.1). Following Baxter (1992:7), whose inventory of phonetic segments is given below, the (i) initial contains a *preinitial* and an *initial*, and the (ii) final contains a *medial*, a *main vowel*, a *coda*, and a *postcoda*. The terms "preinitial" and "postcoda" are introduced since Old Chinese allows consonant clusters in both initial and final position.

Baxter (1992) reconstructs four preinitials (which are now treated as prefixes in Baxter and Sagart 1998; see §4.3.3), thirty-seven initials, three medials, six main vowels, ten codas, and two postcodas. The initials reconstructed for Old Chinese are presented below (this model is largely inspired by Pulleyblank 1962). The spellings *hm*, *hn*, *hng*, and so forth denote the voiceless counterparts of the sonorants *m*, *n*, *ng*:

(4) Old Chinese initials

p	p^h	b	m	hm	w	hw
t	t^h	d	n	hn	l	hl
					r	hr
					y	hy
ts	ts^h	dz			z	s
k	k^h	g	ng	hng		
k^w	k^{wh}	g^w	ng^w	hng^w		
ʔ	x	ɦ				
$ʔ^w$						

Three medial elements have been reconstructed: *-*r*- (on the hypothesis of Jaxontov 1960), *-*y*- (though the reconstruction of the medial *-*y*- has now been replaced by a contrast of vowel length), and, marginally, *-*l*-.

The six main vowels (after Bodman 1980) are as follows:

(5) Old Chinese main vowels

i	ɨ	u
e		o
	a	

The following elements are reconstructed in the coda position:

(6) Old Chinese codas

	k	ng
y	t	n
w	wk	
	p	m

The two postcodas are *-ʔ and *-*s*, which are the respective sources of the rising tone and of the departing tone in Middle Chinese (the rising tone hypothesis is offered by Pulleyblank 1962 and Mei 1970; that of the departing tone by Haudricourt 1954).

This reconstructed Old Chinese phonemic system, the most recently proposed and probably the most complete, is far from being universally accepted. Several of Baxter's propositions are considered controversial and are being actively debated (for a detailed account of the controversial questions, see Pulleyblank 1993 and Sagart 1993a). In fact, several specialists still consider that even today one can do no more than approach a reconstruction of Old Chinese.

3.3 Significant diachronic processes linking Old and Middle Chinese

The main phonological developments from Old Chinese to Middle Chinese can be summarized as follows (for a more detailed account of these changes, see Appendix A of Baxter 1992:565–582):

1. The preinitial position was lost entirely as the preinitial elements (now prefixes) merged with the following initials to form single initial consonants.
2. The Old Chinese initials were also influenced by the following medials. Dentals developed into palatals when followed by *-*y*- or retroflex stops when followed by *-*r*-.
3. The vowel system of Old Chinese underwent radical changes under the influence of the medial and the coda.

There remains an important point of debate: did Old Chinese already have tones? In the past it was proposed that tone is an inherent feature of languages that cannot be derived from nontonal elements; accordingly, as Middle Chinese most likely had tones, Old Chinese must also have had tones. This hypothesis is today highly contested. Studies in recent years have shown that some present-day tonal languages (Vietnamese, for instance) are, indeed, derived from nontonal ancestral languages.

If the rising tone (*shang*) of Middle Chinese can be derived from the glottal postcoda of Old Chinese, as proposed by Pulleyblank (1962) and Mei (1970), and if the departing tone (*qu*) can be derived from the postcoda *-*s* of Old Chinese, as proposed by Haudricourt (1954), then it turns out that there were no tones in Old Chinese. The two other tones of Middle Chinese can be interpreted as follows: (i) the level tone (*ping*) was the unmarked category consisting of those syllables ending in plain vowels or in other voiced segments; (ii) the entering tone (*ru*), as seen above, consisted of all the syllables ending in one of the three stops *p*, *t*, or *k* (for a different point of view, see Ting 1996, who argues that Old Chinese was already tonal).

4. MORPHOLOGY

Chinese is a language of that morphological type called analytic or isolating. Old Chinese morphemes are almost entirely monosyllabic, and most words are monomorphemic.

It is often said that Chinese is a language with an impoverished morphology, a language in which the grammatical processes are almost totally syntactic. Moreover, one usually considers that this lack of morphological marking of grammatical relationships is even more critical in Ancient Chinese than in Contemporary Chinese, since, as noted above, Old Chinese morphemes are almost entirely monosyllabic, and most words are monomorphemic.

Ancient Chinese did indeed possess morphological processes, although none of them was fully productive. These word-formation processes are of the same type as those of

Contemporary Chinese: compounding, reduplication, and affixation. But Ancient Chinese was characterized by yet other derivational processes, ones unknown in Contemporary Chinese.

4.1 Compounding

Not all words in Classical Chinese are monosyllabic; compounds occur which consist of two syllables. Most of these compounds are not yet fully lexicalized. They commonly consist of two independent free morphemes which can occur separately. Nevertheless, there are some exceptions – bound compounds occur which have meanings that cannot be deduced from the meaning of the morphemes from which they are composed. The most striking example is the word *junzi* "gentleman," composed of *jun* "lord" and *zi* "child."

Beginning in the Han period, Chinese develops a greater number of compounds. As new terms are required by the language, compounding is the chief means by which neologisms are introduced (owing to the death of Chinese derivational processes).

There are also in Classical Chinese some bimorphemic monosyllabic words, which result from the fusion of two morphemes. The negative *fu* is thus considered to be formed from the negative *bu* "not" and the third-person pronoun *zhi* "him, her, it."

4.2 Reduplication

Reduplication is a productive morphological process. Archaic Chinese is quite rich in both total reduplicates and partial reduplicates. For the most part, reduplicated forms are expressive or descriptive adjectives or adverbs. Total reduplicates simply repeat the same syllable twice (e.g., *weiwei* "tall and grand"), whereas partial reduplicates only repeat the final part of the first syllable (as in *tanglang* "praying mantis").

4.3 Affixation

Contrary to what is generally thought, affixation is not unproductive in Ancient Chinese, and may represent a vestige of older stages in which such a process was considerably more productive. Several prefixes, suffixes, and infixes have now been reconstructed for Archaic Chinese. These are derivational morphemes changing the meaning or part of the speech of the words to which they are attached (the ensuing discussion closely follows the treatment of Baxter and Sagart [1998]).

4.3.1 Prefixes

The following prefixes are reconstructed:

1. A prefix **N-* (causing a following voiceless obstruent to become voiced in Medieval Chinese) when attached to a verb (or even a noun in some cases) seems to produce an intransitive verb or adjective: thus, *kens* "to see" : **N-kens* "to appear."
2. A prefix **k-* added to a verb or a noun produces, in several examples, a concrete, countable noun of related meaning: for example, **ʔjuj-s* "to fear, be afraid" : **k-ʔjuj-ʔ* "ghost, demon." In some cases in which **k-* is added to verbs, forms with **k-* appear to refer to concrete actions taking place in a specific time frame: for example, **ljuk* "to nourish" : **k-ljuk* "to breast feed."

3. A prefix **t-*, in contrast to **k-*, often appears to produce a derived mass noun, as in **ljuk* "nourish" : **t-ljuk* "rice gruel." The same prefix also appears on some intransitive verbs.
4. A prefix **s-* derives causative verbs from noncausative verbs or even nouns. See Mei 1989.

4.3.2 Suffix *-s

The suffix **-s*, the source of the departing tone of Medieval Chinese (see §3.3), when added to adjectives or verbs produces derived nouns: for example, **drjon* "transmit" : **drjon-s* "a record." Some gradable adjectives also have corresponding noun forms in which the suffix **-s* functions like English *-th*, occurring in pairs such as "deep/depth," "wide/width" (see Downer 1959, Mei 1980).

The same **-s* suffix, in some instances, also makes transitive verbs from adjectives or intransitive verbs, or [+ give] dative verbs from [+ receive] dative verbs: thus, **djuʔ* "receive": **djuʔ -s* "give"; **tsjAK* "borrow" : **tsjAk-s* "lend."

4.3.3 Infixes

Two infixes can be reconstructed in Archaic Chinese. The exact function of the first one, **-j-*, is difficult to establish, but forms with and without **-j-* do appear to be semantically related. The second infix, **-r-*, is said to produce forms that are plural or collective in the case of nouns, and iterative, durative, or indicating effort, in the case of verbs (see Sagart 1993b).

5. SYNTAX

Syntax is all the more critical in Classical Chinese, as words are not usually formally marked for grammatical category or function; words nevertheless do fall into distinct classes such as noun, verb, preposition, and so forth. Word order and the syntactic behavior of words are thus prominent linguistic issues.

5.1 Word order

The three basic word orders in Classical Chinese, as well as in Medieval, Modern, and Contemporary Chinese, are as follows: (i) the subject precedes the predicate; (ii) the verb precedes its object; (iii) modifiers precede the words they modify.

There is little controversy surrounding (i) and (iii), which tolerate only a few exceptions (for instance, the *subject–predicate* order is inverted in exclamatory sentences, as seen below in §5.4.2; see Zhu 1980:191 and Mei 1997 for an inverted order *head–modifier* in Early Archaic). However, things are quite different for (ii), which has been much debated since Li and Thompson (1974) put forward the hypothesis according to which Archaic Chinese was originally of SOV (*Subject–Object–Verb*) order, later being changed to SVO. It has been supposed that Proto-Chinese must have been SOV, and therefore Proto-Sino-Tibetan also since almost all Tibeto-Burman languages have a verb-final order (the only known exceptions being Karen and Bai).

Peyraube (1997a) argues that Pre-Archaic Chinese shows a regular order of SVO and is indeed more thoroughly SVO than later stages (Early or Late Archaic). To suppose, then, that in a more ancient stage, before the oracle-bone inscriptions, the basic order could have been SOV is purely conjectural, not empirically grounded. Moreover, in the later stages of Early and in Late Archaic Chinese, there is also a strong indication that the SVO order is more basic than SOV (see Peyraube 1997b).

5.1.1 VO versus OV

Unlike many European languages which require an overt subject, Chinese does not seem to have such a syntactic requirement. It seems preferable then to frame our discussion in terms of VO versus OV order rather than SVO versus SOV. When the object is a full lexical noun phrase, the basic order in Archaic Chinese is undoubtedly VO, as in the following example:

(7) jun bi shi guo
prince certainly lose state
"The prince [will] certainly lose the State" (Zuo Tradition)

There are a few cases in which the noun phrase object is found in preverbal position, but these cases are marginal and the OV order is then a marked [+ contrastive] order. It is the same when the noun object is followed by a preverbal marker, usually *shi* or *zhi*, as in (8):

(8) jin Wu shi ju
now Wu OBJECT-MARKER afraid
"Now [they] are afraid of [the state of] Wu" (Zuo Tradition)

However, there are also cases of OV order in Archaic Chinese, not found in Contemporary Chinese, in which the object is a pronoun: either (i) an interrogative pronoun (9A); (ii) the demonstrative pronoun *shi* "this" (9B); or (iii) a pronoun in a negative sentence (9C):

(9) A. wu shei qi? qi tian hu?
I who deceive deceive Heaven INTERR.-PCL.
"Whom should I deceive? Should I deceive Heaven?" (Confucian Analects)

B. zi zi sun sun shi shang
son son grandson grandson this supersede
"[His] posterity will supersede this" (Chen gong zi yan, a bronze inscription)

C. bu wu zhi ye
NEGATION I understand FINAL-PCL.
"[You] don't understand me" (Confucian Analects)

Certain observations can be made concerning these various OV orders involving pronouns. First, there are statistical considerations. In a corpus of 2,767 VO or OV sentences drawn from the bronze inscriptions, 88.56 percent of objects (O) are nouns, only 3.3 percent are pronouns (see Guan 1981:88). The ratio of pronoun objects is certainly higher in other documents of the Early Archaic period, and above all in Late Archaic Chinese, but it never exceeds 15 percent of the entire body of VO and OV constructions. Since the OV order is well attested only for pronoun objects, one can conclude with some confidence that the OV order has always been very marginal.

It is also known that in many languages, the position of pronouns is different from that of noun phrases, and that "unstressed constituents, such as clitic pronouns, are often, cross-linguistically, subject to special positioning rules only loosely, if at all, relating to their grammatical relation, so sentences with pronouns can be discounted in favor of those with full noun phrases" (Comrie 1989: 89).

5.1.2 Prepositions or postpositions?

In Classical Chinese, prepositional phrases are usually composed of a preposition (see §5.2.2.3) followed by a noun phrase object, as in the following example:

(10)	Zizhi	bu	neng	shou	Yan	yu	Zikuai
	Zizhi	NEGATION	can	receive	Yan	from	Zikuai

“Zizhi cannot receive [the state of] Yan from Zikuai” (Mencius)

These prepositional phrases can be postverbal (as in [10]), or preverbal, as in the following:

(11)	gu	yi	yang	yi	zhi
	therefore	with	sheep	change	it

“Therefore [I] changed it for a sheep” (Mencius)

Of the two common prepositions of Archaic Chinese, *yu* and *yi*, *yu* has a relatively rigid postverbal position, while *yi* is more preverbal.

More interesting for the problem of word order is that there are cases in which the preposition is found after the noun phrase object. In such instances the “preposition” is thus a postposition. Some scholars (Sun 1991, Mei 1997) have hypothesized that these postpositions are relics of an ancient general order, and, accordingly, that Chinese may have been a postpositional language. Consider the following example:

(12)	shi	yi	zheng	ping
	this	with	politics	pacify

“With this, the politics [will] pacify [the State]” (Zuo Tradition)

However, we should bear in mind that these occurrences are very rare, especially if we exclude the cases in which the object is an interrogative pronoun or the demonstrative pronoun *shi* “this.” The order OP (Object–Preposition) when the object is such a pronoun naturally follows from the rule of positioning these pronouns before the verb (see §5.1.1), as prepositions in Chinese develop diachronically from verbs and still share many properties with them.

To sum up, no OV order needs to be posited for Classical Chinese syntax to capture any sort of linguistic generalization. Classical Chinese has SVO order, just as in the ensuing stages of Medieval, Modern, and Contemporary Chinese.

5.2 Parts of speech

Classical Chinese words are traditionally divided into two categories: *shizi* “full words” and *xuzi* “empty words.” The former are content words (carry semantic content) and form an open class; included in this category are nouns, verbs, and adjectives. The latter are function words or grammatical words, used to express grammatical relationships. They include pronouns, adverbs, prepositions, conjunctions, and particles (for the analysis of Classical Chinese word classes presented here, see Liu 1958:18; other scholars [Wang 1979:36-41; Ma 1983:13] distinguish eleven word classes).

As we will see, words can be used in functions customarily reserved for other words. This does not imply, however, as some scholars have assumed, that there are no parts of speech in Classical Chinese, and that words can be used indifferently in any grammatical category.

5.2.1 Shizi (full words)

Treated under this heading are nouns, adjectives, and verbs, including auxiliary verbs.

5.2.1.1 Nouns

Chinese nouns typically function as subjects or objects. However, under certain conditions, they may function like verbs, as predicates (13), or like adverbs, as adverbials (14):

(13)

jun	jun	chen	chen	fu	fu	zi	zi
ruler	ruler	minister	minister	father	father	son	son

"The ruler acts as a ruler, the minister as a minister, the father acts as a father, and the son as a son" (Confucian Analects)

(14)

shi	ren	li
pig	man	stand-up

"The pig, like a man, stood up" (Zuo Tradition)

Localizers (words showing spatial orientation and direction, like *shang* "above," *nan* "south"), time words (like *ri* "day," *yue* "month," etc.) and measure words (indicating standards for length, weight, volume, area, aggregates, containers – like *dou* "bushel," *bei* "glass") are better considered as subcategories of nouns, though some scholars treat them as independent word classes; see Norman 1988:91; Wang 1979:38. For a history of measure words in Classical Chinese, see Peyraube 1991.

5.2.1.2 Verbs

Fundamentally, verbs are predicative in nature. Unlike nouns, which are negated by the adverb of negation *fei* "is not," verbs are negated by the simple adverb *bu* "not."

Both intransitive (e.g., *yi lai* [lit. doctor come] "the doctor came") and transitive verbs occur; the latter may take a single object or, sometimes, two – an indirect and a direct:

(15)

gong	ci	zhi	shi
prince	offer	him	food

"The prince offered him food" (Zuo Tradition)

One particular use of intransitive verbs in Classical Chinese is in a causative function: thus, *huo* "live" : "make (people) live"; *xing* "go" : "put into motion"; *yin* "drink" : "give to drink."

One verbal subclass is composed of auxiliary verbs. Auxiliary verbs are verbs that take other verbs as their objects and express the modality of the following verb phrase. This modality (ability, possibility, probability, certainty, obligation, volition, etc.) can be characterized as epistemic, deontic, or dynamic. Auxiliary verbs form a closed list and can be classified in the four following semantic groups: (i) verbs expressing mainly possibility and permission, including *ke, neng, zu, de, huo, keyi,* and *zuyi* (see [16A]); (ii) the four verbs of volition, *gan, ken, yu,* and *yuan* (see [16B]); (iii) the two auxiliaries of necessity (certainty and obligation), *yi* and *dang*; and (iv) the passive auxiliaries *jian, wei,* and *bei.* For a detailed analysis of the modal auxiliary verbs in Chinese, see Peyraube 1999.

(16) A.

tian	zi	bu	neng	yi	tianxia	yu	ren
Heaven	son	negation	can	OBJECT-MARKER	Empire	give	other

"The Emperor cannot give the Empire (to) others" (Mencius)

B.

Zi	yu	ju	Jiu	Yi
Master	intend-to	live	Jiu	Yi

"The Master intends to live in Jiu Yi" (Confucian Analects)

5.2.1.3 Adjectives

Adjectives can be considered as a subcategory of verbs. Indeed, they are intransitive verbs of quality, being negated by the adverb *bu*:

(17) ming bu zheng ze yan bu shun
name not correct then word not justified
"If names are not correct, then words cannot be justified" (Confucian Analects)

Like intransitive verbs, adjectives can also have a causative use:

(18) Wang qing da zhi
king beg great it
"Your Majesty, [I] beg [you] to make it great" (Mencius)

In addition, adjectives are also typically found as noun phrase modifiers, as in *bai ma* "white horse," or as verb phrase modifiers, for instance *ji zou* (lit. rapid - run) "run rapidly."

Numerals

Finally, one can consider that numerals constitute a subclass of the category of adjectives. They indeed behave syntactically like adjectives; thus, they can form predicates and are negated by the adverb *bu*. Most commonly, however, they function as modifiers of nouns:

(19) A. nian yi qi shi yi
age already seven ten final-part
"[He] is already seventy years old" (Mencius)
B. wu he ai yi niu?
I why begrudge one ox
"Why [should] I begrudge one ox?" (Mencius)

5.2.2 Xuzi (empty words)

Within this category fall pronouns, adverbs, prepositions, conjunctions, and particles.

5.2.2.1 Pronouns

Several types of pronouns can de identified: personal, demonstrative, interrogative, and indefinite.

5.2.2.1.1 Personal pronouns

Personal pronouns characteristically occur in different forms. The most common ones are as follows, with no distinction being made between singular and plural:

(20) *First person* wu wo yu
Second person ru er ruo nai
Third person zhi qi

If it is relatively easy to distinguish third-person *zhi* and *qi* as accusative and genitive respectively, it is not so for pronouns of the other two persons. Several scholars have tried to characterize their different usages according to case (nominative, accusative, or genitive), but dialectal variation also is a factor: in most instances, the different usages of the pronouns depend on the different texts in which they occur.

5.2.2.1.2 Demonstrative pronouns

The most common demonstratives are (i) *shi*, *ci*, *si*, *zhi*, and *zi* "this, these, here"; and (ii) *bi*, *fu*, and *qi* "that, those, there" (Pulleyblank [1995:85] states that *shi* "this, that" is anaphoric with no implication of closeness or remoteness; *ci* and *bi*, on the other hand, form a contrast between "this (here)" and "that (there)"). Here too, it is difficult to explain formal differences without considering dialectal variation. All of these demonstratives can be used as adjectivals (modifying the following nouns or noun phrases), or as subjects or objects.

5.2.2.1.3 Interrogative pronouns

These are divided into two categories: (i) those that replace subjects or objects (which are usually nouns): *shui* "who," *shu* "which, who," *he* "what"; and (ii) those that replace predicative verbs or adverbs: *hu* "why, how," *xi* "why," *he* "how, why," *an* "where, how," *yan* "how, where," *wu* "how, where." An interrogative pronoun precedes the verb of which it is the object.

5.2.2.1.4 Indefinite pronouns

This class includes *huo* "some, someone, something," *mo* "none, no one, nothing" and *mou* "some, a certain one."

5.2.2.2 Adverbs

Usually positioned in preverbal position, adverbs typically modify the predicate of the sentence. One can distinguish several types: (i) adverbs of degree (*ji* "extremely," *zui* "most," *you* "especially," *shao* "little," *shen* "very," etc.); (ii) adverbs of quantification and restriction (*jie* "all," *ju* "all," *ge* "each," *mei* "every," *wei* "only," *du* "only," etc.); (iii) adverbs of time or aspect (*yi* "already," *ji* "after having," *chang* "once," *jiang* "be going to," *nai* "then," *fang* "just then"; (iv) adverbs of negation (*bu*, *fu*, *fei*, *wu*, *wei*). *Bu* is the ordinary adverb of negation for verbs and adjectives. *Fu* is said to be the result of the fusion of the negative *bu* plus the object pronoun *zhi* "him, her, it" (only found during the Late Archaic period). *Fei* "is not" is the negation used with nouns. *Wu* "do not" could be a blend of *wu* plus *zhi*. *Wei* is an aspectual negative meaning "not yet" or "never."

5.2.2.3 Prepositions

Chinese prepositions are all verbal in origin (i.e., arise from verbs through a process of grammaticalization). There are two commonly occurring prepositions in Classical Chinese: (i) *yu* "at, to, in, from, toward, than, by, etc."; and (ii) *yi* "with, by means of, in order to, because, etc." The first of these, *yu*, can be locative, ablative, dative, comparative, or passive; the second, *yi*, primarily instrumental, also expresses purpose and several other grammatical relationships. One important characteristic of *yi* is that it can also introduce the direct object of a double-object construction (see [10] above). Additional prepositions are *yong* "with," *wei* "for, on behalf of, for the sake of, because," *yu* "with," *zi* "from," among still others.

5.2.2.4 Conjunctions

Generally, simple juxtaposition is sufficient to coordinate nouns or noun phrases, as in *fu mu* (lit. father mother) "father and mother"; or verbs or verb phrases in serial verb constructions. However, some coordinative conjunctions also occur, such as *ji* and *yu* "and," for coordinating noun phrases, or *er* "and" and *qie* "and, moreover" for coordinating verb phrases or clauses.

Liu and Peyraube (1994) have argued that the conjunctions *ji* and *yu* do not directly develop from verbs (as has been claimed), but from prepositions, which are themselves derived from verbs. In other words, two processes of grammaticalization have occurred sequentially: verb > preposition > conjunction (Chinese conjunctions are thus more grammaticalized than verbs).

Subordinating conjunctions also occur: for example, *ru*, *ruo*, or *gou*, all meaning "if" in conditional clauses; *sui* "although, even if" in concessive clauses (see §5.4.5).

5.2.2.5 Particles

This category is usually divided into structural particles (*zhi*, *suo*, *zhe*) and modal particles. For structural particles, see §5.2.3. Modal particles constitute one of the most complex problems in Classical Chinese linguistics; most of the modal notions they express are quite uncertain. Modal particles can occupy the initial, the medial, and, in most cases, the final position of a sentence.

Among the initial particles, we find the following: *qi*, which qualifies a statement as possible or probable; *qi* "how could," which introduces rhetorical questions requiring a negative answer; and *fu* "as for," which announces a topic. Medial particles usually express a pause: for example, *zhe* and *ye*. The final particles can de divided according to the sentence-types in which they occur – declarative, interrogative, exclamatory, and so on. In declarative sentences, one often finds *yi* (a particle of the perfect aspect; see Pulleyblank 1995:112–116), *ye* (transforming a statement into an assertion, a judgment), *er*, and *yan*. *Hu*, *yu*, *ye*, and sometimes *zhe*, are more typically used in interrogative sentences. *Zai* occurs in exclamatory sentences.

5.3 Elements of sentence structure

5.3.1 Subject and predicate

Classical Chinese sentences can, in general, be divided into two main parts, a subject (most commonly a noun phrase) and a predicate (usually a verb phrase), though the subject may be – and indeed often is – unexpressed:

When the predicate is composed of more than one verb, it is said to be *complex*. Such cases involve serial verb constructions of the type $V_1 \ldots V_2 \ldots (V_3) \ldots$ The semantic relationship between verbs in series is varied. It can be a simple narrative sequence (in which case a coordinating conjunction *er* "and" can link the two verb phrases), as in (21A); or the relationship may involve an implication of purpose, as in (21B), where *yi* links the two verb phrases:

(21) A. Shao wang nan zheng er bu fu
Shao prince south invade and not return
"Prince Shao invaded the south and did not return" (Zuo Tradition)

B. Chu ren fa Song yi qiu Zheng
Chu people raid Song for save Zheng
"The people of Chu raided Song in order to save Zheng" (Zuo Tradition)

Complex predicates may also involve a "pivotal construction," in which the noun phrase object of the first verb is the subject of the second verb:

(22) qing jun tao zhi
ask Prince attack him
"[I] ask [you] the Prince to attack him" (Zuo Tradition)

Existential sentences form a special category of subject–predicate sentences. The predicate is composed of either the verb *you* "there is" or *wu* "there is not." In such sentences, the subject is often lacking or expressed by a place name.

Nominal predicates will be discussed below, under copular sentences (§5.4.3).

Finally, an interesting characteristic of the subject–predicate constructions is that they can be nominalized by inserting the subordinating particle *zhi* between the two constituents of the construction:

(23) ren zhi ai ren qiu li zhi ye
person PCL. love person pursue profit him PCL.
"One person loving another person [would] pursue profit [for] him" (Zuo Tradition)

5.3.2 Object and complement

A transitive verb can take one object (usually a noun phrase) or two, an indirect object (IO), and a direct object (DO). The double-object construction is restricted to those verbs with the semantic feature [+ give], [+ say] or [+ teach]: Apart from the pattern *V* + *IO* + *DO*, as in (9) above, two other orders, involving the prepositions *yi* (DO marker) or *yu* ("to," introducing the IO), are possible for the dative construction: (i) *yi* + *DO* + *V* + *IO* (or *V* + *IO* + *yi* + *DO*), also restricted to verbs which are [+ give], [+ say], [+ teach]; (ii) *V* + *DO* + *yu* + *IO*, used with all kinds of verbs (for a detailed analysis of these constructions, see Peyraube 1987):

(24) A. Yao yi tianxia yu Shun
Yao OBJECT-MARKER Empire give Shun
"Yao gave the Empire to Shun" (Mencius)
B. Yao rang tianxia yu Xu You
Yao leave Empire to Xu You
"Yao left the Empire to Xu You" (Zhuangzi)

Transitive verbs, as well as intransitive ones, may be followed by a *complement* (*buyu*), a term used for adjuncts when they follow the verb. When adjuncts precede the verb, they are denoted as *adverbials* (see §5.3.3). As many "complements" may also be placed in front of the verbs, and are thus "adverbials," the function of the complement per se is not very important in Classical Chinese (see Ma 1983:135 for discussion).

Complements are divided into two types, depending upon whether or not they are introduced by a prepositional marker. Those that are introduced by such a marker, of course, constitute prepositional phrases. Most notable of this type are the locative complements, usually introduced by the preposition *yu* "at, to":

(25) bei xue yu zhong guo
north learn at central state
"He went to the north to learn [it] in the Central States" (Mencius)

Compare (26), having a prepositional phrase complement introduced by *yi*, with (19), where *yi* introduces an adverbial:

(26) yi zhi yi yang
change it with sheep
"Change it for a sheep" (Mencius)

Among complements not introduced by prepositions, conspicuous are time complements (though these may at times also be introduced by the preposition *yu*) and durative complements, as in the following example:

(27) Zi	Yi	zai	wei	shi	si	nian	yi
Zi	Yi	be-at	throne	ten	four	year	PCL.

"Zi Yi has been on the throne during fourteen years" (Zuo Tradition)

5.3.3 Adjectivals and adverbials

Adjectivals (*dingyu*) are modifiers of nouns or noun phrases; adverbials (*zhuangyu*) are modifiers of verbs or verb phrases. As a general rule in Classical Chinese, modifiers precede their heads.

Subordinate relations involving nouns are expressed as follows: $N_2 + zhi + N_1$, where N_1 is the head of the phrase, N_2 the modifier (adjectival), and *zhi* the marker of subordination. This marker may be omitted, especially between monosyllables. The same pattern, $X + zhi + N$, is found when the modifier X is a verb or an adjective, as in the following:

(28) wu	duo	ren	zhi	jun
insult	rob	people	SUBORD.-PCL.	ruler

"A ruler who insults and robs [his] people" (Mencius)

Like other modifiers, relative clauses take *zhi* as a marker of subordination.

Two other markers of nominalization are *zhe* and *suo*. The first one may be called an agentive marker. Placed after a verb or a verb phrase, it produces an agent noun phrase: *sha zhe* (kill the-one-who) "The one who kills." The marker *suo*, placed before the verb, gives a noun phrase referring to the object of a transitive verb, as in: *suo sha* (*suo* kill) "that which was killed"; *qi suo shan* (his *suo* good) "that which he considers to be good."

Adverbials (verb phrase modifiers), are most commonly (and expectedly) adverbs, though they may also be nouns (as in [8] above), adjectives (29A), or prepositional phrases (29B):

(29) A. wang	zu	da	bai
prince	finally	great	defeat

"The prince was finally defeated terribly" (Zuo Tradition)

B. wo	yu	Zhou	wei	ke
I	at	Zhou	become	host

"I became a host at Zhou" (Zuo Tradition)

No marker is needed between the modifier and the head.

5.4 Sentence-types

Sentences are customarily divided into simple and complex types. One can also differentiate declarative, interrogative, imperative, and exclamatory sentences.

As the preceding analyses and examples have been concerned principally with the simple declarative sentence, we will treat here the remaining three types of simple sentences (interrogative, imperative, exclamatory). To these we would also add two particular types of declarative sentences: copular (i.e., nominal predicate sentences) and passive. For complex sentences see §5.4.5.

5.4.1 Interrogative sentences

These are of three basic types: (i) yes/no questions; (ii) WH-questions; and (iii) rhetorical questions.

The first type is formed with final question particles which effectively transform statements into questions. As noted above (§5.2.2.5), the most common particles are *hu, yu, ye*:

(30) A. zi yi you yi wen hu?
master also have different hear PCL.
"Master, have [you] also heard of different things?" (Confucian Analects)

B. wang zhi suo da yu ke de wen yu?
prince PCL. PCL. great desire can obtain hear PCL.
"[What] you [the Prince] greatly desire, could obtain a hearing [of it]?" (Mencius)

The second type (WH) contains a question word (one of the interrogative pronouns; see §5.2.2.1.3), generally without a final particle, as in the following:

(31) Zi Xia yun he?
Zi Xia say what
"What did Zi Xia say?" (Confucian Analects)

Note that the interrogative pronoun here follows the verb and is not in a preverbal position, as is usually the case.

The third interrogative-type is more complex. Some rhetorical questions are formed with a final particle (*hu, yu,* or *ye*), but with an adverb of negation placed before the verb, implying an affirmative answer. Others are formed with the modal particles *qi* or *qi* "how could". The final particles *hu* and *zai* are also generally used, though they may be omitted:

(32) yu qi hao bian zai?
I how-could like debate PCL.
"How could I [be one who] loves debating?" (Mencius)

5.4.2 Imperative and exclamatory sentences

Imperatives are not syntactically marked as such in Classical Chinese. The subject is usually deleted, but this in itself is not a sufficient diagnostic of the imperative sentence. However, when the imperative is intended to be understood as a request, and not as an order or a prohibition, the verbs *yuan* "wish" or *qing* "beg" are used:

(33) wang qing du zhi
prince beg measure it
"[My] Prince, please measure it" (Mencius)

The final particle *zai* is the usual marker of the exclamatory sentence. It can be added either to a declarative or to an interrogative. Other particles, like *yi*, may also be used. The subject–predicate order is usually inverted in exclamatory sentences. Consider the following examples:

(34) A. xian zai Hui ye!
sage PCL. Hui PCL.
"[He] is a sage, Hui!" (Confucian Analects)

B. si	yi	Pencheng	Kuo!
dead	PCL.	Pencheng	Kuo

"He is dead, Pencheng Kuo!" (Mencius)

5.4.3 Copular sentences

If one defines the copula as an overt word which, when used in equational sentences, links the subject to a nominal predicate, and expresses (i) an equivalence meaning or (ii) a property or classificatory meaning, then one can identify the presence of copulas in Classical Chinese (even if they are not strictly necessary).

The most common way of creating copular sentences is to add the final particle *ye* at the end of a sentence, transforming it from a statement into an assertion or a judgment (see Peyraube and Wiebusch 1995 for a detailed account of the history of copulas in Ancient Chinese, and especially for a discussion of the status of *ye* as a copula):

(35)	bi	zhangfu	ye	wo	zhangfu	ye
	that	reliable-man	PCL.	I	reliable-man	PCL.

"They were reliable men, I am a reliable man [too]" (Mencius)

In addition to *ye*, other copulas are attested in Classical Chinese. Thus, the negative copula *fei* "be not" is required in all negative nominal predicate sentences:

(36)	wo	fei	sheng	er	zhi	zhi	zhe
	I	be-not	born	and	know	it	the-one-who

"I am not one who was born with [the possession of] knowledge" (Confucian Analects)

In affirmative copular sentences, the verb *wei*, which also means "to do, to regulate, to act, to consider as," and so forth, also acts regularly as a copula:

(37)	er	wei	er	wo	wei	wo
	you	be	you	I	be	I

"You are you [and] I am I" (Mencius)

Finally, the copular verb *shi* "to be," still used today, and which comes from the demonstrative pronoun *shi* "this" through a grammaticalization process, is already attested no later than the Qin dynasty (from an astrological document discovered in a tomb at Mawangdui; second century BC):

(38)	shi	shi	zhu	hui	ren	zhu	you	si	zhe
	this	be	bamboo	comet	man	chief	have	die	the-one-who

"[When] this will be the bamboo comet [coming], the sovereign will die"

5.4.4 Passive sentences

In Classical Chinese there are semantic passives, expressing passivity without any overt morphological marker: a transitive verb can be made passive by placing its object (the patient) in subject position, as in *liang shi* (lit. "supplies eat") "supplies are eaten." However, there are also passive structures marked with some marker, such as a preposition, or an auxiliary verb.

In Early Archaic Chinese, there is only one passive construction, formed with the preposition *yu* "by" used to introduce the agent (*V + yu + Agent*). The construction can still be found in Late Archaic, where it is by far the most common means of producing a passive verb:

(39) zhi yu ren zhe shi ren zhi ren zhe shi yu ren
rule by other the-one-who feed other rule other the-one-who feed by other
"Those who are ruled by others feed others, those who rule are fed by others"
(Mencius)

Two other structures appear in Late Archaic: *wei + V* and *jian + V*. The agent is not expressed, and *wei* and *jian* are best considered to be auxiliary verbs:

(40) A. chen yi wei ru yi
I already AUX.-VERB humiliate PCL.
"I was already humiliated" (Lü shi chun qiu)
B. Pencheng Kuo jian sha
Pencheng Kuo AUX.-VERB kill
"Pencheng Kuo was killed" (Mencius)

Still within the Late Archaic period, these constructions are modified so that an agent can be expressed: *wei + Agent (+ suo) + V*; *jian + V + yu + Agent*. The first of these two will become common, beginning in the second century BC. It is probable that the auxiliary *wei* so used to introduce an overt noun phrase agent has in fact been grammaticalized as a preposition meaning "by":

(41) hou ze wei ren suo zhi
late then by other PCL. control
"[If I react] late, [I] will then be controlled by others" (Records of the Historian)

Yet another passive form appears at the end of the Classical period: *bei + V*, where *bei* is a verb meaning "to suffer," "to be affected." It will later become an auxiliary verb expressing passivity:

(42) Cuo zu yi bei lu
Cuo finally because-of suffer slaughter
"Because of [this], Cuo was finally slaughtered" (Records of the Historian)

One must then wait for several centuries (until the Early Medieval period) before the auxiliary verb *bei* itself comes to be used to introduce a noun phrase agent, and then is grammaticalized into the passive preposition which is still in use today. For a detailed analysis of the passive forms in Ancient Chinese, see Peyraube (1989b).

5.4.5 Complex sentences

Complex sentences are composed of two or more clauses joined through coordination or subordination. The joining of clauses can be accomplished without any overt marking, as in the following examples:

(43) A. lao zhe an zhi pengyou xin zhi shao zhe
old the-one-who soothe them friend trust them young the-one-who

huai zhi
care for them
"As for the old, soothe them, as for friends, trust them, as for the young, care for them" (Confucian Analects)

B. bu duo bu yan
not snatch not satisfy
"[If they] are not snatching, [they] are not satisfied" (Mencius)

A connective may also link the clauses, for instance the conjunction *er* "and, but" or the adverb *yi* "also," in the case of coordination:

(44) renmin shao er qin shou zhong
people few but bird beast numerous
"People are few but [wild] animals are numerous" (Han Feizi)

Subordination may be indicated by subordinating conjunctions or particles, which can occur in the first clause, in the second, or in both.

In the case of conditional sentences, the conjunctions *ru*, *ruo* or *gou* "if" may appear in the first clause (*if*-clause), and the markers *ze* or *si* "then" in the main clause (for an exhaustive analysis of the conditionals in Classical Chinese, see Harbsmeier 1981:229–287):

(45) wang ruo yin qi wuzui er jiu si di ze niu yang
Prince if pain it no guilt and go-to execution place then ox sheep
he ze yan
what choose PCL.
"If [you] the prince were pained by its going without guilt to the place of execution, then what was there to choose between an ox and a sheep?" (Mencius)

In concessive sentences, the most commonly used conjunction of concession is *sui* "although, even if." In the main clause one often finds *er*, which then has its adversative meaning:

(46) sui zhi, er bu bing
though outspoken yet not blame
"Though [he may] be outspoken, [he won't] be blamed" (Zhuangzi)

In sentences expressing cause, the "because" clause may be introduced by the preposition *yi*, and the main clause may contain the connective *gu* "so, therefore":

(47) yi qi bu zheng, gu tian xia mo neng yu
because he NEGATION compete therefore Heaven under nobody can with
zhi zheng
him compete
"Because he does not compete, nobody can compete with him under Heaven" (Laozi)

Time clauses are introduced by the prepositions *ji* or *dang*:

(48) dang zai Song ye, yu jiang you yuan xing
when be-at Song PCL. I intend there-is far go
"When I was in Song, I intended to go far away" (Mencius)

5.5 Significant diachronic developments between Late Archaic and Early Medieval Chinese

The above study is concerned chiefly with the Classical Language as it is fixed during the Warring States period, i.e., the Late Archaic period (fifth–second centuries BC). From the time of the Early Medieval period (second–sixth centuries AD), one can consider that the vernacular language is actually distinct from the literary, deserving a separate description of its own. Here we will only discuss certain important grammatical structures which did not exist in Classical Chinese but which developed later in the vernacular, prior to the sixth century AD. For a detailed review of the developments in the language between these two stages, see Peyraube 1996.

The so-called "disposal form" appears around the sixth century, having the following structure: *Noun Phrase*$_1$*-Agent* + BA + *Noun Phrase*$_2$*-Patient* + *Verb Phrase* where BA is a preposition (*ba*, *jiang*, *chi*, or *zhuo*) which introduces the patient noun phrase. These prepositions were verbs in Classical Chinese meaning "to lead, to take, to hold." Used for V_1 in a serial verb construction $V_1 + O +$ *Verb Phrase*$_2$ in the Pre-Medieval period, they were grammaticalized and became prepositions, probably by analogy with the dative construction *yi* + *DO* + *V* + *IO* discussed above (see §5.3.2), where *yi* was already a marker introducing a direct object (see Mei 1990; Peyraube 1989a).

Locative prepositional phrases introduced by the preposition *yu*, which are postverbal in Classical Chinese, begin shifting to preverbal position in Pre-Medieval. The preposition *yu* is replaced by *zai* around the sixth century, when *zai*, a verb meaning "to be at" (and also used as V_1 in a serial verb construction $V_1 + O_1 + V_2 + O_2$) has already been grammaticalized as a locative preposition (see Peyraube 1994).

The resultative construction, of the type *dasi* (lit. beat-die) "beat to death," also appears in the Early Medieval period, and is not found in Classical Chinese, contrary to what some scholars have argued. What we find prior to the fifth century is a $V_1 + V_2$ serial verb construction in which V_2 is a transitive verb. The resultative compound arises from this serial verb construction, when the transitive verb has become intransitive (see Mei 1991).

Classifiers (CLs) do not exist in Classical Chinese (a classifier being fundamentally a word which, in theory, must occur before a noun and after a demonstrative and/or a number or another quantifier, marking the class to which the associated word belongs). In that period we find only *measure words* (MWs), which are first used in postnominal position, and then in the prenominal position in Late Archaic: *Noun* + *Number* + *MW* > *Number* + *MW* + *Noun*. True classifiers probably begin to appear during the Han period (first century BC), though at that time they still retain many characteristics of the nouns from which they issue, and they are always postnominal.

The grammaticalization process by which classifiers arose, depriving them of their original meanings, is a long one. For a great majority of them, it is completed only around the sixth century. By the time the process has been completed, classifers have moved into prenominal position: *N* + *Num* + *CL* > *Num* + *CL* + *N* (see Peyraube and Wiebusch 1993).

Several other important developments have taken place between the Classical period and the Tang dynasty. I will mention here briefly the following:

1. *Personal pronouns*: A distinction between the two first-person pronouns *wo* and *wu* (see §5.2.2.1.1) gradually disappears. The third-person pronouns *qi* (genitive) and *zhi* (accusative) are replaced by new forms *yi*, *qu*, and (later) *ta*, and are no longer differentiated according to case. True plural forms, with the markers of plurality *deng*, *cao*, or *bei* following the pronouns, develop.

2. *Negatives*: The great number of adverbs of negation found in Classical Chinese is greatly reduced in the later vernacular. *Fu*, which becomes the most common negative, is no longer construed as a blend of *bu* + *zhi*. *Wu*, likewise, is no longer seen as a blend of *wu* + *zhi*.
3. *Localizers*: Monosyllabic in the Classical period, they become disyllabic, beginning in the Pre-Medieval period, by the addition of a suffix *-tou*.
4. *Disjunctive questions*: These appear in the fifth century, with *wei* serving as a disjunctive question marker, used singly or in pairs: $Noun_1$ + $Verb\ Phrase_1$ + *wei* + ($Noun_2$) + $Verb\ Phrase_2$ or $Noun_1$ + *wei* + $Verb\ Phrase_1$ + *wei* + ($Noun_2$) + $Verb\ Phrase_2$ (see Mei 1978).

6. LEXICON

The overall lexicon of Ancient Chinese is quite different from that of Contemporary Chinese. The former is composed of: (i) words that are still attested in the contemporary language, like *shan* "mountain" or *shui* "water"; (ii) words that only exist in the ancient language, and have disappeared from the modern language, such as *yue* "say"; (iii) words that are still used today, but with different meanings, like *zou* "run" (Ancient Chinese) > "walk" (Contemporary Chinese). Of the three types, the first are rare and the last are numerous (see He and Jiang 1980:3).

6.1 Historical development of the lexicon

The Ancient Chinese lexicon has changed considerably since the Pre-Archaic period. From the vocabulary of everyday life (lexemes for food, clothing, housing), we find only fifteen words in the oracle bone inscriptions (fourteenth–eleventh centuries BC), seventy-one in the bronze inscriptions (tenth–sixth centuries BC), and 297 in *Shuo wen jie zi* (second century AD). This naturally does not mean that there were only fifteen words denoting these activities in the Pre-Archaic language, and so forth; many other words must have been used which have disappeared leaving no trace (on the varying richness of Chinese vocabulary in different periods, see He and Jiang 1980:9).

According to He and Jiang (1980:136–137), Classical Chinese has an identifiable basic vocabulary of about 2,000 full words, of which 1,100 occur quite commonly. From four major works of the Late Archaic period (*Confucian Analects, Mencius, Da Xue, Zhong Yong*), He and Jiang have isolated 4,466 distinct words, estimating that about half of these are semantically empty (i.e, are proper personal names or place names). There is no implication that the vocabulary of Classical Chinese is impoverished compared to that of Contemporary Chinese – simply different. For example, there is only a single verb meaning "to wash" in Contemporary Chinese (*xi*), whereas there are five in Classical Chinese: *mu* "to wash (the hair)"; *yu* "to wash (the body)"; *hui* "to wash (the face)"; *zao* "to wash (the hands)"; *xi* "to wash (the feet)."

During the long history of Ancient Chinese, several different processes have led to changes in the lexicon. The major processes of internal development include (i) compounding, a highly productive process beginning in the Han period; (ii) semantic extension (e.g., *zu* "foot soldier" > *zu* "all sorts of soldiers"); and (iii) semantic narrowing (e.g., *zi* "child" (boy or girl) > *zi* "son"). In addition, the Ancient Chinese lexicon was enlarged by borrowing words from other languages.

6.2 Inherited elements and loanwords

There has been a strong tendency in the past to view the Ancient Chinese lexicon as a monolithic linguistic entity, resistant to influences from all surrounding foreign languages. This is certainly a fallacy. Without going as far as Norman (1988:17) who states, "the fact that only a relatively few Chinese words have been shown to be Sino-Tibetan may indicate that a considerable proportion of the Chinese lexicon is of foreign origin," we can doubtless rightly assert that the Ancient Chinese lexicon contains numerous loanwords. Nevertheless, the identification of such words and their sources is often uncertain. Below we mention a few noncontroversial examples of loanwords.

There are two common words for "dog" in Ancient Chinese: *quan*, which is probably the native Chinese word, and *gou*, which appears at the end of the Warring States period. *Gou* is a loanword from a language ancestral to the Modern Miao-Yao languages. The word *hu* for "tiger" might have been borrowed from an Austronesian language in prehistoric times (see Norman 1988:17–20). Other words of non-Chinese origin are *xiang* "elephant" (borrowed from a Tai language?); *putao* "grape" (from Old-Iranian?); *moli* "jasmin" (from Sanskrit); *shamen* "Buddhist monk" (from Sanskrit); *luotuo* "camel" (possibly from an Altaic language).

Bibliography

Principal sources

Baxter, W. 1992. *A Handbook of Old Chinese Phonology*. Berlin: Mouton de Gruyter.
Baxter, W. and L. Sagart. 1998. "Word formation in Old Chinese." In J. Packard (ed.), *New Approaches to Chinese Word Formation: Morphology, Phonology and the Lexicon in Modern and Ancient Chinese*, pp. 35–76. Berlin: Mouton de Gruyter.
Harbsmeier, C. 1981. *Aspects of Classical Chinese Syntax*. London: Curzon Press.
He, J. and S. Jiang. 1980. *Gu hanyu cihui jianghua* (*Talks on the lexicon of Ancient Chinese*). Beijing: Beijing chubanshe.
Norman, J. 1988. *Chinese*. Cambridge: Cambridge University Press.
Peyraube, A. 1996. "Recent issues in Chinese historical syntax." In J. Huang and A. Li (eds.), *New Horizons in Chinese Linguistics*, pp. 161–213. Dordrecht: Kluwer Academic Press.
Pulleyblank, E. 1991. *Lexicon of Reconstructed Pronunciation in Early Middle Chinese, Late Middle Chinese and Early Mandarin*. Vancouver: University of British Columbia Press.
———. 1995. *Outline of Classical Chinese Grammar*. Vancouver: University of British Columbia Press.

Additional references

Baxter, W. 1980. "Some proposals on Old Chinese phonology." In F. van Coetsem and L. Waugh (eds.), *Contributions to Historical Linguistics: Issues and Materials*, pp. 1–33. Leiden: Brill.
Bodman, N. 1980. "Proto-Chinese and Sino-Tibetan: data towards establishing the nature of the relationship." In F. van Coetsem and L. Waugh (eds.), *Contributions to Historical Linguistics: Issues and Materials*, pp. 34–199. Leiden: Brill.
Chou, F. 1963. "Stages in the development of the Chinese language." In F. Chou (ed.), *Zhongguo yuwen luncong*, pp. 432–438. Taipei: Zhengzhong shuju.
Comrie, B. 1989. *Language Universals and Linguistic Typology* (2nd edition). Oxford: Basil Blackwell.
Downer, G. 1959. "Derivation by tone-change in Classical Chinese." *Bulletin of the School of Oriental and African Studies* 22:258–290.
Guan, X. 1981. *Xi-Zhou jinwen yufa yanjiu* (*Research on the Grammar of the Bronzes of the Western Zhou*). Beijing: Shangwu yinshuguan.
Haudricourt, G. 1954. "Comment reconstruire le cinois archaique?" *Word* 10 (2/3):351–364.

Jaxontov, S. 1983–1984 [1960]. "Shanggu hanyu zhong de fufuyin (Consonant clusters in Old Chinese)." *Guowai yuyanxue*, pp. 21–25.
Karlgren, B. 1915–1926. *Études sur la phonologie chinoise.* Leiden: Brill.
_______. 1957. "Grammatica Serica Recensa." *Bulletin of the Museum of Far Eastern Antiquities* 29:1–332.
Li, C. and S. Thompson. 1974. "An explanation of word order change: SVO > SOV." *Foundations of Language* 12:201–214.
Li, F. 1971. "Shanggu yin yanjiu (Research on Old Chinese pronunciation)." *Tsing Hua Journal of Chinese Studies* 9:1–61.
Liu, J. 1958. *Hanyu wenyan yufa* (*A grammar of Classical Chinese*). Beijing: Zhonghua shuju.
Liu, J. and A. Peyraube. 1994. "History of some coordinative conjunctions in Chinese." *Journal of Chinese Linguistics* 22 (2):179–201.
Ma, C. 1983. *Gudai hanyu yufa* (*A grammar of Ancient Chinese*). Qinan: Shandong jiaoyu chubanshe.
Mei, T. 1970. "Tones and prosody in Middle Chinese and the origin of the rising tone." *Harvard Journal of Asiatic Studies* 30:86–110.
_______. 1978. "Xiandai hanyu xuanzewen jufa delaiyuan (The origin of the disjunction question in Modern Chinese)." *The Bulletin of History and Philology* 49:15–36.
_______. 1980. "Sisheng bieyi zhong de shijiancengci (Chronological strata in derivation by tone-change)." *Zhongguo yuwen* 6:427–443.
_______. 1989. "The causative and denominative functions of the **s-* prefix in Old Chinese." *In Proceedings of the 2nd International Conference on Sinology*, pp. 33–51. Taipei: Academia Sinica.
_______. 1990. "Tang-Song chuzhishi de laiyuan (Origin of the disposal form in the Tang-Song period)." *Zhongguo yuwen* 3:191–216.
_______. 1991. "Cong Han dai de 'dong.sha' 'dong.si' lai kan dongbu jiegou de fazhan (The development of the resultative construction since the Han structures 'dong.sha' and 'dong.si')." *Yuyanxue luncong* 16:112–136.
_______. 1994. "Tang dai Song dai gongtongyu de yufa he xiandai fanyan de yufa (The grammar of Tang-Song koine and the grammar of Modern Chinese dialects)." *Chinese Languages and Linguistics* 2:61–97.
_______. 1997. "Hanyu qi ge leixing tezheng de laiyuan (Typological changes in the history of the Chinese language)." *Chinese Languages and Linguistics* 4:81–104.
Peyraube, A. 1987. "The double-object construction in Lunyu and Mengzi." In *Wang Li Memorial Volumes*, pp. 331–358. Hong Kong: Joint Publishing.
_______. 1988. *Syntaxe diachronique du chinois – ēvolution des constructions datives du 14ēmē siēcle av. J.-C. au 18ēme siēcle.* Paris: Collēge de France.
_______. 1989a. "Zaoqi ba ziju de jige wenti (Some problems on the earliest forms of 'ba')." *Yuwen yanjiu* 1:1–9.
_______. 1989b. "History of the passive constructions in Chinese until the 10th century." *Journal of Chinese Linguistics* 17:335–372.
_______. 1991. "Some remarks on the history of Chinese classifiers." *Santa Barbara Papers in Linguistics* 3:106–126.
_______. 1994. "On the history of Chinese locative prepositions." *Chinese Languages and Linguistics* 2:361–387.
_______. 1997a. "On word order and word order change in Pre-Archaic Chinese." *Chinese Languages and Linguistics* 4:105–124.
_______. 1997b. "On word order in Archaic Chinese." *Cahiers de Linguistique Asie Orientale* 26 (1):3–20.
_______. 1999. "On the modal auxiliaries of possibility in Classical Chinese." In H. S. Wang, F. Tsao, and C. Lien (eds.), *Selected Papers from the Fifth International Conference on Chinese Linguistics*, pp. 27–52. Taipei: Crane Publishing.
Peyraube, A. and T. Wiebusch. 1993. "Le rôle des classificateurs nominaux en chinois et leur ēvolution historique: un cas de changement cyclique." *Faits de Langue* 2:51–61.
_______. 1995. "Problems relating to the history of different copulas in Ancient Chinese." In M. Chen and O. Tzeng (eds.), *Linguistic Essays in Honor of William S-Y Wang*, pp. 383–404. Taipei: Pyramid Press.

Pulleyblank, E. 1962. "The consonantal system of Old Chinese." *Asia Major* 9:58–144; 206–265.

———. 1970–1971. "Late Middle Chinese." *Asia Major* 15:197–239; 16:121–168.

———. 1978. "The nature of the Middle Chinese tones and their development." *Journal of Chinese Linguistics* 6:173–203.

———. 1984. *Middle Chinese: A Study in Historical Phonology*. Vancouver: University of British Columbia Press.

———. 1993. "Old Chinese phonology: a review article." *Journal of Chinese Linguistics* 21 (2):338–380.

———. 1995. "The historical and prehistorical relationships of Chinese." In W. Wang (ed.), *The Ancestry of the Chinese Language*, pp. 145–194. The Journal of Chinese Linguistics Monograph Series, 8. Berkeley: University of California Press.

Qiu, X. 1978. "Hanzi xingcheng wenti de chubu tansuo (Explorations on the formation of Chinese script)." *Zhongguo yuwen* 3:162–171.

Sagart, L. 1986. "On the departing tone." *Journal of Chinese Linguistics* 14 (1):90–112.

———. 1993a. "New views on Old Chinese phonology." *Diachronica* 10 (2):237–60.

———. 1993b. "L'infixe *-r-* en chinois archaïque." *Bulletin de la Société Linguistique de Paris* 88:261–293.

———. 1994. "Proto-Austronesian and Old Chinese evidence for Sino-Austronesian." *Oceanic Linguistics* 33(2):271–307.

Starostin, S. 1989. "Nostratic and Sino-Caucasian." In V. Shevoroshkin (ed.), *Explorations in Macrofamilies*, pp. 42–66. Bochum: Brockmeyer.

Sun, C. 1991. "The adposition *yi* and word order in Classical Chinese." *Journal of Chinese Linguistics* 19 (2):202–219.

Ting, P. 1996. "Tonal evolution and tonal reconstruction in Chinese." In J. Huang and A. Li (eds.), *New Horizons in Chinese Linguistics*, pp. 141–159. Dordrecht: Kluwer Academic Press.

Wang, L. 1958. *Hanyu shigao* (*History of Chinese*). Beijing: Kexue chubanshe.

———. 1979. *Gudai hanyu changshi* (*Elements of Ancient Chinese*). Beijing: Renmin jiaoyu chubanshe.

Zhu, X. 1980. *Gudai hanyu* (*Ancient Chinese*). Tianjin: Renmin chubanshe.

CHAPTER 9

Mayan

VICTORIA R. BRICKER

1. HISTORICAL AND CULTURAL CONTEXTS

1.1 Linguistic prehistory and history

The language described herein as *Mayan* is known from a hieroglyphic script that was employed in a large region in Mesoamerica, encompassing much of what is today southeastern Mexico, northern and eastern Guatemala, all of Belize, and the western part of Honduras. The earliest securely dated and geographically provenienced hieroglyphic text from this region is Stela 29 from Tikal in northeastern Guatemala, which bears a date of 6 July AD 292. The script was in continuous use in this region until the second half of the sixteenth century, when it was replaced by the Latin-based alphabet introduced by the Spaniards.

Lyle Campbell and Terrence Kaufman (1985) have classified the thirty or so Mayan languages in terms of five branches, each of which is further divided into groups and subgroups (Fig. 9.1). At the time of the Spanish Conquest, the inhabitants of the region where hieroglyphic texts have been found spoke languages representing the Yucatecan and Greater Tzeltalan groups (Fig. 9.2). The Yucatecan languages were confined to the Yucatan peninsula in the north. South of them was a broad band of Cholan languages, running from Chontal and Chol in the west to Cholti and Chorti in the east. Tzeltal was the only language in Tzeltalan Proper that was spoken in the region under consideration.

Kaufman's (1976) glottochronological estimates suggest that by AD 292 Yucatecan had already separated from Huastecan, and that Cholan and Tzeltalan Proper had already differentiated from each other. This means that the language which is herein called "Mayan" may have represented three quite distinct languages – Yucatecan, Cholan, and Tzeltalan – not dialects of a single language. By AD 600, the Cholan languages had differentiated into Chorti, Chol, and Chontal, and Tzeltal had separated from Tzotzil. The Yucatecan languages, Yucatec, Lacandon, Itza, and Mopan, probably did not emerge as separate languages until after AD 950 (Justeson *et al.* 1985:14–16), and so are outside the scope of this study.

The region inhabited by speakers of "Mayan" can, for the most part, be classified as lowland (which I have defined as land lying below 600 meters; see Bricker 1977). The exceptions include the adjacent highlands of eastern Chiapas and western Honduras, which were inhabited by speakers of Tzeltal and Chorti, respectively, when the Spaniards arrived (Fig. 9.2). The remaining Cholan languages and all the Yucatecan languages were limited to the lowlands at that time (Bricker 1977).

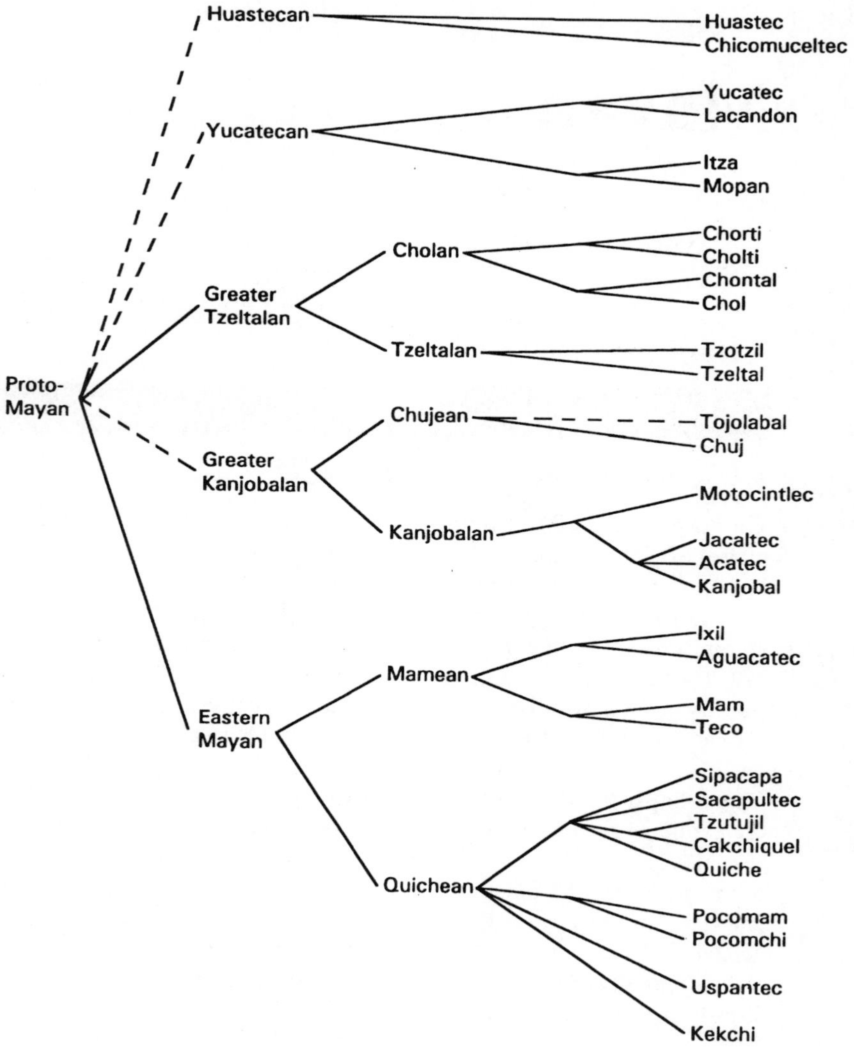

Figure 9.1 Classification of Mayan languages. Dotted lines represent less secure groupings. After Campbell and Kaufman (1985:fig. 1)

1.2 The people and their culture

The ancestors of the people who spoke the languages encoded in the script did not appear in the region until about 1000 BC, which marks the beginning of the period archeologists call the Middle Preclassic (see Sharer 1994:Table 2.1). Historical linguists believe that they came out of the highlands of Guatemala in the south (e.g., Kaufman 1976:106–109). These first Maya settlers in the lowlands were maize farmers who lived in villages and larger, nucleated settlements dominated by terraced platforms and public buildings arranged in clusters connected by causeways (Sharer 1994:80–83). The Late Preclassic that followed (400 BC–250 AD) was characterized by "a rapid growth in population and in the development of stratified organizations, as demonstrated by elaborate funerary remains, massive ceremonial structures housing the artifacts of a variety of ritual activities, and the crystallization of a sophisticated art style, all recognized as typically Maya" (Sharer 1994:85). However, these defining traits of lowland Maya civilization did not yet include writing, which seems

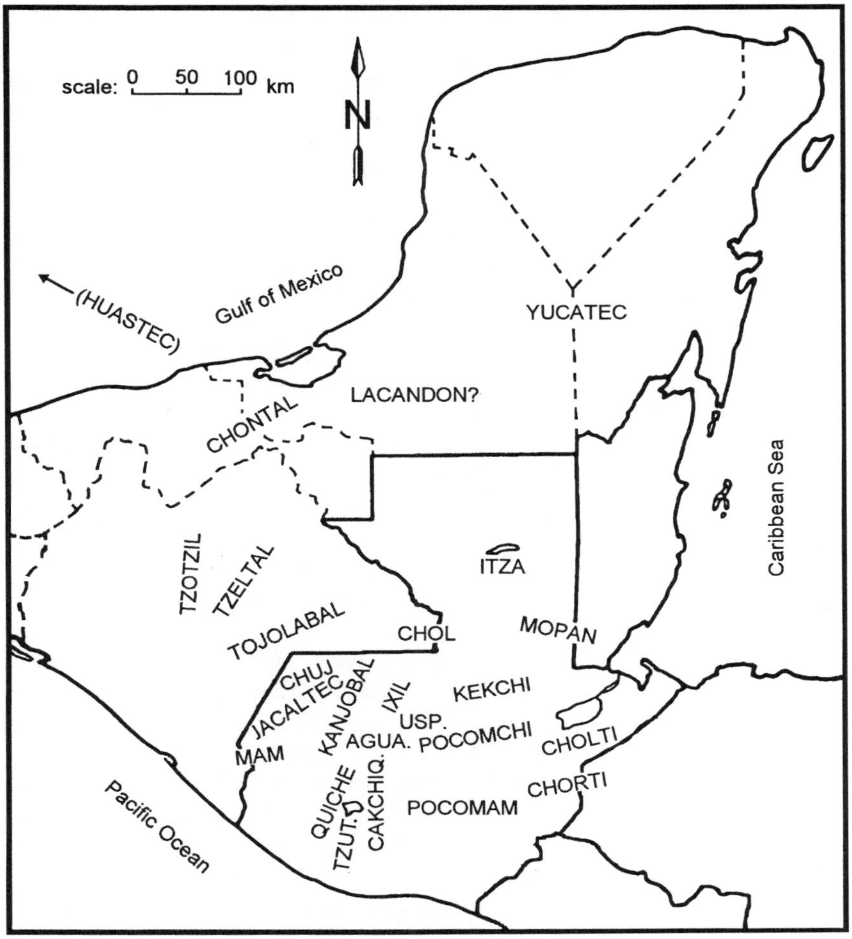

Figure 9.2 Approximate locations of Mayan languages in AD 1550

to have been invented by speakers of non-Mayan languages outside the region in question during the Late Preclassic period (Ch. 10, §2.2) and was not adapted for use with Mayan languages until the very end of this period.

The Late Preclassic period was followed by the Early Classic (AD 250–600), a period characterized by Sharer (1994:138) as "the era when state-level political organizations developed and expanded in the Maya area, especially in the southern and central lowlands." The settlements were larger, with a well-defined central core surrounded by residential areas. The centers contained various specialized structures faced with stone, such as palatial residences for the rulers and their families, ballcourts, and temples on stepped platforms (Sharer 1994:475). Stone was gradually replaced by perishable pole and thatch as building materials for residences, moving out from the center to the periphery of these cities.

1.3 The documents and their content

A strikingly new feature of Early Classic cities was the number of public monuments with inscribed hieroglyphic texts. Texts could be found carved on the walls and in the doorways of buildings, including the lintels, jambs, and steps. They also appeared on the stone rings of ballcourts, through which the rubber ball had to pass in order for a team to score, and on free-standing slabs of stone, called stelae, scattered around the center of a site (Fig. 9.3).

Ceramic vessels had bands of hieroglyphs around their rims, designating the ritual substances for which they served as containers (e.g., chocolate [Stuart 1988]), describing them as plates, cups, or bowls (Houston and Taube 1987), and naming the owners of the vessels and the artists who had painted or carved the texts on them (Stuart 1987:1–11). Pendants and earspools and flares of jade, shell trumpets, animal bones, and even sting-ray spines used in bloodletting often contained short hieroglyphic texts. Elaborate painted murals composed of both text and pictures covered the walls of rooms and tombs. Everything we know about the Early Classic form of the language of Mayan hieroglyphs comes from these sources. There may also have been, as there were in later centuries, screenfold books, or codices, made of animal hide and fig-bark paper (Sharer 1994:272); if so, the humid, tropical climate of the lowlands did not favor their survival into modern times.

The hieroglyphic texts carved on stelae and on the surfaces of buildings were primarily historical in content, containing the biographies of the rulers of the cities, which highlighted the dates of their birth, marriage, accession to office, raids on other cities, and death or burial. They also record genealogical information about the rulers and the rituals they performed at the end of major time periods and on anniversaries of the dates when they took office. Some of the longer texts refer to a succession of rulers, resembling, in this respect, the king lists of the ancient Near East.

The texts relating to a single ruler are often distributed rather widely over a site, with different "chapters" inscribed on separate buildings and stelae in several locations. For this reason, much of the research carried out by epigraphers has involved determining how the texts are related to each other historically and piecing together the biographies of the individual rulers (e.g., Proskouriakoff 1960; Jones and Satterthwaite 1982:124–131). Fortunately, the ancient Maya had a sophisticated calendar that permitted them to specify the chronological position of events in a cycle of more than five thousand years, and they were rather compulsive about dating their texts. Therefore, the histories of the major Early Classic cities are known in considerable detail (see, *inter alios*, Jones and Satterthwaite 1982).

The calendar employed by the lowland Maya was probably borrowed from the people who invented the Epi-Olmec script during the Late Preclassic period. The base of this calendar was a period of 360 days known as the *tun*. The *tun* was divided into eighteen smaller periods called *winals*, each containing 20 days (*k'ins*). Twenty *tuns* formed a larger unit called a *k'atun*, and 20 *k'atuns* were grouped into a *pik*. The complete cycle consisted of 13 (not 20) *piks*, which was known as the Long Count. The beginning of the Long Count was arbitrarily set to coincide with 11 August 3114 (Gregorian) BC, according to the correlation of the Maya and Western calendars that agrees best with ethnohistorical sources from the sixteenth century, and it will end on AD 21 December 2012. Obviously all of Maya history recorded in hieroglyphs falls within this period.

In addition to the Long Count, the Maya calendar contains two other cycles which also have their roots in the earlier Epi-Olmec culture. One is a ritual, or divinatory, cycle of 260 days, composed of two subsidiary cycles based on a sequence of 20 named days (*ʔimiš, ʔik', ʔak'b'al, k'an, čikčan, kimi, manik', lamat, muluk, ʔok, čuwen, ʔeb', b'en, hiš, men, kib', kab'an, ʔets'nab', kawak,* and *ʔahaw*) and the numbers from 1 to 13, which serve as coefficients of the days. The other represents the vague year of 365 days, which is divided into 18 named months of 20 days each (*k'an-halab', ʔik'-k'at, čak-k'at, sots', katsew, tsikin, yaš-k'in, mol, č'en, yaš, sak, keh, mak, ʔuniw, muwan, paš, k'anasiy,* and *kumk'u*) and a five-day intercalary "month," *wayeb'*, that ended the year. The least common multiple of these two cycles is the

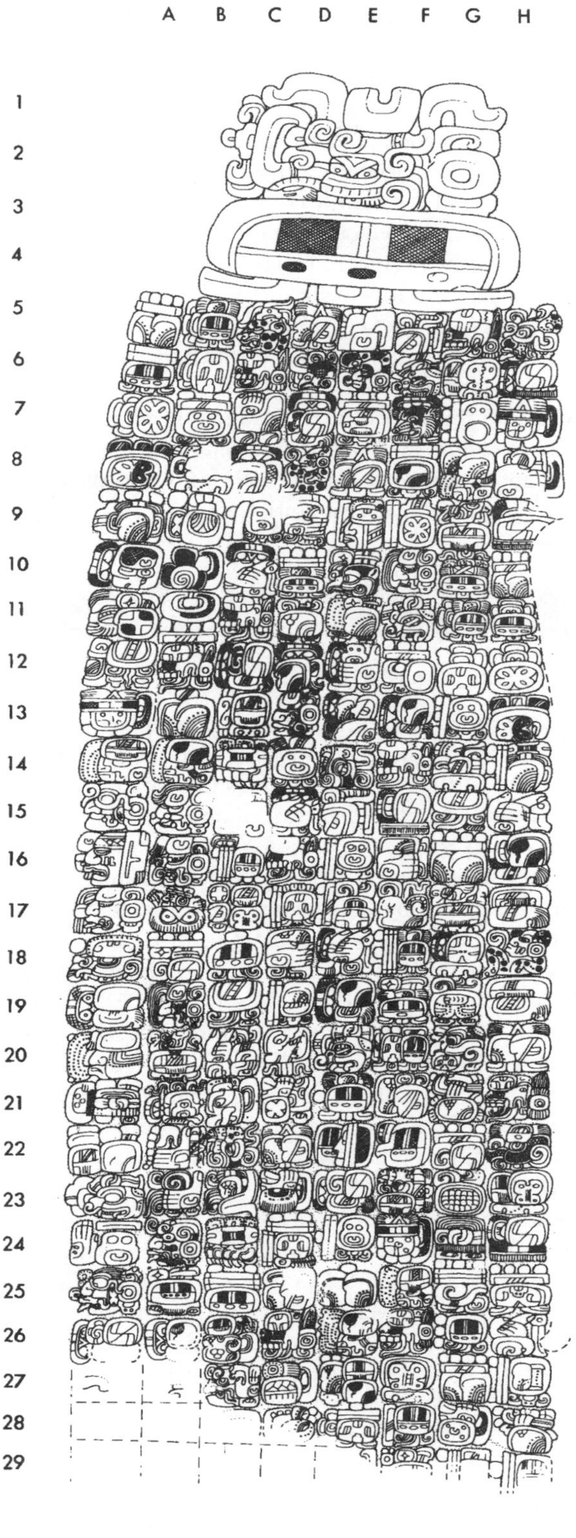

Figure 9.3 Tikal, stela 31, back. After Jones and Satterthwaite (1982:fig. 52b)

so-called Calendar Round of 18,980 days or fifty-two years, which was the Maya counterpart of the European century.

With a firm grasp on the passage of time, the Maya had the tools for recording, and later predicting, astronomical events. By the end of the fourth century AD, they were relating Long Count dates to a lunar calendar, recording several kinds of information: (i) the age of the Moon on the date in question; (ii) the position of the current lunar month in a six-month semester; and (iii) the length of the month as either twenty-nine or thirty days. Eventually, they produced books of tables for predicting dates of solar and lunar eclipses, equinoxes and solstices, heliacal risings of Venus as morning star, and retrograde periods of Mars, examples of which have survived only from much later times (Bricker and Bricker 1983; Bricker and Bricker 1986, 1988).

Both the content of the texts and the media on which they were written suggest that their principal function was to glorify the elite. The focus is on dynastic history, ritual, and on designating the owners and makers of highly valued objects, such as elaborately painted and carved vases and jade and shell ornaments. And although tribute items seem to be mentioned in some Late Classic texts (Stuart 1993), no records of mundane commercial transactions have been preserved in Mayan script.

2. WRITING SYSTEM

2.1 Principles of Mayan writing

The Maya had a mixed writing system, consisting of both logographic and syllabic signs. The total number of different signs that have been identified ranges between 650 and 700 for the corpus as a whole, but the number of signs used at any one time apparently never exceeded 400 (Grube 1994:177). These figures are consistent with the logosyllabic nature of Mayan writing.

The reading order of a Mayan text is from top to bottom and from left to right in paired columns. The columns are labeled by scholars with capital letters and the rows with numbers. A glyph block is normally designated by a combination of a letter and a number, for example A5. In Figure 9.3, for example, after a large introductory glyph that accounts for four rows, the text begins at A5 and moves on to B5, then A6 and B6, A7 and B7, until the end of the first two columns. The reader then moves on to C5 and D5, C6 and D6, and so on through the inscription. The individual glyph blocks are also read from left to right and from top to bottom: prefixes and superfixes appear before the main sign, which in turn is read before postfixes and subfixes. The following transcription conventions are used in this chapter: phonetic transcriptions of the glyphs appear in boldface type, whereas morphemic transcriptions are italicized.

Phoneticism appears quite early in the history of Mayan writing. By AD 320, there is already evidence of the use of phonetic complementation, in which a word is represented by a logogram, but another sign is added to it as a prefix or a suffix to indicate how part of it is pronounced (Justeson and Mathews 1990:117). The first evidence of its use is in a text on a jade plaque bearing a Long Count date and Calendar Round corresponding to 15 September AD 320 in the Gregorian calendar (Fig. 9.4 left). The text records the accession of the ruler who is pictured on the other side of the plaque (Fig. 9.4 right). The collocation in question (at B9 in Fig. 9.4 left; see Fig. 9.5a) consists of the logogram for a verb meaning "sit" (*čum* in Cholan and *kum* in Yucatecan) and the sign for **mu**, which indicates that the final consonant of the word represented by the logogram is /m/ (Ringle 1985:153–154). Note that the vowel in **mu** also echoes the vowel /u/ in *čum*/*kum*.

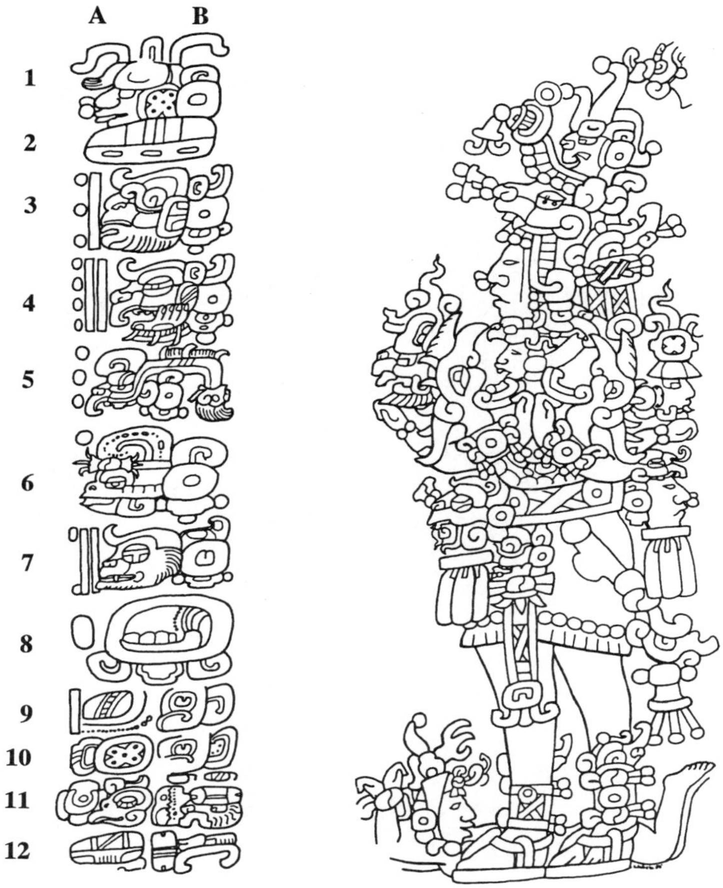

Figure 9.4 The Leyden Plaque (left = back; right = front). Drawing by Linda Schele

The Early Classic inscriptions contain a number of other examples of phonetic complementation, including the words for "day" (*k'in*, spelled as **k'in[ni]** in Fig. 9.5d), "20-day month" (*winal*, spelled as **winal[la]** in Fig. 9.5f), "sky" (*čan* in Cholan and *kaʔan* in Yucatecan, labeled as **čan[na]** in Fig. 9.5h), and "yellow" (*k'an*, spelled as **k'an[na]** in Fig. 9.5j). Examples of the same logograms without phonetic complements (Fig. 9.5c, e, and g) suggest that complementation was optional in Mayan writing.

The original function of phonetic complementation was probably to disambiguate logograms that had several possible readings, but over time it was extended to logograms which had pronunciations that were never in doubt. Justeson and Mathews (1990:118–119) have found evidence that "extensions of orthographic practices are often promoted by similar practices in similar contexts." For example, neither the **winal** nor the **k'in** logograms are polyvalent, so they can be read unambiguously without phonetic complements. These logograms frequently appear side by side in Long Count expressions (e.g., Fig. 9.6a). By AD 425, the **winal** logogram had acquired a phonetic complement (Fig. 9.6b), and less than a century later, in AD 514, the word *k'in* was also being spelled with a logogram plus phonetic complement in contexts where the **winal** logogram employed the same convention (Fig. 9.6c).

The first examples of syllabic writing can also be found in texts dating to the Early Classic period. Two kinds of syllables have been recognized in the script. One consists of a single vowel (V), the other of a consonant followed by a vowel (CV). Mayan words have two basic

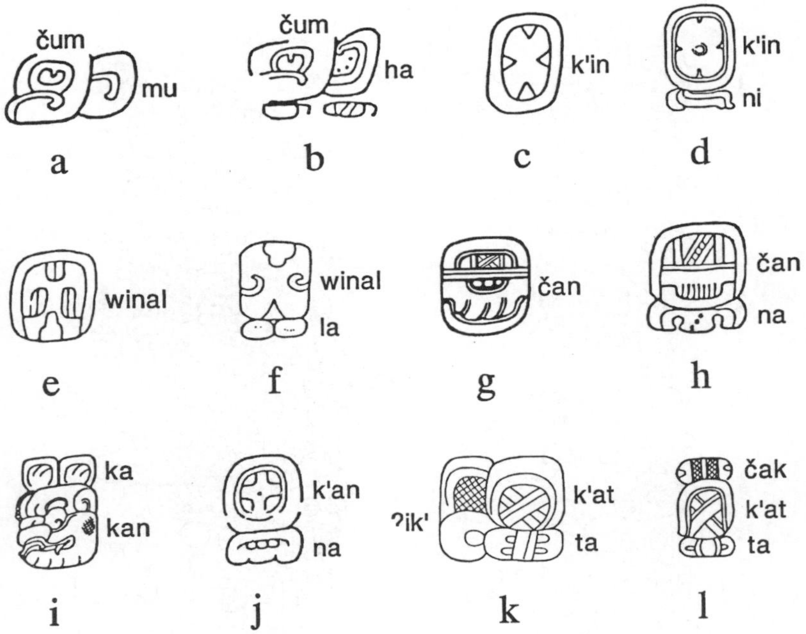

Figure 9.5 Phonetic complementation (a, Leyden Plaque B9. b, Leyden Plaque B10. c, Balakbal, Stela 5 (Justeson and Mathews 1990:fig. 12). d, Palenque, Foliated Cross Tablet, D17 (Maudslay 1889–1902:IV, plate 82). e, Tikal, Stela 31, B6 (Jones and Satterthwaite 1982:fig. 52b). f, Balakbal, Stela 5 (Justeson and Mathews 1990:fig. 12). g, Tikal, Temple IV, Lintel 3, E3b (Jones and Satterthwaite 1982:fig. 74). h, Tikal, Stela 31, C13 (Jones and Satterthwaite 1982:fig. 52b). i, Pomona Panel, L1 (Schele and Miller 1986:fig. III. 12). j, Yaxchilan, Lintel 46, G3 (Graham 1979:101). k, Yaxchilan, Lintel 31, I4 (Graham 1979:71). l, Tila A, B5). a and b from a drawing by Linda Schele. l from *Maya Hieroglyphic Writing: An Introduction*, by J. Eric S. Thompson, fig. 16, *30*. New edition coppyright © 1960, 1971 by the University of Oklahoma Press

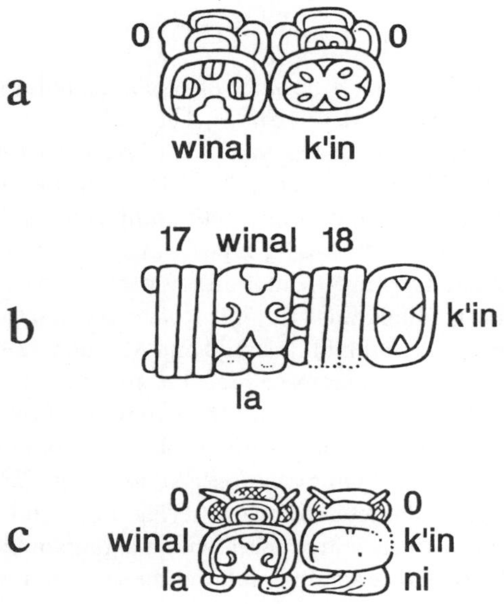

Figure 9.6 Phonetization (a, Tikal, Stela 31, G12–H12. b, Balakbal, Stela 5. c, Caracol, Stela 1, A3–B3). After Justeson and Mathews (1990:fig. 12)

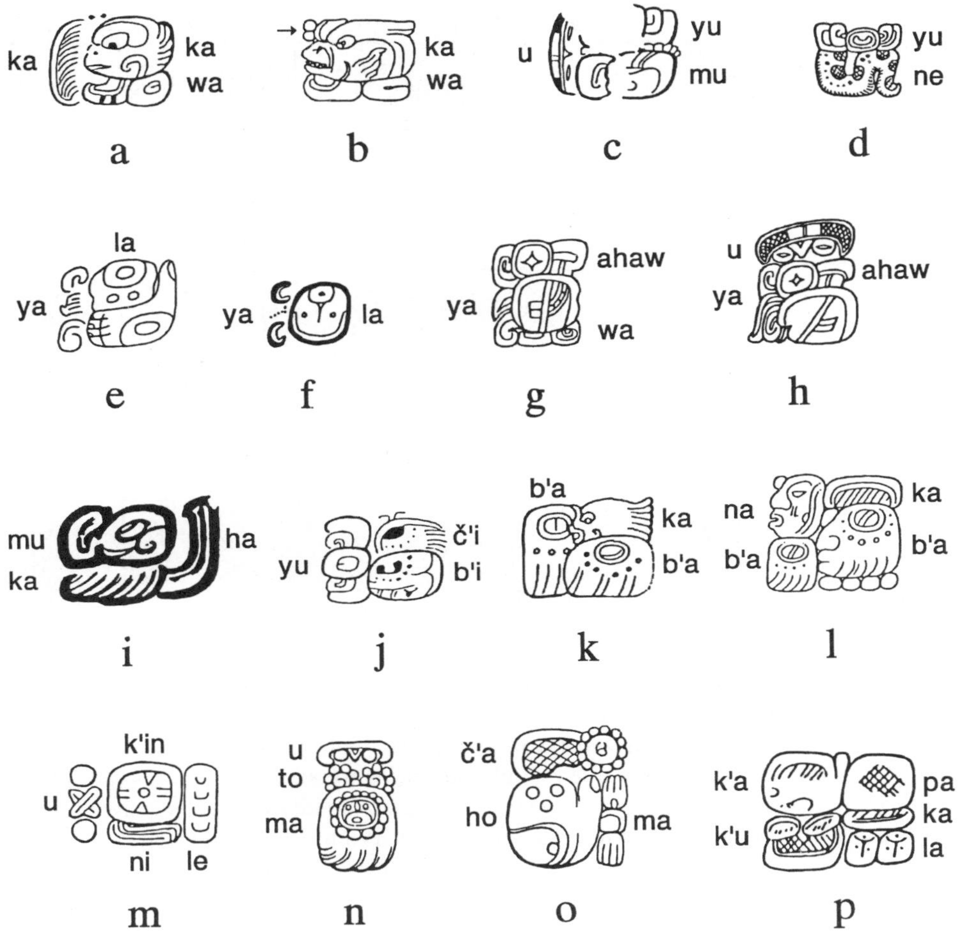

Figure 9.7 Syllabic and logosyllabic spellings (a, Rio Azul, pot, D. (Stuart 1988:fig. 2). b, Piedras Negras Lintel 3, P2. c, Rio Azul, pot, L. (Stuart 1988:fig. 2) d, Tikal, Stela 31, M3 (Jones and Satterthwaite 1982:fig. 52a). e, Caracol, Stela 16, B18 (Beetz and Satterthwaite 1981:fig. 15). f, Naranjo, Initial Series pot, B′ (Coe 1973:103). g, Tikal, Stela 31, L1 (Jones and Satterthwaite 1982:fig. 51a). h, Tikal, Stela 31, P2 (Jones and Satterthwaite 1982:fig. 52a). i, Rio Azul, Tomb 12, C. (Graham and Mobley 1986:456) j, Rio Azul, pot, B (Stuart 1988:fig. 2). k, Yaxchilan, Lintel 2, Q (Graham and von Euw 1977:15). l, Yaxchilan, Lintel 43, D4 (Graham 1979:95). m, Kabah, Structure 1 (Proskouriakoff and Thompson 1947:fig. 1g). n, Copan, Altar S, glyph I (Maudsley 1889--1902:I, plate 94). o, Copan, Stela A, F4 (Maudsley 1889--1902:I, plate 30). p, Chichen Itza, Monjas, Lintel 2A, B1 (Graham 1977:269). b after a drawing by John Montgomery

shapes: CVC and CVCVC. All words end in consonants, but only syllables ending in vowels have been attested in the script. This means that, in order to adapt such syllables to Mayan words, it was necessary to insert an extra vowel, which was never pronounced, at the end of the word. For example, the word *kakaw* "chocolate" was usually spelled syllabically as **ka-ka-wa** (Fig. 9.7a; the second **ka** sign is a variant of the first). This extra vowel is written in parentheses in transcriptions of syllabic spellings of Mayan words: **ka-ka-w(a)**. Another early example of the principle of vowel-insertion is the syllabic spelling of *u-yum* "his father" as **u-yu-m(u)** (Fig. 9.7c). The verb-stem, *muk-ah* "be buried," is spelled as **mu-ka-h(a)** in Figure 9.7i. Note that the syllabic spelling overrides the morphemic boundary between *muk* and *-ah*. The same is true of the syllabic spelling of *y-al* "her child" as **ya-l(a)** in Figure 9.7e and f.

Occasionally a different spelling principle, consonant-deletion, was invoked, as in the rendition of *y-unen* "his, her child" as **yu-ne** (Fig. 9.7d). In words containing more than one instance of the same syllable, one of them might be omitted; in such cases, the scribe sometimes added two small dots beside the upper left corner of the sign, indicating that the syllable should be repeated when the word was pronounced (Stuart and Houston 1994:46 and Fig. 57; compare Fig. 9.7a and b).

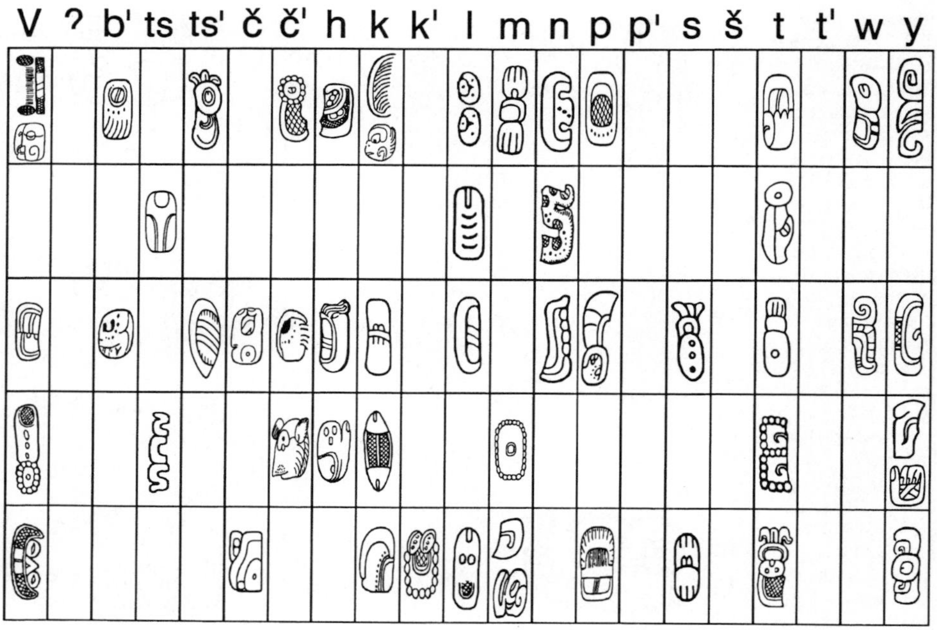

Figure 9.8 Early Classic syllables

The syllabic signs that are known to have been in use during the Early Classic period (AD 250–534) are arranged in the grid shown in Figure 9.8.

For spelling words containing grammatical affixes, a mixture of logographic and syllabic principles was often employed. In Figure 9.7g, the word *y-ahaw* "his ruler" is spelled by prefixing the syllable **ya** to the logogram for **ahaw**. The possessive pronoun, *y-*, is represented by the consonant in **ya**, and the vowel complements the first /a/ in **ahaw**. A similar strategy was later adopted for the representation of grammatical suffixes. Figure 9.7m illustrates the logosyllabic spelling of *u-k'in-il* "on the day." It contains one logogram (**k'in**) and three syllabic signs (**u**, **ni**, and **le**). The first syllabic sign (**u**) represents the clitic pronoun *u-*. The second syllabic sign (**ni**) has two functions: it complements the final consonant of **k'in** and also provides the vowel in the *-il* suffix. The third syllabic sign completes the spelling of the *-il* suffix by adding an /l/ and inserting an unpronounced /e/.

In addition to the phonetic complements that were used for clarifying which of several alternative readings for a logogram were intended, there were also semantic determinatives that served a similar purpose. The sign most commonly used as a determinative was a frame or cartouche that enclosed the glyphs for the days of the Maya week. An example of such a cartouche appears in Figure 9.9a, where it signals that the main sign enclosed by it refers to *kawak*, the nineteenth day of the twenty-day week.

In many cases, the cartouche rested on a pedestal, which served as a second semantic determinative for identifying day signs (Fig. 9.9b). When the main sign appeared without either the cartouche or the pedestal, it could be read in two different ways: as the syllable **ku** or the logogram **tun**. The logographic reading was usually signaled by the phonetic complement, **ni**, which was either postfixed or subfixed to the main sign (Fig. 9.9c, d, and g). During the Late Classic period, the **tun** reading was sometimes indicated by prefixing **tu** to the main sign (Fig. 9.9e), and occasionally both **tu** and **ni** served as complements for this sign (Fig. 9.9f). Finally, Figure 9.9h illustrates the syllabic use of this sign in the personal

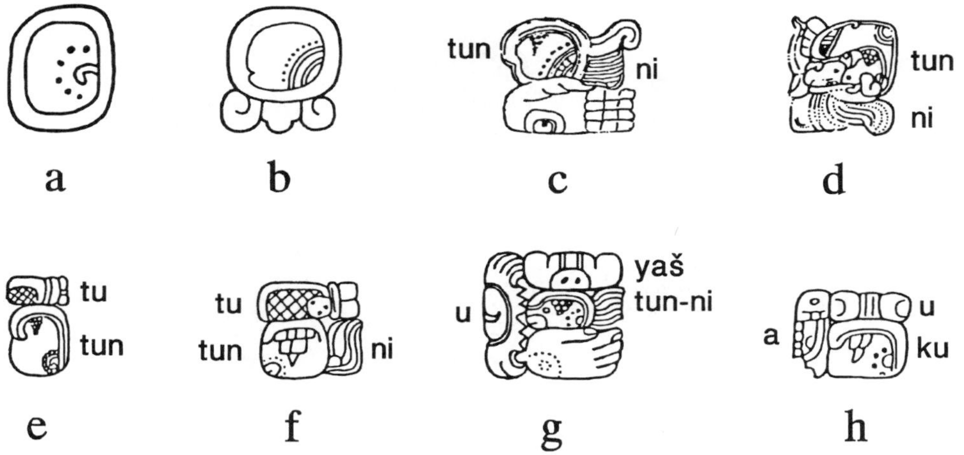

Figure 9.9 Polyvalence. (a, Piedras Negras, Lintel 3, D'6. b, Yaxchilan, Lintel 37, C6a (Graham 1979:83). c, Houston Lintel, E3. d, Piedras Negras, Lintel 12, E1. e, Piedras Negras, Throne 1, L. f, Yula, Lintel 1, B3. g, Piedras Negras, Altar 2 support, G3. h, Yaxchilan, Lintel 42, G3 (Graham 1979:93). a, d, and g after drawings by John Montgomery. c after a field sketch by Ian Graham. e-f from *Maya Hieroglyphic Writing: An Introduction*, by J. Eric S. Thompson, figs. 4 *22* and 33 *31*. New edition coppyright © 1960, 1971 by the University of Oklahoma Press

name, *ʔah-ʔuk* (spelled as **a-u-k[u]**). These examples illustrate the polyvalent nature of many signs (cf. Fox and Justeson 1984). In this case, a single sign had three potential readings – **kawak**, **tun**, and **ku** – that were disambiguated by the presence or absence of two semantic determinatives and two phonetic complements. Other possible semantic determinatives include the hands shown supporting the glyphs for *y-al* "her child" and *tun* "stone, 360-day year" in Figures 9.7e and 9.9c, g, respectively. These examples contrast with other spellings of the same words that appear without the hand in Figures 9.7f and 9.9d.

The economy achieved by using one sign for several words and a syllable was outweighed by the great number of homophonous signs in the script. For example, the word *ʔahaw* "lord, ruler" can be represented by a number of signs that differ markedly from one another. When it refers to the twentieth day of the Maya week, it can appear in a cartouche, with or without a pedestal (Fig. 9.10a and b). In that context, it is often shown as a simian face in frontal view, with two eyes, a nose, and a mouth (Fig. 9.10a and b). It can also be represented by the profile head of a young man, who is often depicted with a black dot in his cheek (Fig. 9.10c). In some cases, the head and the shoulders, or even the entire body of the young man, are shown (Fig. 9.10d and e). There is also a zoomorphic variant of this day sign as the profile head of a vulture (Fig. 9.10l). Still another variant, sometimes called "symbolic" or "geometric," is never enclosed in a cartouche and therefore refers to a human ruler, not a day (Fig. 9.10f). The profile head variant without the cartouche and pedestal sometimes appears with phonetic complements (Fig. 9.10g and h), and there is a syllabic spelling of the same word that also lacks calendrical associations (Fig. 9.10i). The highly pictorial nature of the script has encouraged a multiplicity of sign forms, encompassing geometric, human, and zoomorphic head variants, and, occasionally, even full-figure depictions, that have greatly complicated the task of decipherment and the development of a usable font.

2.2 Evolution of Mayan writing

As the writing system developed, the inventory of syllabic signs shown in Figure 9.8 expanded in two ways: (i) the total number of syllables represented in the grid increased by

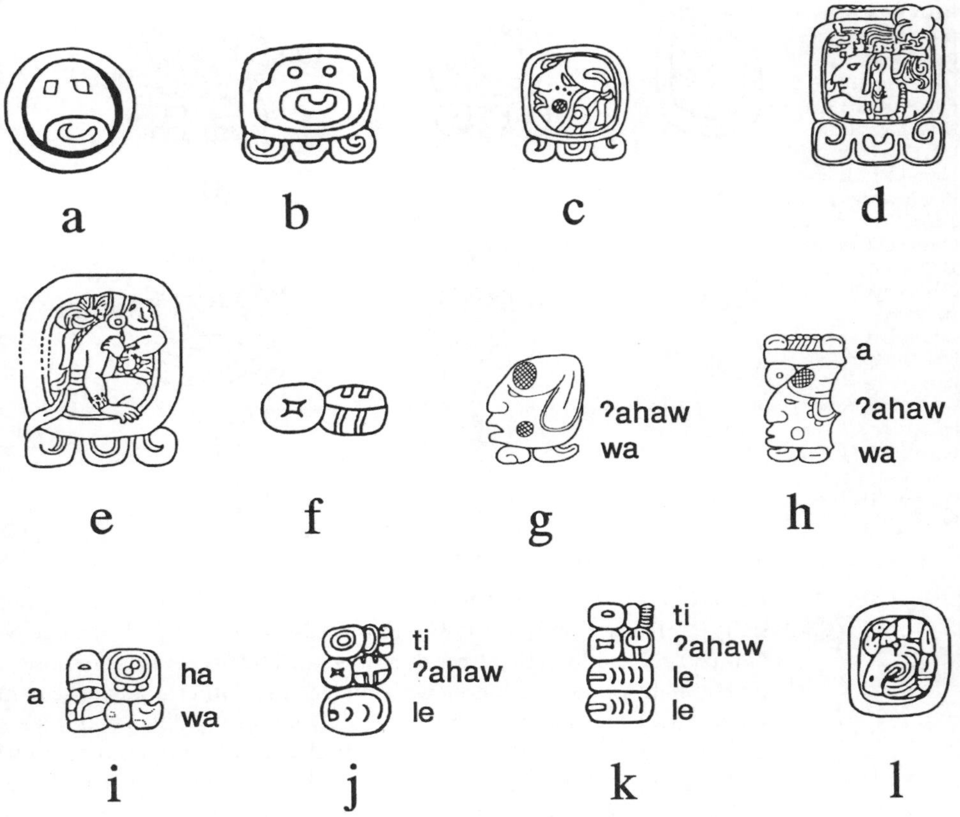

Figure 9.10 Alternative spellings of *ʔahaw* (a, Uaxactun, fresco, glyph 60. b, Tikal, Stela 31, D14 (Jones and Satterthwaite 1982:fig. 52b). c, Copan, Stela C, A2b. d, Quirigua, Stela D, D14. e, Copan, Stela D, A4b. f, geometric variant. g, Yaxchilan, Lintel 23, O5b (Graham 1982:136). h, Yaxchilan, Hieroglyphic Stairway 3, step IV, B3a (Graham 1982:170). i, Yaxchilan, Lintel 3, J1 (Graham and von Euw 1977:17). j, Piedras Negras, Stela 3, F5a (Marcus 1976:fig.12). k, Piedras Negras, Throne 1, H'3 (Morley 1937–1938:fig.111). l, Piedras Negras, Lintel 3, V4). a, c-e from *Maya Hieroglyphic Writing: An Introduction*, by J. Eric S. Thompson, figs. 10 *47*, 11 *24*, *33*, *34*. New edition copyright ©1960, 1971 by the University of Oklahoma Press. l after a drawing by John Montgomery

one-third from 49 to 66; (ii) the average number of signs per syllable doubled. Not all of this homophony was universal. Many signs were limited to a single site or region. But the general pattern was one of increasing variation and artistic elaboration, rather than simplification (Grube 1994:179–184).

Another trend that can be seen over time is an intensification in the use of phonetic complements with logograms to spell polysyllabic words. Whereas during the Early Classic period, it was usually sufficient to spell such words with a single phonetic complement, over time some logograms came to be accompanied by two and even three phonetic complements until the word was written both logographically and syllabically. This can be seen in the different spellings of the word *ʔuniw*, the name for the fourteenth month of the solar year. Figure 9.11a shows the original spelling as **uniw(wa)**. Later it came to be spelled as **uniw(ni-wa)** (Fig. 9.11b). By AD 713, it had acquired a third complement and was spelled as **(u)uniw(ni-wa)** (Fig. 9.11c). Finally, there is a slightly earlier example of the complete replacement of the logogram by the syllabic spelling, **u-ni-w(a)** (Fig. 9.11d).

Nikolai Grube (1994:185) has pointed out that, even though phoneticism increased during the Late Classic period, it did not involve the replacement of logographic with syllabic writing. Both types of writing continued to exist side by side, increasing the possibilities for scribal virtuosity. He attributes the slow development of Mayan writing to the conservatism of a small scribal elite that had little interest in making writing more accessible to the masses.

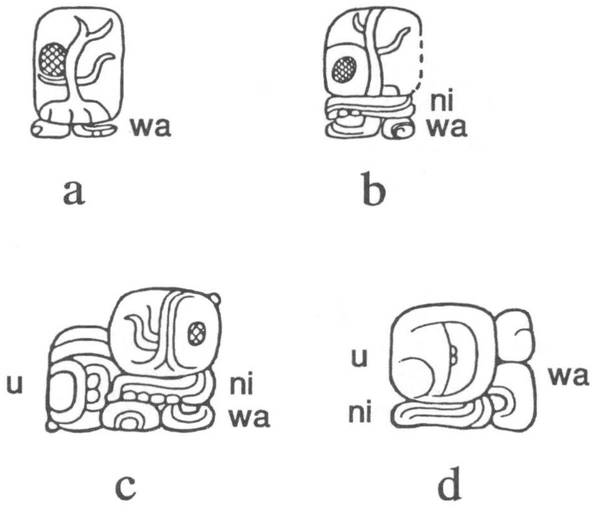

Figure 9.11 Alternative spellings of *ʔuniw* (a, Palenque, Sun Tablet, H2. b, Seibal, Hieroglyphic Stairway, K1a. c, Dos Pilas, Stela 8, I13. d, Yaxchilan, Hieroglyphic Stairway 3, step I, D1a). (Graham 1982:166). a and b from *Maya Hieroglyphic Writing: An Introduction*, by J. Eric, S. Thompson, figs. 18 *23, 27*. New edition copyright © 1960, 1971 by the University of Oklahoma Press. c after a drawing by Ian Graham

2.3 Origins of Mayan writing

The Maya were not the first people in Mesoamerica to use writing, and their script contains evidence of borrowing from earlier scripts that were invented in the region that lies to the west of their highland homeland. Two scripts emerged during the Late Preclassic period, one for an early form of Zapotecan (Whittaker 1992) and the other for an early form of Zoquean (see Ch. 10, §2). The former, and earlier, of the scripts was used in what is today the state of Oaxaca from *c.* 500 BC until *c.* AD 950 (Whittaker 1992:6). The Epi-Olmec script of the Isthmus of Tehuantepec first appeared in *c.* 150 BC and lasted only until *c.* AD 450 (Justeson and Kaufman 1993:1703). Thus, both scripts were contemporaneous with Mayan writing during some portion of their existence.

One feature shared by the Zapotecan and Epi-Olmec scripts was the use of a quinary notation for numbers, with 1 represented by a dot and 5 by a bar. The number 2 was written as two dots, 3 by three dots, and 4 by four dots. For numbers between 5 and 10, a single bar was combined with one to four dots. Two bars were used for 10, two bars and one dot for 11, three bars for 15, and so on. In the Zapotecan writing system, the bar-and-dot numbers were suffixed to main signs, following the order of nouns and their quantifiers in the spoken language (Fig. 9.12a). The reverse was true in Epi-Olmec writing, where numbers were prefixed to main signs (Fig. 9.12b). The Maya used the Epi-Olmec convention for bar-and-dot numbers (Fig. 9.12c), because their languages placed numbers before, not after, the nouns that they quantified, with one exception: in the lunar notations that follow Long Count dates, the bar-and-dot number representing 9 or 10 is postfixed or subfixed to the main sign in the collocation that refers to the length of the lunar month (the main sign is the glyph for 20; Fig. 9.12d). This convention must have been borrowed from the Zapotecan script.

The Long Count and the positional notation for recording it seems to have been invented by the Epi-Olmec people, and it diffused from there into Mayan writing. None of the other peoples of Mesoamerica had the Long Count.

2.4 Decipherment of Mayan writing

A gap of more than three hundred years separates the last practitioners of Mayan writing from the first serious efforts to decipher the script in the late ninteenth century. The closest

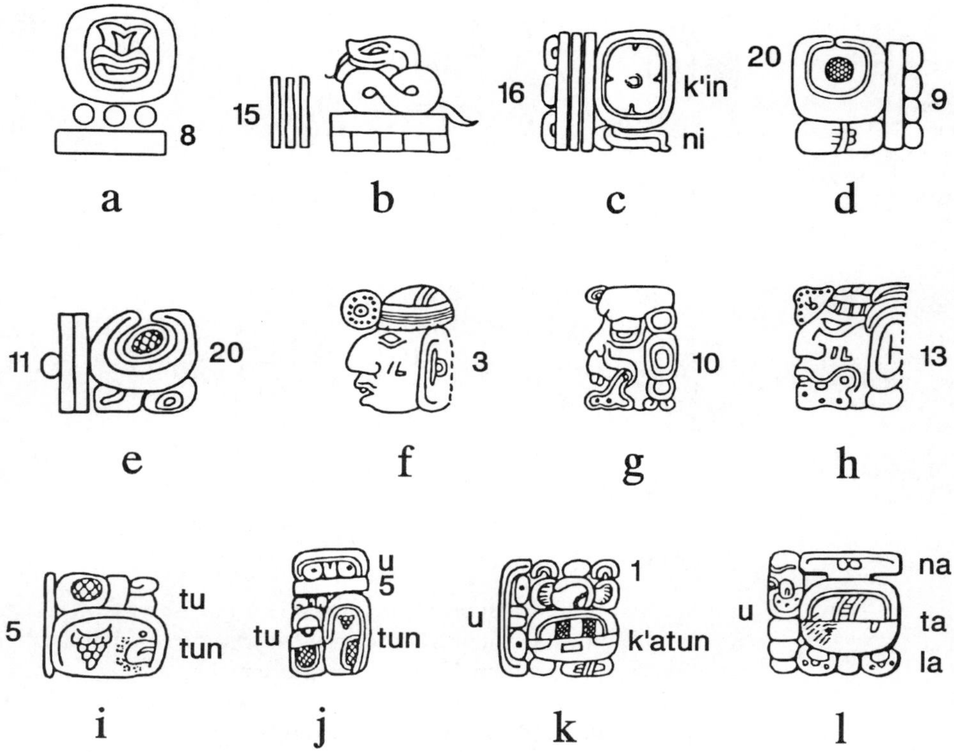

Figure 9.12 Numbers (a, Monte Alban, Stela 12 (Marcus 1976:fig.3). b, La Mojarra, Stela 1 (Capitaine 1988:15), c, Palenque, Foliated Cross Tablet, D17 (Maudsley 1889--1902:IV, plate 82). d, Piedras Negras, Stela 3, A7. e, Balakbal, Stela 5, D10. f, Palenque, Sun Tablet, A6. g, Quirigua, F, C8b. h, Palenque, Cross Tablet, A5. i, Copan, Temple 11, north door, west panel. j, Piedras Negras, Stela 3, F4. k, Piedras Negras, Lintel 3, G1. l, Palenque, Inscriptions Temple, east panel, S9. (Maudsley 1889--1902: IV, plate 60). e-i and k from *Maya Hieroglyphic Writing: An Introduction*, by J. Eric S. Thompson, figs. 4 *16*, 24 *12*, *60*, 25 *11*, 33 *21*, *29*. New edition copyright © 1960, 1971 by the University of Oklahoma Press. d and j after a drawing by John Montgomery

Figure 9.13 Landa's "alphabet". After Tozzer (1941:170)

thing to a Rosetta stone Mayan epigraphers have had to work with is the putative alphabet recorded by the Franciscan priest, Diego de Landa, in the middle of the sixteenth century (see Fig. 9.13).

For the most part, the signs elicited by Landa represented the closest pronunciation equivalents of the names of the letters of the Spanish alphabet (*a*, *be*, *ce*, etc.), which, of course, have a syllabic structure. However, Landa did not include signs for the Spanish letters, *d*, *f*, and *g*, which were not part of the Mayan phonemic inventory, and he included signs for the glottalized consonants, *k'* (written as *k*) and *p'* (written as *pp*), which do not occur in Spanish. Therefore, it seems that he was not simply matching Mayan glyphs to Spanish letters (Durbin 1969). In eliciting different signs for *ca* (= **ka**) and *cu* (= **ku**) (and for *k* (= **k'a**) and *ku* (= **k'u**)), Landa intended only to mark the distinction between *c* and *q* in the Spanish alphabet, but in so doing he was providing a clue to the syllabic nature of a significant portion of the Mayan script. Limited as it was, Landa's "alphabet," together with his hieroglyphic spellings of the names of the twenty days and the nineteen months and a few other Mayan words, have been the key to hieroglyphic decipherment. The brilliant insights of Yuri Knorosov (1963) in the 1950s and the discoveries of more recent scholars (e.g., Lounsbury 1973; Fox and Justeson 1984; Bricker 1986; Stuart 1987) have all taken as their point of departure Landa's efforts to relate Mayan hieroglyphs to Spanish letters.

3. PHONOLOGY

3.1 Consonants

Nineteen consonant phonemes can be distinguished in Mayan:

Table 9.1 The consonantal phonemes of Mayan

Manner of articulation	Place of articulation					
	Bilabial	Alveolar	Palato-alveolar	Palatal	Velar	Glottal
Stop						
Voiceless	p	t			k	ʔ
Glottalized	p'	(t')			k'	
Voiced	b'					
Affricate						
Voiceless			ts	č		
Glottalized			ts'	č'		
Fricative						
Voiceless		s		š		h
Nasal	m	n				
Liquid		l				
Glide	w			y		

One of them, /p'/, is attested only in Landa's "alphabet" (as *pp* in Fig. 9.13), which is a very late source. However, the contrast between /b'/ and /p'/ is an innovation shared by Greater Tzeltalan and Yucatecan (Kaufman and Norman 1984:85), suggesting that the absence of /p'/ in hieroglyphic texts is probably accidental. The glottal stop is not overtly represented in the script, but the epenthetic /y/ that usually replaces it in *ʔ*-initial noun and verb roots when they are inflected with third-person pronominal clitics (see §3.4.1 and Fig. 9.7g and h) is demonstration that it was part of the phonemic inventory of the language, even though the script does not record it.

It is likely that Mayan also distinguished between /t/ and /t'/, as Greater Tzeltalan and Yucatecan have this contrast (Kaufman and Norman 1984:Table 4), but there is no evidence of /t'/ in the script – apparently another accidental gap.

3.2 Vowels

Five vowel phonemes can be distinguished in the hieroglyphic script:

(1) Mayan vowels

	Front	Central	Back
High	i		u
Mid	e		o
Low		a	

Greater Tzeltalan also had only five vowel qualities, but distinguished between long and short vowels. On the other hand, the contrast between long and short vowels was not retained in Proto-Cholan, except for **ā* and **a*. The long vowel **ā* became **a* while short **a* became **ə*. Thus, there are six vowels, not five, in Proto-Cholan (see Kaufman and Norman 1984:85). Proto-Yucatecan had only five vowel qualities and distinguished between long and short vowels.

The hieroglyphic script contains no evidence of more than five vowels. In fact, it used graphemes representing **Ca** syllables indiscriminately for spelling both **a*-medial and **ə*-medial roots. For example, a grapheme representing a gopher (Greater Tzeltalan *b'ah*) was used in spelling both Cholan *u-b'ə* "himself" (Fig. 9.14a) and Tzeltalan *u-b'ah* "he was going" (Fig. 9.16a). Similarly, the **ta** grapheme in Figure 9.8 was used as a syllable for spelling both *təl* "come" (Fig. 9.12l) and *tah* "torch" (Fig. 9.14i) in Proto-Cholan. The lack of a sixth vowel in the script suggests that Mayan distinguished between long and short vowels, but there is no direct evidence for such a contrast in the script.

Houston, Stuart, and Robertson (1998) have argued that roots containing short vowels, CVC or CVCVC, are usually represented by synharmonic spellings, in which the inserted (but silent, i.e., purely orthographic) vowel in the last syllable or the phonetic complement echoes the vowel in the root (e.g., **la-k[a]** = *lak* "plate"; **k'u-k'[u]** = *k'uk'* "quetzal"; **k'an[na]** = *k'an* "yellow"), whereas roots with more complex vowels, either CV:C, CVCV:C, CVʔC, or CVhC, are usually represented by disharmonic spellings, where the inserted vowel does not echo the vowel in the root (e.g., **b'a-k[i]** = *b'a:k* "bone"; **otot[ti]** = *ʔoto:t* "home"; **a-k[u]** = *ʔahk* "turtle"). Their data set does not show a statistically significant pattern of synharmonic spellings for roots with short vowels nor of disharmonic spellings for roots with complex vowels, except for the neutral vowel /a/. Therefore, at present, there is not even indirect evidence for a general contrast between long and short vowels in the hieroglyphic script.

3.3 Syllable structure and phonotactic constraints

Mayan morphemes can have the following syllabic shapes: CVC, CV, VC, and V. Of these, CVC is by far the most common type in terms of either lexical or textual frequency. Many noun roots and all verb roots have this shape, as do a few inflectional suffixes. Examples of CVC roots include *k'in* "day," *ʔal* "woman's child," *k'an* "yellow," and *tun* "stone, 360-day year." CVC suffixes are represented by *-lah* (positional) and *-lel* (abstractive). Most suffixes, such as *-ah* (thematic), *-Vw* (transitive), and *-il* (nominal), have a VC shape. CV is documented by the reflexive base *-b'a* and the preposition *ti* (or *ta*) and V by the third-person bound pronoun *u-*.

The language does not permit sequences of vowels or sequences of consonants within words, so that when such representations occur, phonological processes are applied to eliminate them. This is the cause of the allomorphic variation in the form of third-person

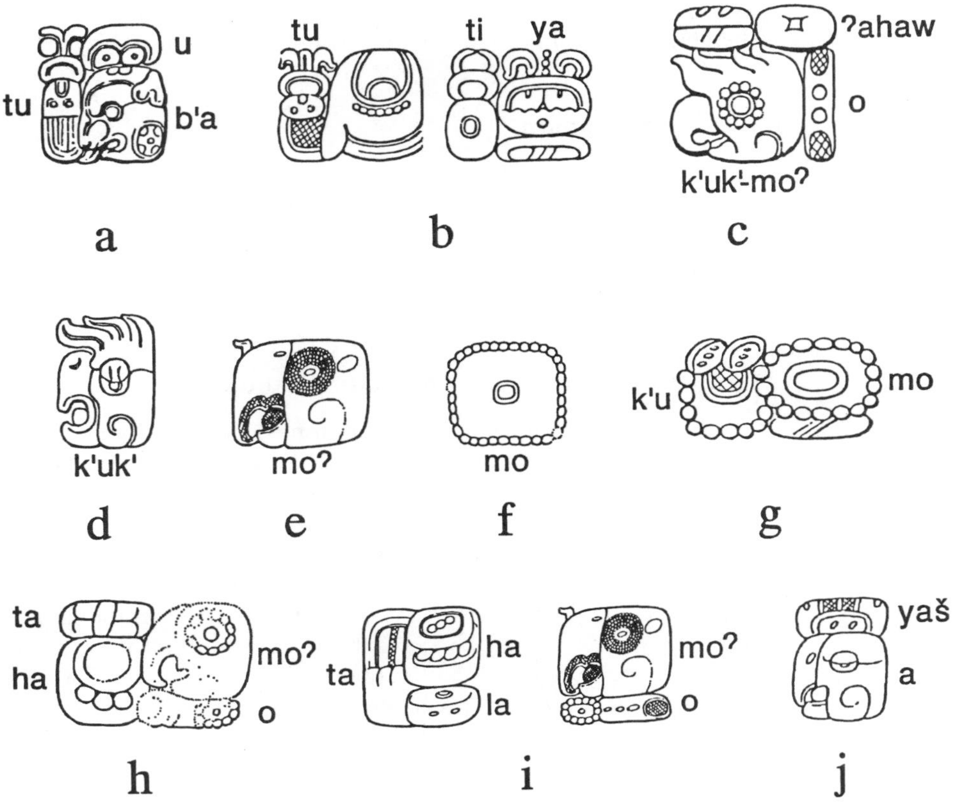

Figure 9.14 Contraction and cluster reduction (a, Palenque, Cross Tablet, S16 (Maudsley 1889–1902:IV, plate 77). b, Tikal, Temple I, Lintel 3, D3–C4 (Maudslay 1889–1902:III, plate 74). c, Copan, Altar Q, A3 (Maudsley 1889–1902:I, plate 93). d, Palenque, Sun Tablet, O9 (Maudslay 1889–1902:IV, plate 89). e, Machaquila, Structure 4, V3 (Graham 1967:fig. 39). f, Uaxactun, Stela 13, A5b (Graham 1986:163). g, Copan, Temple 11, step, glyph 22 (Maudslay 1889–1902:I, plate 8). h, Yaxchilan, Hieroglyphic Stairway 5, glyph 84 (Graham 1982:179). i, Machaquila, Structure 4, V2–V3 (Graham 1967:fig. 39). j, Tikal, Temple IV, Lintel 3, B4 (Jones and Satterthwaite 1982:fig. 74)

pronoun, appearing as *u*-, *uy*-, or *y*-, depending on whether the following noun or verb begins with a glottal stop or some other consonant. However, because the hieroglyphic script does not record glottal stops, vowel sequences appear in constructions involving vowel-final followed by glottal-stop-initial morphemes (e.g., Fig. 9.10j and k).

All the documented consonants in Mayan can begin and end syllables. In CVC syllables, however, there are few restrictions on which consonants can co-occur in initial and final position. If the first consonant in such a syllable is a glottalized stop or affricate, its plain counterpart cannot appear at the end of that syllable, and vice versa (e.g., **k'_k*, **k_k'*). Affricates also exemplify a principle of consonant harmony, a syllable-conditioned process that prevents them from co-occurring in the same syllable if they do not share the same point of articulation (**ts_č*, **ts_č'*, **ts'_č*, **ts'_č'*, **č_ts*, **č_ts'*, **č'_ts*, **č'_ts'*).

3.4 Morphophonemic processes

The following morphophonemic processes can be documented in Mayan: external sandhi, contraction, and cluster reduction.

3.4.1 External sandhi

In Yucatecan and Greater Tzeltalan, most *ʔ*-initial roots have sandhi forms in which /ʔ/ is replaced by /y/ after the third-person pronoun *u*-. This process is reflected in the syllabic spellings of *y-unen* "his, her child," *y-al* "her child," and *y-ahaw* "his lord, ruler" (Fig. 9.7d–h). The contracted form, *y-*, is much more common than *uy-* in Mayan texts.

3.4.2 Contraction

Contraction also occurs when the bound pronoun *u-* follows a preposition (either *ta* or *ti*). In Figure 9.14a, the dative reflexive construction *t-u-b'a* represents a contraction of *ti* (or *ta*) *u-b'a* "by himself." This type of contraction is limited to contexts with the *u-* or *uy-*allomorphs of the bound pronoun. When the preposition precedes *y-*, it is spelled as *ta* or *ti* (e.g., Fig. 9.14b).

3.4.3 Consonant cluster reduction (sandhi)

Mayan sometimes eliminates consonant clusters across word boundaries (on the prohibition of word-internal clusters, see §3.3). Figure 9.14c contains an example of the personal name, *k'uk'-mo?* "quetzal-macaw," in which the logogram for *mo?* (Fig. 9.14e) is infixed in the logogram for *k'uk'* (Fig. 9.14d), and the phonetic complement refers to the vowel in *mo?*. Note that the zoomorphic head in Figure 9.14c has both the distinctive feathers on the head of the quetzal in Figure 9.14d and the characteristic eye of the macaw in Figure 9.14e. The consonant cluster /-k'm-/ is eliminated in Figure 9.14g, where the name is spelled **k'u-mo(o)** (using the symbolic variant of **mo**; Fig. 9.14f). In Figure 9.14i, the name Torch-Macaw (*tahal-mo?*) is written in full; in 14h it is abbreviated to *taha-mo?* or, perhaps, *tah-mo?*, thereby eliminating the consonant cluster /-lm-/ (cf. Fig. 9.14i). Finally, *yaš-ha?* "green water," the name of a large lake in northern Guatemala, has been reduced to *yaš-a?* in Figure 9.14j (Stuart 1985). The motivation for this abbreviated spelling may have been to eliminate the consonant cluster /-šh-/.

3.5 Diachronic developments

The contribution of highland languages can be ruled out by the absence of a distinction between **k* and **q* (and **k'* and **q'*) in the script. This distinction was a characteristic of Proto-Mayan that has been preserved in Eastern Mayan and Kanjobalan, but was lost in Yucatecan and Greater Tzeltalan (Kaufman and Norman 1984:83). In this merger, **q* shifted to **k* and **q'* to **k'*. This change is reflected in the Mayan script, where **ka**, **ki**, and **ku** serve as complements and syllables in spellings that are cognate with highland Mayan words containing either **k* or **q*. For example, **ka** complements /k/ in the logogram for *kan* "snake" (Fig. 9.5i), which is cognate with Proto-Mayan **kān*; it also provides the /k/ in the syllabic spelling of *muk-ah* (Fig. 9.7i), which has a root that is cognate with Proto-Mayan **muq* "bury" (Fox and Justeson n.d.:20).

The shift of Proto-Mayan back velars to front velars in Greater Tzeltalan apparently triggered a concomitant forward shift of front velars to the affricates *č* and *č'*. "In Greater Tzeltalan, all instances of Proto-Mayan **k* and **k'* undergo this shift, except where the shift is blocked by particular phonological environments" (Kaufman and Norman 1984:83–84). The best evidence for this change in Mayan is the grapheme for the syllable **či** (Fig. 9.8). When enclosed by a cartouche it represents the seventh day of the Maya week, which corresponds to days named Deer in other Mesoamerican calendars: **cĭh* was the word for "deer" in Proto-Cholan, compare Proto-Mayan **kehx* (Kaufman and Norman 1984:118).

Yucatecan did not undergo the shift of front velars to affricates. Therefore, it is sometimes possible to identify Yucatecan spellings containing /k, k'/ instead of /č, č'/. A case in point is the use of the phonetic complement **ka** in the collocation shown in Figure 9.5i, which indicates that the main sign refers to the Yucatecan spelling of *kān* "snake," not its Cholan cognate, *čan*.

A phonological change that affected Yucatecan, but not Greater Tzeltalan, was the shift of **t* to **č* in a number of words (Fox and Justeson n.d.). As a result of this change, the Yucatecan word for "house" became **ʔotoč*, whereas the Proto-Cholan word with this meaning remained **ʔotot* (Kaufman and Norman 1984:127). Although there are numerous examples of the *otot* spelling in hieroglyphic texts, the change to *otoč* cannot be documented before AD 950, so it cannot be used for distinguishing among languages using the script during the Early Classic period.

4. MORPHOLOGY

4.1 Word structure

The core of the Mayan word is the root, which is usually monosyllabic and composed of a consonant, a vowel, and a second consonant. Polysyllabic roots have a CVCVC structure and are limited to nouns. Inflectional and derivational processes are signaled by prefixing or suffixing grammatical morphemes with the following shapes to the root: V, VC, CV, and CVC. The language can be characterized as belonging to the agglutinating type because morpheme boundaries in word stems are clear, and words are easily segmented into their constituent morphemes.

Seven root classes have been identified in Mayan: nouns, adjectives, transitive verbs, intransitive verbs, positionals, numerals, and particles. The classification of transitives, intransitives, and positionals as separate form-classes is a characteristic that Mayan shares with Greater Tzeltalan and Yucatecan.

4.2 Nominal morphology

4.2.1 Noun uses

Nouns occur in four morphological environments in Mayan, though the language, like Greater Tzeltalan and Yucatecan, does not inflect nouns for case. There does occur, however, a distinct, but limited, marking of possession; see §4.2.2.

1. In some contexts, they appear without affixes, indicating that they are neither possessed, nor quantified, nor marked for gender: for example, *kakaw* "chocolate"; *tun* "360-day year"; *ʔahaw* "lord, ruler" (see Figs. 9.7a, 9.9d, and 9.10).
2. In others, they are marked for possession, with the possessive pronominal prefixes *u-*, *uy-*, or *y-* (see §4.2.3): thus, *u-kan* "his captor"; *uy-ahaw* "his lord, ruler"; *y-al* "her child" (see Figs. 9.7e, f, h, and 9.17e). For the possessive "declension" see §4.2.2.
3. Nouns can also be quantified in compound expressions with prefixed numerals: for example, *waklahun-k'in* "16 days"; *ho-tun* "five 360-day years"; and *wuklahun-winal* "seventeen 20-day periods" (see Figs. 9.6b and 9.12c, i).
4. The agentive prefixes, *ah-* (male) and *naʔ-* (female) mark some nouns for gender. In Figure 9.9h, the *a(h)-* prefix derives an agentive noun, *ah-ʔuk* "Mr. Uk," from a

personal name. Figure 9.7k illustrates a syllabic spelling of *b'akab'* "sky bearer," a title often used by male rulers. When this title appears in the name phrases of women, it is usually written as *naʔ-b'akab'* "lady sky bearer" (Fig. 9.7l). The absence of *ah-* with *b'akab'* for men and the presence of *naʔ-* with *b'akab'* for women implies that females represented the marked category in Mayan.

A few words should be said concerning plural marking. In Greater Tzeltalan and Yucatecan, number can be marked by plural suffixes, but they are frequently not present. In Cholan and Yucatecan, the third-person plural suffix is *-ob'*, used on both nouns and verbs, though there appear to be no examples of that suffix in Mayan hieroglyphic texts.

4.2.2 Possessive morphology

There is one "declension" in Mayan, for possession, which is represented only by the third-person singular forms in the script. Mayan nouns take either *-Ø* or *-il* when they are inflected for possession. Kinship terms comprise a semantic class that is marked by *-Ø* in possessive constructions: for example, *u-yum-Ø* "his father"; *y-unen-Ø* "his child," and *y-al-Ø* "her child" (see Fig. 9.7c–f). The form *u-kin-il* "the day" represents the inflection of *kin* "day" with suffix *-il* (see Fig. 9.7m).

4.2.3 Pronouns

No examples of independent pronouns have been identified in Mayan writing. The only pronouns observable in the Early Classic script are the clitics and suffixes that refer to third-person subjects, objects, and possessors in their singular forms. As in both Greater Tzeltalan andYucatecan, the marking of plural number was not obligatory in the third person (though it is for first and second) because it could be inferred from references to more than one individual or from other contextual clues.

The third-person transitive subject is usually represented by *(u)y-* before *ʔ*-initial roots and by *u-* before roots beginning with other consonants.

Direct objects are marked by suffixes, of which only that for the third person, which is a zero form (-Ø) in Greater Tzeltalan and Yucatecan, can be inferred in the Mayan script. The subject of intransitive verbs was identified with the direct object of transitive verbs during the Early Classic period (Houston 1997) and was therefore also -Ø. This ergative pattern of pronominal inflection began to change during the Late Classic, resulting in a split-ergative type of system based on aspect (see §4.3.3.2).

The third-person possessive pronoun also appears as *(u)y-* and *u-*, as in Proto-Cholan and Yucatecan. On the possessive construction, see also §4.2.1, **2** and §4.2.2.

4.3 Verbal morphology

4.3.1 Tense-aspect and mood

Most of the verbs that appear in Mayan hieroglyphic texts refer to events that are located in the past. Mayan used Calendar Round dates instead of tense or aspectual particles for placing events in time (cf. Bricker 1981:91–95) and two clitic particles for marking them as earlier (*-iy*) or later (*i-*) in a sequence (e.g., Fig. 9.15i and j; see Wald 2000). On a perfective versus imperfective aspectual distinction, see §4.3.3.2.

Greater Tzeltalan and Yucatecan clearly have a grammatical category *mood* that includes the imperative and optative and is marked by suffixes. Transitive and intransitive verbs have

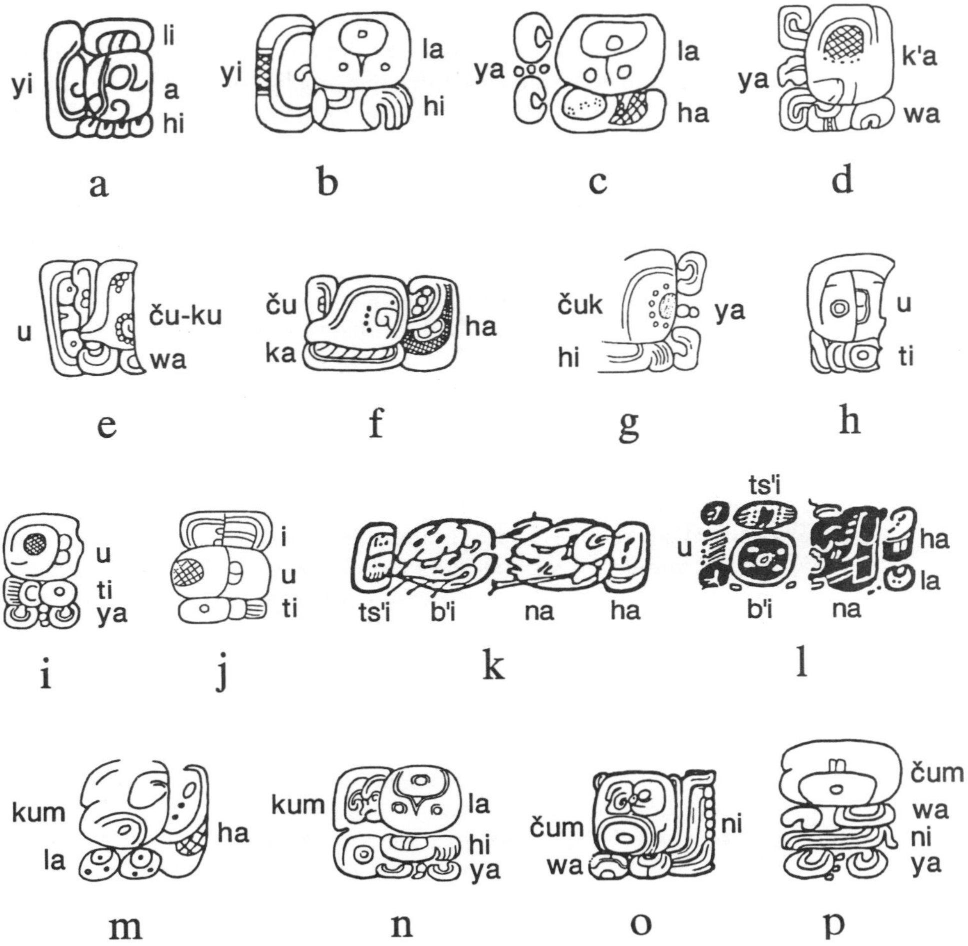

Figure 9.15 Verbal inflection (a, Palenque, Inscriptions Temple, middle panel, H2 (Stuart 1987:fig. 36d). b, Piedras Negras, Lintel 3, J1. c, Piedras Negras, Altar support, A2 (Bricker 1986:fig. 148b). d, Palenque, Inscriptions Temple, middle panel, C8 (Robertson 1983:fig. 96). e, Piedras Negras, Throne 1, A'1. f, Yaxchilan, Hieroglyphic Stairway 3, step I, tread, D1b (Graham 1982:166). g, Yaxchilan, Hieroglyphic Stairway 3, step I, tread, A2 (Graham 1982:166). h, Palenque, Temple 18, jambs, D18a (Sáenz 1956:fig. 5). i, Piedras Negras, Stela 12, A16a. j, Yaxchilan, Lintel 31, 13b (Graham 1979:71). l, Yaxchilan, Lintel 31, I3b (Graham 1979:71). k, unprovenienced ceramic vessel. l, unprovenienced ceramic vessel (Grube 1991:figs. 5i and 9a). m, Deletaille panel, C 2 (Ringle 1985:fig. 2). n, Palenque, Foliated Cross Tablet, N7 (Maudslay 1889--1902:IV, plate 82). o, Dos Pilas, Stela 8, F14. p, Copan, Altar U, K2). (Maudslay 1889--1902:I, plate 98). b, e, and i after drawings by John Montogomery. k after a drawing by David Stuart. o after a drawing by Ian Graham

different mood suffixes. Such suffixes, however, are not represented in Mayan hieroglyphic texts.

Later, there is some evidence of a future participial suffix (*-om*) in association with intransitive stems (e.g., Fig. 9.7n).

4.3.2 Voice

The script contains some information on active versus passive voice distinctions in Mayan during Early Classic times. On passivization see §§4.3.3.1 and 4.3.3.2.

4.3.3 Verb classes

Mayan has three verbal form classes: root transitives, root intransitives, and positionals.

4.3.3.1 *Transitive verbs*

Active root transitives are marked by the suffix *-Vw*. Derived transitives take a suffix *-ah*, which resembles the thematic suffix that is obligatory with derived transitives in the Eastern Cholan languages (Cholti and Chorti; see Kaufman and Norman 1984:98). The third-person clitic pronouns, *u-*, *uy-*, and *y-*, mark agreement with the subjects of transitive verbs, and their objects are cross-referenced on the verb with the third-person suffix, *-Ø*, which, of course, has no graphemic representation.

Mayan examples of root transitives with third-person subjects and objects include *u-čuk-uw-Ø* "he seized it" (Fig. 9.15e) and *y-ak-aw-Ø* "he offered it" (Fig. 9.15d). Derived transitives with third-person subjects and objects are illustrated by *y-il-ah-Ø* "he saw it" (Fig. 9.15a and b) and *y-al-ah-Ø* "he said it" (Fig. 9.15c).

Passive stems were derived from root transitives by suffixing *-ah* to the root (see, e.g., the syllabic spelling of *čuk-ah* in Fig. 9.15f). The rules for inflection are described in §4.3.3.2.

4.3.3.2 *Intransitive verbs*

During the Early Classic period, Mayan had an ergative verb system, in which the intransitive subject had the same form as the transitive object. The only examples in the glyphs are third-person intransitive subjects and third-person transitive objects, both zero (Ø) forms. The root took no stem suffix, and, because the subject pronoun was always *-Ø* in hieroglyphic examples, the inflected intransitive stem was identical to its root form, as in *ʔut* "happen" and *ʔut-Ø* "it happened" (see Fig. 9.15h).

Derived intransitives formed by passivizing root transitives were marked by the thematic suffix, *-ah*, a pattern that is found only in the Eastern Cholan languages (Cholti and Chorti; see Lacadena, forthcoming). Common examples of passives derived from root transitives occurring in hieroglyphic texts are provided by *muk-ah-Ø* "he was buried" and *čuk-ah-Ø* "he was captured" (see Figs. 9.7i, 9.15f).

Passives derived from nouns are also exemplified in Mayan. The passivizing suffix *-n* and the thematic suffix *-ah* follow the nominal root, as in *ts'ib'* "writing," *ts'ib'-n-ah-Ø* "it was written" (see Fig. 9.15k). This pattern is also restricted to the Eastern Cholan languages (Lacadena, n.d.).

The above-described system of pronominal inflection underwent certain changes during the Late Classic period. By the middle of the eighth century AD, there were complement constructions such as *u-b'ah ti ʔak'ot* "he was going to dance" (see §5.2) in the inscriptions of three cities in the region, two in the west (Yaxchilan and Bonampak) and one in the east (Copan), in which the subject of the main verb, the root intransitive *b'ah* "go," was marked by the ergative clitic *u-*, not the absolutive suffix *-Ø*, indicating a shift to a split-ergative pattern of pronominal inflection (see, e.g., Fig. 9.16a).

The form *u-b'ah* also contrasts with *b'ah-iy-Ø* (in identical contexts) during the same period at Copan (compare Fig. 9.16b and c; on the function of *-iy* see §5.3). There are also examples of *u-ts'ib'-n-ah-al* "it was being written" (Fig. 9.15l) contrasting in aspect and pronominal inflection with *ts'ib'-n-ah-Ø* "it was written" (Fig. 9.15k), suggesting that the ergative split corresponded to a distinction between imperfective and perfective aspects, with the former represented by *-al* and the latter by no suffix (i.e., *-Ø*). Clearly the pattern of split ergativity that has characterized the Cholan and Yucatecan languages since the sixteenth century must have had its roots in the Late Classic period. A third aspectual stem-suffix, *-om* "future," occurs with the root intransitive, *ʔut* "happen," as *ʔut-om-Ø* "it will happen" (Fig. 9.7n; Houston 1989) and with the absolutive form of the subject pronoun.

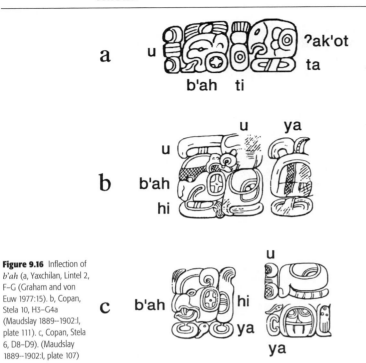

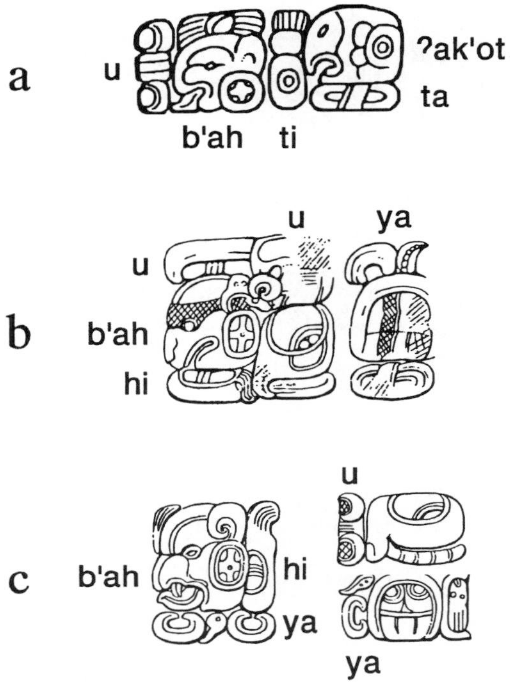

Figure 9.16 Inflection of *b'ah* (a, Yaxchilan, Lintel 2, F–G (Graham and von Euw 1977:15). b, Copan, Stela 10, H3–G4a (Maudslay 1889--1902:I, plate 111). c, Copan, Stela 6, D8–D9). (Maudslay 1889--1902:I, plate 107)

4.3.3.3 *Positional verbs*

Positional verbs can be distinguished from other verbs in terms of both formal and semantic criteria. They refer to physical states or positions, such as standing, sitting, kneeling, hanging, lying down, leaning, bending, and bowing, that human beings, animals, and inanimate objects can assume. Only one positional verb is known from the Early Classic period, *čum* (Cholan) or *kum* (Yucatecan), with the meaning "sit" (Fig. 9.5a–b), and it occurred with what are today the Yucatecan positional suffixes *-l-ah* (Fig. 9.5b). A new positional suffix, *-wan*, replaced *-l-ah* at many sites during the Late Classic period (Fig. 9.15o and p). Stems with these suffixes take the absolutive subject pronoun (-Ø) in Mayan.

4.4 Derivational processes

Mayan derivational processes included not only the formation of agentive nouns described in §4.2.1, **4**, but also the conversion of common nouns into abstract nouns and of transitive roots into instrumental nouns. The abstract *ʔahaw-lel* "rulership, reign" was derived from *ʔahaw* "lord, ruler" by suffixing *-lel* (frequently abbreviated as *-le*) to the noun root (Fig. 9.10j and k). The instrumental suffix *-ib'* was attached to the transitive root *ʔuč'* "drink," and the resulting noun was inflected for possession as *y-uč'-ib'* "his cup" (in Fig. 9.7j; see MacLeod and Stross 1990). Gender-neutral agentive nouns were sometimes derived from nominal or verbal roots by suffixing *-om*, as in *č'ah-om* "caster of incense" (< *č'ah* "drop; incense"; Fig. 9.7o; Schele 1989). These are the only documented types of nominal derivation in Mayan writing.

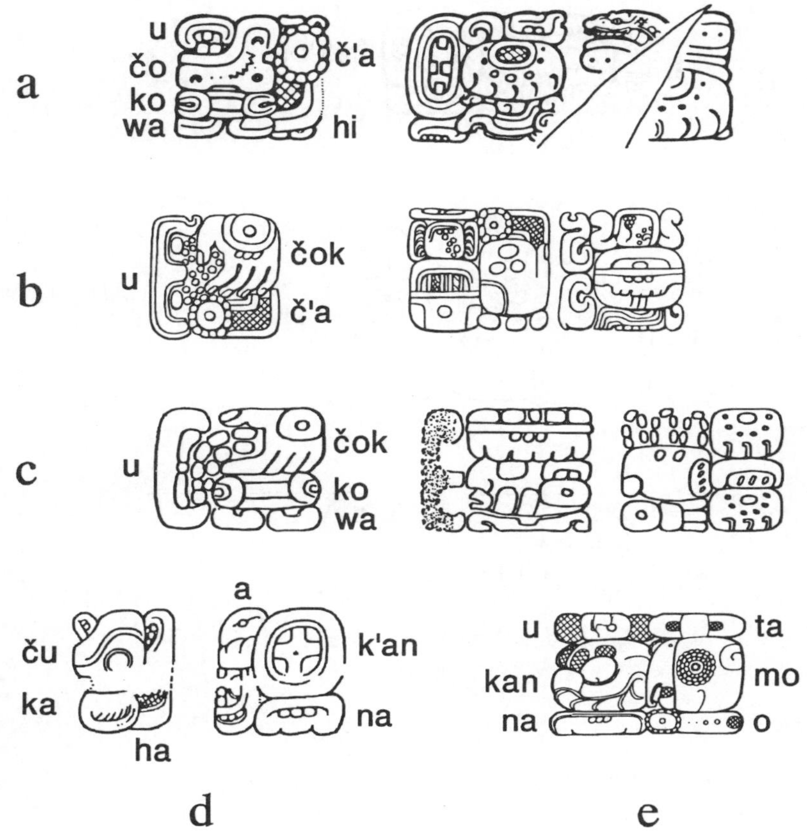

Figure 9.17 Word order (a, Dos Pilas 8, I5–I6. b, Quirigua, Stela A, B16–B17 (Maudslay 1889–1902:II, plate 7). c, Quirigua, Structure 1, G–I (Morley 1937–1938: V, plate 175). d, Yaxchilan, Lintel 46, F3–G3 (Graham 1979:101). e, Machaquila, Structure 4, F1–F2) (Graham 1967:fig. 39). a after a drawing by Ian Graham

4.5 Compounds

Evidence for compounding in Mayan is limited to a few examples of noun incorporation involving the verb *čok* "throw, cast" and the noun *č'ah* "incense." The verb can be represented by the syllables **čo** and **ko** (Fig. 9.17a) or by a logogram depicting a hand casting droplets or granules (Fig. 9.17b and c).

In syllabic spellings of *čok-ow*, the transitive suffix is produced by combining **ko** with **wa** (Fig. 9.17a). The same syllables are often suffixed to the **čok** logogram in logosyllabic spellings (Fig. 9.17c), or the logogram may appear only with **wa**. In Figure 9.17b, the **čok** logogram is followed by the syllable **č'a**, which is an abbreviation for *č'ah* "incense," and there is neither a **ko** nor a **wa** suffix. This collocation cannot represent a transitive verb because there is no *-Vw* suffix. It may, however, be an example of a compound verb-stem with an incorporated direct object. If so, the verb is formally intransitive, and the use of the ergative pronoun *u-* makes it another example of ergative splitting.

4.6 Numerals

Although the bar-and-dot numbers used in writing Mayan had a quinary structure (see §2.3), the number words themselves did not. This can be seen in the head variants of the numbers, which used separate forms for the numbers from 1 through 12 (occasionally 13), but formed the numbers from 13 through 19 by combining the glyphs for 3 through 9 with the glyph for 10 (e.g., Fig. 9.12f–h). There was a separate glyph for 20, and numbers between 20 and 40 were constructed by prefixing the bar-and-dot numbers for 1 through 19 to this sign (e.g., Fig. 9.12e), except for the last collocation in lunar notations, which suffixed the bar-and-dot number to the sign for 20 (Fig. 9.12d). This means that, although the Mayan number system was fundamentally vigesimal in structure, the numbers below 20 had a decimal component. The numbers between 20 and 40 exemplify a principle of "overcounting" based on the previous score. Numbers above 39 usually had calendrical referents and were written in the positional notation employed for Long Count dates and Distance Numbers. For that purpose, there was also a sign for zero that served as a place holder (e.g., Fig. 9.6a and c).

The compounds formed by simply prefixing numbers to nouns are cardinal expressions. Ordinal numbers were formed by prefixing one of the allomorphs of the third-person pronoun to the compound (e.g., *u-ho-tun* "the fifth 360-day year"; Fig. 9.12j). However, there seem to have been three different ways of referring to "the first" in the script: (i) with a *u-* possessive clitic and a single dot for 1 (Fig. 9.12k); (ii) with *yax* replacing the dot (Fig. 9.9g); and (iii) with *na* also replacing the dot (Fig. 9.12l). Alternative words for "first" in the Cholan and Yucatecan languages are *yaš* and *nah* (Schele 1990).

5. SYNTAX

5.1 Word order

The basic word orders in Mayan are Verb–Object–Subject (VOS) in transitive clauses and Verb–Subject (VS) in intransitive and positional clauses. An example of VOS order appears in Figure 9.17a, in which the verb, *u-čok-ow-Ø* "he was casting [it]," is followed by the direct object, *č'ah* "incense," and two collocations that refer to the subject, a ruler of Dos Pilas. The VS order is exemplified by the passive clause, *čuk-ah-Ø ah-k'an* "Mr. Kan was captured," in Figure 9.17d.

Mayan also has verbless, or equational, clauses composed of two nouns, the second of which is inflected for possession with one of the clitic pronouns, *u-*, *uy-*, or *y-*. A case in point is the epithet, *k'ak' u-pakal* "fire [is] his shield," shown in Figure 9.7p, where the possessed noun, *u-pakal* "his shield," functions as a stative verb. There is no verb having the meaning "to be" in Mayan.

At the phrase level, nouns follow their modifying adjectives, and the possessor noun follows the noun that refers to the thing possessed. Phrases such as *ʔik'-k'at* "black cross" and *čak-k'at* "red cross" (< *ʔik'* "black," *čak* "red," and *k'at* "cross"), which referred to the second and third months of the 365-day year, illustrate the syntax of nouns qualified by adjectives (Fig. 9.5k and l). The form *u-kan tah-moʔ* "Torch-Macaw's captor" (lit., "his captor Torch-Macaw") provides an example of a possessor phrase, in which the noun representing the thing possessed (*kan* "captor") is marked by the clitic pronoun *u-* and precedes the noun for the possessor (*tah-moʔ* "Torch-Macaw"; Fig. 9.17e). This word order for possessor phrases is common to most Mayan languages.

5.2 Coordinate and subordinate clauses

Mayan clauses typically begin with a Calendar Round date such as *3 ik' 15 yax-k'in*, which is followed by the verb, the direct object (if there is one), and the subject. The clauses are often linked by Distance Numbers, which express the interval separating the first date from the second in terms of the number of days, 20-day "months," 360-day "years," and so forth, that lie between them. A Calendar Round date may have several clauses associated with it. If the subjects of both clauses are identical, one of them may be deleted, either the one referring to the first verb or the one referring to the second.

Another kind of subject deletion occurs with respect to clauses associated with different Calendar Round dates, but sharing the same subject. In such cases, neither event is introduced by a Calendar Round date; rather, the Distance Number that refers to the interval between them directly precedes the verbs for both events, and the date for the later of the two events appears after the subject at the end of the second clause (Lounsbury 1980):

(2) Distance Number–Verb$_1$–Verb$_2$–Subject–Date

The function of this word order is to focus on the events, rather than the dates that anchor them in time (Josserand 1991). In such cases, the verb that refers to the later of the two events is marked with the clitic particle *i-* (Lounsbury 1980).

Evidence of subordination can be found in complement constructions, in which only the main verb is inflected for subject. The root intransitive, *b'ah* "go," serves as the main verb in such contexts. It is inflected with the ergative pronoun *u-* and is followed by the complementizer *ti* "to" and a verbal noun such as *ʔak'ot* "dance" (Josserand *et al.* 1985). An example of *u-b'ah ti ʔak'ot* "he was going to dance" (Grube 1992) appears in Figure 9.16a.

5.3 Clitics

Mayan employs three clitic particles – *u*, *i*, and *iy* – each with referential functions. The clitic *u* serves as the third-person ergative subject pronoun in transitive stems (and occasionally as the nominative subject pronoun in intransitive stems; e.g., Figs. 9.15e, 9.16a and b) and as the possessive pronoun in nominal stems (e.g., Figs. 9.7c and p and 9.17e). The particle *i* is a focus marker, highlighting or drawing attention to the event in the narrative that follows (Josserand 1991:14). And *iy* is a temporal deictic enclitic that refers to previously reported events (Wald 2000). Thus, *čuk-ah-iy* in Figure 9.15g can be translated as "after he was captured," whereas *čuk-ah* in Figure 9.15f means only "he was captured." Similarly, *ʔut-iy* in Figure 9.15i can be glossed as "after it happened," whereas *ʔut* in Figure 9.15h can only mean "it happened." The forms *kum-lah-iy* and *čum-wan-iy* (in Fig. 9.15m and o) and *kum-lah* and *čum-wan* (in Fig. 9.15n and p) express the same contrast between already reported and not previously mentioned accession events. On the other hand, *i-ʔut* (in Fig. 9.15j) highlights the event that follows – "and then it happened" – contrasting with both *ʔut* "it happened" (in Fig. 9.15h) and *ʔut-iy* "after it happened" (in Fig. 9.15j; see Wald 2000).

6. LEXICON

6.1 The inherited element

Mayan lexemes represent a number of semantic domains that can be grouped into three broad categories: (i) the natural world, including terms for animals, plants, colors and directions, astronomical bodies, and meteorological phenomena; (ii) the supernatural world, with terms for gods and spirits and the rituals used in propitiating them; and (iii) the human world, including terms for social and political relationships.

There is no general term for animal, but the names for eight mammals are known: armadillo (*ʔib'ač*), bat (*sots'*), deer (*čih*), dog (*tsul* and *ts'iʔ*), gopher (*b'ah*), jaguar (*b'alam*), mouse (*č'oh*), and spider monkey (*maš*). Mayan words for birds include the cotinga (*yašun*), hawk (*ʔiʔ*), heron (*b'ak*), macaw (*moʔ*), owl (*kuy*), screech owl (*muwan*), great horned owl (*ʔikim*), quetzal (*k'uk'*), turkey (*ʔulum*), ocellated turkey (*kuts*), and vulture (*k'uč*). Terms for reptiles refer to iguana (*huh*), snake (*kan*), tortoise (*mak*), and turtle (*ʔak*). There are general terms for fish (*kay*) and crab (*b'aw*). Three arthropods are referred to in hieroglyphic texts: ant (*sinik*), bee (*kab'*), and scorpion (*sinan*).

Mayan documents preserve only a few terms for flora. The words for tree (*teʔ* and *čeʔ*), leaf (*leʔ*), seed (*hinah*), and flower (*nik*) are known. The blossom of the maize plant is *hanab'* and of *Pseudobombax ellipticum* (HBK) Dugan is *k'uy-nik*. There are also terms for the gumbo-limbo tree (*Bursera simaruba* [L.] Sargent; *čikah*), the kapok tree (*Ceiba pentandra* [L.] Gaertn.; *yaš-teʔ*), and *Pithecellobium dulce* (Roxb.) Benth. (*ts'iw-teʔ*).

Five primary colors are recognized in Mayan: red (*čak*), black (*ʔik'*), white (*sak*), yellow (*k'an*), and blue/green (*yaš*). The first four colors are associated with the four cardinal directions, the names of only three of which have been deciphered: east (*lak'in*), west (*oč-k'in* and *čik'in*), and north (*šaman*). There are also terms for earth (*kab'*), sky (*čan* or *kan*), day (*k'in*), night (*ʔak'ab'*), sun (*k'in*), and Venus (*k'an*). Among words for natural features of the landscape and meteorological phenomena are the following: water (*haʔ*), stone (*tun* or *tunič*), mountain (*wits*), flint (*tok'*), obsidian (*tah*), rain (*čak*), cloud (*muyal*), rainbow (*čel*), smoke (*b'uts'*), and fire (*k'ak'*).

Words associated with the supernatural world and religious concepts are god (*č'uh* or *k'uh*), demon (*kisin*), hell (*šib'ah*), and alter ego (*way*). The names of several gods and one goddess are known: *čak* (the rain god), *k'awil* (the god of lightning), *ʔitsamna* (the creator god), *ʔahaw k'in* (the sun god), and *čak čel* (the goddess of childbirth).

Rituals involve the casting (*čok*) of incense (*č'ah*) into censers, dancing (*ʔak'ot*), and autosacrifice by perforating (*b'ah*) the tongue (*ʔak'*) or penis (*ʔat* or *ton*) with a pointed object. The gods are offered (*ʔak'*) pieces of paper (*hun*) spattered with blood. Some offerings are made in elaborate painted or carved cylindrical vessels (*ʔuč'ib'*), others on plates (*lak*). There is also a ritual ballgame (*pits*). Hieroglyphic texts refer to two kinds of musical instruments that were used in rituals: the upright drum (*paš*) and the horizontal drum (*tunk'uy* or *tunk'ul*).

Some kinship terms have been identified in Mayan writing: woman's child (*ʔal*), wife (*ʔatan*), father (*yum*), maternal grandfather (*mam*), maternal grandmother (*mim*), older brother (*sukun*), and younger sibling (*ʔits'in*). The head of a lineage is known as the *hol pop* "head of the mat." A number of lineage names that have been attested in Mayan are still in use today in the Maya area (e.g., *b'alam*, *b'atun*, *kokom*, *kupul*, *haw*, *k'awil*, *nik*, and *ʔuk*).

The ruler of a city or polity is called *ʔahaw*. His immediate subordinate, who governed a smaller community, is known as *sahal*. These men are frequently involved in warfare, and there are accordingly words for warrior (*b'ateʔ*), shield (*pakal*), capture (*čuk*), captor (*kan*), captive (*b'ak*), and die (*kim*). Other significant roles in Maya society include priest (*ʔah-k'in* or *čak*), scribe (*ʔah-ts'ib'*), sculptor (*ʔah-pol*), and wiseman (*miyats* or *ʔits'at*). There are also words for writing and painting (*ts'ib'*), hieroglyph (*woh*), and paper or book (*hun*). Other intellectual achievements are related to mathematics and calendrics, the terms of which are listed in §1.3 and §4.6.

Finally, there are terms for buildings and their components: house (*ʔotot* or *ʔotoč* and *na*), lintel (*pakab'*), and sweatbath (*pib'-na*). There are also words for body parts: bone (*b'ak*), tooth (*koh*), hand (*k'ab'*), foot (*ʔok*), fingernail or claw (*ʔič'ak*), and penis (*ʔat* or *ton*). The many other words that were part of the inherited lexicon are shown in Figures 9.5–7, 9.9–12, and 9.14–17 and in the Plates in Davoust (1995).

6.2 Influence of other languages

Only a few loans from other languages have been documented in Mayan. Of these, Mixe-Zoquean has made the largest contribution, including words for chocolate (*kakaw*), child (*ʔunen*), dog (*ʔok*), jaguar (*hiš*), incense (*pom*), and monkey (*čowen* or *čuwen*). Loans from Zapotecan seem to be limited to the day names, *b'en*, *lamat*, and *manik'*. There is one loan each from Totonac (*pak'* "plant") and Nahuatl (*kot* "eagle"; Justeson *et al.* 1985:21–28).

7. READING LIST

The most comprehensive and authoritative single work on ancient Maya cultural history is *The Ancient Maya* by Robert J. Sharer (1994). *Breaking the Maya Code* by Michael D. Coe (1992) is an engaging account of the history of decipherment. The methodology of decipherment is clearly presented in two influential publications, *Ten Phonetic Syllables* by David Stuart (1987) and *Classic Maya Place Names* by David Stuart and Stephen Houston (1994). *L'écriture maya et son déchiffrement* by Michel Davoust (1995) is the best single volume source on Maya epigraphy – encyclopedic, up to date, and profusely illustrated.

Bibliography

Beetz, C. and L. Satterthwaite. 1981. *The Monuments and Inscriptions of Caracol, Belize.* University Museum Monograph 45. Philadelphia: University of Pennsylvania.

Bricker, H. and V. Bricker. 1983. "Classic Maya prediction of solar eclipses." *Current Anthropology* 24:1–23.

Bricker, V. 1977. *Pronominal Inflection in the Mayan Languages.* Tulane University Middle American Research Institute, Occasional Papers, 1. New Orleans.

______. 1981. "The source of the ergative split in Yucatec Maya." *Journal of Mayan Linguistics* 2:83–127.

______. 1986. *A Grammar of Mayan Hieroglyphs.* Tulane University Middle American Research Institute Publication 56. New Orleans.

Bricker, V. and H. Bricker. 1986. "The Mars table in the Dresden Codex." In E. Andrews (ed.), *Research and Reflections in Archaeology and History: Essays in Honor of Doris Stone,* pp. 51–80. Tulane University Middle American Research Institute Publication, 57. New Orleans.

______. 1988. "The seasonal table and related almanacs in the Dresden codex." *Archaeoastronomy* (Supplement to *Journal for the History of Astronomy* 19) 12:S1–S62.

Campbell, L. and T. Kaufman. 1985. "Mayan linguistics: where are we now?" *Annual Review of Anthropology* 14:197–198.

Capitaine, F. 1988. *La estela 1 de La Mojarra, Veracruz, México.* Research Reports on Ancient Maya Writing 16. Washington, DC: Center for Maya Research.

Coe, M. 1973. "The Maya scribe and his world." New York: Grolier Club.

______. 1992. *Breaking the Maya Code.* London: Thames and Hudson.

Davoust, M. 1995. *L'écriture maya et son déchiffrement.* Paris: CNRS Éditions.

Durbin, M. 1969. "An interpretation of Bishop Diego de Landa's Maya alphabet." In *Philological and Documentary Studies,* vol. II, pp. 169–179. Tulane University Middle American Research Institute Publication, 12. New Orleans.

Fox, J. and J. Justeson. n.d. "Hieroglyphic evidence for the languages of the lowland Maya." Stanford University (ms).

______. 1984. "Polyvalence in Mayan hieroglyphic writing." In Justeson and Campbell 1984, pp. 17–76.

Graham, I. 1967. *Archaeological Explorations in El Peten, Guatemala.* Tulane University Middle American Research Institute Publication 33. New Orleans.

______. 1977. "Illustrations of lintels." In J. Bolles (ed.), *Las Monjas: A Major Pre-Mexican Architectural Complex at Chichén Itzá,* pp. 267–275. Norman: University of Oklahoma Press.

———. 1979. *Corpus of Maya Hieroglyphic Inscriptions*, vol. III, part 2: *Yaxchilan*. Cambridge, MA: Peabody Museum, Harvard University.

———. 1982. *Corpus of Maya Hieroglyphic Inscriptions*, vol. III, part 3: *Yaxchilan*. Cambridge, MA: Peabody Museum, Harvard University.

———. 1986. *Corpus of Maya Hieroglyphic Inscriptions*, vol. V, part 3: *Uaxactun*. Cambridge, MA: Peabody Museum, Harvard University.

Graham, I. and G. Mobley. 1986. "Looters rob graves and history." *National Geographic* 169:453–461.

Graham, I. and E. von Euw. 1977. *Corpus of Maya Hieroglyphic Inscriptions*, vol. III, part 1: *Yaxchilan*. Cambridge, MA: Peabody Museum, Harvard University.

Grube, N. 1991. "An investigation of the primary standard sequence on Classic Maya ceramics." In M. Robertson and V. Fields (eds.), *Sixth Palenque Round Table, 1986*, pp. 223–232. Norman: University of Oklahoma Press.

———. 1992. "Classic Maya dance: Evidence from hieroglyphs and iconography." *Ancient Mesoamerica* 3:201–218.

———. 1994. "Observations on the history of Maya hieroglyphic writing." In M. Robertson and V. Fields (eds.), *Seventh Palenque Round Table, 1989*, pp. 177–186. San Francisco: Pre-Columbian Art Research Institute.

Houston, S. 1989. *Maya Glyphs*. Berkeley: University of California Press.

———. 1997. "The shifting now: aspect, deixis, and narrative in Classic Maya texts." *American Anthropologist* 99:291–305.

Houston, S., D. Stuart, and J. Robertson. 1998. "Disharmony in Maya hieroglyphic writing: linguistic change and continuity in Classic society." In A. Ciudad Ruiz, Y. Fernández Marquínez, J. García Campillo, M. Iglesias Ponce de León, A. Lacadena García-Gallo, and L. Sanz Castro (eds.), *Anatomía de una civilización. Aproximaciones interdisciplinarias a la cultura maya*, pp. 275–296. Sociedad Española de Estudios Mayas 4. Madrid.

Houston S. and K. Taube. 1987. " 'Name-tagging' in Classic Mayan script." *Mexicon* 9:38–41.

Jones, C. and L. Satterthwaite. 1982. *The Monuments and Inscriptions of Tikal: The Carved Monuments*. University Museum Monograph 44. Tikal Report 33, part A. Philadelphia.

Josserand, J. 1991. "The narrative structure of hieroglyphic texts at Palenque." In M. Robertson and V. Fields (eds.), *Sixth Palenque Round Table, 1986*, pp. 12–31. Norman: University of Oklahoma Press.

Josserand, J., L. Schele, and N. Hopkins, 1985. "Linguistic data on Mayan inscriptions: the *ti* constructions." In M. Robertson and E. Benson (eds.), *Fourth Palenque Round Table, 1980*, pp. 87–102. San Francisco: Pre-Columbian Art Research Institute.

Justeson, J. and L. Campbell (eds.). 1984. *Phoneticism in Mayan Hieroglyphic Writing*. Institute for Mesoamerican Studies, State University of New York. Publication 9. Albany.

Justeson, J. and T. Kaufman. 1993. "A decipherment of Epi-Olmec hieroglyphic writing." *Science* 259:1703–1711.

Justeson, J. and P. Mathews. 1990. "Evolutionary trends in Mesoamerican hieroglyphic writing." *Visible Language* 29:89–132.

Justeson, J., W. Norman, L. Campbell, and T. Kaufman. 1985. *The Foreign Impact on Lowland Mayan Language and Script*. Tulane University Middle American Research Institute Publication 53. New Orleans.

Kaufman, T. 1976. "Archaeological and linguistic correlations in Mayaland and associated areas of Meso-America." *World Archaeology* 8:101–118.

Kaufman, T. and W. Norman. 1984. "An outline of Proto-Cholan phonology, morphology, and vocabulary." In Justeson and Campbell 1984, pp. 77–166.

Knorosov, Y. 1963. *Pismĕnnosť Indeitsev Maiia*. Moscow: Academy of Sciences of the USSR.

Lacadena, A. n.d. *Passive Voice in Classic Maya Texts: CV-jC-aj and -n-aj Constructions*.

Lounsbury, F. 1973. "On the derivation and reading of the 'ben-ich' prefix." In E. Benson (ed.), *Mesoamerican Writing Systems*, pp. 99–143. Washington, DC: Dumbarton Oaks.

———. 1980. "Some problems in the interpretation of the mythological portion of the hieroglyphic text of the Temple of the Cross at Palenque." In M. Robertson (ed.), *Third Palenque Round Table, 1978*, vol. V, part 2, pp. 99–115. Austin: University of Texas Press.

MacLeod, B. 1984. "Cholan and Yucatec verb morphology and glyphic verbal affixes in the inscriptions." In Justeson and Campbell 1984, pp. 233–262.

MacLeod, B. and B. Stross. 1990. "The wing-quincunx." *Journal of Mayan Linguistics* 7:14–32.
Marcus, J. 1976. "The origins of Mesoamerican writing." *Annual Review of Anthropology* 5:35–67.
Maudslay, A. 1889–1902. *Biologia Centrali-Americana: Archaeology* (1 vol. text, 4 vols. plates). London: R. H. Porter and Dulau.
Morley, S. 1937–1938. *The Inscriptions of Peten* (5 vols.). Carnegie Institution of Washington Publication 437. Washington, DC.
Proskouriakoff, T. 1960. "Historical implications of a pattern of dates at Piedras Negras, Guatemala." *American Antiquity* 25:454–475.
Proskouriakoff, T. and J. Thompson. 1947. "Maya calendar round dates such as 9 Ahau 17 Mol." In *Notes on Middle American Archaeology and Ethnology* No. 79, pp. 143–150. Carnegie Institution of Washington. Washington, DC.
Ringle, W. 1985. "Notes on two tablets of unknown provenance." In M. Robertson and V. Fields (eds.), *Fifth Palenque Round Table, 1983*, vol. VII, pp. 151–158. San Francisco: Pre-Columbian Art Research Institute.
Robertson, M. 1983. *The Sculpture of Palenque*, vol. 1: *The Temple of the Inscriptions*. Princeton: Princeton University Press.
Sáenz, C. 1956. *Exploraciones en la pirámide de la Cruz Foliada*. Instituto Nacional de Antropología e Historia, Informe 5. Mexico City.
Schele, L. 1989. "A new glyph for 'five' on stela E." *Copán Note 53*. Copán Mosaics Project and the Instituto Hondureño de Antropología e Historia. Copán, Honduras.
———. 1990. "*Ba* as 'first' in Classic period titles". *Texas Notes on Precolumbian Art, Writing, and Culture* 5. Austin: University of Texas.
Schele, L. and M. Miller. 1986. *The Blood of Kings: Dynasty and Ritual in Maya Art*. Fort Worth: Kimbell Art Museum.
Sharer, R. 1994. *The Ancient Maya* (5th edition). Stanford: Stanford University Press.
Stuart, D. 1985. *The Yaxha Emblem Glyph as* yax-ha. Research Reports on Ancient Maya Writing 1. Washington, DC: Center for Maya Research.
———. 1987. *Ten Phonetic Syllables*. Research Reports on Ancient Maya Writing 14. Washington, DC: Center for Maya Research.
———. 1988. "The Rio Azul cacao pot: epigraphic observations on the function of a Maya ceramic vessel." *Antiquity* 62:153–157.
———. 1990. "The decipherment of 'directional count glyphs' in Maya inscriptions." *Ancient Mesoamerica* 1:213–224.
———. 1993. "Breaking the code: Rabbit story." In G. Stuart and G. Stuart (eds.), *Lost Kingdoms of the Maya*, pp. 170–171. Washington, DC: National Geographic Society.
Stuart D. and S. Houston. 1994. *Classic Maya Place Names*. Dumbarton Oaks Studies in Pre-Columbian Art and Archaeology, 33. Washington DC.
Thompson, J. 1960. *Maya Hieroglyphic Writing: An Introduction*. Norman: University of Oklahoma Press.
Thompson, J. 1971. *Maya Hieroglyphic Writing: An Introduction* (revised edition). Norman: University of Oklahoma Press.
Tozzer, A. 1941. *Landa's Relación de las cosas de Yucatan*. Papers of the Peabody Museum of Archaeology and Ethnology, Harvard University, 18. Cambridge, MA.
Wald, R. 2000. "Temporal deixis in Colonial Chontal and Maya hieroglyphic narrative." *Written Language and Literacy* 3:123–153.
Whittaker, G. 1992. "The Zapotec writing system." In V. Bricker (ed.), *Supplement to the Handbook of Middle American Indians*, vol. V, pp. 5–19. Austin: University of Texas Press.

CHAPTER 10

Epi-Olmec

TERRENCE KAUFMAN AND JOHN JUSTESON

1. HISTORICAL AND CULTURAL CONTEXTS

The Epi-Olmec language is the most ancient attested member of the Mije-Sokean family (*c.* 300 BCE to at least 533 CE). This family and its internal relationships are presented in Figure 10.1. In the sixteenth century, this family occupied a continuous area of southern Mesoamerica, extending from southern Veracruz to the border of present-day Guatemala, and with no trace of other native languages apart from islands of Nawa. The region seems to have been exclusively Mije-Sokean until the invasion of these Nawas, sometime between 600 and 900 CE; they influenced the vocabularies of individual Mije-Sokean languages but not that of Proto-Sokean or Proto-Mijean.

This region included the entire heartland of the Olmec civilization (1500–500 BCE), and the above circumstances provide a prima facie case that the Olmecs were Mije-Sokeans. Olmecs had widespread influence, diffusing innovations that would become distinctively Mesoamerican cultural characteristics. Evidence from associated linguistic diffusion confirms that at least some Olmecs spoke an early Mije-Sokean language (Campbell and Kaufman 1976); further analysis suggests to us that they were Sokean specifically.

Olmec civilization was originally defined by its distinctive art style, which developed *in situ* in the Olmec heartland, and whose classic form ended after the abandonment of La Venta (*c.* 500 BCE). The *Epi-Olmec* tradition is the Olmec tradition in its later manifestations. Later material remains from the region developed gradually from Olmec canons, a development observable especially at Olmec sites, like Tres Zapotes, that were occupied continuously from Olmec through Epi-Olmec times (Pool 2000).

Linguistic geography had already left little doubt that the Epi-Olmec population spoke Mije-Sokean at least until the breakup of Proto-Mijean and/or Proto-Sokean – *c.* 500 CE according to glottochronology – when our decipherment of Epi-Olmec writing showed that in language, too, the Epi-Olmec tradition was a direct inheritance from the Olmecs. Only ten to twelve Epi-Olmec texts are now known to scholarship (see Table 10.1), and only seven have legible, diagnostically Epi-Olmec signs. Yet these texts spanned the greater part of Mije-Sokean territory. Among Mije-Sokean languages, only Mije lies outside the general area of Epi-Olmec writing.

At this writing, the Epi-Olmec language is known from just four legible Epi-Olmec texts. Several features of its morphology and syntax are specific, in Mesoamerica, to Mije-Sokean languages, and its vocabulary is specifically Sokean. The texts (except the shortest one) include phonological and/or grammatical features that Sokean lost by the Proto-Sokean stage and that today survive only in Mijean (see §7). Two of these three pre-Proto-Sokean texts are dated, to 157 and 162 CE; since the fourth text is centuries older (*c.* 300 BCE),

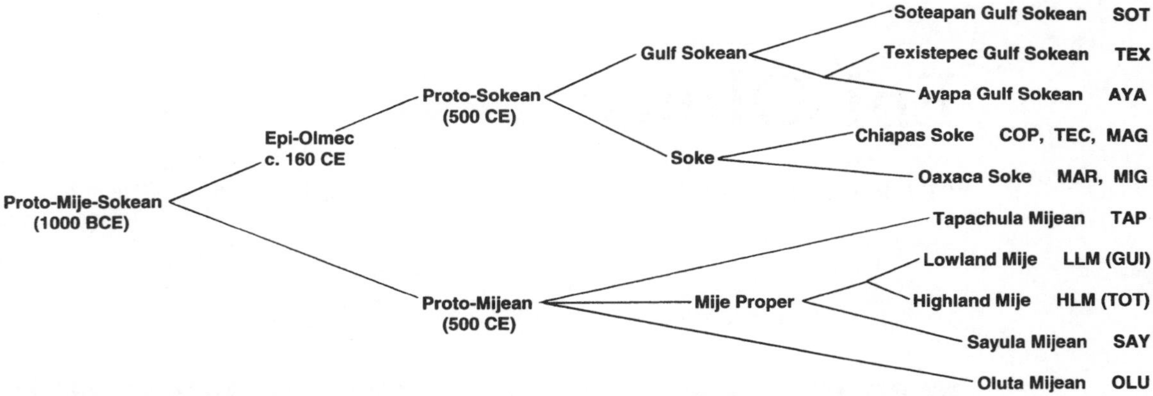

Figure 10.1 The Mije-Sokean language family. Parenthesized dates are Kaufman's current glottochronological estimates for subgroup diversification. The Mije-Sokean languages of Veracruz – those of Sayula, Oluta, Texistepec, and Soteapan – are popularly known as *Popoluca*, and Soteapan Gulf Sokean is specifically known as *Sierra Popoluca*. COP is Copainalá, MAG Magdalena (Francisco León), MAR Santa María Chimalapa, MIG San Miguel Chimalapa, TOT Totontepec, GUI San Juan Guichicovi.

it too must be pre-Proto-Sokean. The latest Epi-Olmec texts (468–533 CE) are almost totally illegible, so their language cannot be identified; if Sokean, as seems likely, they could be Proto-Sokean but hardly much later. Our discussion takes no account of a fifth text that reportedly came to light during or before the summer of 2002, because drawings and photographs of it became publicly available only as the present study was going to press.

2. WRITING SYSTEM

2.1 Decipherment

The Epi-Olmec language has only recently been recovered. Its script was deciphered by the authors in joint work, conducted largely from 1991 through 1994. Just four Epi-Olmec texts were legible enough to provide an empirical basis for establishing the pronunciations or meanings of its signs, or the rules for using them to represent the Epi-Olmec language. The decipherment was initially based only on the data from the two longest texts known at the time, La Mojarra Stela 1 (see Figure 10.2) and the Tuxtla Statuette (see Table 10.1), because available drawings of the other two relatively complete texts appeared to be unreliable. We eventually examined and redrew all of the Epi-Olmec texts; those not previously used were straightforwardly interpretable in terms of the previously established grammatical results and phonetic sign readings, providing independent evidence for the decipherment. The decipherment was supported by another independent test when a previously unseen column of text was discovered on the side of La Mojarra Stela 1 (Justeson and Kaufman 1997).

Summaries of our methods are provided elsewhere (Justeson and Kaufman 1993, 1996 [1992], 1997; Kaufman and Justeson 2001; Kelley 1993). Although cultural and chronological data and inferences played important roles, the decipherment hinged on an understanding of Mije-Sokean grammatical structure and vocabulary as previously worked out by Kaufman (1963); it was facilitated by Wichmann's (1995) expanded list of lexical reconstructions, produced using lexical data unavailable in 1963.

Many grammatical affixes were easily recognized, because of their high text frequency and because most of them were represented by CV syllables that corresponded to a single

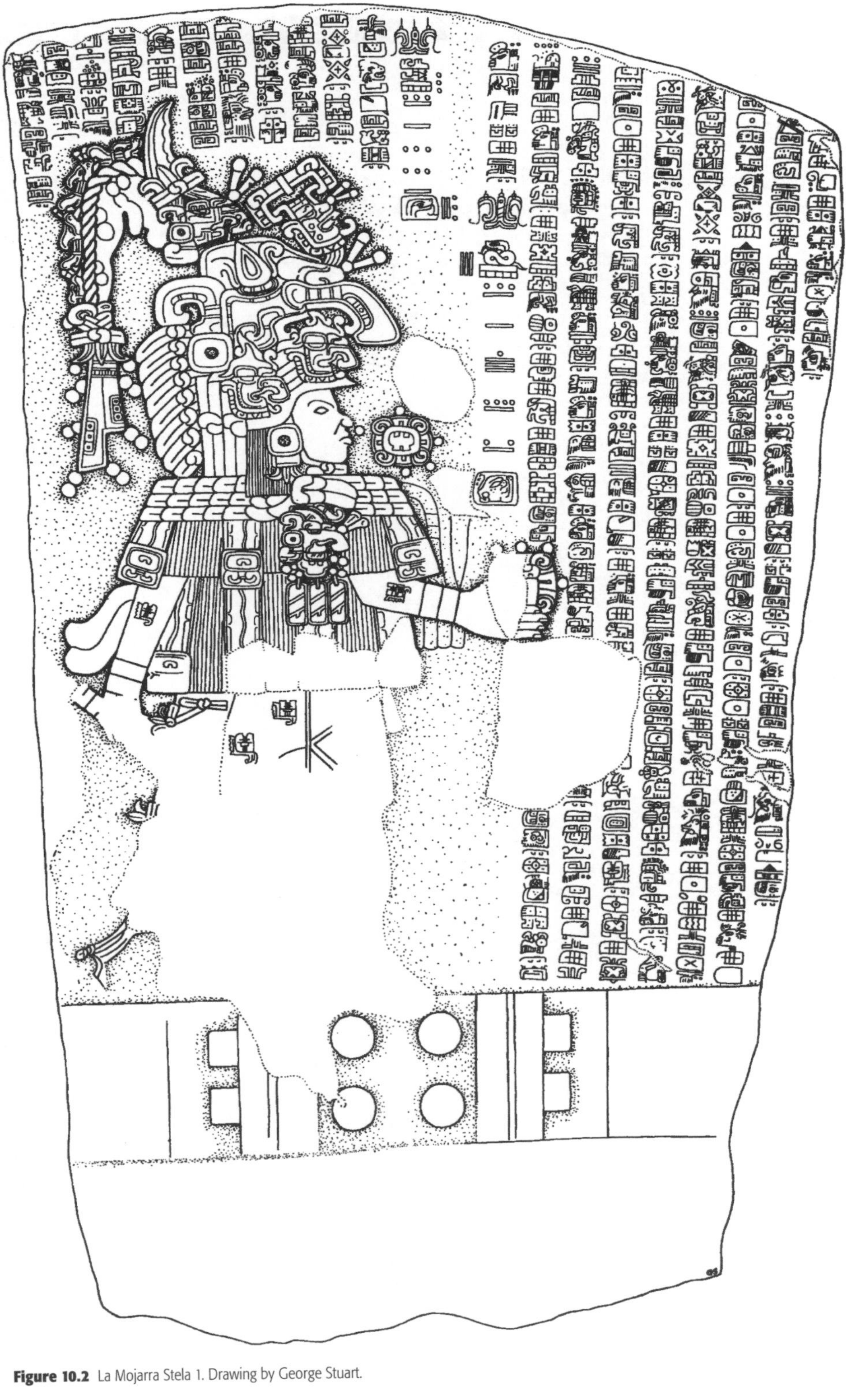

Figure 10.2 La Mojarra Stela 1. Drawing by George Stuart.

Table 10.1 Sources and characteristics of Epi-Olmec and related texts

	Abbr.	Date	Diagnostic Epi-Olmec signs	Total text length	Legible non-num. signs
Chiapa de Corzo					
sherd	CHP-sh	*c.* 300 BCE	6	16+	12
wall panel	CHP-2	36 BCE	(1)	9+	1
Tres Zapotes					
Stela C	3ZP-C	32 BCE	5–7	28	8–10
La Mojarra					
Stela 1	MOJ	157 CE	all	*c.* 544	490
Tuxtla Mountains					
Tuxtla Statuette	TUX	162 CE	all	87	79
79					
Cerro de las Mesas					
Stela 5	MES-5	528 CE	0	*c.* 16	1
Stela 6	MES-6	468 CE	3–4	18	8
Stela 8	MES-8	533 CE	1	*c.* 40	3
Stela 15	MES-15	?468 CE	(1)	4	2
provenience unknown					
O'Boyle mask	OBM	unknown	16	27	27
Teotihuacan-style mask	TEO	??	24–25	104	99
Alvarado					
Stela 1	ALV	?	1–3	12–14	6
El Sitio					
celt	SIT	Late Precl	?	10–12	10–12
Izapa					
various		Late Precl	3		

Legible texts used for decipherment are boldfaced. The standard designation in the literature for the Chiapa de Corzo wall panel is the misnomer "Stela 2"; the label "CHP-2" is used to avoid confusion.

"Diagnostic Epi-Olmec signs" are signs occurring on La Mojarra Stela 1 (MOJ) and the Tuxtla Statuette (TUX) that are distinct from known signs of other Mesamerican scripts. "Text length" is the number of signs originally present in the text, sometimes estimated. CHP-2 and MES-15 are presumed to be Epi-Olmec because, in addition to being from sites yielding demonstrably Epi-Olmec texts, they share a sign form for the day Reed that is distinct from that of neighboring Mayan and Zapotec traditions. MES-8 bears the Epi-Olmec sign ⟨mi⟩.

sign; accordingly, most of the verb and noun morphology was worked out in the first few months of our collaboration. This enabled us to distinguish nouns from verbs, transitive verbs from intransitive, and subordinate from main clauses, and thereby to begin exploring syntactic patterns. As syntactic regularities were identified, they permitted us to refine our analysis of the morphology and vocabulary of ambiguous cases.

We now have almost complete translations and, more importantly, grammatical analyses, for all of the readable Epi-Olmec texts. They conform in all major features, and in almost all details, with what was already known of the grammatical structure of Mije-Sokean languages from the results of comparative reconstruction. A few features were recognized in Epi-Olmec texts before they were known from extant Mije-Sokean languages, and other features of Epi-Olmec texts provided data that have contributed to comparative reconstruction.

Some professional epigraphers who do not know our evidence have expressed doubt about the reliability of the decipherment, but the essentials of the decipherment as it relates to Mije-Sokean linguistic structure are accepted by the leading authorities who do know the evidence (Grube, Kelley, Lounsbury, Mathews, Schele, Urcid). It is not believable that the model presented in this study for the phonological and grammatical structure of the Epi-Olmec language could fit both the comparative Mije-Sokean data and the Epi-Olmec epigraphic data in the detail that it does were it not fundamentally correct (in contrast, no such fit is feasible with a language model based, for example, on Mayan or Oto-Manguean). In particular, the picture we have uncovered of the system of person and aspect/mood marking we consider unassailable. The decipherment is further supported by linguistic features that were not initially known to be reconstructible, but which we found, on gathering and examining more extensive data from the extant Mije-Sokean languages, could be and should be reconstructed (see §§4.3.5, 4.3.6, 4.4.5, 5.1, 5.2.3).

2.2 The Epi-Olmec script

The historical position of the Epi-Olmec script among Mesoamerican traditions is not entirely clear. A text on the El Sitio celt, from the southeastern tip of Mije-Sokean territory, is in either a stylistically divergent form of the Epi-Olmec script or an otherwise unattested script that is its nearest relative. The iconography accompanying this text is considered early post-Olmec. We believe the El Sitio and Epi-Olmec scripts descend from some Olmec script; bare traces of one such script survive, from the end of the Olmec era, on La Venta Monument 13. Several Epi-Olmec signs derive from Olmec iconographic elements. Three signs belonging to the Epi-Olmec script are used as labels on iconography at Izapa, a few kilometers from El Sitio, but no evidence of textual writing survives from the site.

Otherwise, the closest relative of Epi-Olmec writing is Mayan writing. We believe that it arose from an ancestor or sister of Epi-Olmec writing. Mayan writing seems to have emerged from the (set of?) script(s) in Guatemala's southern highlands and adjacent Pacific slopes. That zone's only long, legible text, on Kaminaljuyu "Stela" 10, has some signs otherwise known only from Mayan and/or from Epi-Olmec writing, reflecting some currently unspecifiable historical relation to both Epi-Olmec and Mayan. Complicating the historical picture, some Epi-Olmec signs and their values were adopted by Mayans, and vice versa; other notational and cultural practices also passed between the two groups, like the "long count" calendar and positional numerical notation. Script traditions in the rest of Mesoamerica seem to descend ultimately from Zapotec writing; it is unclear whether Zapotec writing arose from an Olmec (or Olmec-derived) script, but its earliest sure attestation is some 200 years after the Olmec era.

Epi-Olmec signs are arranged in columns, read from top to bottom. Columns were normally read from left to right, and asymmetrical signs faced leftward, but text associated with rightward-facing iconography was reversed in orientation. Successive signs that are part of the same word or phrase often abut, or are set side by side within the space normally occupied by a single sign.

The script is "hieroglyphic" (i.e., its signs have a pictorial quality) and logosyllabic (i.e., it has both logographic and syllabic symbols). Often, sign form relates iconically to sign value. A logogram's form usually relates directly to its meaning – for example, the logogram for

Table 10.2 Epi-Olmec syllabary

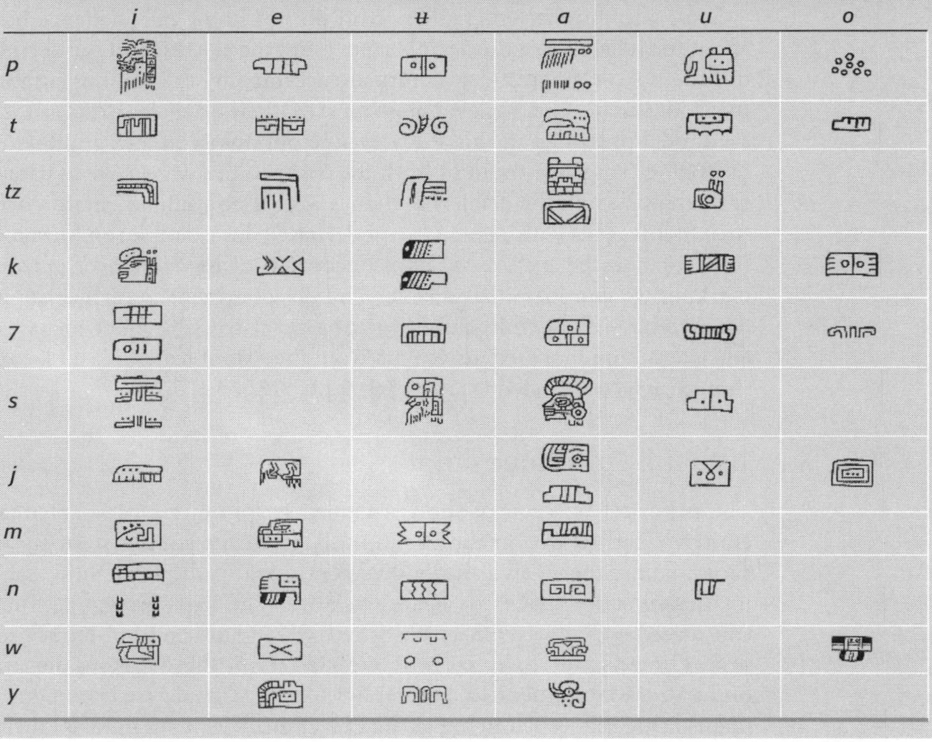
i
e
ʉ
a
u
o
p
t
tz
k
7
s
j
m
n
w
y

piercing depicts a shaft passing through a rectangular field – but sometimes the relationship is more complex, and often it is unknown. The pictorial referent of syllabograms is usually unknown; when this referent is clear, the sign's value is the initial CV(C) of the pre-Proto-Sokean word for the depicted entity: for example, ⟨po⟩ from *pomʉ7* "incense"; ⟨nʉ⟩ from *nʉ7* "water"; ⟨na⟩ from *nas* "earth."

In text frequency, somewhat over half of all signs represent a simple open (CV) syllable, and this is easily the most common type of phonetic sign; for the currently known instances, see Table 10.2. A few signs represent closed (CVC) syllables. No sign represents a simple vowel or VC syllable, because all syllables in Mije-Sokean languages begin with a consonant. Logograms are the most numerous sign type, although they are textually less frequent than syllabograms.

Words and stems of all grammatical classes are spelled by logograms or syllabograms or both. As almost always in all other writing systems, grammatical affixes are spelled using phonetic signs only and, with two restricted exceptions to be discussed, all Epi-Olmec grammatical morphemes are explicitly spelled out.

Spelling with CV signs is straightforward in the case of simple open syllables. In fully phonetic spellings, there is a mismatch between the structure of the Epi-Olmec language and that of the CV syllabary that was used to write it: in the case of syllable codas ending in a consonant, where a consonant in the language is not pre-vocalic, using a CV sign "inserts" an unpronounced vowel, and failing to do so suppresses a consonant. CVC signs are sometimes used, when appropriate ones exist, but they are seemingly rare in Epi-Olmec. In this script, "weak" consonants (/w/, /y/, /j/, /7/) that are not followed by a vowel are never spelled by

CV signs; for example, /j/ is spelled in ⟨ja-ma⟩ for j*ama* 'day,' but not in ⟨we-pa⟩ for *wej-pa* 'he shouts.'

In fully phonetic spellings of words or morphemes, CV signs spell almost all coda instances of the remaining, "strong" consonants. The syllabogram's vowel is always the last preceding vowel in the word, as in the following examples:

(1) ⟨ta-<u>ma</u>⟩   for   +ta7<u>m</u>   'animate plural'
     ⟨tʉ-nʉ-⟩   for   tʉ<u>n</u>+   'inclusive ergative'
     ⟨7i-<u>si</u>⟩   for   7i<u>s</u>   'behold'
     ⟨na-tze-<u>tze</u>-ji⟩   for   na+tze<u>tz</u>ji   'when I chopped it'
     ⟨7i-ki-pi-wʉ⟩   for   7i+ki<u>p</u>wʉ   'they fought against them'
     ⟨na-<u>sa</u>-wʉ⟩   for   na<u>s</u>wʉ   'it passed'
     ⟨mi-<u>si</u>-na-wʉ⟩   for   mi7k<u>s</u>nay7wʉ   'it had quivered'

This principle for choosing the vowel of a CV sign that spells a coda consonant is called *synharmony*. (Our conventions for spelling Mije-Sokean – including Epi-Olmec – words are given at the end of this study.)

One systematic exception is that *k* (and probably *p*) is never spelled before *s*. Four or five words with *k* or *p* before *s* have fully phonetic spellings. In each with *k* before *s*, the *s* is spelled but the preceding *k* is not:

(2) ⟨7i-BLOOD-mi+si₂⟩   for   7i+nʉ7pinmi7ksi   'when he quivered bloodily'
     ⟨mi-si-na-wʉ⟩   for   mi7ksnay7wʉ   'it had quivered'
     ⟨7i-nʉ-si⟩   for   7i+nʉksi   'when it goes'
     ⟨?su+?su⟩   for   su7ksu7   'hummingbird'
     ⟨7o-wa-?ju-si⟩   for   7owaju7psi   'macaw lashing'

In the one possible example with *p* before *s*, what we read as a syllabogram ⟨ju⟩ may be a logogram for LASH, pronounced /ju7ps/.

Besides being used in fully phonetic spellings, syllabograms could be used in a *phonetic complement*, which partially spells the beginning or ending of a word represented (in whole or in part) by a logogram. Vowel choice and consonant representation follow the same principles as in fully phonetic spellings – CV signs for coda consonants contain the last preceding vowel, and weak consonants are only represented prevocalically.

(3)

Word	Gloss	Purely logographic spelling	With phonetic complement
7ame7	'year'	YEAR	⟨YEAR-me⟩
tzap	'sky'	SKY	⟨SKY-pa⟩
7i7ps	'twenty'		⟨TWENTY-si⟩
ni7.jup.7	'body-covering'		⟨LOINCLOTH-pu⟩
na+tzetz-ji	'when he chopped it'		⟨na-tze-tze-CHOP-ji⟩
matza7	'star'		⟨ma-STAR-tza⟩

All of the above spelling conventions are followed without exception in Epi-Olmec texts. Two further conventions apply optionally.

First, the sequence /i7i/ can be spelled as if it were /i/ – otherwise said, the syllable /7i/ is not spelled out in some instances when it immediately follows the vowel /i/. This can be recognized because the syllable /7i/ represents the third-person ergative pronominal prefix, which is grammatically required in some contexts.

We do not believe that this orthographic reduction reflects a phonological process. Although somewhat similar phonological reductions of /7/ are found in some Sokean languages, the pattern is not reconstructible back beyond the separate existing languages, and could easily be recent. As a fast-speech phenomenon, such a phonological reduction is unlikely to be recorded in formal writing.

Second, whenever a verb is spelled with a logogram that represents a verb stem, that sign alone may be read as spelling the verb root plus a suffix of the shape //E(7)// or //A(7)// (where capital-letter symbols are used to indicate that the vowel height alternates: //E// is realized as /i/ after a preceding high vowel, otherwise /e/; //A// is /a/ after a preceding mid vowel, otherwise /ʉ/).

The preceding convention has a plausible source in facts specific to Mije-Sokean grammatical structure. In these languages, no lexical verb can occur without either an aspect/mood suffix or a nominalizing suffix, the two most common of which are {-E} (either the dependent incompletive or the homophonous passive nominalization) and {-A7} (either the imperative or the homophonous active nominalization). A logogram that spelled a verb was probably cited as a nominalization that corresponded to that verb. For example, the sign ⟨PIERCE⟩, which probably spells the verb stem /wu7tz/ 'pierce,' depicts an empty area pierced, and so might have been pronounced /wu7tz.i/ 'pierced (thing).' As a result, such logograms would also be able to represent certain nominalizations of the verb. But these nominalizations were also homophonous with the stem and suffix in certain inflected forms of the same verb, so the citation form could be used for these verb forms as well. The most commonly used of these inflexions is a dependent incompletive form; thus ⟨7i-PIERCE⟩ alone can spell /7i+wu7tz-i/ 'when it gets pierced; when he pierces it,' as it does at MOJ:O*34–35.

When explicit consonant-initial verbal suffixes were spelled out, the verb's logographic (or CVC) representation corresponded to the verb stem without its suffixes.

3. PHONOLOGY

3.1 Phoneme inventory

Proto-Mije-Sokean had eleven consonantal phonemes and six vowel phonemes, and phonemic vowel length. (We write Mije-Sokean forms in a practical, Spanish-based orthography. Most letters have their usual Spanish pronunciation, but *j* represents [h]. *7* represents a glottal stop, *tz* represents a sibilant affricate [c], and *ʉ* represents a high, central-to-back unrounded vowel [ɨ]. *a* is a low, central-to-back unrounded vowel. IPA equivalents are provided in the lexicon [§6].)

consonants						vowels		
p	t	tz	k	7		i	ʉ	u
		s		j		e		o
m	n						a	
		y	w					

The Epi-Olmec syllabary agrees with the phonological system of reconstructed Proto-Sokean, Proto-Mijean, and Proto-Mije-Sokean, in contrasting eleven segmental consonants and six segmental vowels. The following sign series exemplify the contrasts (each syllable listed is the value we have assigned to an Epi-Olmec sign; parenthesized values we do not consider secure):

pi	pe	pʉ	pa	pu	po
ti	te	tʉ	ta	tu	(to)
tzi	tze	tzʉ	tza	(tzu)	
ki	ke	kʉ		ku	ko
7i		7ʉ	7a	(7u)	7o
ji	je		ja	(ju)	jo
si		(sʉ)	sa	(su)	
mi	me	mʉ	ma		
ni	ne	nʉ	na	(nu)	
(wi)	we		(wa)		(wo)
	ye	yʉ	ya		

These phonological units are also essentially identical to the underlying phonological units of all present-day Sokean languages.

One additional segmental contrast is found in some Sokean languages, a phonemic distinction between [w] and the velar nasal [nh]. In those Sokean languages having no phoneme /nh/, the velar nasal is an allophone of /w/ that occurs syllable-finally (i.e., word-finally or before consonants) while [w] occurs before vowels. This allophony is reconstructible back to the time that Proto-Sokean broke up, but we cannot determine how much earlier [nh] developed out of /w/. In particular, we have neither epigraphic nor comparative linguistic evidence for postulating its occurrence as early as the Epi-Olmec stage of Sokean.

Since Epi-Olmec was an ancestor of Proto-Sokean, [nh], if it occurred phonetically, could not have been a phoneme in this language. Consistent with Epi-Olmec being *pre*-Proto-Sokean, the epigraphic evidence is that syllable-final /w/, whether or not it had an allophone [nh], was spelled like any other weak consonant. All Sokean weak consonants – *7*, *j*, *w*, and *y* – are spelled before vowels and nowhere else (see §2.2). Every other consonant, including *n* and *m*, is always spelled (except *k* or *p* before *s*), even when geminate:

(4)	*te7n.na7=*	⟨te-ne-na⟩	'standing upright'
	tʉn+?tʉp(.pʉ7)>jay7-wʉ	⟨tʉ-nʉ-"DEAL.WITH"-ja-wʉ⟩	'we ?speared him/them for him/them' (see [14])
	7i+nʉ7pin=te7n-ji	⟨BLOOD-te-ne-ji⟩	'when he stood upright bloodily'

Proto-Sokean **w* is spelled before vowels, but not before consonants,

(5)	*7otuw-pa*	⟨7o-tu-pa⟩	'he speaks'
	7i+ne7w-ji	⟨7i-ne-ji⟩	'when he set them in a row'
	ne7w-wʉ	⟨ne-wʉ⟩	'they were set in a row'
	puw-wʉ	⟨pu-wʉ⟩	'it was scattered'

so it behaves like a typical weak consonant and not like a nasal consonant.

3.2 Vowel length

A comparison and reconstruction based on the present-day Sokean languages would lead to the conclusion that Proto-Sokean lacked contrastive vowel length, since all the long vowels that appear in any present-day Sokean language are predictable from a Proto-Sokean reconstructed without vowel length. However, Mije-Sokean vowel length survived long enough in pre-Proto-Sokean that some words of Sokean origin were borrowed with long vowels into nearby languages that have contrastive vowel length:

pSo **koya7* ⇐ PMS **ko:y7a7* 'tomato'
⇒ Tzutujil /xko:ya:7/, Awakateko /xko:ya7/ ~ /xko:yi7/
pSo **wetu7* 'fox' ⇐ pre-Proto-Sokean **we:tu7* ⇒ Xinka /we:to/
pSo **yumi* 'high-status person' ⇐ pre-Proto-Sokean **yu:mi*
⇒ Yukatekan /yu:m/
pSo **7amu* 'spider' ⇐ pre-Proto-Sokean **7a:mu* ⇒ Xinka /7a:mu/
pSo **pomʉ7* ⇒ pMS **po:mʉ7* 'incense' ⇒ *po:m* in various Mayan languages

Thus, it is possible that Epi-Olmec had vowel length, but the evidence for reconstructing it is slim, and the orthography of Epi-Olmec does not represent it.

3.3 Phonotaxis and diachronic developments

Proto-Mije-Sokean and Proto-Sokean syllable shapes include CV, CVC(s), CV7C(s) and CVC7. Disyllabic and trisyllabic words could end in V, V7, and Vj. Only *k* and *p* occurred before *s*.

In addition, Proto-Mije-Sokean and Proto-Mijean have syllable shapes of the type CV:, CV:C(s), CV:7C(s), and CV:C7; and Proto-Mije-Sokean (but not Mijean) syllables could have the shape CVC7. Proto-Mije-Sokean di- and trisyllabic words could probably end in V: and V:7 as well, but Mijean points to only V versus V7 or V:.

In the evolution of Proto-Mije-Sokean to Proto-Sokean, the following simplifications occurred:

[a] vowel length was lost
[b] /7/ was deleted between C and V, unless /7/ began a suffix
[c] /7/ was deleted word-finally after C, except when C was a resonant

There is no orthographic evidence that vowel length was preserved in Epi-Olmec (see §3.2), but /7/ was preserved between C and V. The Epi-Olmec words ⟨po-7a⟩ (/poy7a/) 'moon, month,' ⟨HEAD.WRAP-7a⟩ (/ko7=mon7.a/) 'headgear', ⟨PLANT-7i⟩ (/nip7.i/) 'planting', and ⟨SPAN-7ʉ⟩ (/tsat7.ʉ) 'hand-span measure' are evidence for the preservation of /7/ in this environment.

The spelling ⟨kak-SCORPIUS-pe⟩ for 'Scorpius' shows that the Epi-Olmec pronunciation of 'scorpion' was /kakpe7/ as in Proto-Mije-Sokean, and not /kakwe(7)/ as now universal in Sokean. This shows that Epi-Olmec had not undergone the shift of Proto-Mije-Sokean **kp* to Proto-Sokean **kw*.

4. MORPHOLOGY

Mije-Sokean morphology (and syntax) is right-headed or left-branching: modifiers precede heads. This principle is not totally obvious morphologically, since in their inflection and derivation verbs take certain suffixes which are recruited from lexical verbs but have dependent functions grammatically. But with regard to word order, right-headedness is pervasive and obvious, and accounts for SOV, A N, G N, R N, and N Po orders; see §5.1.

In morphologically explicit representations of Mije-Sokean words, inflexional affixes are marked by -, clitics by +, derivational affixes by ., class-changers by >, and compounding, prepounds, and postpounds by =.

4.1 Word classes

Epi-Olmec (like Mije-Sokean languages generally) has the following root and lexeme classes: nominal (noun, adjective, quantifier), verb (transitive, intransitive, positional), and particle (of various functions).

4.2 Person and Number Marking

4.2.1 Person

Mije-Sokean languages distinguish four person categories: exclusive, inclusive, second, and third. While the meaning of inclusive entails at least two persons, all of these categories are subject to optional pluralization.

Proto-Mije-Sokean had an ergative morphology, reflected in two sets of person markers:

1. *The absolutive set*: This set of person markers agrees with (i) the object of a transitive verb (see [7B], [10A], [14], [17], [20AB], [21], [27]); (ii) the subject of an independent intransitive verb (see [6]–[9], [11], [12], [15], [18], [26A], [31]–[34]); and (iii) the subject of a predicate noun or adjective (see [10BC], [13], [16], [19], [22]–[25], [26B], [28], [29]). It forms the basis of independent non-third-person personal pronouns
2. *The ergative set*: This set marks (i) the subject (agent) of a transitive verb (see [7B], [10A], [14], [17], [20AB], [21], [27]); (ii) the subject of a dependent verb (see [9], [17], [19], [34]; and (iii) the possessor of a noun (see [9], [10ABC], [17], [18], [29]).

Person markers are proclitics; the ergative markers are arguably affixes, and the absolutive markers are arguably words. When both an absolutive marker and an ergative marker precede a lexical item, the absolutive marker precedes the ergative.

This Proto-Mije-Sokean system was maintained intact in Soteapan and Texistepec Gulf Sokean (and perhaps in Ayapa Gulf Sokean) and Epi-Olmec, but has been partially and differentially changed in the other individual Sokean languages. The person markers reconstructed for Proto-Mije-Sokean and Proto-Sokean are as follows (affixes that are actually attested in Epi-Olmec texts are in boldface type):

	Absolutive	*Ergative*
First exclusive (X)	**7ʉ**+ [22]	**na**+ [9], [10A], [29]
First inclusive (I)	tʉ+	**tʉn**+ [14]
Second (2)	mi+	**7in**+ [10BC]
Third (3)	Ø (*passim*)	**7i**+ [9], [10A], [17]–[19], [20B], [21], [27] [29],[34]

The inclusive absolutive *tʉ+* is not found in our texts, and the exclusive absolutive marker *7ʉ+* is found only in nominal predicates. Because the third-person absolutive marker is Ø (zero marking), independent intransitive verbs in these texts are spelled without any overt person marker, while transitives and dependent verbs are spelled with overt marking (except for the cases discussed in §2.2 where /i7i/ is spelled like /i/). Inclusive ergative *tʉn+* occurs on just one verb (twice), and second-person ergative *7in+* marks a god as possessor of two different nouns. Exclusive ergative *na+* is well attested and third-person ergative *7i+* is frequent.

4.2.2 Pluralization

The unmarked number is singular. Plural marking has several loci and subdivisions in Mije-Sokean languages; "plurality" refers to a noun or to a person agreement category. It can be marked on a noun, pluralizing the noun or its possessor. It can be marked on a verb, pluralizing a subject or an object. A distinction may be made between third and non-third persons, and between animate and inanimate nouns.

The marking of plurality is optional, even avoided, once plurality for a noun phrase or pronominal category has been established. Complete data on plural marking are not yet on hand for all Mije-Sokean languages, but are known for Soke (Copainalá, Magdalena, Santa María Chimalapa, San Miguel Chimalapa), Soteapan Gulf Sokean, Oluta Mijean, Sayula Mijean, and Lowland Mije.

Originally, the plural marker on nouns was probably Proto-Mije-Sokean *{+tʉk}, found in Mijean and Oaxaca Soke, with no animacy distinction.

The pluralizer for third-person subjects, objects, and possessors in *every* Mije-Sokean language is identical to that language's lexical verb root meaning 'to be finished': Mijean **kʉx*; Santa María Chimalapa Soke, San Miguel Chimalapa Soke **suk*; other Sokean **yaj*. It was probably *{-yaj} in Proto-Sokean; this is also found in Epi-Olmec (see [14], cf. [7A]).

The pluralizer for non-third-person subjects, objects, and possessors was Proto-Mije-Sokean *{-ta7m}; no affix with this function happens to be attested in Epi-Olmec texts.

Proto-Mije-Sokean *{+tʉk} is displaced by certain affixes that are probably to be seen as elite innovations. Gulf Sokean *{+yaj} arises as an extension of *{-yaj} to serve as an inanimate or nonhuman noun pluralizer; in Gulf Sokean and Chiapas Soke, *{+ta7m} arises as an extension of *{-ta7m} to serve as an animate or human noun pluralizer. Both extensions are found in Epi-Olmec as well (see [10C], [20B]).

4.2.3 Gender

Gender is not a grammatical category in Mije-Sokean languages.

4.3 Verb morphology

Verbs begin with (i) obligatory pronominal agreement markers (§4.2.1), optionally followed by (ii) incorporated modifiers (§4.3.3) and various derivational prefixes (§4.3.4). Next comes (iii) the verb root, then (iv) a variety of optional derivational suffixes and class changers (§4.3.5), followed by (v) a variety of optional inflexional suffixes, and finally (vi) a single obligatory aspect/mood marker (§4.3.2). Essential distinctions to be made include that between ergative and absolutive, transitive and intransitive, various aspects and moods, and dependent versus independent status.

4.3.1 Verb classes

4.3.1.1 Transitivity

Any lexical verb is either transitive or intransitive, though a certain percentage are bivalent in that they can be inflected as either transitive or intransitive with no overt intransitivizers or transitivizers.

In the Epi-Olmec texts, the verb stems /ko.wik/ 'sprinkle elsewhere/for others' and /saj/ 'to share' each occur both with and without an ergative prefix. In addition, several independent or optative verbs that are transitive in Mije-Sokean generally are found inflected intransitively in Epi-Olmec, with their single argument being a patient. The reason for this is that approximately one out of every six Mije-Sokean verbs is *bivalent*, occurring sometimes as a transitive and sometimes as an intransitive verb with no transitivizing or detransitivizing suffix. In Sokean, the subject of some of the intransitive forms is an agent, in most a patient;

when the subject is a patient, the verb has a mediopassive interpretation. In Epi-Olmec, only patient subjects occur in the available texts: for example, *puw-wʉ* 'it got scattered.' Precisely which verbs are bivalent is a lexically specific fact that differs from language to language.

4.3.1.2 Positional roots

Positional roots in Sokean are defined by their occurrence with three suffixes: (i) the suffix *{.nay7}, which forms an *assumptive* ('to get into X position/state') intransitive stem; (ii) the suffix *{.wʉ7y}, which forms a *depositive* ('to leave something that is in X position/state') transitive verb; and (iii) the suffix *{.na7}, which forms a *stative* adjective/participle ('that is in X position/state'). The positional root with no derivational suffix can normally be used as a transitive verb with causative function ('to make something be in X position/state'). In Epi-Olmec only the suffix {.na7} (stative) is attested thus far.

(6) *MOJ T24–28*
T te-ne-na-kak-wʉ
R Ø-te7n.na7=kak-wʉ
G 3A-tip.toe-STAT-replace-IC
FT It got replaced upright.

(Here and in other example sentences, the first line presents a transcription of the relevant portion of the cited inscription; the second line offers a pre-Proto-Sokean reading of this; next follows a morpheme-by-morpheme gloss; the last line presents a free translation; a full list of grammatical codes precedes the bibliography.)

4.3.2 Aspect and mood

Each Mije-Sokean verb carries an obligatory aspect/mood suffix as its final morpheme. In Proto-Sokean, there are six to eight such affixes. These are not distinguished by the transitivity of the verb to which they are attached; instead, aspect markers are distinguished on the basis of their dependent versus independent status.

There are apparently at least six categories of aspect and mood in Proto-Mije-Sokean: *incompletive, completive, imperative, vetative, optative,* and *irrealis*. Verbs form matched pairs differing for dependent versus independent function:

	Independent	*Dependent*
Incompletive	*-pa	*-e (> *-i after V_{high})
Completive	*-wʉ	*-ji
Imperative	*-ʉ7 (> *-a7 after V_{mid})	
Vetative		*-wʉ 2
Optative	*-7in (Proto-Sokean)	
Irrealis		*-ʉ (> *-a after V_{mid}; Proto-Soke)

The *vetative* is negative (and dependent) imperative, and has other functions in Soke languages that may not be original. Though homophonous with the independent completive, its functions are quite different, and it probably should be considered a separate morpheme. The *optative* is found in Sokean but is not known from Mijean, where its function may be filled by the descendant of the imperative. Another (dependent) category, *irrealis* or subjunctive, that is pointed to by Soke languages, would have been phonologically eroded in Gulf Sokean and is therefore not directly reconstructible from them. The irrealis occurs with certain subordinating "conjunctions," and in other so far poorly characterized contexts. The *dependent completive* did not survive into present-day Sokean languages, but was still attested at the Epi-Olmec stage. Intransitive verbs with dependent incompletive and dependent completive suffixes use ergative rather than absolutive person agreement markers. This phenomenon is called *ergative shift.*

In Epi-Olmec we have identified independent incompletive *-pa* (see [21], [26AB], [29], [31], [33]); incompletive dependent *-e* ∼ *-i* (see [9], [29], [34]); independent completive *-wʉ* (see [6], [9], [10A], [11], [12], [15], [18], [20B], [27], [32]–[34]); and dependent completive *-ji* (see [9], [14], [17]).

We have not identified any likely imperative, vetative, or irrealis verb forms in the texts. Three verbs appear as optatives, one of them twice (see also [30]):

(7) A. *MOJ U1–3*

T	yaj-7i	"SACRIFICE"
R	Ø-yaj -7i	SACRIFICE
G	3E-finish-OPT	??
FT	The "dripping sacrifice" was supposed to be finished/used.up.	

B. *MOJ R9–17* (with two possible readings given)

T	AFTER-?sʉ	NINE	ja-ma	JAGUAR pʉk-kʉ-7i
R	jʉs	maktas=tujtu	jama	Ø-kajaw=pʉk-7i kajaw Ø-pʉk-7i
G	back	four-past.five	day	3A-jaguar-take-OPT jaguar 3A-take-OPT
FT:	Nine days later he was supposed to take a jaguar [with an incorporated direct object; see §4.3.3]			
OR:	Nine days later [once again] a [tenth] jaguar was supposed to get taken.			

C. *MOJ P*40–Q2*

T	NOW	pʉk-7i	7o-wa-ju/LASH-si
R	ADV_1-ti	Ø-pʉk-7i	7owa=ju7ps.i
G	now	3A-take-OPT	macaw-lash-PN
FT	Now a macaw-lashing/?band was supposed to get taken.		

As the preceding examples show, the optative suffix is spelled ⟨7i⟩ in Epi-Olmec texts rather than ⟨7i-ni⟩, the expected spelling of /7in/; this discrepancy is discussed below (see §7.2.1).

4.3.3 Incorporation

One common feature of Mije-Sokean languages is the incorporation of adjective, noun, and verb stems as modifiers of a verb (so-called incorporees). Their incorporated status is signaled, for example, by the occurrence of the pronominal agreement markers of the verb *before* the incorporee. These texts provide several examples of noun incorporation. Most are intransitive, with third-person subject, whose agreement marker is Ø-, so that no pronominal is explicitly spelled out (also [6], [7B], [12]):

(8) *MOJ Q27–30*

T	SING-ne-DO-pa_2
R	Ø-wan.e=tzʉk-pa
G	3A-sing-PN-do-II
FT	He sings a song.

But there are dependent intransitive cases showing ergative shift (see §4.3.2) in which the sign for BLOOD occurs after the ergative pronominal *7i+* and before the verb (see also [29]):

(9) *MOJ S44–T6*

T	NOW	na-LOSE-ye	7i-saj	7i-BLOOD-SET-ji	mi-si-na-wʉ
R	ADV$_1$-ti	na+yak>tokoy.e	7i+saj	7i+nʉ7pin=tʉ7p-ji	Ø-mi7ks-nay7-wʉ
G	now	XE-CAU-lose-PN	3E-wing	3E-blood-set-DC	3A-quiver-PRF-IC

FT "Then when my overthrown [rival]'s wing/shoulder came to rest bloodily, he/it had been quivering/flapping."

4.3.4 Derivational prefixes

{ko.} 'elsewhere': 'in another's place, on someone else's thing, for someone else'

Proto-Mije-Sokean has a prefix **ko:-* that can be preposed both to verbs (and their nominalizations) and to nouns (i.e., those that are not nominalizations of verbs). Epi-Olmec has examples of both these functions; the following illustrate its attachment to verbs (10A), to nominalizations (10B), and to nouns (10C):

(10) A. *MOJ P3–9*

T	na-BLOOD	7i-ko-LOSE-pʉ-wʉ
R	na+nʉ7pin	Ø-7i+ko.tokoy-pʉ7-wʉ
G	XE-blood	3A-3E-ELSE-lose-ENTIRELY-IC

FT "He spilled/hid my blood in another's place."

B. *TUX C9–D6*

T	to+ke	wʉ	7i$_2$+ni$_2$-ko-SPAN-7ʉ$_2$	TURTLE-ki	wʉ
R	Ø-tok.e	+wʉ7	7in+ko.tzat7.ʉ7	tuki	+wʉ7
G	3A-stain-PN	REL	2E-ELSE-measure-AN	turtle	REL

FT Stained [with blood?] is your elsewhere [otherworldly] handspan measure which is made of turtle[-shell].

C. *TUX C4–8*

T	FOUR	7i$_2$+ni$_2$-ko-SKY+PILLAR	ya$_2$
R	Ø-maktas	7in+ko.tzap=kom	+yaj
G	3A-four	2E-ELSE-sky-pillar	IP

FT Four are your elsewhere [otherworldly] sky pillars.

{ku.} 'away'

Sokean languages have three derivational prefixes beginning with /k/ that are all pronounced /ku+/ in Soteapan Gulf Sokean:

Soke (MAR, MIG, COP)	*Soteapan Gulf Sokean*	
ko7=	ku+	'with respect to the head' (incorporated by verb, prepounded to noun)
ko.	ku+	'elsewhere' (preposed to verb) 'someone else's, step=' (preposed to noun)
kʉ.	ku+	'away,' 'dispersed,' 'separate'

We would be inclined to reconstruct each of these prefixes as it is found in Soke, since Soteapan Gulf Sokean has radically reduced them to a single shape, but while Epi-Olmec has ⟨ko⟩ for the second function (as expected), it has ⟨ku⟩ for the third function, in a so far single example on OBM:C1–3. Here, apparently, Soteapan Gulf Sokean preserves the original phonological shape.

(11) *OBM C1–3*
T BEANS × ARRAY ku=CROSS-wʉ
R sʉk= wʉ=tzʉk.i Ø-ku.jak-wʉ
G bean-good-do-PN 3A-AWAY-cut-IC
FT The bean-bedecked one [Jome7 Sʉk] crossed over.

For the second function Sayula Mijean has {ku+} preposed to verbs and {ko:+} preposed to nouns; and for the third function it has {ku+}, which tends to support **ku+* as the Proto-Mije-Sokean shape for a verb prefix meaning 'away', 'dispersed', 'separate'. Oluta Mijean has {ko7=} 'head,' {ko:.} 'benefactive,' but no correspondent to Soteapan Gulf Sokean and Sayula Mijean {ku+} = Soke {kʉ.} 'away.'

{7aw=} 'with respect to the mouth'

Though the Proto-Mije-Sokean prepound *{7aw=} is clearly the same as the Proto-Mije-Sokean noun root **7aw* 'mouth,' the meaning of the prepound is not at all clear, and only occasionally indicates 'mouth' in any meaningful sense.

The nominalization *7aw=ki7m.ʉ7* 'rulership' appears twice on La Mojarra Stela 1. /7aw=ki7m/ 'to give orders' is reconstructibly Proto-Sokean. Proto-Sokean **ki7m* means 'to go up,' and in some Sokean languages is also a transitive verb 'to mount.' In the case of 'to give orders' there is in fact a plausible reason for mentioning the mouth, even though in Sokean **7aw* no longer means 'mouth,' having been replaced by **jʉp*, a cognate of the word for 'nose' in Mijean.

{ni7.} 'on the body'

This prefix goes back to Proto-Mije-Sokean *{ni:7.}.

(12) *MOJ V25–30*
T SHAPESHIFTER$_2$ ma-sa-ni-APPEAR-wʉ
R jama Ø-masa=ni7.APPEAR-wʉ
G shapeshifter 3A-god-BODY-appear-IC
FT A shape-shifter appeared divinely on his body.

{nʉ.} 'associative'

The meaning is 'to VERB along with someone'.

(13) *MOJ O25-26*
T HALLOW nʉ$_2$=SPAN+EARTH
R (Ø-)ko.nu7ks.i nʉ.tzat7.e=nas
G (3A-)ELSE-greet ASSOC-measure-PN-earth
FT . . . (At) the hallowed ground jointly measured by hand spans. . .
OR . . . The ground jointly measured by handspans had been hallowed.

(Here the associative occurs in a passive nominalization.)

4.3.5 Non-aspect/mood suffixes on verbs

{.pʉ7} 'entirely, completely, all of it'

A suffix *{.pʉ7} can be reconstructed to Proto-Sokean, and on Sayula Mijean evidence possibly to Proto-Mije-Sokean, with the meaning 'entirely, completely, all of it'.

The glyph MS47 occurs three times, in two distinct contexts, in the Epi-Olmec corpus (see [10A], [14]). It follows MS149+50, which we interpret as LOSE/TOKOY, at MOJ:P8 in the string ⟨na-BLOOD 7i-ko-LOSE-MS47-wʉ⟩. If MS47 is a syllabic sign spelling a verb suffix, there are not many possibilities for reading it, given the set of syllables that are established as readings of other signs. The only suffix likely corresponding to an otherwise unread syllable is *{.pʉ7} 'entirely,' which suggests that MS47 spells ⟨pʉ⟩. In some Sokean languages /tokoy.pʉ7/ means 'to spill,' which would fit nicely in the context. This reading is consistent with its other context, as a phonetic complement to a verb referring to how the king's allies dealt with his enemy, or as another instance of the suffix *.*pʉ7* 'entirely'

{>jay7} 'indirective'

The valency-changing suffix {>jay7}, which goes back to Proto-Mije-Sokean, adds an indirect object argument to a verb. When added to an intransitive verb it yields a transitive verb; when added to a transitive verb, it creates a double-object construction in which the verb can agree in person with one object and in number with another object:

(14) *MOJ S7–12*
T tʉ-nʉ-"DEAL.WITH"-pʉ-ja-yaj-wʉ
R Ø-tʉn+?tʉp(.pʉ7)>jay7-yaj-wʉ
G 3A-IE-?spear-?ENTIRELY-NDIR-3P-IC
FT We ?speared/ dismembered him/them for him/them.

This is the only definite example in Epi-Olmec texts of a verb with multiple optional suffixes. It conforms to general Mije-Sokean order restrictions, with {>jay7} before a pluralizer and perhaps after {.pʉ7} 'completely.'

{-nay7} 'perfect/progressive'

In the Epi-Olmec texts, the verb ⟨mi-si-⟩ /mi7ks/ 'to quiver' occurs twice, once with the suffix ⟨-na⟩ /-nay7/ (*perfect/progressive*). From comparative evidence we see that there is a Proto-Mije-Sokean suffix *{.na:y7} ⇒ *{.nay7} in Sokean. In the present-day Mije-Sokean languages this suffix has three standard functions: (i) to form an assumptive intransitive verb from a positional root (see §4.3.1.2; the root may itself occur as a transitive stem); (ii) to form a perfect or back-shifted completive, and a progressive as well; and (iii) to form an iterative intransitive verb from a verb root or symbolic root – in this last function the root is reduplicated.

Since iterative function without reduplication is unknown in surviving languages, if /mi7ks-nay7/ meant 'to quiver repeatedly' it would be anomalous; example (9) shows that /mi7ks-nay7/ is not reduplicated. Example (29) shows that /mi7ks/ is an intransitive stem, so a form with /nay7/ would not be an assumptive based on a positional. Function (ii), the back-shifted completive, is so far known only in Soteapan Gulf Sokean, where it can be glossed as 'has VERBEN,' 'had VERBEN,' 'had been VERBING.'

The suffixes {.pʉ7}, {>jay7}, and {-nay7} occur in this order in present-day Sokean languages; in Epi-Olmec, only the relative order of {.pʉ7} and {>jay7} may be attested.

4.3.6 Nominalizers

{.na7} 'stative'

From positional roots Sokean languages form a *stative adjective* or *adverbial* with the suffix {.na7}; see (6). Such a derivation has not yet been found in any Mijean language. Two such formations are seen in Epi-Olmec texts: /kuw.na7/ '(having been) set aside'; /te7n.na7/ 'standing (upright) on tiptoe.' Both serve as incorporated modifiers, and this function is common, though not universal or necessary, in the present-day languages.

{.kuy7} 'instrument'

Sokean languages have a suffix *{.kuy7} that forms instrument nouns from verbs. (There are relic forms in Mijean that support reconstructing this to proto-Mije-Sokean.) These nominalizations sometimes have readings that suggest they are not only instruments, but may also be nouns naming the action of the verb. One such nominalization is found twice in Epi-Olmec, at MOJ:B5–C4 and MOJ:R4–8, ⟨pak-ku⟩ /pak.kuy7/ "beating instrument" = 'bludgeon.'

(15) *MOJ B5–C4*

T	PIERCE	ma	pak-ku	wʉ	ma-STAR+tza	SHINE-wʉ
R	wu7tz.ʉ7	ma	pak.kuy7	+wʉ7	matza7	Ø-kij-wʉ
G	pierce-AN	earlier	beat-NSTR	REL	star	3A-shine-IC
FT	Piercingly the bludgeon star [Venus] had shone earlier.					

It appears that in some Sokean languages, nouns in {.kuy7} must be formed on intransitive active themes. The result is that for many transitives, an antipassive theme in {.7oy} is the basis of the nominalization in {.kuy7}.

{.7} 'instrument'

In San Miguel Chimalapa Soke, {.7} forms instrument nouns out of particular verbs that contain certain of the possible derivational prefixes. This word-final /7/ is actually pronounced if the verb ends in a resonant (resonants are the consonants after which word-final /7/ is preserved in this language). In all other Mije-Sokean languages, this final /7/ is uniformly lost; this correlates with the fact that, in all Mije-Sokean languages, there is a handful of instrument nominalizations that are not different from the verb itself. Epi-Olmec texts have yielded one instance, ⟨?LOINCLOTH-pu⟩ for /ni7.jup.7/ 'body covering.' The synharmonic spelling of the stem-final /p/ shows that the nominalizer must be {.7} rather than {.A7} or {.E(7)}.

Active and passive nominalizers

The suffixes {.E}, {.E7}, and {.A7} are used to form agent-focus and patient-focus nominalizations in Mije-Sokean languages. Their uses in Epi-Olmec are interpreted as follows:

From a transitive verb a patient-focus (passive) nominalization can be derived with suffixes {.E}and {.E7}, and an agent-focus (active) nominalization can be derived with a suffix {.A7}. Usually, these suffixes are represented in phonetic spellings, whether partial (in final complements) or full, but they are frequently implicit in logograms for the verb stem. Even the same word can be spelled either way: for example, ⟨PLANT⟩ and ⟨PLANT-7i⟩ for *nip7.i* 'plant(ing).'

Passive nominalization with {.E} is abundantly attested: for example, ⟨ne-ke⟩ for /ne7k.e/ 'set aside'; ⟨tu-si⟩ for /tus.i/ 'bristling, prickling'; ⟨tze-tze⟩ for /tzetz.e/ 'chopped off (thing)'; ⟨LOSE-ye⟩ for /yak>tokoy.e/ 'overthrown one'; and ⟨SET.IN.ORDER⟩ for /ne7w.e/ 'set in order (stones)' (see also [7C], [10B], [11], [13], [17], [18], [20B], [22], [26AB], [28], [31]). There is less evidence for active nominalization with {.A7}, but there are enough examples in our small corpus to show that it was a productive, if not entirely regular, pattern: for example, ⟨KNOT+GOVERNOR–7a⟩ for /ko7=mon7.a7/ 'head-wrap'; ⟨?wo-ma⟩ for /wo7m.a7/ 'sprout'; and ⟨LOSE-ya⟩ for /yak>tokoy.a7/ 'overthrower' (see also [10A], [15], [16], [20A], [21], [27], [32], [34]). Examples of {.E7} – such as ⟨PLAY-tai⟩ for /mʉtz.i7/ 'impersonator' (see also [21], [23]) – are rarer still.

The evidence from present-day Mije-Sokean languages shows a fair degree of uniformity concerning passive nominalizations in {.E} and {.E7}, but no unity regarding agent nominalizations. However, in present-day Mije-Sokean languages there are numerous non-productive nominalizations with the suffixes {.A}and {.A7}, and many of these have active readings. Thus, our best current interpretation is that in Epi-Olmec there was an active nominalization in {.A7} that later lost its productivity.

4.4 Nouns and Noun Phrases

Nouns in Mije-Sokean languages do not need to be inflected at all. They are subject to several inflexional and morphosyntactic processes. They may be possessed, with ergative pronominal markers (see [9], [10ABC], [17], [18], [29]). They may be predicate nouns, which have subjects that are expressed by absolutive pronominal markers, as in the following example:

(16) *MOJ P19-22*

T	TIME$_2$+SKY.GOD$_d$=RAIN	ma-TEN	SKY.GOD$_d$=SKY
R	Ø-tuj7=7aw=sʉw=jej.a7	mak	tzap
G	3A-rain-MOUTH-festival-live-AN	Ten	Sky
FT	[The god] Ten Sky is/was a/the rainy season god.		

Both nouns and their possessors may be pluralized. (Plural marking is discussed further in §4.2.2 and §7.2.2.)

A formula that allows for all these markers would look as follows:

Absolutive+	Ergative+	NOUN	+NounPL.	+PossPL.
SUBJECT	POSSESSOR			

4.4.1 Possessive constructions

When a possessor is expressed by a noun or noun phrase, and is thus in the third person, the possessing noun (phrase) precedes the possessed noun, and the possessed noun bears the third-person ergative possession marker *7i+*, as in the following (see also [9]):

(17) *MOJ R28-40*

T	7i-ne-ji	ja$_2$-SYMBOL-si	7i-LOSE-ya	7i-ki-pi-wʉ
R	Ø-7i+ne7w-ji	jay7=ki7ps.i	7i+yak>tokoy.a7	Ø-7i+kip-wʉ
G	3A-3E-put.stones-DC	write-think-PN	3E-CAU-lose-AN	3A-3E-fight-IC
FT	When he placed stones in order he fought against the overthrow(er)(s) of inscribed monuments.			

Adjectives and quantifiers can also occur with possessive markers. Possessed adjectives are interpreted as the corresponding abstract noun of quality ('my/your/its X-ness'), and possessed quantifiers are interpreted as collectives ('the number of us/y'all/them'; 'all of me/us/you/y'all/it/them').

4.4.2 Markers of noun phrase function: core arguments, peripheral arguments, locatives, and manner

Except in Soke languages, Mije-Sokean nouns bear no case markers for such functions as ergative, absolutive, accompaniment, or instrument, and their absence from Epi-Olmec suggests that the postposed enclitic case markers of Soke are an innovation.

For locative (and manner) functions, however, Mije-Sokean languages have a variety of postposed elements with both generic and specific function.

Generic locative markers, roughly glossable as 'at,' include Proto-Mije-Sokean *{+mʉ7}, Proto-Soke *{+ji}, and Proto-Mijean *{+pi}.

Specific locative markers are recruited from the class of nouns, and are called "relational nouns." These include such elements as Proto-Mije-Sokean **kuk* 'middle,' Proto-Mije-Sokean **kʉ7* 'down, under,' Proto-Mije-Sokean **kʉs* 'up, top,' Proto-Mije-Sokean **yuk* 'up, on,' and Proto-Sokean **joj* 'inside.' As nouns these items may be found both alone, and compounded with both nouns and verbs, as prepounds. As locative relators they are followed by one of the generic locators and preceded by the noun they govern, or bear a possessive ergative marker.

Epi-Olmec shows *kuk=* as a prepound (see [18]) and *=joj* as a locator followed by *+mʉ7*. The combination *=joj +mʉ7* is in turn followed by *+k* 'from' (see [19]), which is so far known only from Sokean. The relational nouns are treated as postpounds, and the locative markers are treated as enclitics.

{kuk=} 'middle'

(18) *MOJ N18–29*

T	pe-wʉ	7i-"MACAW.POWER$_1$"	7i-"ECCENTRIC.FLINT"
R	Ø-pey-wʉ	7i+MACAW.POWER	7i+ECCENTRIC.FLINT
G	3A-brandish-IC	3E-??	3E-??

T	7i-ku-MIDDLE-tza$_2$-ja-me
R	7i+ kuk=tza7=jam.e
G	3E-middle-stone-remember-PN

FT His "Macaw.power", his "eccentric.flint", and his pectoral stone memento got brandished.

{=joj} 'inside'; {+mʉ7} 'at'; {+k} 'from'

(19) *MOJ P31–*39*

T	(TITLE$_2$) x x x x x x	?7i-LET.BLOOD	PENIS-jo	mʉ	kʉ
R	ancestor(?)	7i+LET.BLOOD.E	kan=joj	+mʉ7	+k
G	??	3E-let.blood-DI	penis-inside	LOC	FROM

T	PRINCE+BRACE	wʉ
R	Ø-PRINCE	+wʉ7
G	3A-prince	REL

FT (Ancestral(?)) ... when he was blood-letting from inside the penis, he was a prince-type.

OR [When] the ancestral[?]... was blood-letting from inside the penis, he was a prince-type.

4.4.3 Enclitic relativizer

Mije-Sokean languages have a *relativizer*, an enclitic particle that can be added to any word that can serve as the head of a phrase or constituent. The relativizer may have allomorphs distributed according to either phonological or grammatical conditions. The meanings of relativizations vary. When added to a verb, the relativizer produces a relative clause, which always precedes the noun it modifies, according to the right-headedness principle. But a relativized (usually only intransitive) verb can also stand alone as a nominalization, such as "one who kills people" = 'murderer,' "one who teaches" = 'teacher,' "one who has studied" = 'teacher,' "one who studies" = 'student,' "one who gives orders" = 'ruler.'

In Epi-Olmec, the only known relativizer is *+wʉ7*, which is found added only to nouns (no relative clauses based on verbs are attested; see §5.3.1). It is used in three ways, each according with Mije-Sokean usage generally.

When an adjective or a noun modifies a noun, the modifier *may* be followed by the relativizer (type 1: prenominal modifier; see also [15]):

(20) A. *MOJ K5–L3*

T	tzʉ-si	wʉ	"COMMANDING.GENERAL"	tuk	MOUNTAIN+LORD	
R	tzʉsi	+wʉ7	COMMANDING.GENERAL	tuk.ʉ7	kotzʉk	ko.yumi
G	child	REL	??	harvest-AN	mountain	ELSE-leader

FT . . . [said] the youthful "commanding general" Harvester Mountain-Lord.

B. *MOJ D1–F6*

T	KNOT+HALLOW	ma-sa-SPRINKLE	ta-ma
R	X+ko.nu7ks.i	masa=wik.i	+ta7m
G	?-ELSE-greet-PN	god-sprinkle-PSN	AP

T	NOBLE	"WARLEADER"	wʉ	kak+SUPPORT	ta-ma
R	sa7sa7(=pʉn)	WARLEADER	+wʉ7	kak.e=SUPPORT.A7	+ta7m
G	noble(+person)	??	REL	replace-PN-support-AN	AP

T	7i-ki-pi-wʉ
R	Ø–7i+kip-wʉ
G	3A-3E-fight-IC

FT Coronated ones hallowed by sprinkling fought against noble (and) "war-leader"-type succession-supporters [i.e., would-be successors/usurpers].

An adjective or a noun (even when used as an adverb) may be followed by the relativizer but not modify a following noun; in such cases the combination means 'a NOUN/ADJECTIVE-type one.' In this construction, the noun or noun phrase with *+wʉ7* is in apposition to another noun or noun phrase, and that one having *+wʉ7* comes second (type 2: postnominal apposition; see also [10B]):

(21) *TUX F1–10*

T	GOD-ja	ji$_2$-tzi	TITLE$_3$-ne	tu+CLOTH	wʉ	7i$_2$-sa$_2$+pa$_2$
R	jej.a7	ji7tz.i7	TITLE$_3$	tuku7	+wʉ7	Ø-7i+saj-pa
G	breathe-AN	wrinkle-PN	??	cloth	REL	3A-3E-share-II

FT The god Longlip$_2$ was sharing out the "Macaw-Slantbar" cloth things.

This is the only way a noun with *+wʉ7* can follow another noun phrase that it pertains to.

There is also an isolated or independent (type 3) use of the relativizer. The noun or noun phrase to which *+wʉ7* applies is independent of other nouns or noun phrases – it is not a modifier, and it is not in apposition (see also [10B], [19], [26AB], [29]):

(22) *TUX B4–C3*

T	7ʉ₂-DEEDSMAN+ki	BEARD.MASK	sa7-NOBLE	wʉ
R	7ʉ+tzʉk.i=pʉn	BEARD.MASK	sa7sa7(=pʉn)	+wʉ7
G	XA-do-PN-person	??	noble-person	REL
FT	I am a "deedsman," a beard-mask (wearer), a noble one.			

(23) *CHP-sh C1–5*

T	LONGLIP$_2$	CLOTH	wʉ	tu-kʉ
R	ji7tz.i7	tuku7	+wʉ7	Ø-tuk.ʉ7
G	wrinkle-PN	cloth	REL	3A-cut-PN
FT	The thing that is made of pleated cloth has been cut.			

4.4.4 Numerals

Numerals are common in the Epi-Olmec texts but, as is characteristic in Mesoamerica, they occur mainly in calendric expressions. There are a few noncalendrical uses, and only in these instances are the numerals sometimes spelled out phonetically, partly or completely – *metz=* '2' spelled ⟨me-tze⟩; *7i7ps* '20' spelled ⟨TWENTY-si⟩; *mak* '10' spelled ⟨ma-TEN⟩. The uses of numerals that have been observed in the Epi-Olmec texts are the following: (i) as an enumerator/counter (preceding the word it modifies, as in six months, thirteen years, one year); (ii) as an incorporated number of times of an action (as in *metz=* '2'; see [26B]); (iii) as an ordinal numeral (following the word it modifies, as in *7i7ps* '20'; see [32]); (iv) as a coefficient to a day name or month name (preceding the word it is associated with; cf. *mak* '10' in [16]).

4.4.5 Demonstratives

There are three demonstrative roots that can be reconstructed to the Proto-Mije-Sokean stage, and all three are attested in Epi-Olmec: **yʉ7* 'proximal / near speaker / near time of event' (24); **je7* 'distal / far from speaker / far from time of event' (25); **te7* 'near hearer; aforementioned' (26AB):

{yʉ7} 'this'

(24) *MOJ R18–22*

T	SKIN-DRUM	?su+?su	yʉ	"GOVERNOR"
R	Ø-naka=kowa	su7ksu7	yʉ7	GOVERNOR
G	3A-skin-drum	hummingbird	this	"governor"
FT	This "governor"('s headdress) was a skin-drum (and a) hummingbird.			

{je7} 'that'

(25) *MOJ N13–17*

T	SKIN-DRUM	?su+?su	je	"GOVERNOR"
R	Ø-naka=kowa	su7ksu7	je7	GOVERNOR
G	3A-skin-drum	hummingbird	yon	"governor"
FT	That "governor"('s headdress) was a skin-drum (and a) hummingbird.			

{te7} 'the aforementioned' (also [27])

(26) A. *MOJ Q26–33*

T	te	SING-ne-DO-pa$_2$	ja-ma	wʉ
R	te7	Ø-wan.e=tzʉk-pa	jama	+wʉ7
G	that	3A-sing-PN-do-II	shapeshifter	REL

FT The aforementioned one sings a song which is about/of a shape-shifter/day('s length?).

B. *OBM F1–G4*

T	me-tze=UPROOT-si	te	PLANT
R	Ø-metz=wis.i	te7	nip7.i
G	3A-two-uproot-PN	that	plant-PN

FT That planting has/had been uprooted by twos (i.e., two stalks at a time, one in each hand).

Demonstrative roots are used as noun modifiers/identifiers and as noun substitutes, and (among other things) are the basis of adverbs of manner, time, and place (in Epi-Olmec, the bare demonstrative roots are known to occur as noun identifiers and noun substitutes).

/je7.tzʉ/ or /je.tzʉ/ 'thus, that way'

In addition, a manner adverb ⟨je-tzʉ⟩ (/je7tzʉ/ or /jetzʉ/) 'thus, in that way' is attested:

(27) *MOJ M1–7*

T	GO.UP	je-tzʉ	te	7i-si-wʉ
R	ki7m.ʉ7	je7.tzʉ	te7	Ø-⟨7i+⟩7is-wʉ
G	go.up-AN	yon-manner	that	3A-3E-see-IC

FT That was how the latter/aforementioned saw/witnessed the ascent/installation/accession.

{7is} 'lo, behold'

The word *7is* 'lo, behold' (<Proto-Mije-Sokean **7is*) has an indexical function and is attested, alone (in San Miguel Chimalapa Soke) and combined with demonstrative roots, in some Mije-Sokean languages. It is the unadorned verb root 'to see'. At the time that *7is* was recognized as an Epi-Olmec deictic adverbial, it had not yet been reconstructed for any pre-modern form of Mije-Sokean.

(28) *MOJ H3–I4*

T	7i-si$_2$	THIRTEEN	YEAR	BUNDLE-ti
R	7is	mak=tukʉ	7ame7	Ø-pit.i
G	see	ten-three	year	3A-tie-PN

FT [When] behold, there was a prisoner for thirteen years.

4.4.6 Interrogative-indefinites

The words that serve as interrogatives, 'who?' {7i} and 'what?' {ti}, are also used in indirect or indefinite function to mean 'the one who; whoever' and 'that which; whatever' respectively. They are not necessarily used in relative function, and any such use in present-day Mije-Sokean languages plausibly results from the influence of Spanish.

{ti} 'what'

(29) *MOJ S25–34*

T	7i-BLOOD-mi+si$_2$	ti	MACAW	we-pa	na-BLOOD	wʉ
R	7i+nʉ7pin=mi7ks-i	ti	7owa	Ø-wej-pa	Ø-na+nʉ7pin	+wʉ7
G	3E-blood-quiver-DI	what	macaw	3A-shout-II	3A-XE-blood	REL

FT When he quivers/flaps bloodily, what Macaw shouts is:
"It/He is my bloody thing/one."

Though in this usage {ti} is the logical object of a morphologically intransitive verb, this usage is regular and not a grammatical violation in Soteapan Gulf Sokean and San Miguel Chimalapa Soke. Crosslinguistically, it is common (without necessarily being regular or predominant) for intransitive verbs of speaking to have what is spoken mentionable without thereby becoming transitive.

{7i} 'who'

(30) *TUX B1–3*

T	7i	7o-7i
R	7i	Ø-7oy-7i
G	who	3A-take.trip-OPT

FT "Who should go on a trip?"

4.5 Time words

Adverbials are predicate modifiers that specify time, frequency, manner, place, extent, purpose, reason, etc. In Mije-Sokean languages there is no lexical category of adverbs, nor any standard inflexional device that produces adverbials. Many of the words that function as adverbials in these languages are invariant forms of nouns or adjectives; others, while morphologically complex, are not subject to inflexion, and have been formed by non-productive patterns of compounding and suffixation.

In Epi-Olmec texts, the following words function as or act like temporal adverbs:

{ma} 'earlier' (see also [15])

(31) *MOJ Q3–8*

T	ma	ke-ne	FOLD-pa	CLOTH
R	ma	ken.e	Ø-paks-pa	tuku7
G	earlier	see-PN	3A-fold-II	cloth

FT Earlier, (a) garment/cloth(s) was/were getting folded in plain sight.

{jʉs} 'after'

MS89 is a logogram that occurs at MOJ N*38, R9, and T17; in the last-named two it is followed by MS178. In each instance MS89 or MS89 + MS178 is followed by a numeral expression and a spelling of the word *jama* 'day' (see also 23B). Epi-Olmec does not begin clauses with subordinators, and there are no coordinators known in Epi-Olmec or reconstructible to Proto-(Mije-)Sokean. The most likely non-nominal in sentence-initial position is an adverbial of time or manner. MS89 seems to mean 'after.' In Mije-Sokean languages this would be an adverbial formed on the noun **jʉs* 'back,' but plausibly not consisting of the bare root. A unique Proto-Sokean or Proto-Mije-Sokean word 'after' cannot at this time be reconstructed. MS89 and MS89 + MS178 seem to have exactly the same function. MS178, if a syllabogram, may represent /sʉ/, or whatever syllable or morpheme ended the Epi-Olmec word meaning 'after.' For the moment, pending possible improvement in our knowledge, we take the Epi-Olmec word for 'after' to have been or begun with /jʉs/:

(32) *MOJ T13–23*

T	GO.UP-JAGUAR	TWENTY+si-THREE
R	ki7mʉ7=kajaw	7i7ps ko tukʉ
G	go.up-AN-jaguar	twenty-and-three

T	AFTER-?sʉ	THIRTEEN	SHAPESHIFTER$_1$	pʉk-kʉ-wʉ
R	jʉs	mak=tukʉ	jama	Ø-pʉk-wʉ
G	back	ten-three	day	3A-take-IC

FT After thirteen days ascent jaguar [number] twenty-three got taken.

{win} 'in front'

MS8′ is a logogram that we interpret as meaning 'in front,' partly because the preceding glyph (MS90) is plausibly a syllabogram ⟨wi⟩ at OBM:G1, and 'in front' in Mije-Sokean languages is probably based on Proto-Mije-Sokean **win* 'face, eye, surface, front.' We transcribe MS8′ as BEFORE, IN.FRONT/*WIN*... However, we do not know of a Mije-Sokean language where the word for 'in front' is simply /win/: it always has at least one suffix attached, but the attested suffixes differ across the various languages. We take MS8′ to be a logogram for 'in front,' but we cannot at this point specify how the word ended:

(33) *MOJ O*27–33*

T	POUND-wʉ	DRUM	?wi-BEFORE	FOLD+pa$_2$	tu+CLOTH
R	Ø-naks-wʉ	kow.a	win..	Ø-paks-pa	tuku7
G	3A-pound-IC	drum	face	3A-fold-II	cloth

FT The drum got pounded; [then] the garments were getting folded in front.

5. SYNTAX

5.1 Word order

Before 1990, Kaufman had realized that Proto-Mije-Sokean must have had Subject–(Object)–Verb (S(O)V) word order, although no modern Mije-Sokean language was known to preserve this order, as all other word order characteristics are consistent with it, and the verb-initial orders of the modern languages are interpretable as a diffused feature. The Epi-Olmec data indicate that this ancestral word order was preserved, in transitive and in active intransitive clauses, while the position of the subject relative to the verb was variable in nonactive intransitive clauses. Since the Epi-Olmec pattern was worked out, SOV was found to be the basic word order in Santa María Chimalapa Soke, confirming SOV as the basic word order in Proto-Sokean and throughout the pre-Proto-Sokean era.

On La Mojarra Stela 1, within a clause, *every* object encoded as a full noun or noun phrase immediately precedes the verb that governs it (see [10A], [17], [20B], [21]). Similarly, every *subject* of a transitive verb ([20B], [21], [27]) and every *agentive* subject of an *in*transitive verb (see [26A], [29]) precedes the verb. In transitive clauses, subjects precede objects if both are present; otherwise, subjects immediately precede verbs. In addition, subjects and objects can be fronted to outside the clause (see [27], [32]).

Nonagentive subjects usually follow, but sometimes precede, intransitive verbs. Among thirty-six nonactive predicates, the predicate is more likely to precede the subject by a 3:2

margin – whether that predicate is an intransitive stem, a mediopassive, or a nonverbal predicate.

Interrogative-indefinite constituents, no matter what their syntactic function, are fronted to clause-initial position (see [29]).

5.2 Subordination

Eleven clauses in Epi-Olmec texts contain a verb marked with a dependent suffix ({-E} *dependent incompletive* or {-ji}*dependent completive*). Word order is completely regular: each dependent clause precedes its associated independent clause.

There are four or five cases of a dependent clause followed by a clause containing a predicate noun or adjective (see [19]), and six or seven cases followed by a clause containing a verb with an independent aspect suffix ({-pa} *independent incompletive*, see [29], or {-wʉ} *independent completive*, see [9], [17], [34]). Four or five of the independent clauses are completive and two are incompletive; as expected on pragmatic grounds, most (all but one) agree in aspect.

In each case, the contextual meaning of this construction has to be interpreted as either (i) 'when SUBJ$_1$ VERB$_1$-s/-ed, SUBJ$_2$ VERB$_2$-s/-ed' (where SUBJ$_2$ *can* have the same referent as SUBJ$_1$, but need not); or (ii) 'when SUBJ$_1$ VERB-s/-ed, SUBJ$_2$ is/was NOUN/ADJ.' This meaning for the construction was not known from extant Mije-Sokean languages at the time it was found and identified in the Epi-Olmec texts. Since then it has been found to be a living construction in Santa María Chimalapa Soke and in Totontepec Mije. It has not yet been determined whether such a construction exists in other Mije-Sokean languages.

{+7kʉ} 'when; temporal subordinator with past tense reference'

This element is found just once in known Epi-Olmec texts. It occurs attached to a verb with the dependent incompletive suffix, which already has to be interpreted as temporally subordinated. Thus, its use here is presumably optional. (This happens to be the one dependent clause that disagrees in aspect with the independent clause.) A cognate suffix is actively used in Soke (Copainalá Soke {+7k}, 'temporal subordinator [possibly with past tense reference on verbs]'; Magdalena Soke {+7(ʉ)k}, 'temporal subordinator [with past tense reference on verbs]'; Santa María Chimalapa Soke {+7k}, 'temporal subordinator in predicates with past tense reference', and {+k(ʉ)}, 'marker of subordination on preposed dependent clause' and 'marker of fronted verb phrase within a clause'). In addition, in Soteapan Gulf Sokean there are frozen instances of {-k} with the apparent meaning 'temporal subordination' on some temporal adverbs and preposed subordinators. In present-day Soke, the temporal subordinating clitic is used on verbs bearing independent (rather than dependent) aspect suffixes, but still showing ergative shift on intransitive verbs. The usage in present-day Soke suggests that in Epi-Olmec an additional meaning of 'past time' may have been present. The optional (ʉ) in Magdalena Soke is plausibly epenthetic and harmonic in origin, is not compatible with the Epi-Olmec spelling, and probably should not be projected back into the Proto-Sokean reconstruction, which we propose to be *{+7kʉ}.

(34) *MOJ Q18–25*

T …	7i-ko-te	kʉ	PIERCE×NOW
R	Ø-7i+kot-e	+7kʉ	wu7tz.ʉ7 ADV$_1$-ti
G	3A-3E-put.away-DI	WHEN	pierce-AN now

T	"STAR.WARRIOR"	HALLOW-wʉ
R	STAR.WARRIOR	Ø-ko.nu7ks-wʉ
G	??	3A-ELSE-greet-IC

FT When he was putting it away, piercingly now the "star-warrior" got hallowed.

5.3 Unattested traits of Epi-Olmec grammar

Some basic aspects of Mije-Sokean grammar are not yet documented in Epi-Olmec texts. None of the ten grammatical traits discussed below have been found in any of the known texts.

5.3.1 Relativized VPs

In Mije-Sokean languages, relative clauses can be formed by postposing the relativizer to an inflected verb; often a relativized intransitive verb is lexicalized as the name of a type of person who does or undergoes some action. No relative clauses built out of an inflected verb have been identified in Epi-Olmec texts, and they are probably not present in them. The morphemes that mark the relativizing function are various; some languages show as many as three shapes, including /7/, /wʉ7/, /pʉ7k/, /pʉ7/, /7pV/, /pʉ/, and /p/. Proto-Mije-Sokean probably had **wʉ7* and a shape something like **pʉ7*, since both pronunciations are found in languages of both major branches. The form /wʉ7/ is known in Epi-Olmec following nouns; we are not entitled to predict the shape of the relativizer with verbs without explicit spellings, although something that would be spelled ⟨pʉ⟩ is a highly likely one.

5.3.2 Negatives

A predication negator *{ya} (∼ *{yak}) is known from most Sokean languages; most forms of Soke have other or additional predication negators which are higher predicates or auxiliaries. The negator *{7uy} (∼ *{7u}) is found in negative imperatives (vetatives) and some quantifiers. Both *{ya} and *{7uy} are reconstructible to Proto-Sokean. Mijean has a negator of the approximate shape *{ka}, and another, *{ni}, which may be pre-Columbian.

5.3.3 Causative

All Mije-Sokean languages make use of a reflex of the Proto-Mije-Sokean causative morpheme *{yak>} to causativize both intransitive and transitive verbs.

5.3.4 Antipassive

Sokean languages have an antipassivizing suffix {>7oy}, which would be spelled ⟨7o⟩ in Epi-Olmec texts. It has not been observed in our texts, and is probably not present. Mijean languages have no antipassivizing suffix and no cognate to Proto-Sokean *{>7oy}.

5.3.5 Passive and reflexive

All Sokean languages have at least one morphological device (a suffix) for removing the agent from a transitive verb, producing what can be called an agentless passive; the same suffix also has a reflexive reading in most languages (this form is intransitive, having a single argument). However, the Sokean languages do not agree on a single shape for this function, and some languages have more than one suffix that seem to have the same function. A suffix shape *{>Atʉj} may be reconstructible to Proto-Sokean, but nothing like it has been found in Epi-Olmec texts. Mijean languages use a prefix *{yak>} (homophonous with the causative) with a passive reading.

5.3.6 Syntactic reflexive

Besides the morphological agentless passive that may have a reflexive reading, Sokean languages may form a reflexive construction with the noun **win* 'face; surface; front; body.' As a direct object, **win* marks the reflexive person; it is possessed with the same ergative marker that marks the subject of the reflexive transitive verb. This construction has not been observed in Epi-Olmec texts.

5.3.7 Reciprocal

In Mije-Sokean languages generally, a reciprocal form of a verb is formed by preposing *{nay+} to a *passive/reflexive* verb before the lexical stem and after the person markers.

5.3.8 Indefinite subject

In Sokean languages, from any intransitive verb, an indefinite subject form can be made by suffixing *{>Anʉm} to the lexical stem before adding aspect and mood markers. The meaning is 'people VERB,' 'there is VERBing.'

5.3.9 Auxiliaries

All Mije-Sokean languages have constructions in which a small set of *auxiliary* verbs act as the syntactic heads but semantic modifiers of a *main* lexical verb. These auxiliaries encode such meanings as 'go to VERB,' 'come to VERB,' 'want to VERB,' 'finish VERBing,' and a number of other similar notions. From existing languages, it would seem that the most archaic pattern would be

ABS+ (ERG+)MAIN.VERB-suffix # AUX-ASPECT/MOOD

The *suffix* in the above construction would be either a subordinating (dependent) suffix or a nominalizer. Oluta (Mijean) has /-E/ and Santa María Chimalapa (Sokean) has /-A/. Since there are both subordinators and nominalizers with both of these shapes, no clear answer to the identity of these suffixes is likely to be soon forthcoming, although subordinators often induce ergative shift, and the auxiliary construction does not. In general, Mije-Sokean languages do not use non-finite verb forms as the heads/nuclei of verb phrases, so the "subordinator" interpretation is more plausible.

In any case, no auxiliary constructions have been noted in known Epi-Olmec texts. In all Sokean languages the main verb takes a suffix {-wʉ} (probably the vetative suffix {-wʉ$_2$}) when preceded by an auxiliary, but we suspect that auxiliaries were clause-final in Epi-Olmec times and that this Proto-Sokean structure dates from a post-Epi-Olmec period.

Sokean languages use different suffixes after auxiliaries or negatives than elsewhere. These suffixes can be roughly characterized as dependent markers. The *words* that encode negatives are themselves distinguished for completive/incompletive aspect, but do not mark it explicitly. While negative markers are preverbal in all Mije-Sokean languages, and have probably always been so, auxiliaries were probably originally postverbal and their largely or entirely preverbal distribution in most languages is an innovation. The suffix *-*wʉ*$_2$ occurs in post-auxiliary and post-negative constructions in all Sokean languages (in these constructions, *-*wʉ*$_2$ *never* encodes completive aspect).

5.3.10 Independent personal pronouns

Non-third person independent pronouns can be reconstructed for Proto-Mije-Sokean, and Proto-Sokean, as follows: *7ʉ-tz* 'I'; *tʉ-tz* 'we (inclusive)'; *mi-tz* 'you'. All of these could be pluralized by combination with a pluralizing enclitic that does not have a single reconstructible form for Proto-Mije-Sokean or Proto-Sokean. *7ʉ-tz* + pluralizer means 'we (exclusive)'; *tʉ-tz* + pluralizer means 'we (inclusive)'; *mi-tz* + pluralizer means 'you all'. Not all Mije-Sokean languages have a third-person independent personal pronoun. Languages lacking a third-person pronoun use the demonstrative words in this function. Those languages that do have a third-person pronoun typically base it on the demonstrative **je7*.

6. LEXICON

The currently recognized Epi-Olmec vocabulary is almost exclusively Mije-Sokean in origin. This is not surprising. Mesoamerican languages generally are relatively resistant to lexical borrowing, and to date no Proto-Sokean, Proto-Mijean, or Proto-Mije-Sokean words have a recognized foreign origin. In contrast, many other Mesoamerican language groups show reconstructible borrowings from Mije-Sokean. This reflects both cultural attitudes and the culturally prominent roles of Mije-Sokeans over other Mesoamericans in early intercultural interactions. There is one non-Mije-Sokean word identified in Epi-Olmec: /nup/ (spelled ⟨nu-pu⟩) 'counterpart; the other member of a pair', which is borrowed from Greater Lowland Mayan **nuhp* of the same meaning.

Much of the morpheme stock of Epi-Olmec is specifically Sokean. We have identified forty Sokean roots and nine Sokean grammatical morphemes spelled phonetically (in part or entirely): for example, *jama* 'day' spelled ⟨ja-ma⟩, *.na7* 'stative' spelled ⟨na⟩.

It is to be expected that some words that are now specifically Mijean were lost in Sokean in the last few centuries before the Proto-Sokean stage, and therefore that a few such words might be attested in Epi-Olmec texts. We have securely read only two words that are at present restricted to Mijean, *sʉw* 'sun' and *wʉ7m.i* 'nodding'. It was already known that **sʉw* was the Proto-Mije-Sokean word for 'sun.' Commonly in Mesoamerica, a single word means 'sun,' 'day,' and 'festival,' which is the range of meanings of Proto-Mijean **sʉw*; Proto-Sokean has it with the meaning 'festival,' alongside innovated **jama* for 'sun, day.'

The following vocabulary lists all Epi-Olmec lexical items that are spelled phonetically, whether by a fully phonetic spelling or by a logogram with a phonetic complement, as we had identified them by the fall of 2001. The forms are cited in pre-Proto-Sokean phonological garb, first in our practical orthography and afterward in IPA. The stage at which the lexeme is reconstructible within Mije-Sokean is also specified: pMS is Proto-Mije-Sokean; pS is Proto-Sokean. All reconstructions are in the form determined by Kaufman. TK marks cognate sets put together by Kaufman, along with the year it was recognized; SW marks cognate sets put together by Wichmann, all published in 1995.

Grammatical class information is specified as follows: adj = adjective; adv = adverbial; num = numeral; s = substantive; sr = relational noun; sv = verbal noun; vi = intransitive verb; vt = transitive verb; med = mediopassive; pcp = participle; unacc = unaccusative.

7ame7 (< pMS **7a:me7*) s year. Spelled ⟨DRUM/YEAR, DRUM/YEAR-me⟩. IPA: ʔameʔ. (TK 1963)

7i (> pS) pron:interr-indef who?. Spelled ⟨7i⟩. IPA: ʔi. (TK 1963)

7i7ps (< pMS **7i:7ps*) num twenty. Spelled ⟨MOON/TWENTY-si_2⟩. IPA: ʔiʔps. (TK 1963)

7is (< pMS **7is*) vt/unerg to see. Spelled ⟨7i-si-wʉ⟩. IPA: ʔis. (TK 1963)

  7is (< pMS **7is*) expl lo!, behold! Spelled ⟨7i-si, 7i-si_2⟩. IPA: ʔis. (TK 1991)

7otuw (> pS) vi to speak. Spelled ⟨7o-tu-pa⟩. IPA: ʔotuw. (SW 1991)

7owa (< pMS **7owa*) s macaw, parrot. Spelled ⟨7o+wa, MACAW⟩. IPA: ʔowa. (TK 1992)

7oy (< pMS **7oy*) vi to go (and return), to take a trip. Spelled ⟨7o-7i⟩. IPA: ʔoy. (TK 1963)

jak (> pS) vt/vi to cut. IPA: hak. (TK 1963)

ku.jak (> pS) vi to cross over. Spelled ⟨ku-CROSS-wʉ⟩. IPA: ku.hak. (TK 1993)

jam (> pS **jam.ʉj*) vt to remember. IPA: ham. (TK 1963)

kuk=tza7=jam.e. s pectoral stone memento. Spelled ⟨7i-ku-MIDDLE-tza$_2$-ja-me⟩. IPA: kuk=tsaʔ=ham.e. (TK 1963 + TK 1991)

jama (> pS) s day; shape-shifter's animal guise. Spelled ⟨ja-ma, ja$_2$-ma, GUISE$_1$, GUISE$_2$⟩. IPA: *hama*. (TK 1963 + TK 1991)

jay7 (< pMS **ja:y7*) vt/vi to write. IPA: hayʔ. (TK 1963)

jay7=ki7ps.i sv<v+v inscribed monument. Spelled ⟨ja$_2$-SYMBOL-si$_2$⟩. IPA: hayʔ=kiʔps.i.

je7 (< pMS **je7*) dem that. Spelled ⟨je⟩. IPA: heʔ. (TK 1963)

je7.tzʉ (> pS) dem thus, like that. Spelled ⟨je-tzʉ⟩. IPA: heʔ.tsɨ . (TK 1992)

jej (>pS) vi to live, breathe. IPA: heh. (TK 1963)

jej.a7 (> pS) sv < vi god: 'living one'. Spelled ⟨GOD-ja⟩. IPA: heh. aʔ. (TK 1994)

ji7tz (> pS) vt/vi to (get) wrinkle(d). IPA: hiʔts. (TK 1994)

ji7tz.i7 (> pS) sv < vt wrinkled, pleated; earthly Longlip god ("wrinkled one"). Spelled ⟨ji-LONGLIP$_2$, ji-tzi⟩. IPA: hiʔts.iʔ. (TK 1994)

joj (< pMS **jo:tʔ* > pS **joj*) sr inside. Spelled ⟨jo⟩. IPA: hoh. (TK 1963)

jome7 (< pMS **jome7*) adj new. Spelled ⟨jo-me-NEW⟩. IPA: homeʔ. (TK 1963)

jup (< pMS **jup*) vt to cover. IPA: hup. (TK 1992 + SW 1991)

ni7.jup.7 sv body-covering. Spelled ⟨?LOINCLOTH-pu⟩. IPA: niʔ.hup.ʔ.

ju7ps (< pMS **ju7ps*) vt to lash, to tie something onto something else. IPA: huʔps. (SW 1991)

7owa-ju7ps.i sv macaw-lashing. Spelled ⟨7o+wa=ju/LASH-si⟩. IPA: ʔowa=huʔps.i.

jʉs (< pMS **jʉs*) adv after[ward]. Spelled ⟨AFTER, AFTER-?sʉ⟩. IPA: hɨs. (SW 1991+ TK 1993)

kak (> pS) vt/unacc to (get) replace(d). Spelled ⟨kak-wʉ⟩. (SW 1991)

kak.e sv < vt exchange, replacement. Spelled ⟨kak⟩.

kak.ʉ7 (> pSoke **kak.ʉ7*) sv < vt replacer, successor. Spelled ⟨kak⟩. IPA: kak-iʔ. (TK 1992)

kakpe7 (< pMS **kakpe7*) s scorpion; Scorpius. Spelled ⟨kak-SCORPIUS-pe⟩. IPA: kakpeʔ (TK 1963)

ken (> pS) vt to see. (TK 1993)

ken.e (> pSoke) pcp < vt seen: visible, public. Spelled ⟨ke-ne⟩. (TK 1993)

kij (< pMS **kij*) vi to give light, shine. Spelled ⟨SHINE-wʉ, ki-wʉ⟩. IPA: kih. (SW 1991)

ki7m (> pS) vi to go up, accede. Spelled ⟨7i-GO.UP⟩. IPA: kiʔm. (TK 1963)

ki7m.ʉ7 (> pS) sv < vi accession, rising, ascent, installation. Spelled ⟨GO.UP⟩. IPA: kiʔm.ɨʔ (SW 1991)

7aw=ki7m (> pS) vi to rule. IPA: ʔaw=kiʔm. (SW 1991)

7aw=ki7m.ʉ7 (> pS) sv < vi rule (rship). Spelled ⟨7aw-GO.UP, 7aw-GO.UP-mʉ⟩. IPA: 7aw=kiʔm.ɨ ʔ. (TK 1991)

ko.ki7m.i(7) sv < vi accession, or one.who.accedes on.behalf.of.others/elsewhere. Spelled ⟨ko-ki-mi-GO.UP⟩. IPA: ko.kiʔm.i(ʔ).

kip (< pMS **kip*) vt to fight against. Spelled ⟨7i-ki-pi-wʉ⟩. (SW 1991)

ki7ps vt to try, test, think (TK 1963)

ki7ps.i (< pMS **ki7ps.i*) sv < vt symbol(stone) [celt, figurine, stela; badge, token, memento, souvenir]. Spelled ⟨SYMBOL-si_2⟩. IPA: kiʔps.i. (TK 1963 + TK 1992)

kom (< pMS **kojm*) s notched house-post, pillar. (TK 1963)

tzap(=?win)=kom s type s sky(-?face) pillar. Spelled ⟨ko-SKY-?FACE-PILLAR⟩. IPA: tsap(=?win)=kom.

ko.nu7ks (< pMS **ko.nu:7ks*) vt to bless, hallow. Spelled ⟨HALLOW-wʉ⟩. (SW 1991)

ko.nu7ks.i (< pMS **ko.nu7ks.i*) pcp < vt blessed, hallowed. Spelled ⟨HALLOW-si_2⟩. (SW 1991 + TK 1992)

ko.yumi (> pS) s lord. Spelled ⟨ko-LORD-mi⟩. (TK 1963 + TK 1994)

kot (> pS) vt to put away. Spelled ⟨7i-ko-te⟩. (TK 1963)

kuk (< pMS **kuk*) s middle. (TK 1993)

kuk=tza7=jam.e s pectoral stone memento. Spelled ⟨7i-ku-MIDDLE-tza_2-ja-me⟩. IPA: kuk=tsaʔ=ham.e.

kuw (> pSoke) vt to raise; to put up/away. (SW 1991 + TK 1994)

kuw.na7 adv < vt raised; put up/away. Spelled ⟨ku-na⟩. IPA: kuw.naʔ. (TK 1992)

kʉ7 (< pMS **kʉ7*) s hand, arm. Spelled ⟨na-kʉ⟩. IPA: kɨʔ. (TK 1963)

kʉw7 (< pMS **kʉ:w7*) vt/unacc to (get) dye(d). Spelled ⟨kʉ-wʉ⟩. IPA: kɨwʔ. (SW 1991 + TK 1993)

kʉy7 (< pMS **kʉ:y7*) vt/unacc to (get) cover(ed). IPA: kɨyʔ. (SW 1991)

ko.wu7tz=kʉy7 vt + vt/unacc to get pierced and covered for others. Spelled ⟨ko-PIERCE-kʉ-wʉ⟩. IPA: ko.wuʔts=kɨyʔ. (SW 1991)

ma (< pMS **ma*) adv earlier. Spelled ⟨ma⟩. (TK 1963)

mak (< pMS **mak*) num ten. (TK 1963)

mak tzap num+s Ten Sky (a god). Spelled ⟨ma-FIVE-FIVE-SKY⟩. IPA: mak tsap.

masa(n) (< pMS **ma:san* > pS **masan* ∼ *masa=*) s/adj holy (thing), god. (TK 1963 + TK 1992)

masa=wik.i sv something/someone hallowed by sprinkling. Spelled ⟨ma-sa-SPRINKLE-ta-ma⟩.

masa=ni7.*APPEAR* vi to appear divinely on the body. Spelled ⟨ma-sa-ni-APPEAR-wʉ⟩.

matza7 (< pMS **ma:tza7*) s star. Spelled ⟨ma-STAR-tza⟩. IPA: matsaʔ. (TK 1963)

may (< pMS) vt/unacc to count. Spelled ⟨ma-wʉ, ma-$wʉ_2$⟩. (TK 1963)

metz= (< pMS **metz=*) num by twos. Spelled ⟨me-tze⟩. IPA: mets=. (TK 1963)

mi7ks (< pMS **mi7ks*) vi to quiver. Spelled ⟨7i-BLOOD-mi-si_2, mi-si-na-wʉ⟩. IPA: miʔks. (SW 1991)

mon7 (< pMS **mon7*) vt to wrap. IPA: monʔ. (TK 1963)

RULER=***ko7=mon7.a7*** sv ruler's head-wrap. Spelled ⟨"KNOT"+"GOVERNOR"-7a⟩.

mʉtz (> pS) vi to play. IPA: mɨts. (TK 1963)

mʉtz.i7 (> pS) sv < v impersonator. Spelled ⟨PLAY-tzi⟩. IPA: mɨtz.i7. (TK 1994)

nas (< pMS **nas*) vi to pass. Spelled ⟨na-sa-wʉ⟩. (TK 1963)

ne7k (> pS) vt to set aside. IPA: neʔk. (SW 1991)

ne7k.e (> pS) pcp < vt set aside. Spelled ⟨ne-ke⟩. IPA: neʔk.e. (SW 1991 + TK 1993)

ne7w (< pMS **ne7w*) vt to set stones in a row/wall/circle. Spelled ⟨7i-ne-ji⟩ IPA: neʔw. (SW 1991)

ne7w.e sv/pcp (stones) set in order. Spelled ⟨ORDER.STONES = ne⟩. IPA: neʔw.e.

nip7 (< pMS **ni:p7*) vt/unacc to plant, sow; bury. Spelled ⟨PLANT-pi-wʉ⟩. IPA: nipʔ. (TK 1963)

nip7.i (< pMS **ni:p7.i*) sv < vt planting, planted (thing). Spelled ⟨PLANT, PLANT-7i⟩. IPA: nipʔ.i. (SW 1991)

nup (< Greater Lowland Mayan *nuhp*) s counterpart, one of two members of a paɨr. (TK 2001)
nʉks (< pMS **nʉks*) vi to go along. Spelled ⟨7i-nʉ-si⟩. IPA: nɨks. (TK 1963)
pak vt to beat (TK 1992)
pak.kuy7 (> pS) sv bludgeon. Spelled ⟨pak-ku⟩. IPA: pak.kuyʔ.
paki7 (> pS) adj hard, strong, powerful. Spelled ⟨pa-ki⟩. IPA: pakiʔ. (SW 1991)
pey (>pS **pey.e7*) vt unacc to get waved/swung. Spelled ⟨pe-wʉ⟩. (SW 1991 + TK 1993)
pini7 (> pSoke **pini7*) s brother-in-law of man. Spelled ⟨pi-ni⟩. IPA: piniʔ. (TK 1963)
pit (< pMS **pit*) vt to tie (in a bundle). (TK 1963)
pit.i sv < vt bundle; prisoner. Spelled ⟨TIE, TIE-ti⟩.
poy7a (< pMS **poy7a*) s moon; month, veintena. Spelled ⟨po-7a, MOON, MONTH⟩. IPA: poyʔa. (TK 1963)
puw (> pS) vt/unacc to (get) scatter(ed). Spelled ⟨pu-wʉ⟩. (TK 1991)
pʉk (< pMS **pʉk*) vt/unacc to (get) take(n)/acquire(d)/achieve(d). Spelled ⟨pʉk-7i, pʉk-kʉ-7i, pʉk-kʉ-wʉ⟩. IPA: pɨk. (TK 1963)
sa7.sa7 (> pS) adj noble, healthy
sa7.sa7 (=pʉn) (> pSoke) s noble, aristocrat. Spelled ⟨sa$_2$-NOBLE$_2$⟩. IPA: saʔ.saʔ (=pɨn). (SW 1991 + TK 1993)
saj (< pMS **saj*) vt/unacc to (get) share(d) out. Spelled ⟨7i$_2$-sa$_2$+pa$_2$, saj-wʉ⟩. IPA: sah. (SW 1991)
saj (< pMS **saj*) s wing; shoulder. Spelled ⟨7i-sa⟩. IPA: sah. (TK 1963)
si7i7 (> pS) s backside, butt. Spelled ⟨si$_2$-7i⟩. IPA: siʔiʔ. (TK 1992–1994)
su7ksu7 (< pMS **su7ksu7*) s hummingbird. Spelled ⟨?su×?su⟩. IPA: suʔksuʔ. (SW 1991)
te7 (< pMS **te7*) dem the aforementioned; the latter; it; that. Spelled ⟨te⟩. IPA: teʔ. (TK 1992)
te7n (< pMS **te:7n*) vi to stand (on tip-toe), to step (on). IPA: teʔn. (TK 1963)
te7n.na7 (> pS) adv upright(ly), on tip-toe. Spelled ⟨te-ne-na⟩. IPA: teʔn.naʔ. (TK 1963 + TK 1992)
tok (> pSoke) vt to stain. (TK 1993)
tok.e (> pS) pcp stained. Spelled ⟨to-ke⟩. (TK 1993)
tokoy (< pMS **tokoy*) vi to be lost. (TK 1963)
ko.tokoy-pʉ7 vt to cover up/over OR to spill.on.behalf.of.others/elsewhere. Spelled ⟨7i-ko-LOSE-pʉ-wʉ⟩. IPA: ko.tokoy-pɨʔ. (TK1963 + TK 1992)
(yak>)tokoy.a7 sv < v overturning/upsetting/dumping OR overturner/upsetter/dumper etc. Spelled ⟨7i-LOSE-ya⟩. IPA: (yak>)tokoy.aʔ. (TK 1963 + TK 1992)
(yak>)tokoy.e sv < v overturned/upset/dumped one. Spelled ⟨na-LOSE-ye⟩. (TK 1963 + TK 1992)
tuk (> pS) vi to happen. Spelled ⟨tuk×pa⟩. (TK 1963)
tuk (< pMS **tuk*) vt to cut, harvest. (TK 1963)
tuk.ʉ7 sv < vt harvester. Spelled ⟨tuk⟩. IPA: tuk.ɨʔ.
tuk.ʉ7 pcp < vt having been cut. Spelled ⟨tu-kʉ⟩. IPA: tuk.ɨʔ.
wʉ=tuk.i sv well-harvested (thing). Spelled ⟨wʉ-tuk?⟩. IPA: wɨ =tuk.i.
tuki (> pS) s water turtle. Spelled ⟨TURTLE-ki⟩. (TK 1963)
tu7ki (> pGulf Sokean **tu:7ki*) s trogon, quetzal. Spelled ⟨TROGON⟩. [Final /i/ implied by omission of following ⟨7i⟩.] IPA: tuʔki. (TK 1997)
tuku7 (< pMS **tuku7*) s cloth, garment. Spelled ⟨CLOTH, tu+CLOTH⟩. IPA: tukuʔ. (TK 1992)
tus (> pS) vt to prick, sting. (TK 1963)
tus.i (> pS) adj < vt with hair standing on end. Spelled ⟨tu-si⟩. (TK 1992)

tʉp (< pMS **tʉp*) vt to pierce with a shafted or shaft-shaped piercer. Spelled ⟨tʉ-nʉ-“DEAL.WITH”-pʉ-ja-wʉ⟩, ⟨tʉ-nʉ-“DEAL.WITH”-pʉ-ja-yaj-wʉ⟩. IPA: tɨp. (TK 1963)

tza7 (< pMS **tza:7*) s stone. IPA: tsaʔ. (TK 1963)

kuk=tza7=jam.e s pectoral stone memento. Spelled ⟨7i-ku-MIDDLE-tza$_2$-ja-me⟩. IPA: kuk=tsaʔ=ham.e.

tza7yji (> pSoke) adv late in the day. Spelled ⟨tza$_2$-ji⟩. IPA: tsaʔyhi. (SW 1991 + TK 1992)

tzap (< pMS **tzap*) s sky. Spelled ⟨SKY, SKY-pa⟩. IPA: tsap. (TK 1963)

mak tzap num+s Ten Sky (a god). Spelled ⟨ma-FIVE-FIVE-SKY⟩. IPA: mak tsap.

tzat7 (< pMS **tzat7*) vt to measure by hand-spans. IPA: tsatʔ. (SW 1991)

tzat7.ʉ7 sv hand-span measuring device. Spelled ⟨7i$_2$-ni$_2$-ko-SPAN-7ʉ$_2$⟩. IPA: tsatʔ.ɨ ʔ.

nʉ.tzat7.e=nas adj <vt + s ground jointly measured by hand-spans. Spelled ⟨nʉ$_2$-SPAN=EARTH⟩. IPA: nɨ .tsatʔ.e.

tzetz (< pMS **tzetz*) vt to chop (off). Spelled ⟨na-tze+tze-CHOP-ji⟩. IPA: tsets. (SW 1991)

tzetz.e sv < vt chopped off (thing). Spelled ⟨na-tze+tze⟩. IPA: tsets.e.

tzʉk (> pSoke) vt to do (< ?to touch). Spelled ⟨DO-pa⟩. IPA: tsɨk. (TK 1963)

tzʉk.i=pʉn sv deedsman. Spelled ⟨DO$_2$×ki⟩. IPA: tsɨk.i=pɨn.

tzʉsi (> pS) s child under 12. Spelled ⟨tzʉ-si$_2$⟩. IPA: tsɨsi. (TK 1963)

wan (> pS) vt/vi to sing. (TK 1963)

wan.e (> pS) sv < vi song, chant. Spelled ⟨SING-ne⟩. (TK 1963)

wan.e=tzʉk (> pSoke) vi:incorp to perform a chant. IPA: wan.e=tsɨk. (TK 1963 + TK 1992)

wej (> pS) vi to shout. Spelled ⟨we-pa⟩. IPA: weh. (TK 1963)

wen.e7 (> pS) sv < vt (something) broken, piece. Spelled ⟨we-ne⟩. IPA: wen.eʔ. (SW 1991 + TK 1992)

OR ***we7n.e*** (< pMS **we:7n.e*) sv < vt a few, some. Spelled ⟨we-ne⟩. IPA: weʔn.e. (SW 1991 + TK 1992)

wik (> pS) vt/unacc to (get) sprinkle(d). (TK 1992)

ko.wik (> pS) vt/unacc to (get) sprinkle(d) for.others/elsewhere. Spelled ⟨7i-ko-SPRINKLE-ki-pa, ko-SPRINKLE-ki-pa⟩. (SW 1991 + TK 1992)

wik.i (> pS) sv < vt result of sprinkling. Spelled ⟨SPRINKLE⟩. (SW 1991 + TK 1992)

masa=wik.i sv something/someone hallowed by sprinkling. Spelled ⟨ma-sa-SPRINKLE ta-ma⟩. (TK 1992)

win (< pMS **win*) sr in front. Spelled ⟨wi-BEFORE⟩. (TK 1963)

wis (< pMS **wis*) vt to uproot. (SW 1991)

wis.i pcp < vt uprooted. Spelled ⟨UPROOT-si$_2$⟩ or ⟨wi$_2$-si$_2$⟩.

wo7m (> pS) vi to sprout. (SW 1991)

wo7m.a7 (> pS) s sprout. Spelled ⟨?wo-ma⟩. IPA: woʔm.aʔ. (SW 1991 + TK 1993)

wʉ (> pS) adj good. IPA: wɨ. (TK 1963)

wʉ=tuk.i sv < vt well-harvested (thing). Spelled ⟨wʉ-tuk⟩. IPA: wɨ =tuk.i.

wʉ7m (< pMS **wʉ7m*) vi to nod (SW 1991 + TK 2000)

wʉ7m.i pcp nodding. Spelled ⟨wʉ-mi⟩. IPA: wɨʔm.i.

yaj (> pS [elite]) vi:med to be finished. Spelled ⟨yaj-7i⟩. IPA: yah. (TK 1963)

yʉ7 (< pMS **yʉ7*) dem this. Spelled ⟨yʉ⟩. IPA: yɨʔ. (TK 1963)

7. THE PLACE OF EPI-OLMEC IN THE MIJE-SOKEAN FAMILY

7.1 Epi-Olmec and innovations in the diversification of Sokean

The etymological sources of Epi-Olmec vocabulary (see §6), along with a number of grammatical traits, show that the Epi-Olmec language belongs to the Sokean branch of the Mije-Sokean family.

In some ways Epi-Olmec is less evolved than Proto-Sokean as it can be reconstructed from its surviving daughters, as attested (i) *lexically* by *sʉw* 'sun' (see §6); (ii) *morphologically* by {-ji} 'dependent completive' and by the apparently productive use of {.A7} for agentive nominalization; and (iii) *phonologically* by /7/ between C and V, by /p/ after /k/, and by the maintenance of original vowel length (if real). (In fact, the phonological system of Epi-Olmec cannot be distinguished from that of Proto-Mije-Sokean or Proto-Mijean.) Accordingly, when Epi-Olmec agrees specifically with one subgroup of Sokean and diverges from the other, the straightforward conclusion is that the divergent branch is innovative.

The features that are most telling are grammatical; the straightforward cases are provided in Table 10.3 :

Table 10.3 Grammatical innovations in Sokean subgroups

	Features	Epi-Olmec	Proto-Sokean	Gulf Sokean	Soke
			GULF SOKEAN IS CONSERVATIVE		
1.	who?	⟨7i⟩	*7i	SOT 7iH	MAR 7i-wʉ
2.	what?	⟨ti⟩	*ti	SOT tyiH	MAR ti-yʉ
3.	*perfect*	⟨na⟩	*-nay7	SOT {-ne7}	—
4.	that	⟨je⟩	*je7	SOT je7 's/he'	—
5.	like	⟨tzʉ⟩	*+tzʉ	SOT {-tzɄ} frozen	—
6.	away	⟨ku⟩	*ku.	SOT {ku+}	MAR {kʉ.}
			SOKE IS CONSERVATIVE		
7.	this	⟨yʉ⟩	*yʉ7	(SOT yʉ7p)	MAR yʉ7
8.	the	⟨te⟩	*te7	—	MAR te7
9.	from	⟨kʉ⟩	*+k..	SOT {-k} frozen	COP {+k}
10.	when (REL.)	⟨kʉ⟩	*+7kʉ	SOT {-k} frozen	COP {+7k} MAG {+7ʉk} MAR {+k(ʉ)}
11.	*relativizer*	⟨wʉ⟩	*+wʉ7	—	COP {+wʉ7} MIG {+V7k}
12.	completely	⟨pʉ⟩	*-pʉ7	—	COP {-pʉ7}
13.	on the body	⟨ni⟩	*ni7.	—	MAR {ni7.}
14.	*stative*	⟨na⟩	*.na7	—	MAR {.na7}
15.	*word order*	SOV	*SOV	VSO	MAR SOV vs. COP VOS

In Soteapan Gulf Sokean, the symbol H is used to transcribe a morphophoneme that sometimes is realized as vowel length (see §3.2), sometimes as vowel length followed by /j/, and sometimes as nothing. It occurs in a fair number of morphemes, both roots and suffixes; the particular phonological realization is determined by phonological context. The designation "frozen" for Gulf Sokean means that the morpheme occurs in a small number of lexical items, and is not productive, whereas in the corresponding Soke forms the morpheme occurs productively.

7.2 Elite innovations

Certain Epi-Olmec words – for example, *kak* 'to replace,' *kuw* 'to raise, to put up/away' – are now attested only in Chiapas Soke, even though our documentation of other Sokean languages is even more extensive. This suggests the hypothesis that Chiapas Soke maintains some elite forms that have been lost elsewhere. Evidence from three grammatical morphemes, the optative suffix and two pluralizers, supports this hypothesis.

7.2.1 Sokean optative

The optative suffix is spelled ⟨7i⟩ in Epi-Olmec texts (see §4.3.2). This complicates our picture of Sokean morphology. The optative is *-7i* in Chiapas Soke, but the Proto-Sokean form was apparently **-7in*; the presence of the final /n/, for which there is otherwise no straightforward source, is indicated by Santa María Chimalapa Soke *-7in* and Soteapan Gulf Sokean *-7iny*.

One logical possibility is that /n/ was somehow lost in Chiapas Soke. But Epi-Olmec predated the Proto-Sokean phase, and it is implausible that ⟨7i⟩ is spelling /7in/; Epi-Olmecs never failed to spell /n/ (or any other non-weak consonant, except /p, k/ before /s/). The only straightforward solution is that Proto-Sokean had both **-7in* and **-7i*, in conditioned or free variation. If the elite variety (represented earlier in Epi-Olmec texts) preferred /-7i/, while the lower class variety preferred /-7in/ (which may have been more archaic), this would allow both variants and would agree roughly with the hypothesis, for which there is other evidence, that Oaxaca Soke is conservative and Chiapas Soke is at least partly descended from an elite variety of Sokean.

7.2.2 Mije-Sokean plural markers

In two grammatical features, Epi-Olmec agrees with innovations in Gulf Sokean and Chiapas Soke and diverges from conservative forms in Oaxaca Soke.

As noted in §4.2.2, third-person plural markers are always recruited from the particular language's verb root meaning 'to be finished': Mijean **kʉx*, Oaxaca Soke **suk*, Epi-Olmec and other Sokean **yaj*. The remaining plural markers – which are not also known to be roots – are as follows (without their precise functions, which vary from language to language):

{*-ta7m} (Soke, SOT, OLU, LLM)
{*+tʉk} (OLU, LLM, MAR, MIG)
{*jate7} (OLU, SAY, MIG)

Among the Sokean languages, Santa María Chimalapa Soke and San Miguel Chimalapa Soke often differ from the rest and agree instead with Mijean. This might be due either to contact with Mijean, or to conservatism, since certain features common to most Sokean languages might be elite Epi-Olmec innovations preserved in surviving Gulf Sokean (Soteapan Gulf Sokean, Texistepec Gulf Sokean, Ayapa Gulf Sokean) and Chiapas Soke but not in Oaxaca Soke (see the preceding discussions).

On the latter assumption, we would reconstruct the following for Proto-Mije-Sokean:

{*-ta7m}	first- and second-person plural agreement: S/O/P
'to be finished'	third-person plural agreement: S/O/P
{*+tʉk}	noun plural (survives in MAR, MIG, LLM, OLU)
{*jate7}	'each, several' (used to pluralize nouns and adjectives in SAY, pronouns in MIG, first- and second-person subjects and objects in OLU)

A set of elite Epi-Olmec innovations would then be:

animate noun plural ⇒ {+ta7m}
inanimate noun plural ⇒ {+yaj}

Epi-Olmec attests these Proto-Mije-Sokean traits plus the postulated elite innovations, except that no first or second person plural agreement-marker is attested.

Acknowledgments

Our research on Epi-Olmec decipherment, and on the documentation and comparative analysis of present-day Mije-Sokean languages, has been supported mainly by the National Science Foundation (grants SBR-9411247, SBR-9511713, and SBR-9809985), the Salus Mundi Foundation, and the National Geographic Society (4190–92 and 5319–94). We thank Peter Keeler, director of the Maya Meetings at Texas, for supporting our participation and research on Epi-Olmec writing at these annual workshops. Our work was also supported by the Faculty Research Awards Program (grant 320-9753P) at the State University of New York at Albany, and Justeson received research support from the Department of Artificial Intelligence at IBM's T. J. Watson Research Center. We have received smaller grants from the University of Pittsburgh and SUNY at Albany. We thank Roberto Zavala Maldonado for useful comments on this study.

Phonological transcriptions

This paper uses a practical orthography with the following IPA equivalents:

	p	t	tz	k	7	j	s	m	n	nh	w	x	y
IPA:	p	t	ts	k	ʔ	h	s	m	n	ŋ	w	š	y

	i	e	ʉ	a	u	o
IPA:	i	e	ɨ	a	u	o

Morphological transcriptions

In morphologically explicit representations of Mije-Sokean words, inflexional affixes are marked by -, clitics by +, derivational affixes by ., class-changers by >, and compounding morphemes by =.

Example sentence format

T Transcription
  uncertainty that a sign's identification is correct is indicated by a postposed question mark
  less secure readings or interpretations of signs are indicated by a preposed question mark
R pre-Proto-Sokean Reading
  questions and doubts are marked in line T, not here
G morpheme-by-morpheme Gloss (morphemes are separated by hyphens)
FT Free (but still fairly literal) Translation

Grammatical codes

Absolutive person markers

XA	exclusive absolutive: {7ʉ+}
3A	third person absolutive: {Ø}

Ergative person markers

XE	exclusive ergative: {na+}
IE	inclusive ergative: {tʉn+}
2E	second person ergative: {7in+}
3E	third person ergative: {7i+}

Derivational prefixes on verbs

AWAY	away: {ku.}
MOUTH	with the mouth: {7aw=}
BODY	on the body: {ni7.}
ELSE	in someone else's place; elsewhere, for someone else: {ko.}
ASSOC	together, jointly: {nʉ.}
CAU	causative {yak>}

Verb suffixes

ENTIRELY	entirely: {.pʉ7}
NDIR	indirective: {>jay7}
PRF	perfect: {-nay7}

Plural person marking suffixes

AP	animate plural: {+ta7m}
IP	inanimate plural: {+yaj}
3P	third person plural: {-yaj}

Aspect/mood suffixes

II	independent incompletive: {-pa}
DI	dependent incompletive: {-e} ~ {-i}
IC	independent completive: {-wʉ}
DC	dependent completive: {-ji}
OPT	optative: {-7i}

Stative-deriving suffix

STAT	stative: {.na7}

Noun-deriving suffixes

PN	passive nominalization: {.E}, {.E7}, {.A7}
AN	active nominalization: {.A7}, {.E7}
NSTR	instrument noun: {.kuy7}, {.7}

Locative enclitics

LOC	locative: {+mʉ7}
FROM	from: {+k}

Subordinating enclitics

REL	relativizer: {+wʉ7}
WHEN	when: {+7kʉ}

Bibliography

For our discussion of comparative Mije-Sokean linguistics and the features of individual Mije-Sokean languages, we have drawn upon the mostly unpublished results of field work by linguists working with the Project for the Documentation of the Languages of Meso-America. For Oluta Mijean and San Miguel Chimalapa Soke, some of this data is published online at http://www.albany.edu/pdlma/. The Project has lexical databases for all of the Mije-Sokean languages, as follows (language abbreviation, linguist(s) responsible): MIG (Heidi Johnson and Terrence Kaufman), MAR (Terrence Kaufman), COP (Clifton Pye and Terrence Kaufman), TEC (Roberto Zavala), AYA (James Fox and Giulia Oliverio), TEX (Catherine Bereznak and Ehren Reilly), SOT (Terrence Kaufman and Valerie Himes), OLU (Roberto Zavala), SAY (Richard Rhodes and Dennis Holt), GUI (Giulia Oliverio), TOT (Daniel Suslak).

Campbell, L. and T. Kaufman. 1976. "A linguistic look at the Olmecs." *American Antiquity* 41:80–89.

Justeson, J. and T. Kaufman. 1993. "A decipherment of epi-Olmec hieroglyphic writing." *Science* 259:1703–1711.

______. 1996 [1992]. "Un desciframiento de la escritura epi-olmeca: métodos y resultados." *Arqueología* 8:15–25.

______. 1997. "A newly-discovered column in the hieroglyphic text on La Mojarra Stela 1: a test of the epi-Olmec decipherment." *Science* 277:207–210. (An extended version appears in *Science Online* at www.sciencemag.org/features/data/justeson.shl/.)

Kaufman, T. 1963. "Mixe-Zoque diachronic studies." Unpublished monograph.

Kaufman, T. and J. Justeson. 2001. *Epi-Olmec Hieroglyphic Writing and Texts.* Workshop of the XXV Maya Meetings at Texas. Online at http://www.albany.edu/pdlma/EOTEXTS.pdf.

Kelley, D. 1993. "The decipherment of epi-Olmec writing as Zoquean by Justeson and Kaufman." *The Review of Archaeology* 14(1):29–32.

Macri, M. and L. Stark. 1993. *A Sign Catalog of the La Mojarra Script.* Pre-Columbian Art Research Institute, Monograph 5. San Francisco: PARI.

Pool, C. 2000. "From Olmec to epi-Olmec at Tres Zapotes." In J. Clark and M. Pye, eds., *Olmec Art and Archaeology in Mesoamerica.* Studies in the History of Art, 58. Washington, D.C.: National Gallery of Art.

Wichmann, S. 1995. *The Relationship among the Mixe-Zoquean Languages of Mexico.* Provo: University of Utah Press.

Zapotec appendix

Most of what is widely understood about Zapotec (Sapoteko) writing is not linguistic. This knowledge consists of identifications of the signs for numerals from 1 to 19, which are in the same bar-and-dot system as in the rest of Mesoamerica (changed to dots only, later, in central Mexico), and the signs for names of most of the twenty days in the ritual calendar, and, based on it, the fifty-two-year cycle of named years. The current reliable results on the calendar are due mostly to Javier Urcid (1992, 2001), building on work by Alfonso Caso (1928, 1947). Using Urcid's results, Justeson and Kaufman (1996) worked out that the numerical coefficients of a glyph that Caso called *Glyph W* indicate the position of an associated ritual calendar date within a lunation.

Zapotec texts were generally written in columns from top to bottom. Columns were read from left to right, and the signs in these cases face leftward. Above rightward-facing animate beings in accompanying iconography, texts were read from right to left and their signs face rightward; this deviation also usually occurs when columnar text is adjacent to such figures (Kaufman and Justeson 1993–2003).

Almost everything else thus far worked out in the script has taken calendrics as a starting point. People were named for the ritual calendar date on which they were born, so when figures in scenes are accompanied by what seem to be dates, these dates are often to be taken as names of those people (the same practice is found in later Mexican pictorial books, which are famous for their so-called narrative pictography; they have no connected glyphic texts, only glyphic captions for people, places, and dates).

One exception is provided by a set of signs and sign groups occurring above a logogram representing 'hill' on a set of wall panels known as "conquest slabs." Caso (1947) proposed that these sign groups were place names, because their context and arrangement resembled those of Nahua place name glyphs. Marcus (1976) and Whittaker (1980) built on this proposal and attempted to identify specific sign groups with specific places. Justeson and Kaufman (1996) found, to the contrary, that none of these sign groups name places; instead, they give noncalendrical personal names and titles of individuals involved in warfare. Urcid (1992) has identified other glyphic place names, outside the conquest slabs; these names are spelled by glyph groups that are overlaid on the logogram for 'hill.' We agree with Urcid's interpretation of these data and find the same pattern with additional glyphs besides ⟨HILL⟩ that represent places.

Most researchers believe these texts are written in Zapotec because the distribution of the script generally (though not exactly) matches the distribution of Zapotec speech at the time of the Spanish invasion of Mesoamerica. In fact, the very earliest texts in the script are located near the center of the Zapotec region, in the Valley of Oaxaca. Day names occur before their numeral coefficients, an order documented only in the Zapotec calendar (Whittaker 1980). Urcid (1992) observed that two of the day signs relate specifically to Zapotec: Zapotecs had a day named *Knot*, agreeing with the form of a day sign that Caso (1928) recognized as depicting a knotted cloth, and a day named *Corn*, agreeing with the form of a day sign that Urcid recognized as depicting an ear of corn.

Our joint research on the decipherment of Zapotec writing, begun in 1992, is the first to use a systematic linguistic approach based on detailed documentation and reconstruction of Zapotec and other Mesoamerican languages. This has helped us to advance the interpretation of the calendrics, and enabled us to make the first reliable readings of phonetic signs – that is, readings that are supported by distinct semantic and grammatical contexts. We have also identified about half of the most frequent grammatical morphemes that would be expected in a text (Kaufman and Justeson 1993–2003), though nothing as comprehensive or decisive as in the Epi-Olmec case.

These results from the analysis of the grammar of Zapotec inscriptions have been based on Kaufman's models for Proto-Zapotec and Proto-Zapotecan grammar and vocabulary (Kaufman 1988, 1995). Our language documentation project (PDLMA, Project for the Documentation of the Languages of Meso-America; http://www.albany.edu/pdlma/) has gathered data on ten Zapotecan languages for the purpose of reconstructing the vocabulary and grammar of Proto-Zapotecan and Proto-Zapotec. As we now know it, some of the main features of the Proto-Zapotec and Proto-Zapotecan languages are as follows:

Phonology. All syllables in these languages are of the shape CV (except that **k* – in some cases originally probably some kind of deictic enclitic – occurred at the end of some stems;

see Kaufman 2000). The vowel can be short, long, broken/squeezed, or checked. Syllable-initial consonants can be single or geminate (except that **y* and **w* are never geminate, and the marginal loaned phoneme **m* is always geminate). Tone is phonemic.

Morphology. Verbs obligatorily take one of several aspect-mood proclitics, none of which has a zero shape or allomorph. Most verb roots are consonant-initial, but some are vowel-initial; unpredictable allomorphs of the completive and potential proclitics define four verb classes. There are no pronominal agreement-markers; when personal pronouns occur, they do so in the same syntactic slot as any other noun. Pronouns distinguish gender and social status.

Syntax. Word order is VS(O). Sense permitting, any transitive verb that can occur in a VSO frame can also occur without an object. Nuclear case/role categories are unmarked, except by position with respect to the predicate: thus, there is no definitive syntactic evidence for accusativity, ergativity, or agentivity.

Using chronological data to divide up texts into small chunks for analysis, Kaufman and Justeson (1993–2003) have analyzed the structure of about 50 Zapotec texts, exploiting the reconstructed vocabulary and grammar of Proto-Zapotec and Proto-Zapotecan, and have found that the structure of the texts conforms to the structure of these languages. This is clearest in the matter of word order and verb morphology, but also in a number of other details.

The most systematic and compelling results of this analysis involve the identification of a number of grammatical morphemes: three third-person pronouns **kʷe* 's/he: adult nonforeigner', **ne* 's/he: god, high-status human', and **ni* 'thing, bad person, foreigner'; the first-person pronoun **na* 'I'; and a series of aspect/mood markers including the allomorphs **ko-* and *kʷe-* of the completive proclitic. In conformity with Zapotec verb classes, we find **ko-* on verbs represented by logograms for 'to speak' and 'to stand'; and **kʷe-* on a verb logogram seemingly representing 'to punish,' or something similar, which would have occurred with that proclitic in early Zapotec. These morphemes are spelled by CV syllabograms, the values of which were probably based on the acrophonic principle: for example, the sign ⟨na⟩ was based on (Central and Northern Zapotec) **na7* 'hand'; ⟨kʷe⟩ was based on **na7 kʷe* 'right (hand)' (= **na7* 'hand' + *kʷe* 'straight'); and ⟨ne⟩ was based on **nesa* 'road,' using the pan-Mesoamerican icon of paired footprints to indicate a road or path (the identification of the contextual grammatical functions of the signs spelling these grammatical morphemes preceded their phonetic readings).

Apart from signs used for grammatical elements, which are spelled by syllabograms, most words seem to be spelled by logograms. Phonetic complements occur but seem to be rare. It is unclear whether any words are spelled out in full with syllabograms alone. One logogram, representing Zapotec **ko+ kke* 'lord, lady,' is followed by the string ⟨ko-ke⟩ as a phonetic complement. This form provides evidence that consonant gemination, a contrastive feature of Zapotec, need not be written – and there is no known evidence for explicit marking of gemination. Possible further support for this spelling convention comes from a place name ⟨HILL-ko-ti⟩, which can be interpreted as /*tani kotti/ 'hill of the dead'.

The structure of texts fits with what we know about the structure of Proto-Zapotec(an); the acrophonic origins of known syllabograms agree with Zapotec vocabulary; and a few lexical items spelled with syllabograms, the values of which are known through their grammatical uses, are readable as Zapotec words. The earliest texts including complete sentences go back to about 300 BCE, which, according to glottochronology, would be at or a little after the Proto-Zapotecan stage – when the Chatino branch of Zapotecan and the Zapotec branch separated. The latest inscriptions were produced around 900 CE, which must have been centuries after the Proto-Zapotec stage, when the westernmost subgroup of Zapotec broke off from the remaining dialects (*c.* 500 CE). The linguistic markers or traits that we find in the texts have in general not yet been seen to correlate with any of the phonological or grammatical or lexical differentiation that occurred in the history of Zapotecan and Zapotec – with two exceptions: ⟨na⟩ is based on North-Central Zapotec **na7* 'hand' (other Zapotecan **ya7*); **ko+ kke* 'lord, lady' is not known outside Central-Northern Zapotec.

Bibliography

Caso, A. 1928. *Las estelas zapotecas.* Monografías del Museo Nacional de Arqueología, Historia, y Etnografía, Mexico City.

———. 1947. *Calendario y escritura de las antiguas culturas de Monte Albán.* Talleres Gráficos de la Nación.

Justeson, J. and T. Kaufman. 1996. "Warfare in the Preclassic inscriptions of Monte Alban." Unpublished manuscript.

Kaufman, T. 1988. "Oto-Manguean tense/aspect/mood, voice, and nominalization markers." Unpublished manuscript.

———. 1995. "Proto-Zapotec reconstructions." Unpublished manuscript.

———. 2000. "A typologically-odd reconstruction for proto-Zapotecan: stem-final *k." Paper presented at the Eighth Spring Workshop on Theory and Method in Linguistic Reconstruction, March 2000, University of Pittsburgh.

Kaufman, T. and J. Justeson. 1993–2003. "The decipherment of Zapotec hieroglyphic writing." Unpublished manuscript.

Marcus, J. 1976. "The iconography of militarism at Monte Alban and neighboring sites in the Valley of Oaxaca." In H. Nicholson (ed.), *Origins of Religious Art and Iconography in Preclassic Mesoamerica*, pp. 123–139. UCLA Latin American Studies Series 31. Los Angeles: UCLA Latin American Center.

Urcid, J. 1992. "Zapotec hieroglyphic writing." (2 vols.). Ph.D. dissertation, Yale University.

———. 2001. *Zapotec Hieroglyphic Writing.* Studies in Pre-Columbian Art and Archaeology. 34. Dumbarton Oaks.

Whittaker, G. 1980. "The hieroglyphics of Monte Alban." Ph.D. dissertation, Yale University.

APPENDIX 1

Reconstructed ancient languages

DON RINGE

Introduction

This chapter will necessarily be rather different from most of those that precede, since it deals with languages of which no direct record survives – languages which are, by definition, *prehistoric*. Prehistoric languages can only be studied inferentially, and the only sound basis for our inferences is the well-known *uniformitarian principle* (UP). As applied in historical linguistics, the UP states the following:

(1) If the conditions of language use and acquisition cannot be demonstrated to have undergone any relevant alteration between the prehistoric and historical periods, nor between recorded history and the present, we must assume that the same types of language structures and language changes that we can observe today also underlie our historical records and were present in prehistory as well.

Since the only alternative is unconstrained guesswork, all scientific historical linguists must take the UP seriously. It follows that we must not interpret what we find in the written historical record in any way that is inconsistent with the range of structures and changes-in-progress that we can observe in languages currently spoken, nor must we posit for a prehistoric language any type of structure or change that is not actually attested somewhere among the known languages of the world. This very general principle has remarkably specific consequences, especially with regard to phonological change (see §3 below), which constrain and guide our hypotheses with a precision often surprising to interested observers outside the field. Of course the conditional clause in the UP is by no means automatically satisfied, since archeological evidence, modern anthropological work on stone-age populations (e.g., neolithic farmers in highland New Guinea) and the known principles of demography do enable us to judge the conditions of language use in prehistory to a surprising extent; for an eye-opening illustration of the consequences of taking this seriously, see Nichols 1990.

The remainder of this chapter is based squarely on the application of the uniformitarian principle by the whole community of mainstream historical linguists for well over a century.

Since no language system ever remains static, prehistoric languages have all met one of two fates. Some, perhaps even most, have died out without leaving traces of any sort; probably in most cases "language death" occurred because the language's speakers were absorbed by another population or for some other reason abandoned their old language for a different one (cf., e.g., Foley 1986:24–25), though perhaps a few languages died out because of the biological extinction of their speaking populations. Other prehistoric languages survived into the historical period; but since all languages change continually, a language system as it emerges into the historical record is inevitably quite different from what it was sixty or eighty generations earlier – at least as different as, say, Italian is from Classical Latin, and perhaps as different as French is from Latin (to cite two cases which have histories that are known in great detail).

If a prehistoric language has left only one historical descendant – that is, if it has evolved into only one surviving historical language – we may never be able to infer much about its structure at any time substantially before it emerged into history; too much will have changed. Some information about its prehistory will probably be recoverable by the techniques of *internal reconstruction*; but there are many linguistic structures to which they cannot be applied, or from which they lead to incorrect inferences (full discussion of this matter is well beyond the scope of this chapter; see Hoenigswald 1960:68–69, 99–111; Fox 1995:145–216; and Ringe, forthcoming)

But single speech communities often split into two or more new communities, which gradually lose touch and go their own ways, linguistically and otherwise. In each of these new communities language change will continue to occur, *but the specific changes will largely be different in each,* provided that contact between them is minimal or nonexistent. The result will be a family of related languages; in fact, that is the definition of the term *language family.* If two or more such descendants of a prehistoric language survive to be recorded, we can *reconstruct* at least some of the structure of their ancestor by a simple but rigorous mathematical procedure called the *comparative method.* Explication of the comparative method is beyond the scope of this chapter; the definitive codification of the method is Hoenigswald 1960, and a good practical introduction can be found in Fox 1995:17–144.

The ancient languages discussed in this chapter, and all other prehistoric languages about which we have substantial information, have each been reconstructed from multiple historically attested descendants by specialists using the comparative method. That single fact, more than anything else, determines what can be known about them. In the remainder of this chapter I will refer to reconstructed parent languages as *protolanguages*, the standard technical term for such inferred entities.

Most of the examples herein will be drawn from the Indo-European (IE) family, chiefly because that is the family of languages with which the author is most familiar. But there is nothing special about Indo-European; the principles discussed here, and the general statements made, apply equally to all protolanguages.

If any kind of language change proceeded at a constant rate, we could compare a protolanguage with its descendants of known date and calculate when the protolanguage must have been spoken. Unfortunately, rates of linguistic change appear to vary considerably, so that fixing the date of any protolanguage is a matter of informed guesswork. We can attempt to narrow the range of our estimates by seeking to correlate our results with the findings of archeologists, but some uncertainty inevitably remains. To a linguist this does not matter much; the *relative* chronology of important linguistic changes is often recoverable, and *absolute* chronology has little do to with the internal history of a language's structure.

More worrisome is the fact that the linguistic features reconstructed for a single protolanguage can actually be of slightly different dates, so that the reconstruction is temporally "out of focus." This occurs chiefly because the members of a diversifying language family can undergo identical changes even after they have parted company, especially if the changes are natural and easily repeatable; if *all* the daughter languages undergo a particular change early in their separate careers, the effects of that change will naturally – but incorrectly – be projected into the protolanguage.

To consider an example: in most Indo-European languages the so-called laryngeal consonants of Proto-Indo-European (PIE) have been lost when preceded by a vowel, and if that vowel belonged to the same syllable as the laryngeal, it has been lengthened. Even in the Anatolian subgroup, which preserves some laryngeals in some positions, a number of these "contractions" of vowels and laryngeals have occurred (Melchert 1994:67–69, 73). For Proto-Indo-European we must rely on phonological alternations and/or morphological evidence to distinguish, for example, between $^*\bar{a}$ (as in **swād-* "sweet," Stang 1974) and $^*eh_2$ (as in $^*weh_2g$- "break," Kimball 1988:245, Rix *et al.* 1998:605–606) before stop consonants. In reconstructing $^*eh_2$ we are certainly recovering the underlying form, but we cannot be certain that a surface contraction to *[ā] had not already occurred in the last common ancestor of the Indo-European languages. In the absence of relevant alternations or morphologically related forms, we do not always know whether we are dealing with a vowel-plus-laryngeal sequence or an original long vowel. Thus, is PIE "arm" $^*b^h\bar{a}g^hu$- or $^*b^heh_2g^hu$-? Even more uncertain is the historical status of laryngeal "coloring," by which short *e* became *[a] next to $^*h_2$ and *[o] next to $^*h_3$. All Indo-European languages show the results of this change, but can we be sure that it had already happened in Proto-Indo-European? Such problems have led the best historical linguists to be rather cautious about trying to identify the communities that spoke particular protolanguages, recognizing that to a certain extent any protolanguage is an idealized construct which is likely to have a complex relation to "real history."

Strictly speaking, a reconstructed language has no speaking population; yet something very like each competently reconstructed protolanguage must have been spoken by some group of human beings. We can learn something about their society by examining the vocabulary that can be reconstructed for the protolanguage. For example, we know that the speakers of Proto-Indo-European – more exactly, of the actual language that most closely resembled our reconstructed Proto-Indo-European – wore clothes, since we can reconstruct not only such forms as **wéstor* "(s)he's wearing," **woséyeti* "(s)he's dressing [someone else]" (Rix *et al.* 1998:633–634), $^*yeh_3s$- "wear a belt" (Rix *et al.* 1998:275–276), and $^*h_2w\d{l}h_1no$- "wool" (Peters 1980:23–26, fn. 18), but also $^*neg^w nós$ "naked," which implies that people customarily wear clothes.

There are, however, obvious limits to what we can learn in this way. In particular, we can argue only from the presence of reconstructible words for a particular article or concept, not from their absence; the replacement of inherited words by completely different words is a universal and very common type of linguistic change, and that alone can easily account for the fact that there are so many gaps in our reconstructible lexica. This is clearest from a consideration of body-part terms. For example, no Proto-Indo-European word for "finger" is reconstructible; yet surely speakers of Proto-Indo-European had fingers, and (like every other human community) they must have had a word for them!

Apparent breaches of this principle of limitation are just that – apparent rather than real. For example, each major subgroup of the Indo-European family has its own word for "iron" (except that Proto-Germanic **īsarnã* appears to have been borrowed from Proto-Celtic **īsarnom*; for a full discussion see Birkhan 1970:128–137), so that no word for that metal can be reconstructed for Proto-Indo-European; and it's true that virtually all serious scholars believe iron to have been unknown to the Proto-Indo-European speech community. But that belief is *not* based on the fact that no relevant words can be reconstructed; it follows instead from well-known archeological findings about the geographical and chronological distribution of iron among ancient cultures.

The necessary methodology of comparative reconstruction imposes further limitations on what can be known about the prehistory of even the most solidly reconstructible protolanguages. For example, we are mathematically constrained to reconstruct a more or less unitary dialect as the ancestor of each attested family. Yet experience with living languages leads us to infer that most of these reconstructed dialects must have been members of dialect networks – all the other dialects of each network having more or less completely died out.

Our ability to reconstruct the relative chronology of the changes that occurred as each protolanguage diversified into a language family is likewise limited: we can recover the relative chronology of those changes that interacted (one change producing the conditions under which another could then take place, or removing examples which would otherwise have undergone a later change), but changes that had nothing to do with one another cannot be ordered chronologically.

Finally, an unpleasant fact of language change imposes the most drastic limitation on what can be known. All languages gradually replace their inherited vocabulary with completely different and unrelated vocabulary items, and also replace, lose, and restructure the affixes with which full words are formed. "Basic" vocabulary is, of course, replaced at a relatively slow rate, and inflectional affixes are also resistant to change; but in the long run every word will be replaced, and inherited inflectional patterns will be transformed beyond recognition. When the vast majority of even the most tenacious items have disappeared, the few remaining cognates shared by genuinely related languages will be indistinguishable from chance resemblances – so that the relationship will be undiscoverable, and reconstruction of a protolanguage will be impossible. There is, therefore, a temporal limit beyond which we will probably never be able to penetrate prehistory; and though estimates of that limit differ, it seems clear that a threshold even ten millennia before the earliest attested documents of a language family is beyond our reach for all practical purposes.

Phonology

Regularity of sound change

It is the phonology of protolanguages that is most solidly reconstructible, for a simple reason: in any line of linguistic development, *sound changes* (changes in pronunciation) are overwhelmingly regular. That is, in a given line of development – say, from Latin into some specific dialect of Italian – within a given span of time, either a given sound x always develops into x' (which may or may not be phonetically identical with x), or else the conditions under which x becomes x' are statable entirely in terms of other sounds in the same word or phrase. Since the sound changes that took place in the development of a given language L_1 from its ancestor P are regular, and the sound changes that took place in the development of another given language L_2 from the same ancestor are likewise regular (though different from those that occurred in L_1), we will find *regular correspondences* between the sounds of L_1 and the sounds of L_2 to the extent that both languages have preserved words and forms inherited from their common ancestor P; and we can exploit those correspondences to "triangulate" back to P by the comparative method. The regularity of sound change operates on contrastive units of sound – that is, on phonemes, whether "classical," lexical, or underlying, depending on one's analysis – as Hoenigswald 1960 demonstrates; thus the comparative method recovers a protolanguage's phonemic system and the phonemic shapes of its words and affixes (insofar as their reflexes survive in two or more daughters).

Modern work in sociolinguistics has shown that the scenario just summarized is slightly oversimplified; most importantly, sound changes pass through a variable phase before "going to completion," and occasionally the progress of a sound change is arrested in the variable phase, giving rise to irregularities (see, e.g., Labov 1994 for discussion). But the statistical preponderance of regular sound changes remains impressively massive, and it is almost always methodologically advisable to treat explanations involving irregular sound changes with suspicion (essentially for the same reason that one always hesitates to draw to an inside straight). The correctness of this view has been confirmed repeatedly. For example, late in the nineteenth century a strict application of the comparative method – assuming the absolute regularity of sound change – led Karl Brugmann and others to reconstruct for Proto-Indo-European three sets of dorsal stops, conventionally called palatals, velars, and labiovelars. Such a reconstruction was repeatedly denied by some linguists, partly on grounds of sheer implausibility (though see below) and partly because no single Indo-European language then known clearly preserved different reflexes of all three sets. Yet Melchert 1987 showed that the three Proto-Indo-European voiceless dorsal stops do have different reflexes in Cuneiform Luvian, a language whose records were discovered only in this century (namely, PIE $*\hat{k} >$ Luvian *z*, $*k > k$, and $*k^w > ku$), thus vindicating the traditional reconstruction of Proto-Indo-European and the comparative method. (For a striking vindication of the regularity of sound change from a quite different empirical perspective, using a wide range of modern data, see Labov 1994:419–543.)

Proto-phonetics

The *phonetics* of proto-phonemes, on the other hand, are not fully determined by the distribution of sound correspondences; inferences about proto-phonetics are probabilistic, and the best we can do is to maximize our chances of arriving at the correct solution by using all potentially relevant information at our disposal. The most solid basis for inferences about proto-phonetics is (naturally) the phonetics of a proto-phoneme's reflexes in the attested daughter languages; a hypothesis about the phonetic identity of any proto-phoneme will be plausible to the extent that its attested phonetic reflexes can be derived from the posited proto-sound by natural, plausible sound changes. Unfortunately, our judgments of the naturalness of sound changes rest on experience, and even the collective experience of the whole community of historical linguists is insufficient to solve some puzzles; for example, most Indo-Europeanists remain noncommittal about the phonetics of the so-called laryngeals reconstructed for Proto-Indo-European (see *WAL* Ch. 17 §2.1.3) simply because the historical record does not provide us with many examples of sounds that become dorsal fricatives in some daughter languages but vowels in others. For similar reasons it is less than clear whether the emphatic stops of Proto-Afro-Asiatic (see *WAL* Ch. 6 §1.3.1) were glottalized or pharyngealized.

It has become customary to bring typological arguments to bear on problems of proto-phonetics; but both our knowledge of the full range of typological possibilities in human language and the usefulness of typology in general have been at times abused. A notorious case is the *glottalic hypothesis* regarding Proto-Indo-European stop consonants, according to which the traditional voiced stops should be reconstructed as glottalized, the traditional voiceless stops as aspirated, and the traditional voiced aspirated (i.e., breathy-voiced) stops as voiced (with or without aspiration; see e.g., Gamkrelidze and Ivanov 1973, Hopper 1973). One motivation for this revision was the supposed typological impossibility of the system of Proto-Indo-European stops as usually reconstructed; yet a remarkably similar system is found in present-day Madurese (Stevens 1968:16, 38) and some other Indonesian languages, as Hock (1986:625–626) observes. Moreover, adopting the glottalic hypothesis would force us to posit serious implausibilities in the phonological development of early Iranian loanwords in Armenian (Meid 1987:9–11). In other words, what is known about the phonetics of the reflexes of Proto-Indo-European stops actually furnishes hard evidence *against* the glottalic hypothesis. Brugmann's reconstruction of three sets of Proto-Indo-European dorsal stops was also rejected in part because of its supposed implausibility; yet similar systems are well attested in the languages of the Caucasus and of the northwest coast of North America, and new evidence has vindicated Brugmann directly (see §2.1). Debacles of this kind reveal that typological arguments should be used with considerably more caution than they have been used with by some investigators.

Limitations on reconstruction

In view of these facts it is not surprising that the prosodic phenomena of protolanguages may or may not be recoverable, and that any interesting allophony of proto-phonemes is likely to be recoverable only under favorable circumstances. Moreover, the reconstruction of phonological rules, phonotactic constraints, syllable structure, and the like depends largely on being able to reconstruct sufficient vocabulary and paradigms.

Even above the level of the phoneme, some types of linguistic development can make reconstruction difficult or impossible. A well-known example is the phonological rule called *Bartholomae's Law*, by which the "breathy voice" of a voiced aspirated stop spreads rightward to an adjacent apical stop or fricative. The rule still affects stop + stop clusters in Sanskrit (e.g., bud^h- "awaken" + *-tá-* (part.) → $budd^h$*á-* "awake, enlightened"; see Ch. 2 §3.4.2.1); and though voiced aspirated obstruents have merged with voiced obstruents in Avestan, the most archaic dialect of that language (Gāthic Avestan) still contains numerous stop + stop and stop + fricative clusters the voicing of which shows that they had been affected by Bartholomae's Law before the merger. Bartholomae's Law can then be reconstructed for Proto-Indo-Iranian (the latest common ancestor of the Indic languages, including Sanskrit, and the Iranian languages, including Avestan) with certainty (see Schindler 1976).

It seems clear, however, that Bartholomae's Law is easily lost from a language's grammar. In Sanskrit it has ceased to apply to stop + fricative clusters, so that corresponding to Avestan *dißža-* "deceive" (from Proto-Indo-Iranian $*d(^h)ib^h z^h a$-) we find Vedic Sanskrit *dipsa-* "want to deceive." In Younger Avestan (later than Gāthic) it has largely been eliminated in all environments, so that in place of Gāthic *aogdā* "(he) proclaimed" ($< *aug^h d^h a < *aug^h$- + **-ta*) we find *aoxta* (note that underlying /k/, or inherited **k*, normally appears as *x* before consonants in Avestan).

This raises an obvious question: is it possible that Bartholomae's Law was a phonological rule of Proto-Indo-European, and that it has been lost in all branches of the family other than Indo-Iranian? Such a hypothesis is by no means implausible, but proof would depend on finding unarguable relic forms in at least one other branch. Unfortunately the evidence is equivocal, and among specialists no consensus has emerged (see Mayrhofer 1986:115–117 with references).

Reconstruction of phonemic systems

The degree of similarity that obtains between the phonological system of a reconstructable protolanguage and those of its historically attested daughters is not a constant; it depends on what sound changes have occurred in each of the daughters. At one end of the spectrum, the phonemic system of Proto-Semitic is almost identical with that of Classical Arabic (Bergsträsser 1928:3–5, 134), simply because few sound changes occurred in the development of the latter. Similarly, the sound system of Proto-Algonkian strongly resembles those of many of its daughters, the most notable deviation being the presence of a consonant, conventionally symbolized as $*\theta$, which has merged with other consonants in most daughter languages (Bloomfield 1946:85–90). On the other hand, the phonemic system of Proto-Indo-European is fairly different from that of any daughter language:

(2) The Proto-Indo-European phonemic system

Obstruents					*Sonorants*		
p	t	k̂	k	k^w	m	m̥	
b	d	ĝ	g	g^w	n	n̥	
b^h	d^h	$ĝ^h$	g^h	g^{wh}	l	l̥	
	s	h_1	h_2	h_3	r	r̥	
					y	i	ī
					w	u	ū

Vowels		
e	a	o
ē	ā	ō

The position of the laryngeals (*h_1, *h_2, *h_3) is speculative; it does not affect the discussion that follows. There was also some sort of pitch-accent system.

Of the attested daughters, Sanskrit best preserves the stop system but has merged the laryngeals with other sounds. Hittite best preserves the laryngeals but has undergone mergers in the stop system (Melchert 1994:60–62, 117–120). The labiovelar stops are especially prone to change; in only a few attested daughters can they be shown to survive as distinctive unit phonemes. The very distinctive Proto-Indo-European system of sonorants, in which the nonsyllabic sonorants alternated with their syllabic counterparts under well-defined conditions, has nowhere been preserved without alteration. As might be expected, the vocalic portion of the system (*y ~ *i and *w ~ *u) survives longest (in Indic and Germanic). However, it does not follow that the above reconstruction is in any way doubtful; the comparative method reconstructs with confidence the system of phonological contrasts reported here, and the fact that all attested systems of Indo-European languages are more or less different is a straightforward consequence of the regular sound changes they have each undergone.

The uniqueness of sound change

Since sound change is the only type of language change that exhibits statistically overwhelming regularity giving rise to clear patterns that pervade comparative data, it is the only type of change that can be exploited directly to reconstruct protolanguages. The recovery of all other aspects of protolanguage structure depends on our ability to reconstruct individual words and affixes by exploiting regular sound change. The methodological observations of the following sections therefore will not amount to a complete and coherent procedure comparable to the (phonological) comparative method.

Morphology

The nature of morphological reconstruction

Much of what has traditionally been subsumed under morphological change appears in the light of current theory to be essentially phonological or syntactic. For example, the leveling of morphophonemic alternations is sometimes described as the restriction or loss of a phonological rule; and the complete loss of grammatical categories, such as the loss of the instrumental case within the history of Old English, is clearly a syntactic phenomenon, though it obviously has morphological consequences. The irreducible residue of morphological changes does not seem to be governed by any regular "rules"; one repeatedly finds that although some particular type of change is quite common, its converse is not rare. For instance, systems of nominal case-marking are frequently simplified over the course of a language's development (as in many European languages), but we also find that new case-markers evolve by the accretion of postpositions (most spectacularly in Tocharian, but also in Lithuanian and Armenian); aspect-based verb systems often evolve into tense-based systems (e.g., in Latin), but new systems of aspect can and do arise (e.g., in Russian; see further below).

For these reasons the reconstruction of a protolanguage's morphology simply cannot be pursued on the basis of matching functional categories in the daughter languages without regard to their formal expression. On the contrary, reliable reconstruction of morphological categories depends almost entirely on reconstructing the morphemes that instantiate them by exploiting the regularity of sound change in the usual way. This can be illustrated by considering the reconstruction of two details of the Proto-Indo-European verb, namely the system of voices and the tense and aspect system.

Reconstructing morphology

The morphological expression of voice in the verb systems of the oldest, well-attested representatives of each major branch of the Indo-European family is summarized in (3):

(3) Morphological voice in selected Indo-European languages

	System of oppositions	*Deponent verbs?*
Hittite	active vs. mediopassive	yes
Sanskrit	active vs. middle vs. passive	yes (middle only)
Avestan	active vs. middle vs. passive	yes (middle only)
Greek	active vs. middle vs. passive	yes (both middle and passive)
Latin	active vs. passive	yes
Armenian	active vs. mediopassive	yes
Gothic	active vs. passive	no
Old Irish	active vs. passive	yes (distinct from passives)
Tocharian	active vs. mediopassive	yes
Old Church Slavonic	(active only)	—
Lithuanian	(active only)	—
Albanian	active vs. mediopassive	yes

A large majority of these languages exhibit an opposition of at least two voices in their verb morphologies; it would, however, be rash to project such a situation back into Proto-Indo-European without further investigation, as it is conceivable that the nonactive voices evolved independently in these languages. Such a development can be demonstrated for Russian and Icelandic, which have created new middle-voice forms by the accretion of a reflexive clitic to active forms. In fact, the Albanian mediopassive appears to be a new formation as well: its only nonperiphrastic forms (made to the present stem) are constructed with a suffix *-(h)e-* and ordinary, active-looking endings, and there are no clear cognates in any other language. A closer look at the three-voice systems of Greek and the Indo-Iranian languages (Sanskrit and Avestan) shows that their morphological opposition between middle and passive is likewise the result of secondary developments: in all three languages those two voices are distinguished only when there is a separate passive stem (Greek aorist *-(t^h)ę̄-* and future *-(t^h)ę̄-se/o-*; Sanskrit and Avestan present *-ya-* and aorist [third singular only] *-i*), and though some of those stems have cognate formations in other languages, they do not exhibit passive function in those languages.

To demonstrate that Proto-Indo-European had a morphological opposition between an active and a nonactive voice we must be able to reconstruct at least some clear and distinctive morphological markers for the latter, and in fact that can be done. For example, in past tenses we find the following cognate set for the third singular *nonactive* ending: Sanskrit, Avestan *-ta* = Greek *-to* = Tocharian B *-te* = Tocharian A *-t* < PIE **-to*. Moreover, the same nonactive **-to* appears with further suffixes in Hittite past third singular *-(t)tat(i)* < **-to-ti* (cf. Melchert 1994:60) and in Latin third singular *-tur* < **-to-r* (Latin does not systematically distinguish past from non-past endings; there is much more to be said about *-tur* and its cognates, but that is beyond the domain of this discussion [see further below]). For the *active* past third singular ending we have a quite different cognate set: Hittite, Sanskrit, Avestan *-t* = Greek, Tocharian Ø = Old Latin *-d* < PIE **-t*. The opposition between these two reconstructible endings, and between the members of other, similar pairs, establishes an active: nonactive contrast for the Proto-Indo-European verb.

In the case just sketched, enough of the daughter languages have preserved the same morphological markers in comparable functions to enable us to reconstruct part of the proto-system. We are not always so lucky, as the following case will show.

The Hittite verb system is remarkably simple. Except for a tiny handful of anomalies, each verb has only one stem. Conjugation is effected by means of endings; each finite ending expresses person, number (singular vs. plural), voice (active vs. mediopassive), and tense-mood (present vs. past vs. imperative). The only notable complication is the fact that there are two lexical classes, called the *hi*-conjugation and the *mi*-conjugation after the shape of their first singular present active endings (see *WAL* Ch. 18 §4.4.7).

In the other archaic Indo-European languages, the situation is vastly different. Simplifying somewhat, we can say that Greek exhibits a rich and elaborate inflectional system based on aspect: most verbs exhibit an imperfective stem (called the "present stem") and a perfective stem (called the "aorist stem"), and many also have a stem which in Homeric Greek is still usually stative (called the "perfect stem"), though verbs lacking one or more of these stems are not rare. On each stem are built a non-past and a past indicative tense (except that there is no perfective non-past), as well as subjunctive, optative, and imperative mood forms, participles, and infinitives; as noted above, there are three voices. In addition, there are future tense stems with a defective set of forms. The system of the Indo-Iranian languages is strikingly similar; in purely formal terms, a large proportion of its morphology corresponds point for point with that of Greek, though some functional shifts have occurred. The Armenian system also shows a fundamental contrast between perfective and imperfective stems, though there is nothing corresponding to the Greek and Indo-Iranian "perfect" (i.e., stative); and though the Latin system has been more extensively restructured, there are numerous clear indications that it closely resembled the Greek system at no very great remove in its prehistory. The same can be said of the Old Church Slavonic verb, which still shows, for example, a clear contrast between "present" and "aorist" stems. Even the Baltic and Germanic verb systems, which are based on a simpler opposition of tenses (present vs. past), exhibit *two different stems* per verb: in both groups the present stem is cognate with the "present" (imperfective) stem of Greek, etc.; the Germanic past of strong verbs is cognate with the "perfect" (stative) of the more southerly languages, while the Germanic weak past and the Baltic past appear to be innovations. The verb systems of Tocharian, Old Irish, and Albanian show more unique features and present many more puzzles; but in those languages too it is normal to find at least two stems per verb, and a large proportion of each of those systems can be explained as late developments of a Greek-type system without great difficulty.

Should we reconstruct for Proto-Indo-European, then, a complex verb system much like that of Greek and Indo-Iranian, and suppose that the Hittite verb system, in spite of its very early date of attestation (mid-second millennium BC), has undergone radical simplification? Some scholars have concluded that that is correct, but there is a further fact that gives cause for doubt. Roughly speaking, the endings of the Hittite *hi*-conjugation are cognate with those of the "perfect" (stative) of the other archaic Indo-European languages, in spite of the fact that most *hi*-conjugation verbs are not stative in meaning, while the endings of the *mi*-conjugation are cognate with those of the "present" and "aorist" (perfective and imperfective) of the other languages. There is, thus, a complete and irreducible lack of "fit" between the functional categories of the two systems:

(4) Anatolian and the other Indo-European languages: cognations in the verb system

Hittite		*Greek, Sanskrit, etc.*
hi-class vs. *mi*-class	≈	"perfect" (stative) vs. "present" and "aorist"
(lexical classes)		(imperfective and perfective)
one stem per verb	:	more than one (aspect-)stem per verb

It is not easy to imagine a system of Proto-Indo-European verb categories that could have given rise to two systems as different as these by uncontroversially natural changes. Not surprisingly, specialists have been arguing about the matter for decades, and there is still no consensus.

This shows clearly that, even in a thoroughly researched family of languages for which we have abundant early evidence of high quality, the very structure of the data can frustrate our attempts to arrive at a plausible reconstruction of parts of the morphological system. The basic reason for this difficulty is that there seem to be no general "laws" of morphological change comparable to the regularity of sound change; morphological systems, idiosyncratic by nature, seem to change in idiosyncratic ways, and when we are presented with a pattern of data that has no close parallels in the attested history of languages, we can do no better than make informed guesses about the changes that might have produced it.

Sometimes, however, distributional factors can be exploited to tell us more than we could otherwise have figured out. Let us return to Latin passive third singular *-tur* (see above). Though Latin has largely eliminated an inherited contrast between past and non-past endings, many related languages have preserved it, and it is clear that *-tur* is cognate with a set of non-past third singular nonactive endings. But there are two cognate sets in that function:

(5) Indo-European non-past mediopassive third singular endings

Set 1: Hittite *-(t)ta* ~ *-(t)tari* < *-*tor* (± *-*i*; on the complex development of this ending see Yoshida 1990)
Phrygian *-tor*
Tocharian A and B *-tär* < *-*tor* (Ringe 1996b:86–87)
Latin *-tur* < *-*tor*
Old Irish (conjunct) *-thar* < *-*tor*

Set 2: Greek *-toi* (Arkadian dialect) / *-tai* (most dialects)
Sanskrit *-tē*, Avestan *-taē* < *-*toi* or *-*tai*
Gothic *-da* < *-*toi* or *-*tai*

Which set reflects the Proto-Indo-European ending? Two distributional facts suggest that Set 1 does, and that the correct Proto-Indo-European reconstruction is *-*tor*.

In the first place, note the formal relations between the full set of Proto-Indo-European (nonimperative) third singular endings if **-tor* is the correct reconstruction:

(6) Proto-Indo-European third singular endings

	Past	*Non-past*
Active	*-t	*-ti
Mediopassive	*-to	*-tor

It seems clear that the consonant **-t(-)* is what marks the third-person singular, and that an additional suffix **-o(-)* marks the mediopassive. Moreover, the non-past endings are distinguished from the past endings by yet a further suffix, **-i* in the active and **-r* in the mediopassive. If these reconstructions are correct, we have a plausible source for **-toi*, the most probable reconstruction for Set 2 in (5): the system has been simplified by extending the scope of **-i* from the active to the mediopassive, replacing **-r* so as to create a unitary non-past marker (and **-o-i* > **-oi* is not problematic; cf. the similar summary of Yoshida 1990:117). On the other hand, if the correct Proto-Indo-European reconstruction for the lower right-hand cell of (6) were **-toi* or **-tai*, we would have no plausible source for the **-r* of Set 1 **-tor*. This is a strong distributional argument (though not sufficiently strong to convince all specialists).

The other distribution that favors a reconstruction of **-tor* for Proto-Indo-European is geographical. Of the subgroups that show reflexes of **-tor*, nearly all are unarguably geographically peripheral: Celtic and Italic are at the western edge of the (known) Indo-European speech area, Tocharian at the eastern edge; and since the Anatolian languages are found in what is now Turkey in the second millennium BC, when nearly all other Indo-European-speaking groups that we know about seem to have been living further north and northwest, it is overwhelmingly likely that they were then at the southern margin of the Indo-European speech area (the geographical position of Phrygian at that date is completely obscure). By contrast, the groups that exhibit Set 2 endings are all more centrally located. We are accustomed to thinking of Indo-Iranian as the far southeastern corner of the Indo-European speech area, but it is abundantly clear that Indo-Iranian spread east (and later south) from the Eurasian steppe, where speakers of Iranian languages continued to be an important part of the population in the last few centuries BC (cf., e.g., Schmitt 1989:92–93 with bibliography). Speakers of Balto-Slavic must have been to the northwest throughout the last two millennia BC, with speakers of Germanic still further northwest (and all three in contact, for which there is abundant linguistic evidence; cf., e.g., Porzig 1954:139–147, 164–166; Stang 1972; Hock 1986:442–444, 451–455, 667 with bibliography). While the position of Greek at an early date is less clear, it seems at least to have been less peripheral than Anatolian. We can therefore suggest that the Set 2 endings reflect an innovation that occurred in the central part of the Indo-European speech area but did not spread to the margins; and that is a reasonable hypothesis whether we regard the central languages as a valid subgroup exclusively sharing an immediate parent (in which the change could have occurred) or as a group of diversified dialects still in contact (in which case the change could have spread from dialect to dialect). In the former case we must suppose that Balto-Slavic, and perhaps also Armenian and Albanian, shared the change before losing the mediopassive voice; in the latter it is at least thinkable that some of those groups had already lost the mediopassive before the change in the endings occurred. Of course this line of reasoning too can be challenged; in particular, it is not completely clear that the innovation that produced the Set 2 endings could not have occurred more than once independently (Jay Jasanoff, personal communication).

It can be seen from these examples that reconstructing the morphological system of a protolanguage involves procedures much less mechanical and much less rigorous than the reconstruction of a protolanguage's phonology and of the shape of its words and affixes. In effect, we use every bit of information that we have in morphological reconstruction – including everything that linguistic theory, the description of modern languages, and the historical record can tell us about morphological structure and change. Nevertheless, the results are often less clinching than in phonological reconstruction, and morphology is both the area in which the most intensive and interesting work on many language families is being pursued and the area in which disagreements between specialists are most prevalent.

Syntax

Theoretically well-informed work on the syntax of protolanguages is still in its infancy. Most Neogrammarian work (e.g., Delbrück 1893–1900) treated syntax as an adjunct of morphology, so that syntactic constructions were discussed in terms of the morphological categories that mark them; and though the rich body of data amassed by our predecessors continues to be useful, modern work in syntax shows all too clearly that a theory which treats syntax as an extension of morphology cannot be correct. It should be noted, however, that at least one line of Neogrammarian research, Wackernagel's pioneering work on the placement of "second-position" clitics (Wackernagel 1892), has proved to be very fruitful in a modern theoretical context (see further below).

Within Indo-European studies, an approach to syntactic change that was developed before the mid-1980s concentrated on the basic order of major constituents in the clause (cf., e.g., Lehmann 1974); that approach has been disappointing, since the *surface order* of constituents is not a primitive of Proto-Indo-European syntax. A promising beginning to syntactic reconstruction had been made in the 1960s (see Watkins 1963, 1964, Kiparsky 1968); but syntactic theory has developed so rapidly that those early studies need to be thoroughly reevaluated in a more modern syntactic framework, and so far that has not been attempted. Indeed, there are good reasons why the attempt has been postponed: cogent reconstruction of the syntax of protolanguages will become possible only when the processes of syntactic change are much better understood, and syntactic change can be investigated in the requisite detail only in the context of a highly articulated theory. Chomskyan Government and Binding theory and a number of its competitors reached a suitable level of sophistication and precision in the mid-1980s, and since then a steadily increasing amount of useful and detailed work on syntactic change has appeared. (A thorough and up-to-date discussion of what is known and what remains to be done is Kroch 2001; for discussion of a large quantity of interesting crosslinguistic data on syntactic change from a theoretically detached perspective, see Harris and Campbell 1995.)

Lexicon

As noted above, the reconstruction of a protolanguage's lexicon by the comparative method must always remain incomplete because of the replacement of lexical items in the daughter languages; the inferences that can be drawn from our lexical reconstructions are therefore limited. A particular problem is the fact that changes in the meanings of words seem to be very idiosyncratic indeed; for that reason we are occasionally unable to specify the meaning of a proto-lexeme with any precision even when its form is uncontroversially reconstructable. A case in point is the protoform of Greek *stóma* "mouth," Avestan (acc.) *stamanəm* "jaws (of a dog)," and Hittite _ištaman_, Luvian _tūmmant-_ "ear." From these reflexes we can reconstruct a Proto-Indo-European noun _*stéh$_3$mr̥_ ~ _*sth$_3$mn̥-_ (Melchert 1994:73–74), and it is reasonable to infer that it referred to some orifice of the head; but given that we can also reconstruct Proto-Indo-European _*(h$_1$)éh$_3$s_ "mouth" (Melchert 1994:115–116) and _*h$_2$éusos_ "ear" (Szemerényi 1967), the exact referent of _*stéh$_3$mn̥_ remains indeterminable. An even more spectacular case involves the Proto-Indo-European words for "head" and "horn"; see Nussbaum 1986 for a full and fascinating discussion which does achieve firm results.

Occasionally the evidence for a proto-lexeme's meaning unanimously supports a reconstruction which is demonstrably anachronistic. For example, a Proto-Algonkian word _*paaškesikani_ can be reconstructed from cognates in several daughter languages, all of which mean "gun, firearm" (Fox _paaškesikani_, Ojibwa _paaškəsikan_, Cree _paaskisikan_, Bloomfield 1946:106). Yet it is clear that the Proto-Algonkian speech community, which must have existed roughly two millennia ago, cannot possibly have known and used firearms. In fact, the attested words are all instrument nouns derived from a verb meaning "shoot with a gun" (Bloomfield, loc. cit.), and that verb is actually a complex formation which literally means "make things burst by means of fire" (Bloomfield 1946:114, 120). Either the verb and its derived instrument noun have been created independently in the languages in which they occur, or (more probably) the word was coined in one language and translated morpheme-by-morpheme into the others as firearms spread from community to community. This case, in which the anachronism of a prima facie reconstruction is obvious, should alert us to the possibility of similar pitfalls in cases over which we have fewer or less reliable means of external (dis)confirmation.

A possibly relevant case is provided by the Proto-Indo-European terms for "wheel." Two etymological groups of words are well attested throughout the family. On the one hand, Vedic Sanskrit _ráthas_ "chariot" reflects substantivization of an adjective _*(H)roth$_2$-ó-s_ "having a set of wheels." That adjective is evidently derived from _*(H)roté-h$_2$_ "set of wheels," the source of Latin _rota_ "wheel"; and _*(H)roté-h$_2$_ is in turn the collective of _*(H)rót-o-s_ "wheel," the ultimate source of German _Rad_ and Lithuanian _rãtas_ "wheel" (Rix _et al._ 1998:459; note that in the preceding Proto-Indo-European reconstructions the identity of the laryngeal is uncertain [hence noted as H], and, moreover, parentheses indicate that the very presence of the laryngeal is uncertain – the data _underdetermine_ the reconstructions of these words, a fairly common problem). On the other hand, we can also reconstruct a term _*k^{w}ék^{w}lo-s_ "wheel," collective _*k^{w}ek^{w}lé-h$_2$_, which is the source of English _wheel_, Homeric Greek _kúklos_ (pl. _kúkla_), Sanskrit _cakrám_ (pl. _cakrā́_), and so on.

Both of these words are transparently descriptive. _*(H)rót-o-s_ is literally "(act of) running," an unproblematic action noun derived from _*(H)ret-_ "run" (cf. Old Irish _rethid_ "(s)he runs"), while _*k^{w}ék^{w}lo-s_ is a reduplicated derivative of _*k^{w}el-_ "turn" (cf. Sanskrit _cárati_ "(s)he wanders," Homeric Greek _peri-tellómenos_ "going around, revolving," etc.). Thus, neither of these words by itself is watertight evidence for wheeled vehicles in the Proto-Indo-European speech community, as opposed to its immediate daughters.

In contrast, the reconstructibility of Proto-Indo-European _*h$_2$iHséh$_2$_ or _*h$_3$iHséh$_2$_ "thill" (cf. Hittite _hiššaš_, Sanskrit _ī̥ṣā́_; Melchert 1994:78, 152), which is completely opaque, and of a basic verb _*wéǵ^{h}eti_ "(s)he transports . . . in a vehicle," is better testimony for Proto-Indo-European wheeled-vehicle technology; and the fact that an entire technical vocabulary for wheeled vehicles (including, of course, the two terms for "wheel") can be reconstructed adds further weight to the argument (Mallory 1989:275–276, fn. 25; Anthony 1995:556–558).

It is sometimes possible to find patterns among proto-lexemes from which we can make inferences about the deeper prehistory of a protolanguage. The reconstructible

Proto-Indo-European lexicon is especially amenable to this procedure because of a quirk of Proto-Indo-European word structure.

Both the inflectional and the derivational morphology of Proto-Indo-European exhibit a relatively simple but pervasive system of vowel alternation (*ablaut*). Literally hundreds of reconstructible paradigms and word-families, including the vast majority of reconstructible items, participate in the system, which is consequently well understood. One general principle of Proto-Indo-European ablaut is that we expect to find only one full vowel (**e*, **o*, or **a*, either long or short; on PIE vowel gradation see *WAL* Ch. 17 §2.2) per form, except for a closed list of derivational and inflectional morphemes (such as the *thematic vowel*, a stem-final vowel which always appears as full **-e-* or **-o-* no matter what ablaut grade appears in the root-syllable; see *WAL* Ch. 17 §3.4). It is therefore rather startling to find that almost every word for "ax" that might be reconstructible for Proto-Indo-European violates that principle, or fails to conform to the usual *sound laws* that reflect regular sound change (see §2.1), or both. Thus, **pelek̂u-s* (Gk. *pélekus*, Skt. *paraśús*) exhibits two full-grade **e*'s in its root, whereas we expect to find only one (and note that the attested reflexes do not agree on the position of the accent). The Greek word *aksī́nē* seems to be related to Germanic forms such as Gothic *aqizi* and Old High German *acchus*; but the first consonant of the Germanic words should reflect Proto-Indo-European **g^w*, which in Greek ought to appear as *-p-*, not *-k-*, before an immediately following *-s-*. The Germanic words also point to a protoform with two full vowels in the root (**ag^w esiH-*). Most stunning of all is the apparent connection between Hittite *ates* "ax" and Old English *adesa* "adze" – there are no other cognates – which, if it is not a mirage, can only reflect a preform **ad^h es-*, again with two full vowels (see Puhvel 1984:227–228). The only "ax" word that makes sense in Proto-Indo-European terms is the one reflected in Latin *secūris* and Old Church Slavonic *sěkyra*, both derived from **sek-* "cut" (though the Slavic form reflects a long **ē* in the root) with a suffix containing the sequence **-ūr-* or **-uHr-* (though the final stem-vowel differs). It would be reasonable to infer from this pattern of data that all the "ax" words but the last were borrowed into Proto-Indo-European (or some of its immediate daughters) from languages of quite different structure – and that axes were important trade items in early Indo-European communities.

Patterns like these can be exploited to identify probable loanwords in proto-lexica, provided that the reconstructible structure of the protolanguage is idiosyncratic enough and well enough understood. Sometimes we are even luckier: occasionally two or more protolanguages between which no genetic relationship can be demonstrated exhibit words so similar in form and meaning that some sort of historical relationship can reasonably be inferred, and in such cases borrowing is by far the best hypothesis to account for the similarities. Proto-Indo-European **pelek̂u-s*, for example, might be connected with Semitic Akkadian *pilaqqu* by a chain of lexical borrowings between geographically intermediate languages, and a similar situation probably accounts for the similarity between Proto-Indo-European **táuros* and Proto-Semitic **θauru* "bull." (The archeology of Proto-Indo-European groups puts direct borrowing out of the question in both cases; see in general Mallory 1989.) But it should be clear that questions like these must be addressed on a case-by-case basis.

Conclusions

The foregoing discussion can be summarized as follows.

1. Because protolanguages can only be reconstructed inferentially from the data of their historical descendants, the methodology according to which the inferences are drawn

is a matter of the utmost importance. Over the past century and a half, historical linguists have evolved a thoroughly reliable methodology for reconstructing protolanguages, based on what is known about language structure and language change from contemporary and historical records.

2. Reconstruction of the phonological systems of protolanguages and the phonological shapes of their words and affixes is based on the observation that sound change is overwhelmingly regular; that basis guarantees both the realism and the rigor of phonological reconstruction. Proposed alternative methodologies (such as reliance on the phonetic similarity of words) are unrealistic and lack rigor; for both reasons they are unacceptable.
3. Reconstruction of the phonological rules and morphological systems of protolanguages (and of their syntax, when that becomes feasible) depends crucially on a thorough knowledge of the daughter languages and of relevant areas of linguistic theory and description, since in these components of the grammar we have no regular patterns of change that can be exploited directly.
4. Reconstruction of proto-lexica, especially with regard to the meanings of the lexemes, presents us with the greatest range of possible pitfalls; we can best deal with this situation by adhering rigorously to the regularity of sound change and treating all other aspects of the work with caution.

At this point it should be clear to the reader that rigor, caution, and a general knowledge of linguistics that is as wide as possible are crucial to the reconstruction of protolanguages. Those considerations alone refute the claims of some scholars to have established so-called long-range genetic groupings of languages that include several recognized families (such as "Nostratic" and "Amerind"), because *without exception* their work fails to meet the best standards of mainstream historical linguistics (see refutations in, *inter alios*, Campbell 1988, Vine 1991). It is also true that simple, robust statistical tests reveal such claims to be untenable (see Ringe 1995, 1996a, 1999; Nichols and Peterson 1996 with references).

The prospects for further reconstruction of protolanguages are therefore clear: we must continue as we have begun, paying close attention to the data, employing the comparative method with the greatest rigor we can muster, and bringing to bear on our reconstructions of morphology and lexica all the tools of linguistics at our disposal.

Bibliography

Anthony, D. 1995. "Horse, wagon and chariot: Indo-European languages and archaeology." *Antiquity* 69:554–565.

Baltin, M., and C. Collins (eds.). 2001. *The Handbook of Contemporary Syntactic Theory.* Oxford: Blackwell.

Bammesberger, A. (ed.). 1988. *Die Laryngaltheorie.* Heidelberg: Carl Winter.

Bergmann, R., H. Tiefenbach, and L. Voetz (eds.). 1987. *Althochdeutsch, Band I: Grammatik, Glossen und Texte.* Heidelberg: Carl Winter.

Bergsträsser, G. 1928. *Einführung in die semitischen Sprachen.* Munich: Hueber.

Birkhan, H. 1970. *Germanen und Kelten bis zum Ausgang der Römerzeit.* Vienna: Österreichische Akademie der Wissenschaften.

Bloomfield, L. 1946. "Algonquian." In Osgood 1946, pp. 85–129.

Campbell, L. 1988. "Review of Greenberg 1987." *Language* 64:591–615.

Cowgill, W. and M. Mayrhofer. 1986. *Indogermanische Grammatik*, vol. I, 1–2. Heidelberg: Carl Winter.

Delbrück, B. 1893–1900. *Vergleichende Syntax der indogermanischen Sprachen.* Strasburg: Trübner.

Foley, W. 1986. *The Papuan Languages of New Guinea.* Cambridge: Cambridge University Press.

Fox, A. 1995. *Linguistic Reconstruction.* Oxford: Oxford University Press.
Gamkrelidze, T. and V. Ivanov. 1973. "Sprachtypologie und die Rekonstruktion der gemeinindogermanischen Verschlüsse." *Phonetica* 27:150–156.
Greenberg, J. 1987. *Language in the Americas.* Stanford: Stanford University Press.
Harris, A. and L. Campbell. 1995. *Historical Syntax in Cross-Linguistic Perspective.* Cambridge: Cambridge University Press.
Hock, H. 1986. *Principles of Historical Linguistics.* Berlin: Mouton de Gruyter.
Hoenigswald, H. 1960. *Language Change and Linguistic Reconstruction.* Chicago: University of Chicago Press.
Hopper, P. 1973. "Glottalized and murmured occlusives in Indo-European." *Glossa* 7:141–166.
Janda, R. and B. Joseph. Forthcoming. *A Handbook of Historical Linguistics.* Oxford: Blackwell.
Kimball, S. 1988. "Analogy, secondary ablaut, and *OH_2 in Common Greek." In Bammesberger 1988, pp. 241–256.
Kiparsky, P. 1968. "Tense and mood in Indo-European syntax." *Foundations of Language* 4:30–57.
Kroch, A. 2001. "Syntactic change." In Baltin and Collins 2001, pp. 699–729.
Labov, W. 1994. *Principles of Linguistic Change. Volume 1: Internal Factors.* Oxford: Blackwell.
Lehmann, W. 1974. *Proto-Indo-European Syntax.* Austin: University of Texas Press.
Lunt, H. (ed.). 1964. *Proceedings of the Ninth International Congress of Linguists.* The Hague: Mouton.
Mallory, J. 1989. *In Search of the Indo-Europeans.* London: Thames and Hudson.
Mayrhofer, M. 1986. "Lautlehre (segmentale Phonologie des Indogermanischen)." In Cowgill and Mayrhofer 1986, pp. 73–216.
Meid, W. 1987. "Germanische oder indogermanische Lautverschiebung?" In Bergmann *et al.* 1987, pp. 3–11.
Melchert, H. 1987. "Proto-Indo-European velars in Luvian." In Watkins 1987, pp. 182–204.
_______. 1994. *Anatolian Historical Phonology.* Amsterdam: Rodopi.
Nichols, J. 1990. "Linguistic diversity and the first settlement of the New World." *Language* 66:475–521.
Nichols, J. and D. Peterson. 1996. "The Amerind personal pronouns." *Language* 72:336–71.
Nussbaum, A. 1986. *Head and Horn in Indo-European.* Berlin: de Gruyter.
Osgood, C. (ed.). 1946. *Linguistic Structures of Native America.* New York: Viking Fund.
Peters, M. 1980. *Untersuchungen zur Vertretung der indogermanischen Laryngale im Griechischen.* Vienna: Österreichische Akademie der Wissenschaften.
Porzig, W. 1954. *Die Gliederung des indogermanischen Sprachgebiets.* Heidelberg: Carl Winter.
Puhvel, J. 1984. *Hittite Etymological Dictionary*, vols. I–II. Berlin: Mouton.
Ringe, D. 1995. "'Nostratic' and the factor of chance." *Diachronica* 12:55–74.
_______. 1996a. "The mathematics of 'Amerind'. " *Diachronica* 13:133–154.
_______. 1996b. *On the Chronology of Sound Changes in Tocharian*, vol. 1. New Haven: American Oriental Society.
_______. 1999. "How hard is it to match CVC-roots?" *Transactions of the Philological Society* 97:213–244.
_______. Forthcoming. "Internal reconstruction". To appear in Janda and Joseph (in press).
Rix, H., M. Kümmel, T. Zehnder *et al.* 2001. *Lexikon der indogermanischen Verben.* Wiesbaden: Dr. Ludwig Reichert.
Schindler, J. 1976. "Diachronic and synchronic remarks on Bartholomae's and Grassmann's Laws." *Linguistic Inquiry* 7:622–637.
Schmitt, R. 1989. "Andere altiranische Dialekte." In R. Schmitt (ed.), *Compendium Linguarum Iranicarum*, pp. 86–94. Wiesbaden: Dr. Ludwig Reichert.
Stang, C. 1972. *Lexikalische Sonderübereinstimmungen zwischen dem Slavischen, Baltischen und Germanischen.* Oslo: Universitetsforlaget.
_______. 1974. "Ieur. **swad-/*swād-*." *Norsk Tidskrift for Sprogvidenskap* 28:99–101.
Stevens, A. 1968. *Madurese Phonology and Morphology.* New Haven: American Oriental Society.
Szemerényi, O. 1967. "The history of Attic οὖς and some of its compounds." *Studi micenei ed egeo-anatolici* 3:47–88.
Vine, B. 1991. "Indo-European and Nostratic." *Indogermanische Forschungen* 96:9–35.
Wackernagel, J. 1892. "Über ein Gesetz der indogermanischen Wortstellung." *Indogermanische Forschungen* 1:333–436.

Watkins, C. 1963. "Preliminaries to a historical and comparative analysis of the syntax of the Old Irish verb." *Celtica* 6:1–49.

———. 1964. "Preliminaries to the reconstruction of Indo-European sentence structure." In Lunt 1964, pp. 1035–1045.

Watkins, C. (ed.). 1987. *Studies in Memory of Warren Cowgill.* Berlin: de Gruyter.

Yoshida, K. 1990. *The Hittite Mediopassive Endings in -ri.* Berlin: de Gruyter.

APPENDIX 2

Full tables of contents from *The Cambridge Encyclopedia of the World's Ancient Languages*, and from the other volumes in the paperback series

Table of contents of *WAL*

Table of contents of *The Ancient Languages of Asia Minor*

Table of contents of *The Ancient Languages of Europe*

Table of contents of *The Ancient Languages of Mesopotamia, Egypt, and Aksum*

Table of contents of *The Ancient Languages of Syria-Palestine and Arabia*

Index of general subjects

Index of grammar and linguistics

Index of languages

Index of named linguistic laws and principles